SYSTEMATIC
CORPORATE
PLANNING

Consulting Editor

John Perrin
School of Business and Organizational Studies
University of Lancaster

John Argenti

SYSTEMATIC CORPORATE PLANNING

A HALSTED PRESS BOOK

John Wiley & Sons
New York

Published in the U.S.A.
by Halsted Press, a Division
of John Wiley & Sons, Inc., New York

First published in Great Britain 1974

Library of Congress Cataloging in Publication Data
Argenti, John.
   Systematic corporate planning.
   "A Halsted Press book."
   1. Planning.   2. Industrial management.   I. Title.
HD38.A6813 1973   658.4'01   73-12093
ISBN 0-470-03265-0

Printed in Great Britain

Contents

Part two

Introduction

I have written this book for what I believe are two good reasons. The first is that I felt like writing it; the second is more complicated because it has to do with the present stage of development that corporate planning has reached.

Corporate planning began to emerge as a discrete management discipline in the United States in the Nineteen Fifties. By the mid Sixties approximately three quarters of the largest five hundred companies in America and Japan were reported to be using formal systems of long range strategic planning or were about to do so. But by the early Seventies there were still some very large companies in America and Japan who were not using the corporate planning approach; in Europe there were many; all over the world the number of medium-sized companies not using it must have been enormous; hardly any other types of organization – national and local governments, government agencies, charities, institutions, trade unions and so on – hardly any of these were using it. As I understand it, then, the position by the early Seventies was that although many very large companies had adopted corporate planning the actual *number* of organizations to have done so was derisory.

I also have the strong impression that many corporate planners, professional managers and management academics were unhappy at the rate at which corporate planning was being adopted and a number of reasons for its lack of progress have been put forward. My own opinion is that those who were expecting corporate planning to have spread much faster than it actually has must have been expecting something of a miracle. I am not suggesting that faster progress would not have been beneficial – I firmly believe that corporate planning is an essential ingredient of modern management – but I am suggesting that the average manager adopts new ideas in management far more cautiously than is generally recognized. There are still many companies not using any form of Method Study which was developed and proven as far back as five decades ago and it is almost impossible to find a single instance of say, Utility Theory having been used in real life in spite of its having been featured in almost every management textbook for the past thirty years.

My interpretation of the situation is that while the rate of diffusion of corporate planning is slower than is desirable, it is not unreasonably slow, its spread is continuing and an enormous number of organizations of all types and sizes will adopt some form of corporate planning over the next two or three decades. This is why it seems to me that the time is ripe for a book on corporate planning in which the really important conclusions about the subject are brought together into a coherent whole.

Not a practical guide

It might be thought that if a large number of organizations are indeed about to adopt corporate planning then what is really needed is a new practical guide. I have no doubt that the time for such a volume will come again, but there are three reasons why I do not think one is needed now. The first is that there already exist a fairly large number of excellent practical guides on the subject including, of course, one of mine.* The second reason is that I believe several rather serious misconceptions and misunderstandings have arisen within the subject and ought first to be cleared up or at least discussed further. These misconceptions are mainly philosophical and logical in character but they lead to some extremely damaging practical consequences. I believe that if a manager tries to put into practice a theory that is misconceived he will inevitably be dissatisfied with the results however great his practical competence as a manager may be; and conversely even a relatively inexperienced manager can often achieve useful results if he understands the basic essentials of a theory provided that it is logically sound and consistent.

The third reason why I do not think another practical guide is required at present stems from the changes taking place in management education. Until fairly recently most managers learned their skills in the field and therefore needed a practical explanation that was above all brief. But today an increasing number of managers take time off away from their desks to give serious formal study to the subject. I have written this book, therefore, for the serious student of management who wishes to delve rather deeper into this subject than a practical guide can take him.

The student of management

Unfortunately for the authors of management books, management students are even more heterogeneous than students in many other fields of study. They range from seventeen year old sixth formers with no practical knowledge of business whatever to the mature executive who is about to take up a very senior post with an organization of international dimensions and repute. Some of these students will end their period of study with a formal written examination, others will simply return to their management duties after a few days or weeks of post-experience study. But nearly all management students have one thing in common, namely that they intend using their knowledge of management in real life practical situations and in this respect they differ from the student of history, literature and so on. In view of this I think it is appropriate that even a

---

* *Corporate Planning—a practical guide* published in Britain by Allen & Unwin, in U.S.A. by Dow Jones Irwin, in Germany by Verlag Moderne Industrie, in Holland by Samsom Uitgeverij, in Spain by Oikos-Tau and in Japan by Sangyo Nohritsu Tanki Daigaku.

book that is intended for students should be practical rather than academic. Although this book is not intended as a practical guide, therefore, I hope it is not an impractical guide. But it is not a traditional textbook either; I doubt very much if the management student of today needs to strive for the level of academic excellence implied by the traditional college textbook, with its detailed discussion of semantic minutiae and innumerable cross-referenced footnotes.

No, what I think today's student of corporate planning requires is neither a practical guide nor a traditional textbook, but a volume in which the philosophy of the subject is stated as a coherent whole together with its existing technology. Armed with these two facets of the subject the student will then be equipped to play a valuable role as a member of a corporate planning team or to co-operate with any such team from whatever managerial position he may hold.

If I am right about the future course of corporate planning – that it will spread to a very large number of organizations of every size and type over the next two or three decades – then an enormous number of people who are now students will become involved in it and a very large number of people who are now managers will wish to make a formal study of it.

The two facets of the subject

Back in the Fifties and Sixties, when corporate planning was in its infancy, it had no technology of its own. Since then, however, corporate planners have developed or adapted a wide range of techniques; they now use computer models, forecasting techniques, risk analysis and a host of others. I imagine most new subjects worthy of study develop in this way, from a simple powerful concept to a highly specialized and complex technology – but in the case of corporate planning it has had somewhat ironic consequences. The fundamental idea behind corporate planning is the suggestion that senior executives should try to look at their organization as a corporate whole – they should, in other words, try to see the wood, not the trees. Unfortunately, as the number of corporate planning techniques has multiplied it has become progressively more difficult for practitioners to keep their minds on the wood; the simple but immensely powerful concept of corporate planning is tending to become buried under the complexity of its technology. I think that many corporate planners have lately fallen into this trap – it is the same trap that, for example, architects and town planners appear to me to have fallen into. In their case they have become hypnotized by the technological advances of their professions which allow them to design surprising and sometimes beautiful habitations but they have forgotten the simple, but rather important first consideration, namely that people are going to have to live in them. I think the same thing is happening to corporate planners; they now seem to be devoting immense energy to making detailed cash flow calculations on a computer or to building elaborate manpower models while having given no thought whatever to such crucial questions as whether their company is too large or too small or how it should behave in civilized society – in other words they have become so intrigued with the application of their new technology to the study of the trees that they have forgotten to look at the wood.

I happen to believe that it is a thousand times more important to apply the basic fundamental principles of corporate planning systematically than it is to be able to manipulate the tools of its technology and I suspect that many of those who believe they are doing corporate planning are really only applying such techniques as financial planning or manpower planning. If I am right about this then the number of companies who are using the principles of corporate planning – as opposed to merely its techniques – is even lower than the various surveys suggest.

Why this book is in two parts

This book is set out in two parts because of my obsession with the importance of the distinction between the principles of corporate planning on the one hand and its technology on the other. Part 1 deals with the principles and Part 2 with the technology. In both parts I have tried to gather together all the most important conclusions reached by the various authors on the subject; however, since no two corporate planners agree on every aspect of their subject I have had to be ruthlessly selective in order to preserve coherence. I have not attempted to imitate the traditional textbook in which the various views of a number of noted authorities are paraded before the student but where no reconciliation of conflicting opinion is made for him. On the contrary, I have tried in Part 1 to present a single coherent view of the principles of corporate planning and have indicated where this differs from some of the other views that have been expressed by noted authors. In Part 2 I have selected only those aspects of the technology of the subject which, in my opinion, are likely to prove useful to those who will be studying and using corporate planning within the next decade – and this means, quite simply, that some of the newer and very advanced techniques are not described because I believe that some of these will remain far beyond the practical requirements of the vast majority of corporate planners for at least the next decade.

Because Part 1 deals with the principles I have been able, I hope, to preserve a relatively simple style of writing with the minimum use of jargon words; I hope this will make it suitable for sixth formers and busy executives as well as for the advanced student. Part 2 is necessarily more technical in content and in style.

Case studies and exercises

I have used case studies in three different contexts. In Part 1 I have used them to illustrate particular points of principle and these cases are therefore extremely brief since only one point is being exemplified by each case. In Chapter 10, however, I describe two cases at very considerable length because each of these is intended to illustrate all the major principles of corporate planning. Although all these cases are based on real life, I have heavily disguised the companies, products, locations, markets and the people involved. I have done this because I cannot see any advantage to be gained by revealing the name of the organization – especially since Part 1 is only concerned with principles rather than with particular practical problems. On the other hand there are serious disadvantages for the organization concerned if its name is revealed, not the least of which is that its competitors may gain an important insight into its strategic thinking. But there are other reasons for preserving anonymity which I describe more fully in Chapter 10.

I have also included some case studies among the exercises for students in Part 2. These exercises are intended to serve two functions. Firstly I hope that students will find them useful as a means of testing out their grasp of the principles and techniques of corporate planning. Secondly I hope they will help the teacher of corporate planning to mount practical projects based on them for the further enlightenment of his students. I hope teachers will also find the specimen syllabus for corporate planning courses useful.

References

As I have written this book for use in schools, colleges, universities, management schools and company training colleges – wherever management is taught – I have assumed that the student will have ready access to a small selection of journals and books on corporate planning. I certainly hope he will have access to the *Journal of the Long Range Planning Society* and to Ansoff and Steiner and perhaps one or two others. However, as explained earlier, this is not a traditional textbook with hundreds of references to previous works on the subject for the student to follow up. He may, however, wish to verify some of my remarks about other authors' statements and to enable him to do this I have indicated the relevant chaper in that author's standard work. Thus when I refer to something that Ansoff says in Chapter 6 of his *Corporate Strategy* I write, '... as Ansoff (Ch. 6) says ...' or to something that Steiner says in Chapter 12 of his *Top Management Planning* I write, '... as Steiner (Ch. 12) remarks. ...'

The standard works to which I make reference throughout this book are as follows:

Russell L. Ackoff   *A Concept of Corporate Planning*
H. Igor Ansoff   *Corporate Strategy*
J. Thomas Cannon   *Business Strategy and Policy*
Basil W. Denning   *Corporate Planning; Selected Concepts*
David W. Ewing   *The Practice of Planning*
D. E. Hussey   *Introducing Corporate Planning*
Bruce Payne   *Planning for Company Growth*
George A. Steiner   *Top Management Planning*
Isay Stemp   *Corporate Growth Strategies*
B. H. Walley   *How to Apply Strategy in Profit Planning*

E. Kirby Warren *Long Range Planning; the Executive Viewpoint*
E. H. and G. F. Weinwurm *Long-term Profit Planning*

Acknowledgement
I particularly wish to thank Mrs P. J. Henley for typing this book from my manuscript.

JOHN ARGENTI

PART ONE

PART ONE

1 Corporate planning and management

People and organizations

Human beings have certain needs, wants, desires and instincts which can be satisfied in either of two ways. We can try to get what we want on our own, each person acting for himself in rugged isolation, or we can form an organization. We can do some things very much better on our own; we should be grateful that Beethoven did not form an organization to write his Ninth. But to land a man on the moon we need an organization.

An organization consists of two or more people working together to satisfy a need – one of their own needs or of someone else. The closer these people work together the more likely is the organization to be effective and this implies that certain things have to be agreed and understood between them; the nature of the need that their organization has set out to satisfy has to be agreed, for example. So have the means to be employed, what each person in the organization is to do, when he is to do it, and so on. The process of deciding such things, of communicating these decisions, of controlling the organization in its progress towards achieving its purpose, is known as the process of management. No organization can be effective unless this process exists. In large organizations one can see and hear the process being carried on because certain employees called managers have been invited to conduct the process and they have at their disposal an array of charts, telephones and computers to help them. One has only to watch them at work to see the management process in action. In smaller organizations it may be more difficult to see this because it is carried on so informally – there may not be a 'manager' as such at all in some organizations. Nevertheless the process is going on formally or informally, deliberately or subconsciously, autocratically or democratically, conscientiously or negligently. It is important to distinguish between what management is and the manner in which it is performed.

The process of management

Although wide differences in definition can be found in the management literature the process of management can be reduced to a minimum of four steps. For any given manager in any organization the process starts when he agrees to carry out the instructions of his boss. Step 1 of the management process can thus be described as 'Accept Task'. Step 2 consists of deciding the best way of carrying out this task – call this 'Decide How'. The manager will then give instructions to his subordinates so that each of them will be acting to contribute to the successful completion of his task. That is Step 3 – 'Give Instructions'. Finally, the manager sets up some form of reporting procedure by which he can judge what progress is being made towards the successful completion of his task; this Step 4 could be called 'Check Results'. It should be noted that if, when the manager checks results, he finds that his task may not be successfully completed he returns to Step 2 and re-decides how to tackle the job in the light of the new circumstances. If, on the other hand, he finds that the task has been completed or that it will definitely not be then he will report to his boss. The process is shown in Exhibit 1·1.

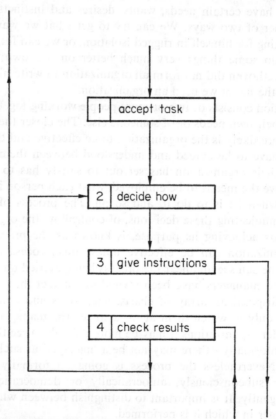

Exhibit 1·1   The four-step management process
(for one manager for one task)

Some authors believe that the minimum management process contains far more than four steps. Very often 'Motivating' is included but although motivating is certainly something that managers may have to do it is not an additional step in the process of management; it merely describes how some managers take some of the four steps. Some authors, Ernest Dale for example, include 'Innovating' as a step. Innovating is certainly something that managers may do but they would do it in Step 2 – 'Decide How', where, on occasions, they may well decide not to innovate. Motivation and innovation are not *extra* activities of the process; they are the taking of some of the steps in a particular manner. (I suggested above that it would be helpful to hold in our minds the distinction between what management is and the manner in which it is performed). Some authors add 'Controlling' as a further step, but controlling is not an additional activity, it is the repeated performance of two of the four steps in a cyclic sequence. 'Controlling' is the cycle: Deciding – Checking Results – re-Deciding – re-Checking – re-Deciding, repeated until the task is complete. All other complex management activities, such as co-ordinating, can be seen as composites of these four basic steps.

The four-step process is valid for all managers at all levels in all organizations. The chief executive goes through exactly the same sequence as the charge-hand does; the style, the content and the nature and scale of their respective tasks are different, but the basic logic of the management process is always the same.

The process of planning

Consider now the second of the four steps of the management process, the one called 'Decide How'. When a manager has been given an urgent task he may take Step 2 in the few seconds that it takes him to dial his subordinate's telephone number. As soon as the subordinate answers, the manager is ready to give him his instructions i.e. he is ready to take Step 3, 'Give Instructions'. But if this manager had been given a very complex task by his boss the 'Decide How' step might take hours, days or even years to complete. Even though it is possible to complete Step 2 in a fraction of a second it is nevertheless a rather complex process even at its simplest.

Consider what happens immediately after a manager has been given a task by his boss. His first thought will be to weigh up the size and importance of the task; it may be simple and urgent or complex and urgent or important but not urgent. Depending upon his evaluation of these factors he will decide what resources it would be appropriate to allocate to the decision-making process itself. We might call this Stage A of Step 2, 'Decide How to Make the Decision'. In the second stage the Manager will consider the various alternative ways by which his task might be completed. In the third stage he will evaluate each of these and select the best one – the act of making this choice being the actual moment of decision. Finally, before he can give instructions to his subordinates he may have to draw up some form of plan of action for each of them to follow. Exhibit 1·2 shows this four-stage sub-process of decision making within the context of the four-step management process.

It is interesting to note that this description of the decision making process is also a description of the planning process. The two appear to be identical; indeed they *are* identical in logic. They are distinguished in practice only in one respect – the extent to which a manager takes deliberate and conscious care over a decision. When a manager makes a decision in an instant we say he has taken a decision. When he makes a decision carefully, deliberately, systematically and formally we say he has planned. Planning is merely one way of making a decision. Planning is taking a decision carefully and deliberately.

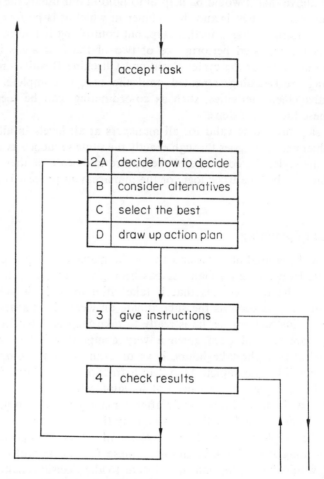

Exhibit 1·2 How the deciding or planning process fits into the process of management

Planning is often defined as taking decisions before one takes action. Ackoff (Ch. 1) for example, calls it '*anticipatory* decision-making'. But although this definition is entirely correct it implies that some alternative to planning exists, such as the taking of an action *without* first deciding what action to take. This alternative does not exist. Even in an emergency – an impending car crash, for example – one must decide what to do before one does it, even if the time for thought is only milliseconds. Perhaps, therefore, this is not the key distinction between planning and not planning; the key difference is the quality of thought that goes into a decision. We talk of 'hatching a plot' and 'laying a plan', popular expressions which imply incubation, a gestation period, a period of careful systematic thought that precedes a *decision* rather than preceding an action. Planning is taking deliberate care over a decision. But even this definition, while perfectly correct, is no more helpful because 'taking care' and 'deliberate' and 'systematic' are relative terms. They do not allow us to place a definitive line between planning and not planning. We cannot say that a manager who took ten hours over a decision has planned while his colleague who only took nine hours (or nine minutes) has not.

A better way to define planning is to describe it as the process that leads to a plan. A plan is a set of instructions to someone and the planning process ends when these are ready to be issued. The planning process, then, starts after a manager has accepted a task from his boss and when he first considers how much effort to devote to it (Stage A). If he decides that the task warrants the exercise of great care and thought then he will deliberately search for imaginative alternative ways of performing the task (Stage B), he will carefully examine the merits of each before making up his mind (Stage C), and he will then prepare detailed plans for each of his subordinates (Stage D). But if at Stage A he decides that prompt action is indicated he will perform the remaining stages at such a speed that they will be reduced almost to vanishing point. Thus his decision at Stage C will consist of selecting the best out of a very few alternatives after a necessarily hasty and superficial examination and the action plans that he draws up for his subordinates at Stage D may be no more elaborate than a few words probably spoken rather than written. Deciding, then, is a truncated form of planning. Planning is an extended form of deciding. Both lead to the giving of instructions but in the one case they usually are brief and simple and in the other usually complex and carefully devised.

The hierarchy of managers

At every level in every organization managers go through the same four-step process of management and the same four-stage process of planning or deciding within it, although the style, the manner and the content differ for each manager and each task. Thus just as a manager's style of managing may be conscientious or negligent so may a manager go through the planning process carefully or quickly. What planning is and how it is done should be distinguished. The content of plans also differs widely from manager to manager; thus there is production planning, project planning, manpower planning and so on for almost as many types of planning as there are management tasks.

In most organizations the relationship between the managers is hierarchical; that is, each manager reports to a boss above him and has several subordinates below him for whom he is responsible. We can show the essential logic of this arrangement by simply placing several Exhibit 1·1s one on top of the other as in Exhibit 1·3. The decisions taken by managers near the top of the hierarchy will usually be more important than those taken by managers lower down – that is, these decisions will have a more far reaching effect upon the organiza-

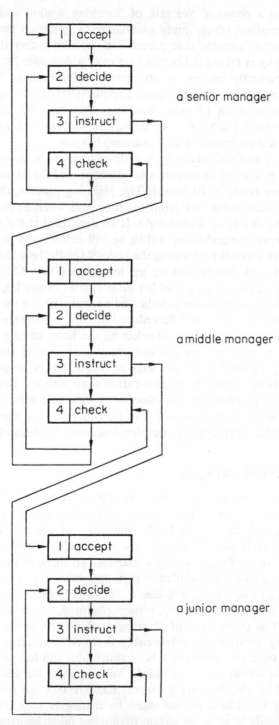

**Exhibit 1·3   Three managers is a hierarchy
(Only one subordinate is shown for each)**

tion's ability to achieve its purpose than those taken lower down. One would expect that senior managers would spend more time planning (as opposed to 'deciding') because, at Stage A in their planning process they would recognize that the importance of their decisions justifies the expenditure of considerable resources at the decision-making step. Managers in the upper levels of the hierarchy take some decisions of such importance to the organizations that they are categorized as being 'strategic'. Unfortunately it is not possible to define strategic planning in such a way as to draw any sharp line between it and tactical or any other sort of planning. Steiner (Ch. 2) lists no less than fifteen differences between strategic and tactical planning but adds that both in theory and in practice all these lines of demarcation are blurred. Ansoff (Ch. 1) suggests that strategic decisions are those that arise because of external influences on the company (i.e. from its environment) as opposed to tactical decisions which arise from internal problems. He adds that some operational or tactical problems might be more important to the success or failure of the firm than some strategic problems – i.e. that strategic problems cannot always be said to be 'more important' than tactical.

In this book I will use the words 'strategic decision' to mean a decision that affects or is intended to affect the organization *as a whole* over long periods of time as opposed to parts, sections, departments or elements of it. This definition does not help to sharpen any of the blurred lines of demarcation that Steiner lists but it does place emphasis on the one distinction between strategic and other planning that is most relevant to the study of corporate planning, namely the *corporate* nature of this type of planning. This definition suggests that production planning, project planning and product planning, for example, are not strategic because they are concerned with only parts or elements of an organization rather than with the organization as a corporate whole. By this definition *very* few types of planning are strategic.

It may be thought that the proper definition of strategic planning is a matter of indifference to anyone other than a lexicographer. In later chapters, however, we must attempt to draw up a list of duties for the corporate planner; unless these can be stated with some precision there is a danger of friction between him and those who work in areas adjacent to him.

Strategic planning, then, is the careful, deliberate, systematic taking of decisions which affect, or are intended to affect the organization as a whole (as opposed to only parts of it) over long periods of time.

Planners and managers

Some managers manage without the assistance of any advisers. They make their own decisions, give instructions unaided, check results themselves. But most managers today have access to advisers; there are operations research experts who help the manager to select the best of alternative actions; there are behavioural scientists to advise on the best way of giving instructions; there are accountants and statisticians to help managers to check results.

A planner is strictly speaking someone who helps or advises a manager how best to perform his Step 2 of the management process. However, in practice the planning of a task is intimately linked with checking results in Step 4. We often speak of Planning and Control as if it was one activity; in fact, as can be seen from Exhibit 1·1, it consists of the sequence Decide – Check Results – re-Decide – re-Check – re-Decide. Because of this close linkage it often falls to the planner not only to advise and help the manager to plan but also to check and interpret results. Furthermore, managers who have been given a complex task by their boss very often invite a planner to help him to clarify exactly what the task is – in other words to clarify the objectives he has been set by his boss. Thus in practice planners advise managers not only on Step 2 of the management process but also on Steps 1 and 4 as well. Managers do not normally invite planners to help them with Step 3 – 'Give Instructions' – because this is the step at which a manager's authority is exercised. Planners are advisers and have no authority to give instructions.

Corporate planning

I suggested above that planning is the careful, systematic taking of decisions. In just the same way corporate planning is the careful systematic taking of strategic decisions.

I also suggested that the word planning has come to mean more than just the process of planning that managers carry out in Step 2 of the management process. It has come to include the Step 2 – Step 4 control or co-ordination cycle and the clarification of objectives at Step 1 as well. In the same way corporate planning includes not only the systematic taking of strategic decisions but the checking of strategic results also; perhaps it should be called 'Corporate Planning and Control'. And it also includes the clarification of objectives. But, since it is *corporate* planning the objectives it is concerned to clarify are the corporate objectives for the organization as a whole as opposed to parts of it. We may describe corporate planning as follows:

'Corporate planning is a systematic approach to clarifying corporate objectives, making strategic decisions and checking progress towards the objectives. (See Exhibit 1·4). Corporate objectives are the objectives for the organization as a whole, not for parts of it; strategic decisions are decisions which affect, or are intended to affect, the organization as a whole over long periods of time'.

We have also reached several conclusions about the nature of corporate plans in this chapter. A corporate plan is very much like any other type of plan in that it is a carefully considered set of instructions to someone. A sales manager's plan may be a set of instructions to the salesmen that they should do this on Mondays and that on Tuesdays. A corporate plan is no different to this, except, of course, that the content and style is different. We can describe a corporate plan as follows:

'A corporate plan is a set of instructions to the managers of an organization describing what role each constituent part is expected to play in the achievement of the organization's corporate objectives'.

We have also seen that a corporate planner's function is not significantly different to that of any other specialist planner; only the content of his advice and the level in the hierarchy at which he gives it is different. We can describe him as follows:

'A corporate planner helps the chief executive (or the top executive body) to clarify corporate objectives, make strategic decisions and check results. Corporate planners do not give instructions to managers'.

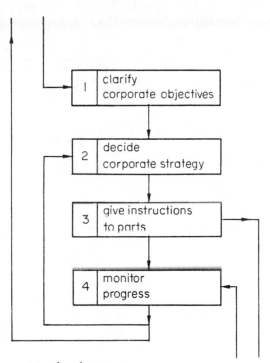

Exhibit 1·4   The corporate planning process

Finally it should be noted that all organizations make strategic decisions and have done so since the dawn of history. Corporate planning is nothing more than a particular way of taking these decisions. Strategic decisions can be taken carefully or negligently, deliberately or haphazardly or systematically. When an organization declares that it is 'introducing corporate planning' it means that it will in future clarify its objectives and make its strategic decisions in a more deliberately systematic manner.

Summary of Chapter 1

In this chapter I have suggested that we should try to distinguish between what management is and the manner in which it is performed. Conceptually management is a comparatively simple process containing four basic steps. One of these is called 'deciding' and one way of deciding is called 'planning'. Planning is taking decisions carefully and systematically. Corporate planning is taking corporate decisions in this way and corporate decisions are ones that affect the organization as a whole as opposed to decisions that affect only parts of it. Corporate planners are specialists who advise and help managers take these decisions and help to clarify corporate objectives and exercise control.

2   The need for a systematic approach

In this chapter I shall examine the reasons behind the recent surge of interest in corporate planning systems and then identify some of the essential features that any such system must have.

Many of the trends that have forced senior managers to adopt corporate planning in the past two decades have had precisely the same effects at all levels of management; more managers at all levels are now having to do more planning. However some trends have affected the activities of senior managers more than those of middle managers so that although most managers now have to do more planning the senior ones have found that they have to do far more. One of the trends that affects senior managers in particular is society's growing interest in the behaviour of organizations.

Society's growing interest and concern

I suggested in Chapter 1 that one subject for study in corporate planning is the clarification of corporate objectives. Until quite recently most chief executives probably felt confident that they knew with some accuracy what the objectives of their organization were. In the past few decades, however, their confidence has been progressively undermined and, by the late Sixties, the debate over corporate objectives for companies, nationalized corporations, certain professional bodies, some of the organized churches, some charities and even the nation state itself became the subject of considerable public debate. The fundamental role of these organizations in society came under scrutiny not only from the press, politicians, sociologists and academics but, more directly from protest groups and even the man in the street.

As a matter of fact this heightened interest in objectives has affected all levels of management and has recently resulted in the appearance of a wide variety of management techniques (such as Management by Objectives and Program Budgeting) designed to systematize the clarification of objectives. However, the debate on objectives has nowhere been more inconclusive and unsatisfactory than for the top level of objectives, i.e. those to be set for organizations as a whole. It is because this debate has so far been both sterile and even at times heated that many chief executives now have to devote much more time and resources to that part of corporate planning in which corporate objectives are clarified.

One of the reasons why society's interest in corporate objectives has recently become so keen is that many organizations, especially multinational companies, have become large enough to rival the power of the nation state itself. The activities of these companies, together with some trade unions and some other organizations now have a significant political and social impact in national and international affairs.

Employees are also now showing a much greater interest in the corporate objectives of the organizations for which they work. Senior managers have always shown this interest – indeed some authors maintain that corporate objectives are largely determined by the formation of a consensus of opinion among senior managers – but lately employees on all levels have shown a greater awareness of the meaning and importance of objectives. Not so many years ago shop floor employees were interested only in pay and conditions of work; lately they have become more interested in the content of their own jobs and those of their boss – and, more recently, they have begun to show a preference for working for organizations whose corporate objectives appeal to them personally and with which they can identify themselves.

But there is yet another reason why the centre of interest has moved up to the area of corporate objectives; it is that the spotlight of study has for decades been moving upwards through the hierarchical levels of management. The first areas of management to be subjected to systematic study were those of the shop floor and office floor and this resulted, decades ago, in the development of such systematic management techniques as Work Measurement and Organization and Methods. Then the centre of interest moved up to the middle levels resulting in such techniques as Operations Research. In much the same way the techniques of selling were developed during the Thirties and Forties but in the Fifties came the study of marketing – marketing being a more general field of study than selling and one that is usually practised by managers higher up the hierarchy. In the Sixties the spotlight moved up again, to strategic decision-making at the chief executive level and in the Seventies it moved up again to the area of long term fundamental corporate objectives which are set to the chief executive by those above him right at the top of the hierarchy. It appears that as soon as one area of management becomes systematized it then becomes apparent that the validity of that system depends upon decisions made by a manager higher up the hierarchy and so the spotlight of attention moves up.

Size, complexity and variety

The size of organizations in virtually every field of human activity has been increasing. There have been more mergers between churches, professional bodies, trade unions and, most notably, companies then ever before – indeed the rate of merger between companies in the Sixties was such as to lead Professor Perlmutter to predict that, in the Eighties, over half the needs of the Western world would be provided by a mere two hundred companies. Now a decision taken by a manager in a large organization will commit more resources than one taken by his opposite number in a smaller organization; the larger the decision the more carefully must it be taken. Larger decisions demand more planning.

One consequence of size is complexity; the larger an organization becomes the more complex will each decision become if only because there are more people to consult. But complexity is not caused only by size; many of the new technologies are more complex than the older technologies; there are now more regulations controlling the activities of companies, some of which are extremely complex. The causes of the increasing complexity of management decisions are many; the consequence is that before a decision can be taken it is necessary to do more planning.

Both these trends, which affect managers at every level in the hierarchy, are mentioned by all the authors in this field. Less often mentioned, but of major significance, is the increasing range of choice in all goods and services. Just as the choice of packaged foods available to the housewife has grown in the past few decades so have the different sources of capital available to the finance director, the choice of machine tools to the production manager, of advertising media to the marketing manager. Now a decision is the act of choosing between alternatives; if there are more alternatives the act of choosing becomes more difficult and requires more care. Taking more care over a decision is another way of saying more planning. There is a second consequence of this increased variety in the modern world; organizations which provide this growing range of goods and services of all kinds find that they have to invest in progressively more specialized equipment. If one of their investment decisions turns out to have been wrong the residual market value of this equipment is often negligible. In other words the penalty for error rises as the trend towards specialization proceeds.

The rate of change and the time span of decisions

It is widely acknowledged that the rate of change in the modern world is now much greater than even a few decades ago. New technologies appear and old ones disappear more quickly, new social patterns form and re-form, new roads and bridges appear and old ones disappear faster than ever before. The consequences of this upon a decision-maker are that he will now have less confidence that a decision that is correct for today will still be valid tomorrow. He has therefore to examine what would happen if his decision becomes invalid and this represents an important *additional* criterion by which he must judge the best of the many alternatives that lie before him.

Now the position of the decision-maker has come to this; because his decisions are larger and more complex and the range of alternatives before him is greater he must now spend more time on planning. Because he spends more time on planning the period of time that elapses between the moment he is given a task and the moment it is successfully completed has grown. It has grown because the planning stage has grown; but in addition the total time for

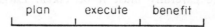

plan   execute   benefit

time taken to plan, execute and obtain benefit from
a task a few decades ago

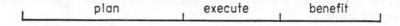

plan   execute   benefit

time taken to plan, execute and obtain benefit from a task today

Exhibit 2·1   The lengthening time spans of tasks

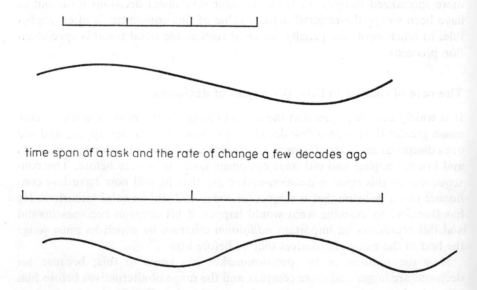

time span of a task and the rate of change a few decades ago

time span of a task and the rate of change today

Exhibit 2.2 Larger time spans and faster change lead to much greater risk

completion of the task may well have grown even more because, since his current tasks are larger than his previous tasks (because his organization has grown) the time to execute them may also have grown. Exhibit 2·1 shows this lengthening Time Span of Decisions. But that is not all; not only may it now take, say five years to plan and complete a task where before it took only three, during those five years the number of changes that may occur has increased due to the increased rate of change. This is shown in Exhibit 2·2. Thus the decisions made during the planning stage are at risk for a longer period of time and are also at a higher level of risk for that time.

All types of planning, including strategic, have lately entered this vicious circle. Decisions are becoming more difficult; so it is necessary to spend longer on planning. If one spends longer on planning one must plan further ahead. If one plans further ahead it means making forecasts further into the future. The further ahead one forecasts the greater will be the level of uncertainty. The greater the uncertainty the more difficult the decision – and so back to the start of the vicious cirle of spending longer on the planning, planning still further ahead with still more errors in the forecast and so on.

This vicious circle is very real and its effects are everywhere to be seen, not least in the way in which some advanced planning techniques, described in Part 2, have been developed to meet it. Perhaps the most interesting effect has been the development of new styles of management and organization that have emerged not to meet the demands of the circle but to break it. (See page 24).

Human factors

The increase in the volume of planning at all levels and the growing time horizon of plans are caused partly by the purely technical factors, such as physical lead-times, reviewed above. In addition there are some more subtle but powerful psychological forces working in the same direction.

In the past few decades the pattern and style of management has changed. In the past managers would tell their subordinates not only what to do but also how to do it – often in great detail. Having done so the manager would check up on the subordinate's progress and exercise control over him at frequent intervals. This emphasis on detail and short time horizons is typical of the now declining authoritarian style of management. The new style places far more emphasis on allowing much wider discretion to subordinates and this is achieved in practice by giving instructions to them that are much less detailed and cover a longer period and also by checking up on their progress much less often. Typically the modern sales manager, for example, will now set his salesmen their objectives for a period of a month at a time, whereas before he would have set objectives for only a week ahead.

We know from our discussion above that severe difficulties arise when the time span of a decision is increased; there are severe disadvantages in setting objectives and laying plans further ahead than is absolutely necessary. When a sales manager sets his salesmen their objectives for a month ahead instead of a week he is almost certain to face some of the technical problems associated with the 'vicious circle' but he reaps no compensating technical advantages whatever. The sole justification for setting objectives for further ahead than is technically necessary is that, in modern conditions, it has a compensating motivational value. It seems probable that the time horizon of plans will lengthen all the way up the hierarchy for this psychological reason quite apart from the effect of lengthening lead-times. Managers may have to plan further ahead than is technically necessary.

Centrifugal forces

One further trend that has emerged strongly in more recent years is one that specifically affects the managers at the top of the hierarchy. It is a phenomenon found mainly in the larger organization; namely the difficulty of holding the organization together as a coherent whole. It is not only a matter of maintaining control – manifestly this must be more difficult for the chief executive of a large organization than of a small one – there is also the problem of deciding which new activities will best complement the existing ones, how the existing ones should be altered to maintain the organization's balance in a changing environment and, in general, the problem of managing change in a large, complex and widespread organization. The problem is one of deciding what changes to make as well as giving effect to them and controlling them.

Companies appear to be responding to this problem in two very different ways. One of these leads to the formation of conglomerates, to bottom-up management, to venture management – and in some cases to loss of control and even anarchy. The essence of this response is for managers to abdicate, partially but deliberately, from their responsibilities as managers who, traditionally, have always decided what their subordinates should do and what role they should play within the organization. Thus a true conglomerate is composed of autonomous subsidiaries having no synergistic relationship with each other; the chief exective of the parent company has, in effect, decided not to attempt to plan the future shape of the group. His strategy is to have no strategy. In fact it is extremely doubtful whether a true conglomerate exists or has ever existed; all the so-called conglomerates are to some degree designed by the parent, nevertheless in theory a true conglomerate could exist and some companies come close to being intentionally unplanned in this sense. Managers who adopt Venture Management have the same principle in mind; they allow certain of their subordinates to form new business enterprises the nature of which rests entirely with the subordinate. In much the same way true Bottom-up Management consists of allowing subordinates to take their own decisions rather than carrying out their boss's instructions, with the result that presumably the company does what they want it to do and it becomes what they want it to become. One company, Jewel Companies Inc., claims to have adopted an inverted pyramid form of organization in which the traditional hierarchy has been turned upside down (see *International Management*, July 1971).

One disadvantage of this philosophy is that it may lead to complete loss of control and even to anarchy – it probably has in some cases. Another is that the organization may lose sight of its fundamental purpose or pursue so many different objectives that few of them can be achieved. But this approach does have two advantages; its philosophy is more in line with the modern trend towards allowing subordinates greater discretion and, secondly, it breaks the 'vicious circle'. It does this because the manager avoids planning; he delegates his decisions to his subordinates.

The opposite response to these increased centrifugal forces is to try to bind the organization together more tightly so that it can continue to be managed as a corporate whole by the chief executive. Amongst the techniques in this category are the Overlord system, the Matrix form of organization, project managers, program budgets, company models (all of which are discussed in Part 2) and, of course, corporate planning.

One of the functions of corporate planning, then, is to assist the chief executive to hold his company together against the increasing forces of disintegration. This function is peculiar to corporate planning and distinguishes it from all other types of planning. Indeed one can go further and suggest that one of the causes of disintegration, of lack of cohesion in companies, is that there are so many other types of planning. Companies, even quite small ones, have become so departmentalized that only an overall or *corporate* plan could weld together all the production plans, marketing plans, project plans, long range plans, strategic plans, manpower plans, financial plans, schedules, charts and budgets. But this statement, while true, implies that a corporate plan is merely the co-ordinated sum of all these specialized plans; it is nearer the truth to say that all these plans should spring *from* the corporate plan. In theory, if each departmental plan is derived from a corporate plan, then each of them will be consistent with all the others, thus creating a fully coherent organization.

When corporate planning is necessary

A company's need for corporate planning depends, then, upon a large number of factors. Its size is one, another is its complexity, another is the time span of strategic decisions, another the rate of change to which its environment is subject. The extent to which it provides specialist goods or services to a segmented market is another; another is the nature of the style of management it has adopted and yet another is the centrifugal forces to which it is subjected. The growing public interest in corporate objectives is another.

In theory it might be possible to calculate how much corporate planning any company should do by measuring the extent to which it was affected by each of these factors; nothing of the sort is possible in practice although Denning (Ch. 14) has examined the relationship between the duties of corporate planning departments and the size, capital intensity, rate of technological change and so on of the companies in which they operate.

It might be thought that some relationship between the extent of corporate planning actually done in a company and the extent to which it was affected by these factors could be established. Although very little formal research has been published there does not appear to be any such link. Many well-known companies can be clearly seen to be facing major long term problems but have not adopted corporate planning and are making no attempt to tackle their problems systematically.

It might be thought that companies which practise corporate planning would show a better record of profit or earnings per share or some other long term criterion of success than those that do not. Although 75% of the largest American companies have now set up formal corporate planning systems there does not appear to be any clear evidence that success and corporate planning are correlated. Ansoff (*L.R.P.* Vol 3, No 2, 1970) brings evidence to show that acquisitions have generally been more successful if they have resulted from long range planning then if they were unplanned. There is evidence that managers believe that corporate planning has resulted in better decisions, in a greater awareness of company policy, in improved awareness of problems, in clarifying objectives – many authors quote testimonials to corporate planning by satisfied managers (see, for example, Warren or Weinwurm). It may be the case that all attempts to prove that corporate planning brings success are doomed to failure for it is not possible to predict what might have happened to a company if it had not used corporate planning or what might have happened to a company not using it if it had.

It is questionable whether improved profit is really the main justification for corporate planning. It is true that textbooks emphasize the positive aspects, such as the search for opportunities, 'making the future happen as we want it' and so on, all of which may be valid, but many companies appear to adopt corporate planning *after* they have been through a period of rapid growth. It is difficult to avoid the impression that dramatic successes come mainly to companies headed by a vigorous entrepreneur rather than ones in which corporate planning is highly developed. (see *Is Corporate Planning Necessary?* published by the British Institute of Management). Corporate planning, then, should perhaps be regarded not so much as an offensive weapon by which to achieve spectacular success but as a defence against the increasingly difficult problems of management in the modern world such as those listed in the above sections.

How much corporate planning?

If the largely defensive nature of corporate planning is accepted then the resources that a company should devote to corporate planning will be related to a company's need to defend itself against the effects of the growing complexity of its decisions, the rate of change, the increased interest that society takes in its objectives, the immediacy of a major strategic decision and so on. All these multifarious factors combine to produce one consequence of transcending significance for estimating the need for corporate planning; this is the penalty for error.

Many of the factors listed in the above sections of this chapter conspire together to increase the penalty to a company for making a mistake; it is against this possibility that a company most needs defence. Larger decisions, more specialized equipment, higher rates of change – they all point in this direction. The minimum resources that a company should devote to corporate planning therefore are those that will ensure that no strategic decision is made that contains a penalty of unacceptable magnitude. If corporate planning achieves nothing else it should at least do that.

It is possible to state the maximum resources that should be devoted to corporate planning; additional resources should not be committed to planning beyond the point when they result in a decision that is better by less than these marginal resources. In other words one should not attempt to search for the best strategic plan but only for the plan that is good enough to convince one that it is not worth searching for a better one. Neither of these statements can be quantified in practice; there is no practical method for calculating how much to spend on corporate planning. But these two statements do provide the essential bracket within which resources may be allocated to corporate planning even though the allocation can only be made subjectively and qualitatively.

Failure to use corporate planning

There are four main reasons why companies do not employ the corporate planning approach even when it becomes manifestly clear that they should be doing so.

Warren (Ch. 3) describes three 'roadblocks' to planning. One is the overwhelming pressure for short term results; the urgent always receives more attention than the important. This roadblock is mentioned by many authors in this field (see Weinwurm (Ch. 2), for example) and it must be considered the most important of all. I shall refer to it frequently in later chapters. The second roadblock is the nature of the personality of chief executives. One of the characteristics of men who achieve high executive positions is their ability to get things done. They have to know how to act quickly and decisively. That does not inevitably imply that these men are incapable of reflective thought – to suggest that chief executives are incapable of the disciplined thought that must be exercised in systematic corporate planning is of course ridiculous. Nevertheless it may be true that many chief executives prefer to get things done rather than think about getting them done. Even if they do not have this preference, the pressure for short term results may force it on them. Since Warren drew attention to this roadblock in 1966 it has received wide recognition and, as a result, it may now be less valid. Most chief executives today are on their guard against it and recognize the need to involve themselves more closely with the development of corporate objectives and strategy. Many of them deliberately set aside a substantial proportion of their time for these activities and it may be that, increasingly, candidates for senior executive positions who cannot do so will not be appointed.

Warren's third roadblock concerns the personality of planners. It is often suggested that planners and executives tend to represent two opposite human categories. It is said that planners have all the necessary theoretical knowledge to prepare a plan but lack the political skills and judgement to make it a practical proposition in the real world. This may well be why the central problem in the relationship between planners and executives is that of convincing executives that real practical tangible advantages can be obtained from the planning process. Executives will feel no commitment to a plan, however brilliantly conceived and technically excellent it may be, unless they are convinced that the results will be better than one of their own snap decisions vigorously executed. It is because tangible results do not appear from the corporate planning process for so many years that senior executives tend to be so sceptical of the value of time spent on this type of planning. But it seems probable that increasingly only those candidates for senior planning positions who know how to take account of the earthy nature of reality in their plans will be appointed.

Any system of corporate planning must be designed to take account of these three roadblocks. These three are not the only causes of failure to introduce corporate planning and to use it effectively – Hussey lists several more (Chs. 1 and 2), Steiner presents a long list in Denning (Ch.15), Payne adds several more (Ch. 1) – but they are three of the most important. There is one other of equal importance, namely the execrable quality of the information available to corporate planners.

The quality of information

Consider the three main areas of interest to corporate planners. First there is the clarification of corporate objectives; here opinions vary widely as to what these are and even what the words mean is open to discussion. It is a cliché that if an organization has not determined what its objectives are it cannot decide how to achieve them and yet this is precisely what the position is today; entrepreneurs used to know very well what their objectives were – chief executives are not so sure as I pointed out above. Thus the corporate planner may not even know what his company's corporate plans are intended to achieve.

At the second stage, where the corporate plans themselves are drawn up, much reliance has to be placed on long range forecasts; all plans are based on forecasts, but corporate plans are based on forecasts that may extend so far into the future that confidence in their validity falls to nearly zero. It is not only the forecasts that are suspect – the validity of many statements about the present position of the company are frequently suspect also. (Many companies do not know what contribution each activity makes to their overall profits now – let alone what this may be in a few years' time.) Most of the statements made about the strategic position of the company within its current environment are subjective; very few of them can be stated objectively and quantitatively.

The third stage of corporate planning consists of monitoring the progress of the company towards its objectives. Even assuming that these objectives are known with infinite accuracy, which they are not, so variable are company results from year to year that many years may elapse before even the most advanced statistical analysis can reveal a significant trend (see Case Study 1 in Chapter 10, for example).

The central core of corporate planning is the hard fact that there are very few hard facts. This accounts for much of the scepticism shown towards it by pragmatic executives. To suggest that corporate planning can be useful in spite of the poor quality of information available is to state only a fraction of the truth. The full truth is that corporate planning is necessary *because* information for strategic decisions is so poor. Corporate planning *is* the study of major decisions based on poor information.

The need for a system

The need to adopt a systematic approach to corporate decision-making stems from two of the problems mentioned in previous sections of this chapter. The first concerns one of Warren's roadblocks – that it is the pressure for short term results that is mainly responsible for a company's failure to give enough thought to long term results. The most effective counter to this phenomenon is for senior executives to set aside a proportion of their time for discussing matters of strategic importance. Even if their discussions are unstructured, even if they merely identify what strategic problems they face, even if their skills and knowledge of techniques of corporate planning are minimal, the mere setting aside of a period for thought on a routine basis would be better than nothing. If they decide that they have no strategic problems and therefore need not think about them, at least this decision would be deliberate, conscious, explicit and overt. The minimum requirement for any corporate planning system then, is a *deliberate procedural device* designed to focus attention upon corporate problems. How this should be achieved and what part the corporate planner should play in it is discussed later.

The second requirement derives from the assumption that there must be a right and wrong way to make corporate decisions. It must be presumed that better decisions will be obtained with less effort if certain steps in the decision-making process are completed in this sequence rather than that, if certain pieces of information are obtained in this form rather than that and so on. Weinwurm shows repeatedly that many companies have omitted whole sections of the corporate planning process (for example, about a fifth of the companies studied failed to identify objectives) and have failed to use vital information (for example, failure to co-ordinate the figures in a finance plan with those in a sales plan). Many companies omit the whole of the third element of corporate planning – monitoring progress towards objectives – and this renders the entire corporate planning exercise virtually useless. It is, then, essential to design a system to guide managers through this long and often complex process.

I shall later consider what essential features any corporate planning system must have; but first consider the use of flow charts as illustrative aids to the description of a system.

The use of flow charts

Many of the authors in this field attempt to clarify the details of possible corporate planning systems by means of flow charts. A typical example was the one described by F. Gilmore and R. G. Brandenberg in the *Harvard Business Review* of Nov-Dec 1962. Steiner (Ch. 2) displays several including one of his own. Ackoff shows one (fig. 6·1 in Ch. 6) of remarkable complexity.

Some of these charts are designed to show how particular companies organize their planning or how companies should organize it. However, experience suggests that companies do not adhere to elaborate systems for very long, not even when these are programmed on to a computer and recorded in detailed instruction manuals. Many systems are changed quite frequently, some are abandoned, and many others operate successfully only because managers take action outside the official system. Much the same is true of the detailed forms and documents (see Weinwurm's Exhibits, for example) which companies claim to use – no doubt they do use them but a high proportion of information exchanged in a company is transferred verbally, in special reports, at meetings and so on. None of these charts can show all the details of a planning system. Thus, for example, the Stanford Research Institute diagram (part of which is reproduced by Steiner (Chart 2·3 in Ch. 2) and by Weinwurm (Exhibit 1)) shows how the various types of planning are interrelated but although it includes plans for products, markets, finance and administration no plans for the purchasing function are shown. Neither the charts designed to show how planning should be done nor those showing how it is actually done can be expected to be accurate; some may be positively misleading.

A second difficulty is that there is some doubt whether all these detailed charts are logically consistent. The more detailed they are the more difficult it is to verify this point but where some boxes are labelled with activities (such as 'evalute') and others with sources of information (such as 'the environment') others with groups of people ('the planning committee') it is difficult to discern what meaning the lines joining them can have. Some of the lines must mean 'this is done next', others mean 'the data is used here', some of them must be feed-back loops. Unless immense care is taken with the definitions used in these charts they may do nothing more than mislead and confuse and this is true whether a diagram is drawn as a flow chart, as concentric circles, as hierarchical pyramids or multidimensional honeycomb structures. Students of planning may like to examine, for example, Friedmann's conceptual model for the analysis of planning behaviour to be found in Denning (fig. 4·1 in Ch. 4).

A third warning should be made. Stripped of all the details many charts appear as Exhibit 2·3 where a feed back is shown from the box marked 'review' to the one marked 'objectives'. This implies that when a manager reviews the progress he is making towards the achievement of a task (i.e. his objective) he will, if necessary, alter the objective in response to the progress he is making. Diagrams reflecting this layout can be found in Hussey (fig. 2 in Ch. 1), in Walley (fig. 3·1 in Ch. 3), in Stenier (fig. 2·1 in Ch. 2). Ackoff (fig. 6·1 in Ch. 6) does not show this feed back to objectives, however; his diagram, although vastly more detailed, has more in common with the diagram I showed in Exhibit 1·4 where the feed-back loop returns not to the 'objectives' but to the 'strategy' box. It is vital to understand why the point being raised here is not trivial but fundamental.

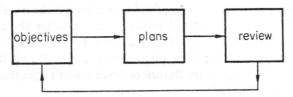

Exhibit 2·3   The Management Process as a closed loop

Fundamental conflicts in systems design

The question that these two rival types of diagram raise is whether a manager, fearing that he will not achieve the objectives set to him, may alter those objectives. One would think not; one would imagine that a manager faced with failure would either determine to find some new means of achieving the task or he would report the unhappy situation to his boss. His boss would then decide whether to alter the objective or to bring in extra resources to help the manager achieve the original objective. Thus a manager's objectives are altered by his boss, not by the manager. This cycle continues all the way up the hierarchy but just as the end link in a chain is logically different from all the others so the top objectives of an organization may be logically different from all other management objectives. Why this is so will be discussed in the next chapter; the consequence of this difference may be that top objectives cannot be altered by any manager and may not be affected by performance at all. Corporate objectives may be fundamentally different from management objectives. It is questionable whether Exhibit 2·3 is a valid representation of the corporate planning process; flow charts which take this form may be incorrect not merely in detail but in principle.

Another rather similar difference of opinion can be identified among the various flow charts in the corporate planning literature. Some flow charts imply that the first step in corporate planning is the clarification of corporate objectives. Others suggest that setting objectives is only the second step, the first being an examination of the company and its environment. This latter sequence implies that managers should set corporate objectives according to the prospects for the company; if the omens are favourable, then ambitious objectives will be selected, if unfavourable then objectives will be set at a lower level of achievement. This sequence is the one adopted by W. W. Simmons of IBM (see *L.R.P.* Vol. 1, No. 2, 1968) in which he suggests that the strategic thought process moves in the sequence; environment, objectives, strategy. He illustrates this sequence with a flow chart. Steiner (Ch. 2) quotes Smalter's *Steps in Planning and Problem Solving* which adopts the same approach. Figure 1·5 in Cannon (Ch. 1) suggests the same rationale. However, Steiner's own chart of the process (Chart 2·1 in Ch. 2) shows fundamental objectives first, so does Denning (fig. 1·9 in Ch. 1) and Hussey (fig. 2 in Ch. 1). It may be thought that perhaps it does not matter whether a planner studies the environment or sets objectives first, or even does both at once. In fact there must be occasions when it does matter.

Another very similar difference of opinion exists on the question of whether it is reasonable and logical to alter the objectives after the plans had been prepared. Ansoff suggests that objectives may be altered in the light of the confidence managers feel in their plans; he says (Ch. 2) that if a firm cannot find any means of achieving its Return on Investment target then it reduces the target. He calls this 'adaptive'.

Three pairs of opposite views are represented by these various charts and diagrams:

Some writers say that objectives are affected by results. Others say they are not.
Some writers say that objectives should be set only after a study of the environment has been made. Others say objectives should be set first.
Some writers say that objectives should be altered according to the manager's confidence in his plans. Others say that managers should search for a plan that will achieve the objectives.

I believe that any confusion these differing views may cause is due partly to differences in the definition of 'objectives', 'environment', 'strategy' rather than to any fundamental misconceptions, and partly to the author's need to simplify the flow charts for the sake of intelligibility.

The essence of a corporate planning system

The system to be described here has six essential elements – see Exhibit 2·4. It will be immediately observed that it is composed of two interlinked cycles. The cycle on the left of the diagram concerns the determination of corporate objectives and keeping them under review while the cycle on the right concerns the determination of strategy and keeping that under review. The cycles are linked by an arrow in one direction only, indicating that a strategy is selected only after the objectives have been decided – a strategy is valid only to the extent that it achieves the objectives – and that objectives are not affected by strategic decisions.

It should be noted that the factors that affect the choice of corporate objectives are, or may be, wholly different from the factors that are taken into account when selecting a strategy; that is why I have separated them into two different boxes in the chart. It should also be noted that the need to review objectives arises from stimuli that may be different from and independent of the stimuli that cause a review of strategy and each of the two cycles may take place at different times and over different periods of time.

Exhibit 2·4 is somewhat different from many of the charts that other writers devise. The justification for these differences lies in these two statements: (1)

that corporate objectives are in a different logical category to management objectives and may be determined by people who are not managers after consideration of factors that may be different from the factors taken into account in management decisions; and (2) that the sole justification for any given strategy is that it will achieve the corporate objectives and that, if it does not, then it is the strategy that is changed, not the objectives. If no strategy can be devised to achieve corporate objectives then the organization itself has failed (because the objectives are *corporate*) and it will be disbanded. I will discuss these conclusions again in the next chapter.

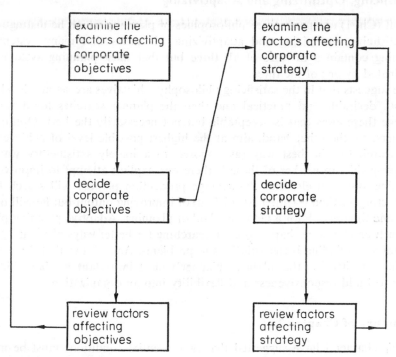

Exhibit 2·4   The objectives cycle and the strategy cycle in the corporate planning process

In the previous section I drew attention to three pairs of opposite views that appear in flow charts of the corporate planning process – Exhibit 2·4 suggests that corporate objectives are not affected by results nor by a manager's confidence in his plans. It also suggests that objectives cannot be determined until *some* of the environmental factors have been examined, i.e. those factors that affect the selection of objectives have to be examined before the objectives can be selected but those that affect strategic decisions may be examined before, during or after the determination of objectives – Exhibit 2·4 is neutral on that point – but it does show that strategic decisions cannot be taken until both the objectives and the factors affecting strategic decisions have been determined.

The layout of the remainder of Part 1 of this book is conditioned by Exhibit

2·4. Thus in the next chapter I shall consider the factors affecting the selection of corporate objectives, the nature of these and the need to keep them under review – Chapter 3 deals therefore with the left-hand cycle in Exhibit 2·4. In Chapters, 4, 5, 6 and 7 I shall consider the factors affecting strategic decisions, how the data concerning them is collected, and how such decisions are made. In Chapter 8 I shall discuss the last part of the right-hand cycle, namely the review of progress towards the corporate objectives and the revision of strategy that this review may provoke.

'Satisficing, Optimizing and Adaptivizing'

Ackoff (Ch. 1) compares three philosophies of planning which he distinguishes as satisficing, optimizing and adaptivizing. He notes that many systems of planning contain a mixture of all three but that most planning systems are dominated by one of the three.

He suggests that in the satisficing philosophy, objectives are set at a level that is both desirable and practical and then the planner searches for a way to achieve these aims that is acceptable but not necessarily the best. Optimizing planners, on the other hand, aim at the highest possible level of achievement and search for the best way (as opposed to a merely satisfactory way) of achieving this. In neither of these is there any explicit attempt to improve the planning system itself; thus the average production planner will search for a satisfactory method (or the best method) of improving output but he will not at the same time search for a better method of planning. Adaptive planning places as much emphasis, perhaps more, on searching for better ways of planning and control as on finding better solutions to problems. Ackoff says that the process of planning itself is the adaptive planner's most important product; his aim being to build responsiveness and flexibility into an organization.

Summary of Chapter 2

In this chapter I have suggested that two essential conditions must be met if corporate planning is to be used successfully. The first is that a *deliberate procedural device* must be employed which demands that managers periodically examine their strategic problems formally and conciously in order to overcome their natural preoccupation with short term problems. Secondly that there should be an understanding of the logic of the corporate planning process itself so that they tackle strategic planning *systematically* as suggested by the flow charts devised by various authors. The differences in design and layout of these charts may only be due to differences in definition and Exhibit 2·4 is an attempt to bring these into the open.

The need to use the corporate planning approach has recently increased because society and employees have become keenly interested in corporate objectives, because of the size of companies, the complexity of decisions, the variety of alternatives, the rate of change, growing lead times, changes in management style and the growth of centrifugal forces.

Corporate planning is probably of much less value as a device for dramatically improving results than as a defence against the rising penalty for error; it may be said that the study of corporate planning is largely the study of taking corporate decisions under conditions of severe uncertainty.

3 Corporate objectives

In this chapter I shall examine the various meanings of the word objective and discuss the factors that have to be considered when selecting objectives for a company.

Definition of corporate objectives

Most writers accept the idea that there is a hierarchy of objectives just as there is a hierarchy of managers. At each higher level in the hierarchy the objectives are more general and are relevant to a greater proportion of the company's activities so that the objectives at the top of the hierarchy are relevant to one hundred per cent of the company. In Exhibit 3·1, for example, those at the top are corporate objectives, those in the second level are departmental while at the lowest levels we find the objectives set to individual operators. In theory each operator should only do those things that contribute to the departmental objectives and departments should only do those things that contribute to the corporate objectives. The distinction between corporate and all other objectives is that they validate *all* the activities of the organization without exception. Thus if profit is the only corporate objective of a given company then any activity that contributes to profits is valid, any that does not is invalid. The sole justification for any activity in that company is that it contributes to profits. If increasing sales turnover improves the company's profits then sales should be increased, if not then sales should not be increased. It is clear that 'increase sales turnover' is not a corporate objective because it validates only those activities relevant to increasing sales and does not validate other profit-increasing activities such as, for example, improving labour productivity. 'Increase sales turnover' is a partial or departmental objective. But even objectives such as 'maintain our leading position in technology' or 'diversify into microelectronics' have no validity on their own; their validity depends solely and exclusively upon what the *corporate* objectives are. If one of those is profit and if leading in technology or diversifying into microelectronics improves profits then these are valid activities. If not, not.

If this hierarchical view of objectives is correct it will be seen that the means for one manager are the aims of the manager below him. Thus a manager may be asked to increase sales turnover – that is his aim or his objective. To achieve this he may decide to ask his subordinate to recruit ten new salesmen – that is the *means* by which he hopes to achieve the objective, but it is also the *aim* of his subordinate. The word 'objective' includes anything one is trying to do, i.e. both aims and means. While this is a legitimate use of the word it conceals the important distinction between aims on the one hand and means on the other. It is because of this usage of the word that companies often declare their objectives in the form of a list which may include statements concerning profit (a corporate *aim*) alongside statements concerning turnover or technology or markets which are corporate *means*. The danger in this confusion is the possibility that managers may fail to observe that aims are logically distinct from means and are determined as a result of quite different arguments. Thus corporate aims are determined from a consideration of largely social, personal and political factors while corporate means, or strategies, may be largely determined on strictly pragmatic and rational criteria.

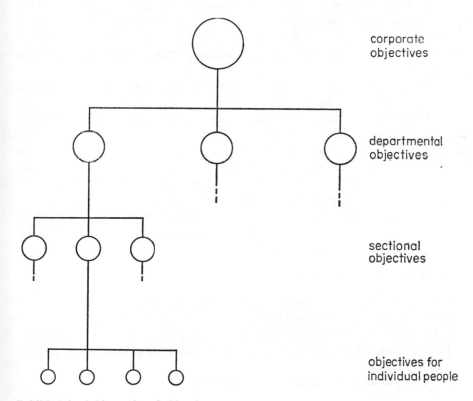

Exhibit 3·1   A hierarchy of objectives

Corporate aims, with which this chapter is concerned, themselves fall into two rather different categories which I shall distinguish as Purpose and Ethos. (The word objectives, then, is commonly used with *three* distinct meanings; means, purpose and ethos.) The fact that corporate aims can be regarded as being of two varieties implies that the hierarchy of objectives is more complex than is usually supposed or that there are two hierarchies, one for purpose and one for ethos, or that the hierarchical concept is invalid or inadequate.

Purpose and ethos

I suggested in Chapter 1 that an organization is simply a group of people working together to satisfy a need – either one of their own needs or of some-one else. All organizations are originally formed with the intention of yielding some form of benefit to certain beneficiaries. Thus a group of socially concerned people may form an organization to find homes (benefit) for the homeless poor (beneficiaries); or to relieve famine, i.e., to send food (the benefit) to the starving (the beneficiaries); or preserve an unspoilt village from the depredations of property developers. Again, the purpose of a school is to provide education to its students. The purpose of any organization is the provision of a benefit to beneficiaries. The purpose of a company is to generate a return on the shareholders' capital – that is why any company is formed and it is the only reason one is ever formed. The word 'company', when used synony-mously with 'firm' or 'business', denotes that the purpose of that organization is to make profits.

Now whenever an organization comes into being it interacts with people and other organizations including the people who work within it or for it. The manner in which an organization behaves towards these employees and others may be termed its ethos. Both purpose and ethos are *corporate* objectives because both condition the activities of every part of the organization. While the corporate purpose provides the sole justification for one set of activities the corporate ethos may justify another set of activities. The two sets may be complementary, non-interactive or even mutually exclusive.

Consider the following list of corporate objectives, a list that is typical of many that are drawn up by companies – see examples in Steiner (Ch. 6), Weinwurm (Exhibits), Payne (Ch. 3);

Objectives for Penguin Parachute Company.

1 We aim to lead our industry in technical developments.
2 We will provide our shareholders with a satisfactory return.
3 We propose to provide comfortable working conditions for employees.
4 We will contribute generously to worthy community projects in the locality of our factories.
5 We aim to increase our share of world markets.

Now this list of five items contains the following different categories of 'objective'. There is one statement of purpose (item 2); there are two statements of ethos (items 3 and 4) and all of these are corporate objectives; there are also two statements concerning strategy (items 1 and 5) and these are corporate means rather than corporate aims. The reasons why I consider it so important to distinguish between these three categories is not only that each type of objective is determined on different grounds but also that strategic objectives cannot be determined until ethological objectives have been, and these in turn cannot be determined until the purpose has been defined. We should clearly distinguish between these three types of objective;

Purpose: the reason why the organization was first formed or why it now exists. All organizations are originally formed to provide a specific benefit for specific groups of beneficiaries.

Ethos: how an organization behaves towards its employees and all other people or groups of people with whom it interacts. These include customers, the state, the local community, employees, suppliers, and so on including even casual visitors. The way in which it has decided to behave constrains and modifies the means it uses to achieve its purpose.

Means: how the organization proposes to carry out its purpose and ethos. If an activity is thought likely to contribute to its purpose or ethos then that activity will be undertaken, if not, not. Some activities which might contribute to the purpose have to be rejected or modified because of the organization's ethos.

It might be thought that if the shareholders are the intended beneficiaries of a company, then their demands upon it would be given priority over all other demands. In fact it is doubtful if this has ever been the case (even in the days of smash and grab capitalism); those who say that it is the case may have misunderstood the relationship between purpose, ethos and means. The true position is probably that the shareholder is, and always had been, the 'residual legatee'; that is to say, a company is set up to benefit the shareholder but that

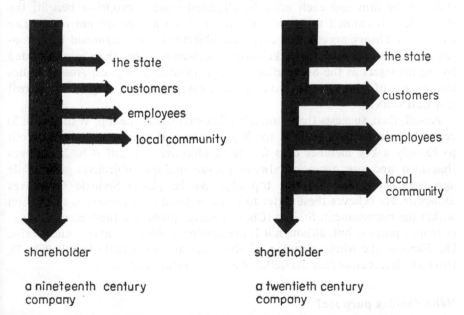

Exhibit 3·2   The shareholder as residual legatee'; his share has declined but his role remains unchanged

no benefit accrues to him until the company has discharged its obligations to all the other groups of people that are recognized by its ethos. I believe this is true of all types of organization; their intended beneficiaries are residual legatees. Of course, where an organization adopts an ethos that reflects a very high standard of morality then its intended beneficiaries will receive less benefit than if it adopts a lower standard. (see Exhibit 3·2) Most organizations today – not only companies – are adopting higher standards and, unless the quality of their management improves, the intended beneficiaries obtain less benefit. It can be argued that this phenomenon may be observed in the case of a wide variety of organizations today.

Purpose of companies

Although Drucker at one time suggested that Survival is the only corporate objective most authors now agree that, for a company, profit is the only one or is an important one among several. Ansoff (Ch. 3) suggests that the top objective is something financial and points out that objectives are not synonymous with social responsibilities, a remark which seems to accept that there is a logical distinction between purpose and ethos as I suggested earlier. This point of view is certainly not universally accepted – both the Stakeholder Theory and the Consensus Theory maintain that companies do not exist to benefit only shareholders but to benefit everyone. The stakeholder theory maintains that the objectives of the firm are derived by balancing the conflicting aims of the various stakeholders in the firm. Thus workers, shareholders, managers, suppliers, customers, the State, the local community are all deemed to have a stake in the firm and each must be allocated some appropriate benefit; the shareholder is entitled to his return but his is not a predominant stake. The Consensus Theory argues that corporate objectives are determined by a consensus of view amongst the stakeholders themselves rather than being decided by the managers as the Stakeholder Theory apparently implies. Ansoff argues that neither of these theories have yet been developed far enough to be of real practical value.

Ansoff, then, suggests that something financial lies at the top. Walley (Ch. 3) certainly believes that profit is the key objective. Hussey (Ch. 3) holds profit to be only a key member of a family of objectives. Ackoff (Ch. 2) believes that men and organizations always pursue multiple objectives and while agreeing that profits are one top objective he places Stylistic Objectives alongside. He believes these latter to be determined by a consensus of opinion within the management. Steiner (Ch. 6) believes profit is a fundamental socio-economic purpose but, although it is the dominant objective, many others exist. He discusses the whole question of objectives at considerable length (Ch. 7), from which it is clear that the debate has by no means ended.

Who decides purpose?

It is quite clear that a charity working for the relief of famine has as its purpose the relief of famine. This is so both *de jure* and *de facto*; no other group of people, and certainly not the employees, would expect any benefit for themselves from this organization. It is, however, entirely possible for a powerful pressure group to infiltrate this organization and turn it to their own ends. Such a thing has occurred to organizations of every sort and size. When this happens the purpose of the organization is changed *de facto* if not *de jure*. Nor need this change be brought about malevolently, it may just as well be benevolent, but the central point is that the purpose of any organization is whatever is decided by those who have the power to decide it.

It can be said categorically that all companies are formed for the sole purpose of making a return on the founders' capital. So long as they continue to retain their sole authority over the company, profit will remain its sole purpose although the company may fully recognize its social responsibilities towards other people and groups. However if the power of the shareholder declines, for any of a variety of reasons, or if the power of another group grows, then the company may well become multipurpose as many may have now become. At present, for these companies, this change is *de facto*; *de jure* the purpose of most companies is to make a profit for the shareholders and this is reflected in the body of commercial law, in 'articles of association' that are drawn up in the formation of a company and in the laws of property and ownership. However, some companies, when they fail as companies, do become something else both *de facto* and *de jure*; for example, when a company is nationalized.

It has always been possible, then, for the purpose of an organization to change at the will of the people for whose benefit it was called into existence or to be changed by the exercise of power by some other group. Normally, however, except for a transition period, very few organizations are required to serve more than one group of beneficiaries, either *de facto* or *de jure*. If it is now the case that some companies are required to provide appropriate, and therefore various, benefits to a variety of beneficiaries then, as Steiner remarks, the door is wide open for business to assume a variety of social responsibilities. But it is not yet possible to say how corporate objectives may then be determined, nor by what criteria allocations of benefit should be made to whom nor on what grounds any request or demand made upon the company could be refused. The stakeholder theory or the consensus theory should provide answers to these questions. They do not do so, as both Ansoff and Steiner point out. They do not give us grounds for stating whether the local community is a Stakeholder or not, nor, assuming it is, whether a company *must* contribute to the cost of say, building a community swimming pool. If there is only one intended beneficiary, the shareholder, then there is no argument; it is not mandatory on the company to contribute to the swimming pool. If there are many intended beneficiaries, among them the community, then it should or must contribute – but how much, and at the expense of which of the other stakeholders?

If, as the stakeholder theory suggests, a company is now really a social institution run for the benefit of all, then some means must be found to identify who the beneficiaries are, the nature of the benefit they require and how much of it is enough – in other words a company of this sort requires all the complex

representational apparatus of a constitutional democracy.* The consensus
theory may well be valid, that is, benefits may be allocated as a result of
agreement among the beneficiaries but this is, or could be, little more than a
euphemism for the philosophy that 'might is right'.

The stakeholder theory appears to have gained considerable support in
recent years but as yet the consequences of this acceptance have not been faced.

Among the consequences are these:

(a) if it falls to the senior managers to allocate benefits and to approve or
refuse demands made to a company, they will have to be trained to make
socio-political decisions, rather than business decisions.

(b) the criteria for strategic decisions will cease to be those of return on
capital and risk and become something else as yet unspecified.

(c) it will become less difficult for managers or any pressure group to turn a
company's resources to their own benefit.

(d) if the managers do not make these allocations of benefit, some other
authority must do so but the study of how several disparate groups can
make their views known to an executive is in its infancy.

(e) if the shareholders' interests are to be further diminished the capital
structure of companies will have to change to lessen or eliminate risk capital
participation.

My own conclusions are these; there are at present a very large number of
organizations which we call companies. Their sole purpose is to generate a
return on shareholders' capital while recognizing certain ethological objectives
which, as will be shown later in the chapter, are today very comprehensive and
powerfully constrain the manner in which companies may try to achieve their
purpose. That is my first conclusion – that companies as defined, do exist. My
second conclusion is that some companies are or may be in the process of
transition from ownership by one group of shareholders to another or to a
different category of beneficiary such as the employees, the State, a foreign
state, and so on. During that transition no clarity can exist as to corporate
objectives but that when it is complete the objectives can again be clearly stated
in terms of benefit to the new beneficiaries. My third conclusion is that there
may be some organizations which are still *de jure* companies but are *de facto*
non-companies or social institutions in that the intended beneficiaries are no
longer solely shareholders. At present there are no rules to show how their
corporate objectives should be set or by whom. As they must therefore be wide
open to exploitation by any group of people having the power to do so, it can
be argued that their social institution status should be made explicit and *de jure*
without delay.

When I suggested in Chapter 2 (page 32) that corporate objectives are determined by factors that are quite different from the factors affecting strategic
decisions I had in mind that the most important factor of all in deciding a

* In the belief that the spotlight of study will turn to precisely this area over the next decade
I have included a discussion on Supervisory and Representative Boards in Part 2.

company's purpose is the assertion of power by actual or potential beneficiaries – a factor that may play very little part in strategic decisions.

Return on shareholders' capital

Both Ansoff (Ch. 3) and Ackoff (Ch. 2) state that it is difficult to measure profit and that this is therefore a highly unsatisfactory choice of corporate objective. The same may be said of return on capital employed or return on net assets for the same reasons, namely that accounting practice varies so widely from company to company and from nation to nation. As all writers on this subject agree that the shareholder is one of the beneficiaries of a company it may be more appropriate to use return on *shareholders'* capital as one definition of purpose, especially as it has the striking advantage that it can often be measured with complete precision. It is only necessary to know the amount of capital a shareholder invests in a given company to be able to calculate the rate of return represented by the stream of dividends he receives over the years together with the value of his shares when he sells them.

It should be noted that Return on Shareholders' Capital is *not* the same as Return on Assets Employed. They are not designed to measure the same aspects of performance and they do not move up and down together – indeed they can move in opposite directions (when, for example, a manufacturing company makes a capital gain on property). Return on Shareholders' Capital is a central concept (I will refer to it as ROSC in future) because it is not only a *de facto* and *de jure* corporate objective of any company, it can also be measured with complete accuracy. It must also be distinguished from ROI. Return on Investment is the term applied to the return on the capital invested in a *project*. ROSC refers to the return on the shareholders' capital invested in a company.

Whether one accepts the view that a company exists to benefit only the shareholder or the shareholder among others, it becomes necessary, at some point in the process of deciding corporate objectives, to state how much return the shareholder may expect. It is not sufficient to declare 'one of the corporate objectives of this company is to make a return on shareholders' capital'; the statement must include a target level at which the company may aim over a period of several years and the target must be stated in such terms that the company's progress towards that level can be empirically verified. If an objective is quantified, managers can plan and control within closer limits of accuracy, and the act of quanitifying both clarifies the objective and assists in its unequivocal communication to other people.

Because some confusion exists concerning the setting of targets I shall discuss this in general terms before returning to setting ROSC targets.

Targets, forecasts and actuals

Managers use figures in three different roles (perhaps only in three); Targets, Forecasts and Actuals. A Target is the statement of an objective in quantified terms. Thus, 'increase sales turnover' is a possible objective for a sales manager and 'increase sales turnover by 10% before August' could be his target. A target is a quantified aim, goal, mission, objective. A forecast is a prediction about the future; it reflects someone's opinion of what will happen. Thus this sales manager may predict that he will only be able to increase sales by 5% by August. An Actual is a measurement of fact; by August sales turnover had in fact risen by 7%. Ackoff (Ch. 2) refers to targets and forecasts as wishful projections and reference projections respectively. (He adds that there are really two types of forecast; reference projections which are a manager's forecasts of what may happen if he does nothing while a planned projection is what may happen if he carries out a certain plan. I shall use the same distinction in Chapter 5).

Failure to distinguish between target and forecast is a very common error (Vera Lutz noted this even among very senior civil servants in the French national planning commission – see Chapter 3 of her book, *Central Planning for the Market Economy*). Part of the confusion here may be due to the indiscriminate use of jargon words by professional planners and economists such as normative, projection, indicative, imperative.

A second common error is the failure to understand that all these figures may be inaccurate. It is generally recognized that forecasts cannot be accurate and that any forecast expressed as one figure (a point forecast) will usually be wrong. But nor is it possible often to measure precisely what actually is; while it may be possible accurately to count the number of items in stock, for example, it is not possible accurately to value them. Nor is it often meaningful to set point targets; it cannot be claimed that a manager who has been set the target of increasing turnover by 10% has missed the target in any meaningful sense if turnover actually rises by 9·9% or 10·1% – nor even perhaps by 9% or 11%. All figures used as targets are more or less arbitrary.

At those levels of management at which managers deal with physical objects over short planning horizons, the point target, the point forecast and the point actual may be used without severe loss of validity, but single figures all become progressively misleading, inaccurate and inappropriate as the level of abstraction rises and the planning horizon lengthens.

A third common error is particularly relevant to target setting. The figure set as a target to a subordinate may represent a level of achievement that is considered acceptable by his manager, or is considered challenging or is considered to be the minimum that his manager will tolerate. Targets may be set at any level on an infinite scale of values. To select one figure to represent *the* target is tantamount to selecting one particular point on a scale which ranges from 'totally unacceptable' to 'achievement of unprecedented brilliance'. When managers set targets, they should, in order to avoid misunderstandings, either select a single figure on the scale and state where it lies on the scale or should set a bracket of targets indicating the range within which results will be considered acceptable.

With these comments in mind we should return to the setting of ROSC targets.

Selecting the ROSC target

Most writers appear to agree that the traditional statement that companies exist to *maximize* profits is invalid. Steiner (Ch. 7) points out that maximization was the ideal of the classical economists who noted that profit would be at a maximum when marginal revenue equals marginal costs. Companies cannot in practice measure marginal revenues or costs accurately enough to know when they are equal, as Steiner says. A more severe criticism is that even if they could measure these for existing products no one can say whether the company could have made even more profit by introducing an entirely new product – or by taking any other strategic decision. The key disadvantage of the maximiza-tion ideal is that it is not empiricaly verifiable. Ansoff rejects maximization (Ch. 3) so does Hussey (Ch. 3) and Ackoff (Ch. 2).

If companies do not aim to maximize ROSC, what do they aim for? Many authors suggest they aim to make a satisfactory ROSC, others that they aim at one that is equal to or better than the average for the industry. Steiner (Ch. 7) prefers *'required* profits', i.e. those needed to satisfy all the claims made upon the enterprise. Ansoff suggests (Ch. 4) a range of targets including a minimum threshold – a view that echoes the remarks I made above on point and range target setting.

It seems to me that 'satisfactory', 'average', 'outstanding', 'required' and 'minimum threshold' are all valid target levels. Companies do, and should, aim at any or all of them. They each represent points on a scale of performance and companies are entitled to aim at any point on this scale so long as it is not below the minimum threshold point. It is possible to state, in figures, what this minimum threshold is for any company in any nation at any moment in time. Thus no public company in Europe in 1973 should have been aiming at an ROSC of less than approximatley 6% (in real terms); to have aimed below 6% would have been tantamount to aiming to achieve an unacceptable result, one that would be below the minimum threshold.

The special status of a minimum threshold figure rests on the definition of corporate purpose proposed earlier, that organizations are formed to provide a benefit to their beneficiaries. If an organization fails to do this it fails *as an organization,* and eventually, when it becomes clear to the beneficiaries that it has failed, it is wound up – this is the proper fate of all organizations that fail, from the abandonment of the League of Nations to the dissolution of a marriage. In the case of a company the founders invest their capital in the explicit hope that a return will be earned upon it that is not less than they could obtain in any other investment; they appoint managers with specific instruc-tions to take whatever action they may to achieve this return and managers are dismissed if they fail to do this. At any given time and in any given circum-stances there is a 'going rate' of return on risk capital, which, for the past few decades has been, approximately, 6% (in real terms and, say, 9 to 10% in money terms). No shareholder would invest capital in a company if he thought he could not obtain this minimum over a period of years. However, so difficult is it to forecast whether a given company will earn this return that shareholders will allow a company to retain their capital right up to the moment the company is forced into liquidation – a statement that is well in accord with the remarks I made on page 44 concerning point and range targets, i.e. that it is only possible to state whether a target has been achieved or not within wide limits of uncertainty.

However, it is doubtful if shareholders invest capital with the sole aim of achieving 6% return; they also hope for more, say 10% or 20% or even 40%. They have a range of expectations.

The performance-risk curve

It seems probable that what shareholders really have in mind when they invest capital is a Performance–Risk Curve. They are seeking an investment which stands a good chance of yielding a high rate of return and *at the same time* a very low risk of achieving a poor rate of return. The words 'the same time' are crucial, for if a shareholder has both these expectations at the same time it must distort these expectations to try to express them as a single figure.

It follows that a company should not seek to make a satisfactory profit nor required profits nor to aim at spectacular success, nor to avoid an unsatisfactory return; it should aim at *all* these – but each associated with a different level of risk. In Exhibit 3·3 I show a performance–risk curve for a shareholder which

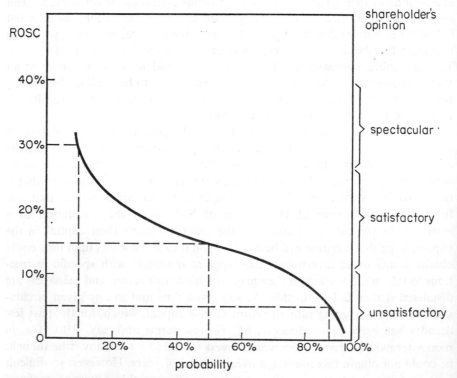

Exhibit 3·3   A shareholder's performance–risk curve

indicates that he is searching for an investment that will, in this example, give him a 90% chance of achieving a 6% ROSC, a 50% chance of achieving a 15% ROSC, and a 10% chance of a 30% ROSC. I should make some further explanatory comments on the performance–risk curve.

Valid in principle for all shareholders

Exhibit 3·3 is, I suggest, valid in principle for all shareholders of all companies (and the performance–risk approach is valid for all beneficiaries of all organizations). Whether it is practicable to place a figure on a shareholder's attitude to risk is much more questionable and the figures in my diagram were intended to illustrate the ideal. (On page 280 in Part 2 I discuss some of the newer techniques designed to estimate subjective probabilities and to quantify value judgements). The small shareholder, solely dependent upon his investment income, may select a very flat performance–risk curve as in Exhibit 3·4. The shareholder with an instinct for gambling would select Exhibit 3·5 where there is a possibility of a very high return but he also recognizes a very high risk of severe losses. While in Exhibit 3·4 the level of return the shareholder most wishes to see is close to the prevailing level of return on non-risk capital, in Exhibit 3·5 this criterion is almost irrelevant.

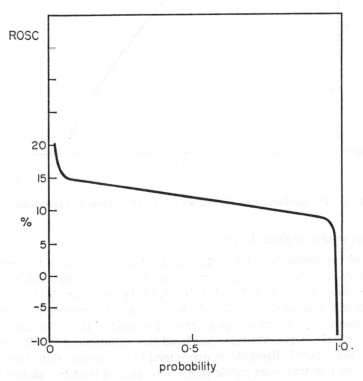

Exhibit 3·4 The performance–risk curve for a small shareholder

The curve for the proprietor of a small business, who may be prepared to trade off part of the return on capital for the personal satisfaction of running his own company, may choose any of the shapes that other shareholders might adopt but the whole curve may be moved downwards by a few percentage points.

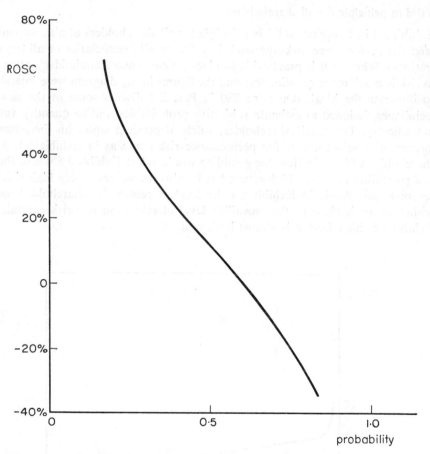

Exhibit 3·5   The performance–risk curve for an adventurous shareholder

Changes in the shape of the curve

Very few companies have taken steps to determine what shape the performance risk curve may have for their own shareholders. One shareholder survey in Europe (described in *L.R.P.* Vol. 3, No. 3, 1971), conducted by Fisons Limited, showed that private shareholders looked for 'a safe investment', among other requirements. I interpret this as an explicit request to that company to aim for a relatively flat curve. On the other hand this requirement was less prominent among institutional shareholders questioned in this survey, thus drawing attention to the fact that most public companies serve at least two classes of shareholder who may have different curves in mind. One conclusion that may be drawn is that shareholders tend to invest in a given company because they believe that the managers of that company have a performance–risk curve in mind which is not significantly different to their own; it is questionable therefore whether a company may significantly alter its traditional curve without reference to shareholders. I shall consider the factors relevant to changes in shareholder requirements on page 52.

In view of the extreme difficulty of placing meaningful figures on shareholders' requirements it may be more reasonable to concentrate attention upon only two sections of the curve. One of these is the point of inflexion at the lower ROSC rates where the curve must reflect the existence of an area of special concern around the minimum threshold figure of 6% return (in Europe). The other area of major importance is that length of the curve representing the 'satisfactory' level of ROSC at approximately 8 to 12% in real terms. Returns of this magnitude, while not quite 'glamour' performance are considered to be satisfactory or more than satisfactory by most shareholders today. (Unilever, for example, is widely reported to be aiming at a very long term growth in earnings per share of 10% per annum; assuming inflation at, say 5% p.a. this target becomes 5% growth in real terms.* If one also assumes a divided yield of, say 4% then Unilever's reported growth target implies a ROSC target of 9% in real terms and 14% in money terms. This is within the 'satisfactory' area I was suggesting above and is typical of many companies' aims in the developed world.)

Shareholders and managers

I am suggesting that each individual shareholder has in mind a particular performance–risk curve that reflects his own requirements modified by his knowledge or beliefs about how companies perform; his curve may be realistic or unrealistic. Each institutional shareholder also has a curve in mind. All shareholders have different curves in mind even for the same company. It falls to the managers, or their financial advisers to choose one curve rather than another to represent these differing views but, inevitably, the managers will inject their own ambitions for their company into this consensus. Although they have no mandate to do this, it is difficult to believe that it does not happen with the result that quite often, presumably, the company strives to achieve a much flatter or much steeper curve than the shareholders require.

Performance-risk curve and strategy

The traditional explanation of the link between a target and a strategy is that the target provides a criterion by which a strategy may be selected. Thus if a company aims at a ROSC of 15% then any strategy that is capable of yielding 15% will be acceptable, any that is not will not. If one rejects the single figure target as being an oversimplification one has to admit to a more complex set of criteria for the selection of strategies.

---

* To be quite correct, 5% plus 5% is not 10%. The correct calculation is, of course, 105% multiplied by 105% equals 110·25%.

In the simplest case, a company aiming for a good chance of achieving a satisfactory return and, at the same time, a low risk of achieving a poor return, will be searching for a strategy that will achieve precisely this performance–risk curve. In practice it is questionable whether any single strategy could satisfy this complex criterion or even whether any company can have a *single* strategy. It may be more realistic to visualize a company pursuing a set of strategies or a portfolio of strategies. If so then it follows that when managers refer to 'a strategy' they are drawing particular attention to only one out of a set; and any statement made about that strategy should be seen in the context of the whole portfolio. No single strategy will achieve all the aims of the company; a single strategy will only *contribute* to the performance-risk curve. This leads to the concept of the 'strategic structure' of a company. The aim of the corporate planner may therefore be conceived not as 'to search for a strategy to achieve the company's target' but 'to search for a Strategic Structure to achieve the company's performance-risk curve.' I shall consider this concept in detail in Chapter 4.

ROSC and growth

For several decades now growth has been accepted as a major corporate objective; some believe it to be *the* corporate objective (Stemp Ch. 1). 'Growth' may refer to growth of profits or earnings or share values – i.e. something financial – or it can mean growth of sales or number of employees – i.e. something physical. It is said that everyone connected with a company requires that it grows; shareholders look for more profit each year, trade unions expect the firm to employ more men at higher wages, suppliers anticipate larger orders, the state gathers more tax, the managers hope for more rapid promotion and wider horizons. It has even been said that if a company is not expanding it is dying.

Recently many of these dogmas have been called into question. The environmentalists claim that economic growth will destroy the ecology of our planet; managers have recognized that too rapid rates of growth bring more problems than they at first appreciated and that greater satisfaction in their work can come from other sources than empire building; many employees now feel that working as a larger cog for a smaller machine might be more rewarding; the state is jealous of the growing power of some large companies; the local community may become too dependent upon one large company – and so on.

It is possible that growth may lose its premier position in the hierarchy of objectives and, if it does, it may be asked what should replace it. One answer is dividends. A company may achieve a return on shareholders' capital by any permutation of income and capital gain provided that these discount to the target ROSC. Low dividend yields and high levels of retained earnings for growth have become traditional in many parts of the world, but there is no theoretical reason why a company should not pay out 100% or more of its earnings as dividends. The alternatives to growth are zero growth and de-growth.

The point being made then is this; growth has become accepted as an essential part of the definition of corporate purpose. I am more inclined to classify growth as a strategy; I consider that growth should be adopted if the company's managers believe their shareholders will receive a better return on their capital if the company grows than if it is static or declining. Growth is a means to an end, therefore, not an end in itself. If this is the case then it must be right for managers to give as much consideration to the alternatives to growth as they would give to any other strategic option such as alternatives to a merger or alternatives to building a new factory.

'The purpose cycle'

I suggested on page 33 that corporate planning consists essentially of two inter-linked cycles of which one was concerned with deciding corporate aims and the other with deciding strategy as shown in Exhibit 2·4. However, if it is true that there are two distinct types of corporate aim, purpose and ethos, it may follow that the cycle for deciding corporate aims is more complex than implied by Exhibit 2·4. I am now suggesting that there are indeed two corporate aim cycles, not one, and Exhibit 2·4 must therefore be modified to show this. So far in this chapter, however, I have only given detailed consideration to deciding and quantifying purpose – I consider ethos below – so I will illustrate 'the purpose cycle' only at this stage; see Exhibit 3·6.

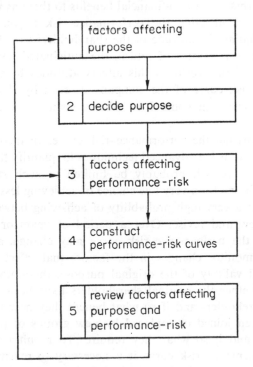

Exhibit 3·6   'The purpose cycle'

Exhibit 3·6 represents the steps in the process of deciding corporate purpose and it differs in two important respects from Exhibit 2·4. Firstly, as noted above, it illustrates only the process of deciding purpose and does not concern ethos while Exhibit 2·4 showed both being decided together. Secondly it shows five stages in the process, not three as shown in Exhibit 2.4. The explanation for this modification is that 'setting a target' is the act of attaching a suitable figure to an aim that has already been decided conceptually and qualitatively. Thus the act of setting a target (or as I prefer, 'constructing a performance–risk curve') can only be performed after a decision as to the purpose – furthermore the factors that determine the purpose are not the same as those taken into account when placing a target figure to it.

Exhibit 3·6, then, shows the stages through which one has to pass in the process of deciding (and reviewing) the ROSC performance curve for a company. These stages can be summarized as follows:

First, the factors affecting purpose. The only factor here is power. The purpose of any organization is determined by those who have the power to determine it. In the case of a company the shareholders are indisputably intended to be the *de jure* and *de facto* beneficiaries at its foundation.

Second, the decision as to purpose. As long as shareholders retain power over the company they will decide the nature of the benefit they require from it. This will universally be return on their capital and possibly, especially with family firms, other non-financial benefits to them as well.

Third, factors affecting the performance–risk curve. Many factors are involved including the attitude of the shareholders to risk, the general level of risk and non-risk rates of return, the anticipated level of inflation, the general state of the world as this affects attitudes to risk, the traditional performance–risk curve of the company as seen by shareholders, and the attitude of society in general to what constitutes a reasonable rate of return.

Fourth, construct the performance–risk curve. In theory it is possible to construct a curve using advanced techniques to quantify the factors above. In practice the curve will probably be limited to such statements as, 'The company is aiming for a very low chance of achieving less than 6% ROSC in real terms but a very high probability of achieving between 8 and 12%'.

Fifth, review and revise. Over a period of years or decades both the purpose and the performance–risk curve may change, and it is necessary therefore to monitor changes in the factors that affect them. To monitor the continued validity of the original purpose, therefore, it is necessary to determine whether the original shareholders have been replaced by a new group of shareholders and if so what benefit they now require, or whether they have been joined or replaced by new groups of people who are not shareholders and if so what they require. To monitor the validity of the original performance–risk curve it is necessary to review current views on future interest rates, attitudes to risk, inflation and so on.

As previously suggested, I have excluded from the list of factors affecting purpose or performance–risk any mention of current or future expected performance of a company. Shareholders do not, I suggest, alter their requirements according to the future outlook for their company. If they lose confidence in it they sell their shares (or sell the company) or change the management. Any new shareholder buys the shares at a price which he believes will give him his required ROSC. If the company goes into liquidation, it ceases to exist *de facto* and *de jure*; if it is taken over by the employees or the state it also ceases to exist as a company *de facto* and often *de jure*. It may be objected that if the outlook for a company is highly promising it would be reasonable to raise the target levels. This could be so if a single target level had originally been set and if this now appeared to be too easily obtainable. I am suggesting, however, that shareholders are already aware that their company may, with good management and good fortune, achieve a high ROSC for years at a time and that this awareness is already built into their performance–risk curves as would be made explicit if they were invited to state their views. The possibility that their company may achieve or has achieved a high ROSC does not alter their performance–risk curve, it merely gratifies them (and the managers) to discover that the actual performance is in the higher reaches of the curve they already have in mind.

In Part 2 I deal extensively with the technical problems of deciding ROSC targets, the conflict between short and long term profits, dividend policy and so on.

Ethos

The distinction between the two types of corporate objective, purpose and ethos, lies in the fact that all organizations are originally formed to generate a specific benefit to specific beneficiaries and for no other reason – this is their purpose. Thus a hospital is formed solely to heal the sick, a school solely to educate students. But in each case the act of formation creates a body which interacts with its environment; how it behaves towards people in its environment is its ethos. It may be objected that when a company is formed it also benefits the employees because it satisfies their need for work; this is true, but this is not why a company is formed any more than it is a reason for founding a hospital or school. It may *become* part of its purpose to provide employment but if it does its managers will meet all the problems inherent in the consensus and stakeholder theories for which, as I remarked on page 41, no solutions have yet been found. Until these problems are solved, I believe there is no alternative either in logic or in practice to continuing to distinguish between what a company is for and the manner in which it pursues that aim; i.e. between its purpose on the one hand and its ethos on the other. It should be noted that when a company fails to make a profit we say that it has failed *as a company*. When a company dismisses a large number of employees at short notice, or gives its customers short weight, or pollutes a river, we do not say it has failed as a company, we say it has behaved immorally. People still clearly recognize the distinction between purpose and ethos in ordinary conversation.

Factors affecting ethos

I am suggesting, then, that a company's purpose is determined by a process
that may approximately be illustrated by Exhibit 3·6 which I call the Purpose
Cycle. A company's ethos is determined in a very nearly identical cycle, illustrated in Exhibit 3·7, consisting of: factors affecting ethos, the decision as to
ethos, factors affecting performance risk curves, the construction of the curves
and finally the review feed-back loops.

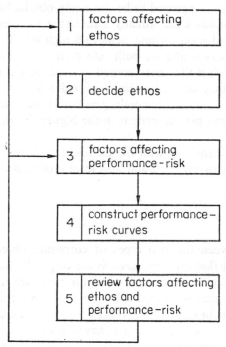

Exhibit 3·7   The 'ethos cycle'

The first stage of the Ethos cycle, then, is to identify what are the factors that
determine how a company behaves in society. One of these is the fact that it is
a company as opposed to, say, a charity or a branch of the armed services.
Different types of organization adopt different attitudes to employees and
others. Another factor is the shape of the performance–risk curve for ROSC
decided in the purpose cycle; companies whose curve is traditionally rather flat
may behave differently towards employees and others than high-performance
high-risk companies. A third factor is the attitude of top managers (a factor
emphasized by Steiner (Ch. 7) and most other authors). A fourth is the ethological tradition of the company. A fifth, and one that is of growing influence,
is the activities of protest groups. The sixth is the most important because most

of the other factors are partially derived from it, namely the attitude that society in general adopts towards corporate behaviour as revealed by common law, opinions expressed in the press and so on. Most top executives take their ethos from this social consensus although some will disagree on specific points; most company traditions accord well with the social consensus, although some are distinctive in specific areas; many protest and protection groups reflect the general social consensus on corporate ethos but, of course, reflect it with unusual vigour. Another factor determining a company's ethos is legislation.

Ethological objectives

The determination of a full set of ethological objectives would be an almost endless task. It would be necessary to state how the company was to behave towards competitors, customers, employees, the state, foreign states, visitors, suppliers, government officials, casual passers by, the local community, trade union officials, female employees, coloured employees, the disabled....

Ackoff (Ch. 2) examines what he calls Stylistic Objectives, by which he means the kind of business a company's managers would like to be in. He quotes a company making hand tools which decided to manufacture electronic parts – a decision made on stylistic grounds (the managers thought it would be fun) rather than on grounds of reasoned economics. Ackoff is clearly using the word 'style' in a different sense to my 'ethos', although I certainly recognize that ethos may affect strategic decisions as powerfully as economic reasoning does. Ansoff (Ch. 3) divides 'non-economic' or ethological objectives, as I call them, into two categories; responsibilities on the one hand (such as when a company supports a charity) and constraints on the other (such as when a company excludes certain actions it might otherwise have taken to improve profits). My view appears to be identical in this respect – see page 39. Walley (Ch. 3) draws particular attention to job security for managers and employees and to environmental injury.

Those companies that do attempt to write down their ethological objectives usually concentrate upon such obviously important areas as their attitude to employees, customers and the local community. A typical statement would be, 'we aim to give our employees reasonable job security' or 'we aim to give our customers good value for money'. It is questionable whether such statements have much value; in an attempt to add a touch of realism, therefore, it may be desirable to quantify these objectives in the same way as I suggested that purpose should be quantified.

Factors affecting ethological performance—risk curves

Very few ethological objectives are as yet quantifiable even in the simplest terms. However, some certainly are. Many nations now legislate on job security, for example, so that the statement 'we aim to give our employees reasonable job security' can now be quantified as, 'we will give our employees not less than three months notice and severance pay will not be less than six months full pay', or whatever. Many companies have set themselves target levels for complaints from customers, for permissible levels of pollution, for factory safety, donations to charity and so on. A few companies are beginning to set target scores on a job satisfaction index for their employees. However the number of companies who have determined point targets for ethological objectives remains small and very few have determined any performance–risk curves. It is not surprising that they have not done so in view of the extreme difficulty of quantifying value-judgements. Nevertheless many companies do set quality control specifications for their products. Quality control specifications usually take the form of a statement that not more than $X\%$ of products may fall below a given standard of quality and this is a statement identical in principle to the 'very low chance of achieving an unsatisfactory ROSC' I proposed on page 46. Quality control statements may reflect the managers' interpretation of the expectations of their customers. In the same vein it might be possible to quantify parts of the performance–risk curves for many other ethological objectives such as the probability of an employee being promoted, of a river being polluted, and so on.

The factors that determine ethological target levels are the same as those that determine their selection. That is to say, where an ethological objective is capable of being quantified, the company will select a figure which reflects society's current consensus, modified by the values of top managers, the company's traditions, the activities of protest groups and legislation. Some companies accept a minimum threshold for some ethological objectives that is far above the consensus and these are fully prepared to go out of business altogether rather than act immorally. Others, of course, set targets so low that they continually flout normal standards of decency in the pursuit of profit.

Reviewing the factors affecting ethos

The factors affecting a company's ethos change rapidly today; society is taking a much closer interest in the behaviour of companies and, almost daily, new moral or aesthetic dilemmas appear and are discussed on television, in the press, in the boardroom and on the shop floor. Increasingly the ethological objectives are constraining and limiting the actions that companies may take in the pursuit of profit – actions they used to take without a qualm are now taboo. A company does not have to step far out of line today to bring down upon itself the full glare of modern publicity methods together with the wrath of a protest movement.

In Part 2 (page 208) I give some detailed examples of ethological objectives and on page 282 I describe some of the techniques of quantification that may be used in this area.

Deciding corporate objectives is a sequential process

In part of the book I am concerned only with the theoretical, conceptual and logical aspects of corporate planning. I believe that, in theory, corporate objectives may only be determined in the sequence: Purpose, Ethos, Strategy (and I believe that this sequence is the best in practice also). Strategic decisions are heavily dependent upon both purpose and ethos and must be determined last. Ethos depends partially on purpose. Purpose is not influenced by either ethos or strategy.

Until a company has identified its purpose it cannot consider its ethos. Thus if it is decided that a company's sole purpose is to make a return on shareholders' capital it may then consider how it should behave towards other groups of people while in pursuit of this aim. If, on the other hand, it is decided that the company exists to make a return to shareholders *and* to benefit the local community, then its ethological decisions may be very different with respect to all other groups – and certainly with respect to the local community. Thus purpose is a factor in determining ethos but not vice versa – the acceptance by a company of a very high standard of social behaviour does not alter the performance–risk curve for shareholders, it merely makes it more difficult to find a strategy that will result in a high ROSC – a fact that is becoming increasingly evident to managers as society demands progressively more responsible behaviour from companies.

In Exhibit 3·8 I show the purpose, ethos and strategy cycles and the way they are linked together. (The strategy cycle is incomplete in this diagram, I shall discuss it in detail in the following chapters).

Summary of Chapter 3

The use of the word objective to mean 'anything one is trying to do' conceals the fact that it covers three quite different concepts which I call purpose, ethos and strategy. The purpose of any organization is to generate a specific benefit for a specific group of people; ethos refers to the manner in which an organization behaves towards other people while generating this benefit. Strategy refers to the activities it chooses to carry out in order to generate this benefit or to ensure that its behaviour accords with its chosen ethos.

Very severe theoretical problems face any organization having more than one homogeneous group of beneficiaries, for no rationale exists to justify any one proposed distribution of benefit between them rather than some other. In practice the decision may be made by a consensus, or by the exercise of power, or by a formal constitutional democratic apparatus, or by the managers, or some other authoritative body. Very little consideration has yet been given to this important problem – important because it is now widely argued that the shareholder is not the sole intended beneficiary of some companies.

Whether the shareholder is the sole intended beneficiary or only one of many it is necessary to set targets in terms of return on capital to the shareholder. The figure selected may represent a satisfactory level, a very satisfactory one, or a minimum threshold, but each of these, except the minimum, represents an arbitrary point on a continuous scale of performance. It may more accurately reflect the requirements of the shareholder if the entire scale is adopted and linked to a scale of risk levels resulting in a performance–risk curve. This

C

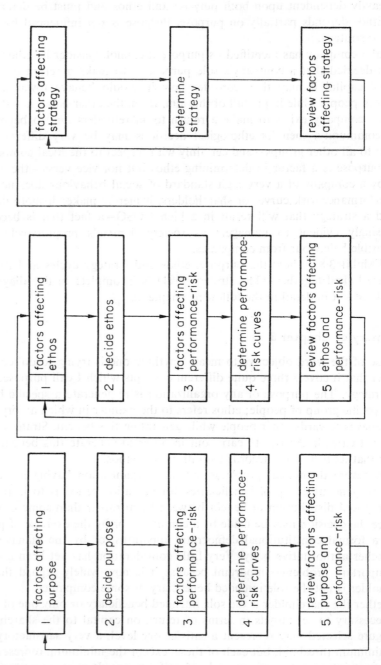

Exhibit 3-8

approach has the additional merit that the managers do not have to alter the target every time a forecast shows that the target will be missed or exceeded. A similar performance–risk curve could be drawn up to represent the requirement of any other intended beneficiaries.

A company has to decide how it proposes to behave towards those people who are not intended beneficiaries but who nevertheless have dealings with it or are affected by it. The ethos adopted by most companies is mainly conditioned by a consensus of opinion in society modified by the traditions of the company, legislation, the value judgements of top managers. It is theoretically possible to draw up a performance–risk curve for any ethological objective but in practice many value judgements cannot be quantified at all and most only very arbitrarily.

In theory, and perhaps in practice, strategic decisions (i.e. decisions which set out what role each major part of an organization shall play in the corporate whole) cannot be made until ethos has been determined and this in turn can only follow the identification of the purpose. The phrase 'determine corporate objectives' implies that this part of corporate planning may be performed as one simple step; I am suggesting that it really contains three linked cycles (see Exhibit 3·8).

4 The strategic structure

Performance–risk and strategic structure

In the previous chapter I put forward the idea that when a shareholder makes an investment decision he has in mind not one single criterion but a multiple one. He is not motivated by the thought of say, a 15% return but by the possibility of a good return coupled with a low probability of a poor return. I do not think that the literature reflects this rather complex situation; almost every author recommends that a single target should be set for return on capital (and each author recommends a different method of measurement) and, usually in some later chapter, but quite separately, he discusses the problem of risk. In putting together these two concepts I am conscious of creating severe intellectual difficulties; instead of writing the simple word 'target' I have to write 'performance–risk' or some equally clumsy phrase. Instead of stating that a given company is 'aiming at a 15% return' I have to write that it is 'aiming for a good chance of achieving 15% and a low probability of 8%,' or whatever. Although this multiple criterion carries the severe penalty of its inherent complexity I believe it does more accurately reflect the fundamental quality of the business situation, namely that business is essentially a risky occupation.

I also mentioned the concept of 'strategic structure' in the previous chapter and said that the concepts of performance–risk and strategic structure go together. Indeed I suggested that the goal of the corporate planner was not 'to devise a strategy to achieve a target' but to 'devise a strategic structure to achieve the performance–risk curve', and later I will suggest that the corporate plan is complete when, and only when, the management of the company is confident that a strategic structure has been devised that has performance–risk characteristics similar to the performance–risk curves for the company's purpose and ethos.

Definition of strategic structure

The idea that a company has a strategic structure is not new; Steiner (Ch.9) draws attention to the difference between a 'master' strategy and a 'pure' strategy where the former embraces the entire basic company mission and the means to pursue it while the latter refers to a single particular ploy in some specific area such as a change made to the price of a product to counteract some action by a competitor. My concept of the strategic structure is close to Steiner's master strategy but perhaps more comprehensive and it is certainly more comprehensive than Ansoff's product-market strategy which concerns products and markets only. The strategic structure of a company, then, is the totality of its individual strategies.

The most significant feature of the definition of an individual strategic decision is that it is intended to have a major influence in achieving the purpose or ethos of the company (see page 15). The strategic structure of a company consists therefore of all those features of the company that will have a major effect upon achieving its purpose and ethos. Its present structure is the resultant of a multitude of strategic decisions made and left unmade during the past few years or decades of the company's history. Its structure in ten years' time will be consequent upon many of these strategic decisions together with those made in the next decade. Thus the structure that the corporate planner should have in mind is essentially a coarse-grained picture of the company in the future. I believe the phrase 'the coarse-grained strategic structure' of a company closely reflects what a corporate plan should describe.

The decision to open up a new market is almost certainly a strategic decision. But this decision does not merely have the effect of increasing turnover and profits for the company, it does something else of more lasting significance; it alters the strategic structure of the company. Now the fundamental distinction between corporate planning and strategic decision-making lies in the sequence in which such decisions are taken. In corporate planning the management will first design a suitable coarse-grained strategic structure for the company and then search for means of achieving it. In strategic planning the management will take their strategic decisions *ad hoc* and the strategic structure of the company will be the consequential sum of these individual strategic decisions. Thus when a company decides to open up a new market its management may either have argued thus; 'our company now operates in n different markets but it would be better if we operated in $n + 1$. Therefore we will search for a new market'. Or they may have argued; 'here is a promising market – let us open it up', and, as a consequence the market structure of the company is shifted from n to $n + 1$.

Consider the following case: Cormorant Components Limited supplies electrical components to the British automotive industry. Over the past two decades profits have risen by an average of 15% p.a. partly due to the growth in the industry and partly due to Cormorant's policy of introducing new products every year or two. The management still holds to this policy and has several new components on the drawing board. But consider this; over these two decades the number of customers to whom they supply these components has fallen from sixteen to four due to mergers within the industry – and one of these remaining four takes no less than sixty per cent of Cormorant's output.

The points I wish to illustrate with this simple case are as follows. Firstly notice how the strategic structure has changed over the two decades;

Cormorant used to supply eighteen different components to sixteen different customers, now they supply thirty different components to four customers. Secondly we can assume that their present policy will result in a continued rise in profits over the next few years – Cormorant's management are certainly confident on this point. Thirdly, and this is the key point, it must occur to us that the riskiness of the business has increased out of all recognition so that while the management are saying 'here is another splendid new product idea, let us launch it into the market', we might argue 'Cormorant only has four customers; let us therefore find some way of reducing the riskiness of the present strategic structure'. We would then consider such risk-reducing alternatives as increasing the number of customers, developing exports, diversifying or whatever. The one strategy we would *not* consider appropriate is introducing more products to the same four customers. Thus while Cormorant's managers had not considered altering the structure of their company, we would alter it; while they were content to approve a new product so long as it increased profits we are now searching for any new profit-making venture so long as it alters the strategic structure. As soon as we have decided what shape the new structure is to have we can then narrow the area of search to those projects that will (a) be profitable and (b) bring about the desired structure.

I hope that this case illustrates the two ways in which a company's strategic structure can emerge. In the one it results from a number of individual *ad hoc* strategic decisions; in the other it is designed in advance, and individual strategic decisions are then taken to bring it about. Sometimes the structure of a company needs to be redesigned so as to alter the company's exposure to risk (as in the case of Cormorant), sometimes to improve profits, more often a combination of both. Sometimes only one element in the structure has to be altered (Cormorant, for example, might only need to search for a few more customers in the British automotive industry), more often many of the elements in a company's strategic structure have to be changed (as would be the case if Cormorant decided to diversify).

I have already suggested that the strategic structure of a company is complex; it would be a mistake to emphasize the importance of markets or products or customers only because a company's capital structure, the distribution of skills amongst its employees, its management structure and so on can be of equal importance. Some of these are of such importance to some companies that they *must* be included in the design of the future structure, others may be excluded – which elements are included and which are excluded is one of the most important decisions that have to be made in the corporate planning process.

A company, then, may be seen as the present sum of past strategic decisions. A corporate plan is a statement of the coarse-grained strategic structure of a company towards which the management has decided to work and from which individual strategic decisions can be deduced. Corporate planning *is* the process of selecting a strategic structure for a company.

The elements of a strategic structure

A company is composed of many elements or parts. It may operate twelve factories or only one; it may employ ten people or a million; it may manufacture four products or forty thousand. Furthermore these elements may appear in every permutation; a company may make 4 products in 12 factories or make 4,000 in one factory. Its employees may be mainly skilled or mainly unskilled; its capital may be mainly equity or mainly long term loan and may be invested mainly in inventories, or mainly in property, it may lease all its physical facilities or none of them. Clearly the number of elements and their possible permutations and combinations are nearly infinite but the precise permutation or combination of these is unique for any given company at any moment in time. The totality of these elements is the company; no other company has the same structure.

Among the elements that are often of strategic importance are markets, products, physical facilities, services, finance, employees, supplies, distribution and management. All companies need to determine some aspects of some of these elements many years ahead; some companies must decide most of them, occasionally all of them. How many of them must be planned depends upon the factors mentioned on pages 19–27 which include the size of the company, its degrees of specialization, the rate of change and so on. Each element is briefly described below together with an indication of the changes that many companies need to consider.

Markets

It is usual to divide a market into geographical area and type. Thus a company may sell to the North of Spain but not the South, to New York but not to Washington, to Asia but not to Australia. Or it may supply the chemical industry but not the petroleum industries or the AB consumer, not the CDE, the public sector but not the private sector. Which markets a company supplies is, of course, a critically important element in its total strategic structure and, probably without exception, all companies need to decide what their market structure should be years or decades ahead.

Thus consider a small Canadian company manufacturing earth-moving equipment. At present it sells 80% of its products to the Canadian public work authorities, 12% to private contractors in Canada, and 8% to other nations. One of the vitally important elements in its structure ten years hence will be the proportions then obtaining – should it by then be selling 90% to the Canadian government or only 40%? To whom ought it to be selling the other 10% or 60%. Does it matter? Should this be decided now or can the decision be postponed?

Products

A car company manufactures 12 different models. In five years time should it still be making 12 models or 8 or 20? Of these 8 (or 20) should one of them be the mainstay of its profits or would it be better if 80% of its profits came from 4 of them? Should it aim for a reputation of reliability or safety or performance?

It is clear that the type, number, profitability, and so on of products is closely related to the market strategy. Ansoff (Ch. 2) refers to 'product-market' strategy. However it is not only these two decisions that are interrelated; the supply strategy may be intimately linked to product-market decisions, as are also finance and research and so on. Not only is research, finance, etc. dependent upon the products or markets but vice versa. Many of these strategic elements must be considered individually in turn but a plan is not a corporate plan unless the interactions are fully taken into account. That is why it may be preferable to talk of 'strategic structure' rather than product-market strategy or financial strategy or manpower plans. Each of these are useful and legitimate decision areas on their own but none of them is corporate planning.

Physical facilities

These include factories, offices, warehouses, plant and equipment, transport fleets and other assets. The number, size, type, and location of these are often of strategic importance. Of equal importance is the decision to own or not to own any given physical asset. Many oil companies own a percentage of the tanker capacity they require but the percentage varies from company to company; for any given company one percentage will be more appropriate over the following years than some other. Whether to reap the economies of scale of one large factory or to obtain the advantages of better human relations from several small factories may be another strategic decision.

Services

The number and variety of services required by a company are immense. It requires such management services as an accounting system, computing, auditing, personnel services, consultants in special management practices, pension schemes, invoicing, banking and so on. It needs many business services: transport, electricity, warehousing, and so on. Most of these services are now so universally available that they may not need to be planned years in advance and need not be specified in the strategic structure. Some, on the other hand are so crucial to some companies that they must be included in a corporate plan, especially if they are to be provided within the company itself.

Research

The extent to which a company invests in scientific research is frequently of strategic importance. Some companies, even in areas of high technology, spend virtually nothing on research but rely entirely on the imitation of others, obtaining licences for products developed elsewhere and making no effort whatever to lead their industry in innovation. At the other end of the scale companies invest as much as 15% of their total income in scientific research and pride themselves on their position of leadership. Some companies devote a high proportion of their expenditure on scientific research into new processes, some concentrate upon the development of new products, others on a search for new materials and yet others concentrate upon the consumers' use of their products. Some companies devote at least a small proportion of their research expenditure to basic fundamental scientific research (what used to be called 'pure science') while others concentrate solely on problem orientated research; others again sponsor research at universities and others seek government grants for their research efforts. Of all the many factors that determine a company's long term strategic structure and its position within an industry there is little doubt that the volume of expenditure of research and the direction in which that expenditure is channelled are of major importance.

Finance

The extent to which a company is financed by cash flow, by new equity, by loans or leasing during a given period of time determines its financial structure at the end of the period. Up to a point the financial structure of a company determines the nature and certainly the size of any proposed venture into a new market or product. The opposite also obtains; the nature of its product-market strategy partially determines its financial structure for although in theory any company could justify a 200% gearing in practice this is possible only for companies in low risk fields of business such as property or hire purchase.

One of the elements of a company's strategic structure that may have to be specified years in advance, then, is its financial structure; its equity valuation, price earnings ratio, income and capital gearing, dividend policy, amortization rates and so on may have to be decided. In the case of a family business the question of going public will certainly arise.

Employees

Many companies will need to decide how many employees it will employ in five or ten years' time, what skills they must have, their age distribution, the total cost of remuneration, where they are to work, their nationality. What these should be partly depends upon what the company's products, markets, physical assets will be and these in turn depend to some extent upon the present and future employment structure.

Some strategic decisions are independent of others; for example, almost regardless of any other factor, the practice of dividing employees into rigid categories of those paid weekly and monthly will decline. Many companies may have to decide these changes years ahead and some of the decisions can probably be taken independently of the product-market decision. But the distribution of skill and knowledge among the employees probably cannot be determined until many other strategic decisions have been made.

Supply lines

A company may now purchase 70% of its turnover; should it aim to increase that to 80% over the next decade or cut it to 60%. Need it decide this? How should the decision be made?

A company may be buying a crucial component from one supplier – should it try to reduce this dependence? The suppliers may be vulnerable to strikes, or the transport facilities between the company and its suppliers may be vulnerable or the supplies themselves may be liable to price fluctuation or perhaps even to total depletion within a few decades.

Distribution

A company may now distribute its output through two dozen merchants – or it may own the entire distribution network to the eventual consumer. Either may be better in today's conditions; is any change required over the next few years? What changes? How will the company's products be distributed in ten years' time? How will this affect the employee structure, the financial structure, the products?

Management

How the company is managed tomorrow may have to be very different from today. The organization structure will change, the number of managers and managed will change. The methods of inspiring innovation, controlling projects, using computers will change.

Complexity of the strategic structure

The first major task in corporate planning is to determine the financial and ethological targets. The second is to design a strategic structure that will give the company a good chance of achieving satisfactory results and a low probability of achieving less than satisfactory results. This second task is, of course, far more complex than the first. It is difficult partly because of the poor quality of the information available at the strategic level of decision-making, as will be described in later chapters, but mainly because of the complexity that springs from the innumerable alternative structures that any given company could in theory adopt.

Even at the most coarse-grained level, where the definition of each element in the strategic structure is at its most general, the number of alternatives is legion. Take, for example, a company in which there are only three elements, namely three subsidiary companies – let us, in other words, ignore such 'detailed' elements as the company's product or market or financial structure. Let us further simplify by assuming that each subsidiary now contributes one third of the group's total earnings of £300m. Let us assume that the company wishes to achieve minimum earnings of £600m in ten years' time. Now the strategic structure towards which the company could aim might take an infinite number of permutations. Exhibit 4·1 (a) shows the present situation; Exhibits 4·1 (b) to (d) show the company as it could become in ten years' time – and there are infinite variations on any of these structures, not to mention the ones shown in Exhibits 4·1 (e) and (f) where one subsidiary has been sold or closed down or, alternatively, a fourth has been added.

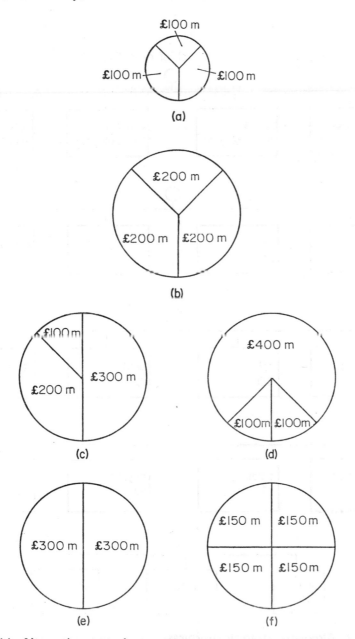

Exhibit 4·1   Alternative strategic structures

Regardless of the way the strategic structure is analysed this complexity is always present. In Exhibit 4·2 (a) for example, I show the four main departments of a small company employing 100 people. Its departmental structure could change in any of the ways shown in Exhibits 4·2 (b) (c) (d) and (e), in one of which, for example, the company has decided to cease production entirely.

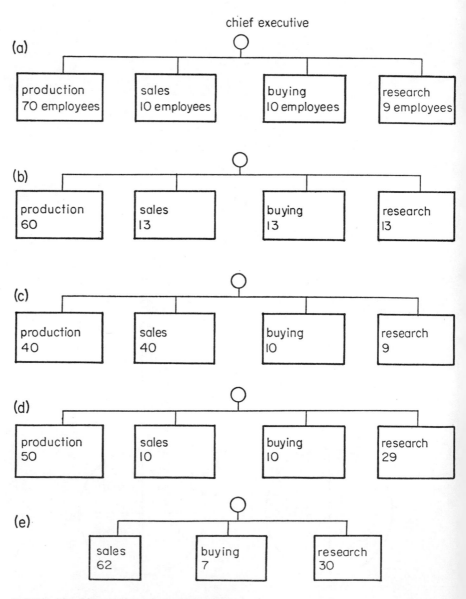

Exhibit 4·2   Alternative strategic structures

Even with only three or four elements in the strategic structure, then, this complexity exists; it rises to progressively greater levels of incomprehensibility as the number of elements to be considered is increased. It is of profound importance therefore that the corporate planner does not attempt to determine any part of the strategic structure that need not be determined. It is important for the corporate planner to consider, at the start of the strategic planning process and throughout it, just what has to be decided and what does not. Confidence is the key criterion; a corporate plan should contain enough detail to allow the managers to gauge their confidence in it. If they do not have this confidence then either there is not sufficient detail in the plan or, if there is, then the plan is itself suspect. In Chapter 10 I give an example of a plan which contains more than enough detail but which fails to secure confidence (see Case 1 on page 141) together with a plan which contains very little detail but which does inspire confidence (see Case 2 on page 157).

It should be noted here that every statement and every figure that appears in a plan represents a decision. It must be as wrong to take too many strategic decisions as too few and it is often the case that the longer one can leave a decision unmade the greater is the probability that more relevant information will come to light. As the number of decisions made in the plan increases so the number of occasions when managers can take advantage of an unexpected opportunity decreases.* At the same time, the more that has been decided the more there is to be redecided when circumstances change. It is questionable, for example, whether corporate plans should include provision for the introduction of a specific product in a particular market; it may make for better planning if the plan makes provision only for the introduction of a P-like product into a M-like market so that only the *type* of product and market are specified together with, perhaps, the size of the project and other overall desiderata. It is then the task of the marketing department to create a product to this specification thus preserving the general rule I suggested above – that projects are selected to bring about a desired strategic structure rather than the future structure being the sum of individual projects.

While this philosophy – the less planning the better – is doubtless correct in principle, in practice such an underspecified plan may not provide enough information to allow the managers to test their confidence in it. They may not be convinced that a P-like product is a realistic proposition in this M-like market unless they are given more information about either P or M and the corporate plan cannot be said to be complete until the product or market have been sufficiently fully and precisely identified for the decision-makers to be able to gauge their confidence in the practicability of the total plan.

---

* I must add that, in my opinion, the past few decades have taught us that the penalties of too much planning are very severe. I believe that the skill of deciding how much to decide is as vital a part of the planner's job as his knowledge of the technical planning skills upon which so much attention is always focused.

Designing the strategic structure

There must be as many methods of designing a strategic structure as there are companies. I shall consider only five: hunch, the 'business question', budgets, projects and strategic decision systems.

Let us first consider hunch (or intuition or entrepreneurial flair). I have already suggested (page 26) that many of the companies that have a record of spectacular success appear to owe it to one man (or occasionally a group or a succession of individuals), who by some unanalysable magic, achieve feats of astonishing business success, often over a period of several decades. Such men usually have a major financial stake in their companies, are usually autocratic, are blessed with energy, imagination, courage and self-confidence. They are also very rare and their style of management is such that, almost by definition, they lose control of their organization when it grows in size beyond a certain critical mass. It is highly questionable whether companies run by such men would benefit from the introduction of a corporate planning system. Even if a system was introduced, the entrepreneur would surely not value it above his own intuitive judgement. I believe it is generally agreed, in other words, that entrepreneurs have no need of corporate planning and that their style is incompatible with it. It is probably also true that shareholders (and employees) recognize that the entrepreneur's company will display a high performance, high risk characteristic as compared with the flatter, more pedestrian performance–risk curve of the professionally managed company.

The entrepreneur's approach to strategic decision-making has been proven over many generations as being one of exceptional power in certain conditions and in the right hands. The three methods I shall discuss below have perhaps less validity in the modern world.

'What business are we in?'

One of the most often quoted examples of this approach is that of Cunard, the shipping company, who, it is said (Steiner Ch. 6 for example), asked themselves what business they were in. Their answer was not 'shipping' but 'floating hotels'. This ingenious answer led them into the expanding leisure industry, with what might be exciting prospects, but whether it is a success or failure is not as important as the principle involved. This was to identify a whole new area of business by asking the simple question, 'what business are we in?' It is interesting that this was the second occasion on which Cunard is believed to have asked itself this question and was the second answer it had obtained. Earlier the company had decided that it was not in 'shipping' but in 'transport' and had purchased an airline company. This was not a total success; they later sold the airline.

Now the moral of this story is that this question can be answered in so many ways that it may be a matter of pure good fortune if the answer found happens to be the right one. Thus a cabinet-maker may decide either that he is a carpenter (and should therefore expand his business into making anything made of wood) or that he is a furniture maker (and that he should expand into making furniture whether of wood or any other material). Again a company making venetian blinds may be either in the home decoration business (and therefore expand into paints, veneers, wallpapers) or that it is in the keeping-the-sun-out business (and therefore develop a photosensitive device which alters the degree of sunlight passing through glass according to the intensity of the sun).

The value of this question lies in its role as a provocation to wider thinking on the part of managers. It is a stimulus to creative thought, not an analytical tool. It does not solve strategic problems, it merely widens the contexts in which a company's strategic problems can be solved. The answer to the 'what business are we in' question provides some answers but it does not provide *the* answer nor does it provide *all* the answers. To arrive at *the* answer requires the use of analytical tools. To arrive at *all* the answers requires the use of other creative tools.

This question, then, is useful as a stimulus to creative thought. It is by no means the only stimulus that should be used. Nor is it an analytical tool.

Budgets

It is generally recognized that corporate planning is not the same as budgeting. The distinction is important. When a manager is asked to draw up his budget the question he is being asked is, in effect, 'What do you propose to do next year, or for the next few years?' The budget is his formal quantified answer. When his budget, together with those of all the other managers in the company are received by the chief executive they are 'co-ordinated'. What does this mean? It can mean two quite different things. It may mean that the chief executive adjudicates between rival aims or that he compares each manager's aims with an overall company strategy.

In the first sense of the word the chief executive adjudicates between departments. In the second between departments and the company as a whole. The first activity is normal among all companies, the second is possible only where the chief executive has a desirable strategic structure in mind with which to compare the individual budgets. If no such strategic plan exists, no comparison can be made and the company becomes merely the sum of the aims of the managers.

The budget procedure was devised and introduced into many companies in the era just before the rate of change began to accelerate a few decades ago. At that time few managements had to take strategic decisions at the rate they have to today and all the advantages of the budget procedure were reaped without meeting its signal disadvantage – namely that it is a procedure for planning the use of existing resources. It does not encourage managers to think beyond their current operations, indeed the very design of the forms used in budgeting often precludes managers from entering figures that are not relevant to their existing activities. No provision is made, for example, for considering acquisitons and mergers on the average budget forms.

Budgets should come out of the corporate planning process rather than form an input.

Project appraisal

The budget usually reflects the aims of those managers who are responsible for on-going activities. Projects are designed to bring about a change in the company. Project proposals represent the second major method of communicating intentions between managers. In companies using the bottom-up approach a manager will submit a project proposal to his superiors who 'evaluate' it. According to most descriptions of this process it is necessary to pass each proposal through two main tests, the first is a financial one to verify that the proposal can be expected to yield a rate of return on capital that lies above the cost of capital and the second that it is in line with company policy.

It can be argued that the second test cannot be adequately applied unless the strategic structure of the company has been determined. A proposal to launch Product P into Market M cannot be evaluated against company policy unless that policy lays down that a P-like product in an M-like market is to form part of the company's long term structure.

If a company has determined its strategic structure it can indicate what projects its managers should be searching for. They can see not only what type of projects are required but their size and timing. If it has not determined the structure then they cannot be expected to make relevant proposals. What is more serious in practice is that, because project proposals are submitted for approval sequentially over quite long periods of time, one proposal may be approved rather than another simply and solely because it happens to be submitted first.

Strategic decision-making systems

In the absence of entrepreneurial flair there are only two other ways of making strategic decisions. One is to take them *ad hoc* whenever it is thought that a decision should be taken and the other is to devise a system. The system I am describing is very similar to those that will be found elsewhere in the literature. Mine contains three cycles, as shown in Exhibit 3·8 because I believe there are three types of corporate objective; purpose, ethos and strategy. Each author's system reflects his definition of words as well as his personal knowledge and experience of corporate planning in practice. In the next few chapters I will describe the 'strategy cycle' that forms the third and most difficult part of the corporate planning system I am describing. Before turning to this, however, I will list 'the factors affecting strategic decisions' (see Exhibit 3·8). The list I give below is very similar to the lists shown by other authors. They are: purpose, ethos, expected performance, strengths and weaknesses, changes in the environment and risk.

Purpose

Clearly it is possible to determine the strategic structure of an organization only if the purpose of the organization is known. The more accurately it is known the more precisely can the structure be tailored to achieve it. A change in purpose results in a change in strategy.

Ethos

Some ethological objectives reflect obligations upon a company, others impose constraints. (See page 55). While most of the strategic decisions that a company makes are designed to achieve its purpose, some (an increasing number) are directed to meeting obligations. Ethological constraints, which are becoming increasingly severe, set limits to the methods, actions and activities that a company may adopt. A change in ethos results in a change in strategy.

Expected performance

If the managers are confident that their current strategy will result in an acceptable performance then they need take no further strategic decisions. If this confidence declines then they will reconsider their strategy. It is the opening and closing of the 'gap' between target results and forecast results which acts as the signal for a review of strategic decisions.

Strengths and weaknesses

A strategic decision is one that is intended to have a major effect on the company's ability to achieve its performance—risk curves. There is general agreement that a strategy that employs a company's known capabilities is less risky than one that does not. Before a strategic decision can be taken, then, it is necessary to know what strengths and weaknesses the company has.

Changes in the environment

The design of a strategic structure must obviously depend heavily upon how the managers believe the company's environment will change.

Risk

Risk is a major element in business. Risk was built into the performance–risk curves and there must therefore be a corresponding preoccupation with risk when making strategic decisions. The riskiness of the strategic structure taken as a whole will be related to the risks inherent in the individual strategic decisions.

I shall discuss each of the last four of these factors in detail in later chapters. It is now clear that the strategic structure of a company must accord with this rather complex specification:

* It must have a performance–risk profile close to the performance–risk curves adopted by the company for purpose and ethos.
* It must not contain any action or activity that may infringe the company's ethos.
* It should make use of the company's major strengths or correct major weaknesses.
* It must take account of relevant changes in the company's environment.

The 'strategy cycle'

It is now possible to fill in some of the details of the strategy cycle shown incomplete in Exhibit 3·8. In the section above I listed the factors affecting strategic decisions, earlier in this chapter I described the strategic structure and suggested that individual strategies can be deduced from the structure. The decision-making sequence, then, runs: the factors, the structure, individual strategies – in that order. However, because the managers' confidence in their company's strategic structure often depends heavily upon their confidence in the individual project proposals, any proposed strategic structure will probably not be accepted until these proposals have been made. There is a final stage, therefore; the evaluation stage which can only take place after concrete proposals have been devised for the existing operations and for new projects. If these, taken together, meet the performance–risk curves, then the managers will approve the strategic structure together with these concrete proposals. Instructions are then issued to all concerned and the planning stage is complete. There then follows a period when no results can be expected to emerge from the strategic decisions just taken but, eventually, results should begin to come through. When they do the managers will compare them with their expectations expressed in the plan and, depending upon these results the strategy will be reviewed or confirmed. However, results are not the only criterion of confidence in a strategy; if any of the assumptions, forecasts or targets built into the strategic decisions are invalidated then confidence in these decisions will decline. It is therefore necessary continuously to review the validity of the performance–risk curves (shown as separate cycles in Exhibit 3·8), the strengths and weaknesses and the expected changes in the environment. In Exhibit 4·3 I show the whole corporate planning system as shown in Exhibit 3·8 but now with more of the details of the strategy cycle.

In the next chapter I will discuss how managers may forecast the expected performance of their company and show how Gap Analysis is used. In Chapter 6 I will consider how strengths and weaknesses and the environmental factors enter the strategic decision-making process. In Chapter 7 I will consider how to evaluate alternative strategies and finally in Chapter 8 will discuss the review mechanisms.

It will be observed that this system is rather complex; it is greatly more complex than budgeting or asking what business a company is in. It is vastly more complex than 'hunch'. And yet I doubt if it is very much more complex than the systems of planning employed in many production departments or

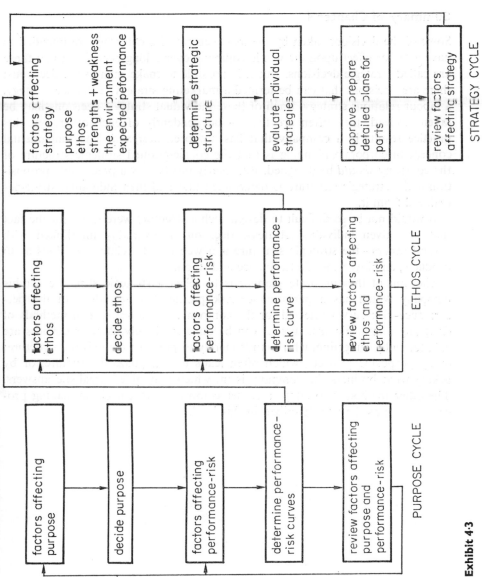

Exhibit 4·3

project management departments or marketing departments, and many of the strategic decisions that emerge from this system are arguably more important to the future of the company than the decisions emerging from production or project planning systems.

Summary of Chapter 4

Some of the decisions taken by the management of a company are intended to have a major effect upon the whole company over a long period of time; these are called strategic decisions. But it is possible to make many such decisions; there are decisions that can be termed a marketing strategy, a finance strategy, a labour relations strategy. Each of these individual strategic decisions may be taken – indeed, they often are taken – independently of each other, but this practice results in a company that has not been *designed*. The fundamental concept in corporate planning is that the coarse-grained strategic structure of the company *should* be designed. But clearly this is only a practicable proposition if the strategic structure is determined first and then individual strategies deduced from it.

It would not be so difficult to design such a structure were it not for the fact that any given individual strategic decision is invariably interlinked with several others – the strategic structure is a web of interrelated decisions as to products, employees, markets, finance and so on.

The aim of the corporate planner is to select a strategic structure for his company which has a performance–risk profile that accords with the performance–risk curves selected for the company. There are several methods of designing a strategic structure; it can be done intuitively as entrepreneurs are said to, or by budgeting, which tends merely to preserve the existing structure; or by proposing projects, which often leads to a haphazard structure, or by asking what business the company is in, which may give unrealistic answers. The other method is to adopt a rather complex formal decision-making procedure such as the one described in this book.

5 Expected performance and gap analysis

Types of forecast

I have already suggested that if the managers of a company are confident that their present strategies stand a good chance of achieving good results and a low probability of achieving poor results then they will probably decide to make no more strategic decisions at that time. The most satisfactory method of testing confidence is to make a forecast of probable results and compare these with the targets, basing the forecast on the assumption that no changes are made to the strategic structure as currently conceived. Thus, if, for example, a company now maintains a gearing ratio of 40% and if no decision has been made to alter this then this forecast will be based on the gearing continuing indefinitely at 40%. Or if the company markets its products only in Italy then the forecast is based on continuing to do only this.

As to external events, the forecast should be based on the assumption that the company will react to any event in the same way as it has reacted in the past; thus, for example, if in the past the company has normally reacted to a competitor's price increase by making a similar increase for its own products then the forecast should be based on the same policy being continued into the future.

I prefer to call this type of forecast 'the F_0 forecast' rather than 'reference projections' (as Ackoff calls them in Ch. 2), because this symbol brings out their salient feature that they are based on doing nothing new. Ackoff also refers to 'planned projections' by which he means a forecast based on the assumption that the company does do something new; it is the expected result of carrying through a plan. I prefer to call this type the F_P forecast. As will be seen much later I believe that corporate planners have to make a large number of F_P forecasts during the evaluation stages of the planning process and, when an F_P has been found that is satisfactory it is then approved by the managers – this one I call the F_A forecast indicating that it is the one that has been approved.

The F_0 forecast

It might be objected that a forecast that is based on the assumption that the company was going to behave in the future exactly as it had in the past would be wholly unrealistic. This is true; but there are four reasons why this is a valuable exercise. The first, and most important, is that the whole point of making this forecast *is* to determine whether any new strategic decisions need to be taken – it would destroy the purpose of the F_0 forecast if new policies were built into it. Secondly a forecast that includes some new activity of which the company has no experience will be more inaccurate than one that reflects only those policies the company has hitherto pursued. Thirdly, any forecast for any company consists of a complex mix of individual assumptions, forecasts and calculations, and it is perhaps sensible to keep this complexity within bounds by all possible means. There is a fourth justification for the F_0; sometimes a company that is facing a threat decides to take vigorous action to avoid it without first calculating the consequences of not avoiding it. It must sometimes be the case that standing still is preferable to stepping into the unknown and the F_0 shows what the consequences of doing nothing might be.

The F_0 forecast, then, is a simple approximation of the consequences to the company of continuing to behave as it has done in the past. The function of the F_0 forecast is to indicate, by comparing it with the targets, whether any change in policy is required. It is the on-off switch for the company's policy-makers; if there is a gap between target and forecast, then they must reconsider the company's strategy. If there is no gap, they need not.

It has two other useful subsidiary functions. The first is that in order to forecast future earnings the planner has to review the salient features of the company's past. In doing so he is certain to discover, or rediscover, a number of trends or events that may have a profound effect upon the formulation of future strategy. The second subsidiary function is that this examination of the company's past may place into perspective the size of the changes to which the company has been subjected over the past decade, say, and will therefore indicate the scale of changes that may be expected over the next decade.

Typical of such changes are those listed below for a large company in Britain – one which was certainly not noted for the reforming zeal of its management. The changes are nevertheless substantial and pervade all the major departments;

Item	1956	1966
number of factories in UK	15	7
number of basic raw materials in use	4	9
number of products manufactured	42	110
profit margin on sales %	12	6

The executives working for this company expressed considerable surprise when these figures were presented to them. No one could say whether any of these long term trends were intentional, or were merely the consequences of many individual piecemeal decisions. No decisions had been made for their future – the company did not know, for example, whether the number of products should double again by 1976 or whether to call a halt, nor whether they should aim at having only 3 factories by then or to retain 7 or build 6 new ones.

It may be that none of these decisions mattered – that none of these items was of sufficient long term significance to warrant its appearance as an element in a strategic plan – but that was not the opinion of the company's executives in this case. These slow, long term movements had occurred without conscious direction. Their scale was also significant, for if changes of this magnitude can occur without conscious planning and direction it suggests that, over the next ten years, the shape of the company may change even more dramatically.

Although many senior executives know the current figure for earnings or earnings per share for their company and may know these figures for the past year or two, very few indeed know what long term rate of growth their company has achieved. Thus one of the functions of the F_0 forecast is to remind executives of the salient features of the history of their company and by doing so to identify those items that really matter to its future.

A simple example of an F_0 forecast

Consider a company, let us call it Sparrow Engineering, which has developed steadily over the past two decades. By now certain management ratios have become established as norms of performance and, using these, a forecast of earnings can be made with some confidence. The assumptions that are to be used in Sparrow's F_0 forecast are as follows:

1 The market for Sparrow's products is almost static but Sparrow is gradually increasing its share of the market and unit sales will continue to increase at about 3% p.a.
2 Price inflation has allowed small price increases to be made almost every year for the past decade. This will continue, in the management's opinion, at the slightly increased rate of 4% p.a.
3 The materials and components bought in by Sparrow's have been rising in price at a faster rate than the selling price of their products and it is forecast that this will continue. Sparrow's managers think the rise will be at 8% p.a.
4 Labour productivity on the shop floor has only been rising at $4\frac{1}{2}$% p.a. No plans exist to improve this so that is the figure used in the forecast.
5 Wage rates have been rising at about 5% p.a. but this is expected to increase to an average of 7% p.a.
6 Overheads have been rising rapidly due to salary inflation and rent on offices and other factors outside Sparrow's control. The managers forecast overheads to rise at 10% p.a.
7 Taxation is at 50% on profits. This is expected to remain the tax rate for many years.

Using these assumptions it is now possible to draw up a forecast of earnings for any future period. This is shown in Exhibit 5·1 for a five year period. Profits and earnings, it will be seen, rise rather slowly (at approximately 5·5% p.a.). The accuracy of this forecast depends solely upon the validity of the assumptions; if they are faulty then the forecast will be wrong. In view of this there is little merit in attempting to make F_0 forecasts either in great detail or with great accuracy; it is entirely legitimate to round figures off to only one or two significant places. (I deal extensively with forecasting techniques in Part 2).

The gap

In principle the gap for any company can easily be calculated. Suppose Sparrow Engineering have a target of 10% p.a. growth in earnings then, since their earnings in year 0 were $1m (see Exhibit 5·1) their earnings by year 5 would have to have risen to $1·6m. The F_0 forecast shows that earnings are only going to rise to $1·3 so there is a gap of $0·3m by Year 5. This concept of the gap has considerable value in corporate planning.

Exhibit 5·1   An F_0 forecast for Sparrow Engineering

Year	0	1	2	3	4	5
Units sold (rising at 3% p.a.)	10000	10300	10600	10900	11200	11600
Unit price $ (rising at 4% p.a.)	1000	1040	1080	1130	1170	1220
Turnover $m	10·0	10·7	11·4	12·3	13·2	14·1
Materials $m (rising at 8% p.a.)	3·0	3·2	3·5	3·8	4·1	4·4
Labour Productivity Index (rising by 4.5% p.a.)	100	104	109	114	119	125
Number of Employees	1000	985	970	955	940	930
Average pay per employee $ (rising at 7·0% p.a.)	3000	3200	3400	3650	3900	4200
Total wages $m	3·0	3·1	3·3	3·5	3·7	3·9
Total direct costs $m	6·0	6·3	6·8	7·3	7·8	8·3
Overheads $m (rising at 10% p.a.)	2·0	2·2	2·4	2·7	3·0	3·2
Profits $m	2·0	2·0	2·2	2·3	2·4	2·6
Tax at 50%	1·0	1·0	1·1	1·15	1·2	1·3
Earnings $m	1·0	1·0	1·1	1·15	1·2	1·3

If a company has determined upon a target rate of growth of, say, 10% per annum in earnings per share and if its current earnings are $1m then a simple exponential curve can be drawn on a graph as in Exhibit 5·2. It will be seen that earnings should have doubled by the eighth year, trebled by the twelfth and so on. Now if the F_0 shows that earnings will probably only rise to $1·3m by the eighth year then a gap of $0·7m exists in that year, see Exhibit 5·3, and the company will have to consider whether this shortfall demands their immediate attention or not. It is clear from Exhibit 5·3 that this company's current strategy is sufficient to generate the target rate of growth for the next five years. Only by Year 6 does any shortfall occur and even then it is small compared with the then level of earnings. So the question becomes this very precise challenge; is five years long enough in which to find a whole new source of earnings sufficient to close the gap in the sixth, seventh … , years? Where the company concerned is operating in a field of business where lead times exceed five years, then, in this example, they should start the search at once.

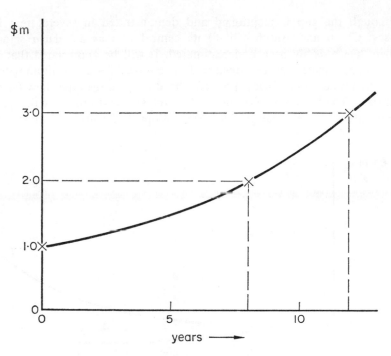

Exhibit 5·2 A simple earnings per share growth target

Where lead times can be expected to be only a year or two then the company need take no action for as many as four more years. And, of course, if the lead time to find extra earnings of $0·7m exceeds seven years then they are already too late.

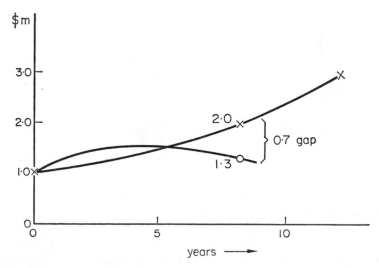

Exhibit 5·3 A simple gap analysis chart

Although the gap is mentioned and demonstrated in several text books (Hussey, Ch. 6 and Ansoff Ch. 8) its central role as an alarm signal for planners has possibly been underestimated. It will be appreciated that it not only acts as an alarm – as demonstrated in Exhibit 5·3 – it also illuminates two other difficult decisions. One is how far ahead to plan, the other how far ahead to forecast. The key to the first decision is the size and timing of the gap that remains after a new strategy has been adopted. Exhibit 5·4(a) shows the

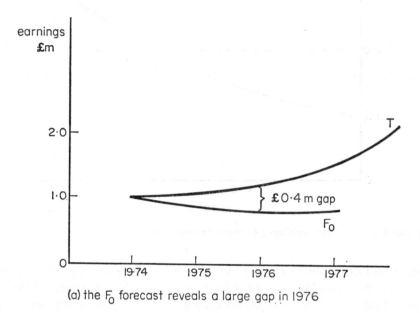

(a) the F_0 forecast reveals a large gap in 1976

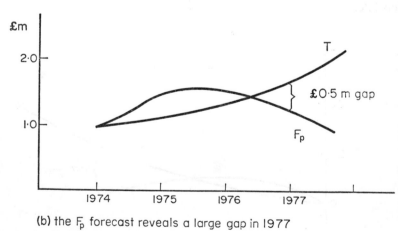

(b) the F_p forecast reveals a large gap in 1977

Exhibit 5·4   Deciding the planning horizon

position of a company in January 1974. There is a large gap in the very near future. Clearly a new strategy is required. By September 1974 this company believes that it has found a satisfactory new strategic structure that will generate new earnings as shown in Exhibit 5·4(b). Whereas the F_0 showed a gap of £0·4m in 1976 this new forecast F_P shows the gap closed for this year but £0·5m for 1977. Should they adopt this new strategy? Of course the answer would depend on the practical conditions in real life, but on the face of it they should not adopt this strategy. Its profile is too sharp; it yields too much over too short a period. They have not done enough planning or, at least, have not found the right answers.

The gap also illuminates the choice of the forecasting horizon. Exhibit 5·5 (a) shows a typical gap situation. The company concerned may well be entitled to believe that no major strategic decisions need be taken for, perhaps, two years. However, let us now forecast ahead for two further years and the posi-

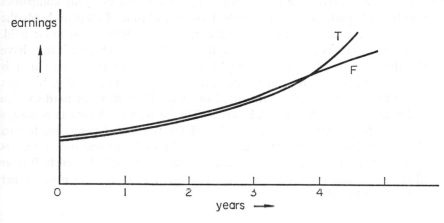

(a) no strategic decision required

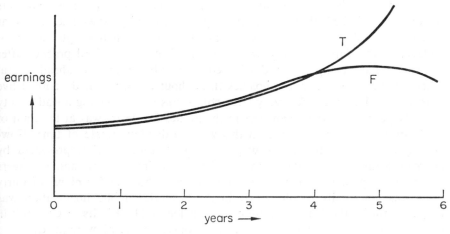

(b) a major gap is revealed

Exhibit 5·5 Deciding the forecast horizon

tion shown in Exhibit 5·5(b) might be revealed. Either this now suggests that an immediate start be made to devise a new strategy or it does not. If it does, then of course, the previous four-year horizon was inadequate.

Now these two principles are valid regardless of whether the gap analysis is used or not, but the process of drawing the two curves from which the gap is derived serves to illuminate and clarify the planning choices open to management. The two principles regarding the time horizons for planning and forecasting can be summarized as follows: 'Plans should be made to close the gaps just far enough ahead to exceed the lead time required to close a remaining gap'. Forecasts should be made 'far enough ahead to ensure that the result of forecasting still further ahead would not alter the planning horizon'. These two statements are of considerable practical importance. At the strategic level it may mean that the five-year forecasting horizons selected by many companies are wholly inadequate. The task with the longest lead time of all is probably the extrication of a company from one field of business into a dissimilar field. Unless a company has forecast far enough ahead to know whether it may have to take this step it will have left too little time to make the change if it is necessary. Companies that are large or in a highly specialized field of business may have to forecast twenty years ahead or more. They may not need to *plan* ahead for more than a few years, however. The horizon for forecasts is always greater than for plans; the horizon selected for the one depends on factors wholly distinct from the others. Indeed it may be said that one only forecasts in order to determine whether one needs to plan. One only forecasts further ahead than one has already forecast to discover if one needs to plan further ahead that one has already planned.

Very long range planning

As Weinwurm (Ch. 2) points out, early in the twentieth century most managers felt that it would be rather risky to try to predict formally for as much as a year ahead. Before World War II, however, many companies had adopted a formal budgeting procedure for one year ahead. This became standard practice after the war in many companies and a few companies began looking ahead several years. In the Sixties many companies throughout the world had adopted five years as standard and a few very large companies began looking ahead twenty or thirty years. For most managers in the Sixties five years was at the limit of acceptance; anything further than this was a ridiculous waste of time. However, late in the Sixties the new profession of 'futurology' (represented by Herman Kahn among others) caught the public imagination and managers began to accept that a time horizon for forecasts (but not for plans) of thirty years was not totally risible. Early in the Seventies public imagination was caught again by the MIT exercise on the ecology ('The Limits to Growth') in which forecasts extending some hundreds of years ahead were made.

There is little doubt that ten years will be adopted as a standard forecasting horizon by a great many companies during the Seventies when many of the very large companies in the world will be forecasting ahead several decades. It will be appreciated that corporate planning is mainly concerned with the strategic structure of a company and most of the elements in this structure take decades to change. The style of management does, new technologies do, so does the development of a new world-scale market; all these changes have to be made, of course, while the company continues to grow in size and profits.

Performance–risk gap analysis

In order to illustrate the value of gap analysis in the above sections I assumed that the company had selected a single figure target (for example, growth in earnings per share of 10% p.a.) and that a single point forecast could be meaningfully prepared and shown as a line on a graph. Neither of these assumptions is valid. In Chapter 3 I suggested that a single figure target merely distorts what shareholders and managers really want from their company and that point

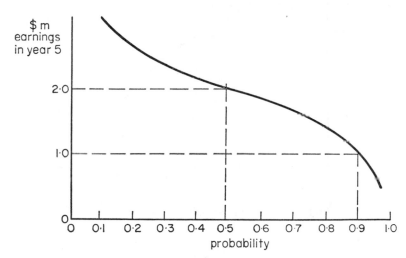

(a) Sparrow Engineering's performance-risk curve

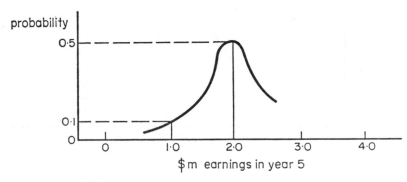

(b) the same

Exhibit 5·6

forecasts are almost certain to be wrong. Although the use of the performance risk concept makes gap analysis more complex it also greatly increases its value as a planning tool.

Let us assume that Sparrow Engineering Company have decided the two critical points on their ROSC performance–risk curve, namely that there must be a 50% chance of exceeding $2m earnings by year 5 and a 90% chance of exceeding $1m. Exhibit 5·6(a) shows this curve; Exhibit 5·6(b) shows the same curve transformed to the usual 'Normal' shape. Now let the management of Sparrow Engineering make their forecast as before but this time they should take account of any possible errors in the forecast. Let us assume this forecast shows a 50% chance of achieving $2m by Year 5 but only an 80% chance of

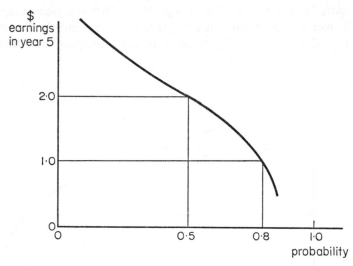

(a) Sparrow Engineering's F_0 forecast

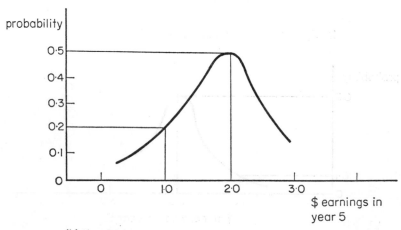

(b) the same

Exhibit 5·7

achieving $1m. This will appear as Exhibit 5·7(a) or (b). When the target and forecast curves are superimposed as in Exhibit 5·8(a) or (b) the management can see at a glance that the company's present strategic structure is 'too risky'. From this curve the management might well decide that no further measures are needed to improve earnings but that measures are required to protect the company from risk – the precise nature of the risk may well have become apparent during the forecasting procedure. Thus the company may have calculated that earnings in Year 5 would be $2m if Event E did not occur but only $1m if it did; the management would know therefore that they must take steps to prevent E happening or protect their company from its consequences.

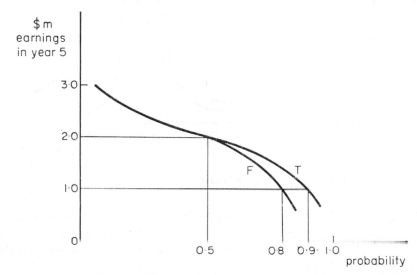

(a) Sparrow Engineering's performance – risk gap analysis

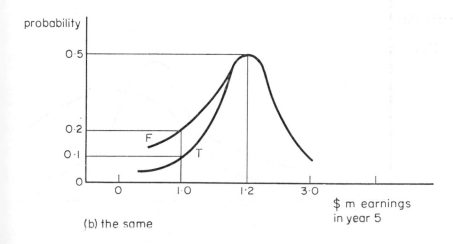

(b) the same

Exhibit 5·8

Of course, the forecast might show the opposite situation; where the risks were not out of line with those considered acceptable but where, instead, the earnings were inadequate – a situation reflected in the target and forecast curves shown in Exhibit 5·9. In this case the company might decide to launch a

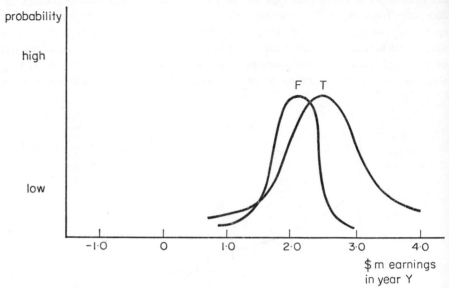

Exhibit 5·9   A low risk, low earnings forecast

small high risk project. Equally, it is perfectly possible for a forecast to *exceed* a target earnings figure but to have a poor risk characteristic as shown in Exhibit 5·10 where (and in the absence of any other data) it might be appropriate to search for a low risk project.

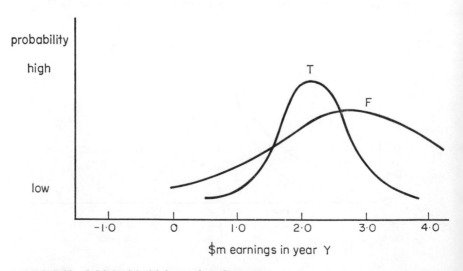

Exhibit 5·10   A high risk, high earnings forecast

In theory it is possible to use this performance–risk gap analysis to specify precisely what changes are required to the strategic structure of a company – this analysis does not determine the *nature* of the changes but it does indicate the *size* and *risk profile* of the projects required. (I deal at length with probability estimating, risk analysis techniques and portfolio selection in Part 2). Thus if an F_0 forecast shows there is a 90% chance of achieving $1m earnings in Year Y and if the performance–risk target calls for an 80% chance of achieving $1·5m then a project having a 90% chance of achieving an extra $0·5m is required. If, at the same time the performance–risk target calls for a 50% chance of achieving $3m and the F_0 shows a 70% chance of $2m then this project must show a 70% chance of achieving $1m. If no single project having these characteristics can be found it may be necessary to search for two projects that together fit the specification. Of course the launching of a project is not the only route to new profits; less dramatic, but sometimes of far greater importance to many companies, is to concentrate upon the existing business. Many companies must have launched major schemes to diversify into new fields, often beyond their knowledge or competences, thus adding new risks to an already risky company profile with disastrous results. Conceivably they could have remained in their existing business and concentrated upon reducing the causes or effects of existing risks.

The 'significant gap'

Gap Analysis is important. It is the most useful mechanism available to guide managers in the difficult decision of whether to rely upon existing plans or to set out to search for additional profits; it shows how far ahead to forecast and how far ahead to plan, it shows when enough planning has been done; it can be used to show the probability of achieving a target. But its most important use is as an on-off signal for the planner. It is necessary, however, to distinguish clearly between a gap that exists beyond the lead time to close it, in which case it is not significant, and one that lies within the critical horizon. The latter will be termed 'the significant gap'. The appearance of a significant gap is the signal for strategic planning to start, or re-start.

Summary of Chapter 5

Even at its simplest, where both the target and forecast are treated as single figures, Gap Analysis is a useful diagnostic tool in corporate planning. It may be used to demonstrate whether a major strategic decision is required to allow the company to reach its target. It illuminates the very difficult questions of how far ahead it is sensible for a given company to forecast and to plan. It helps managers to decide whether a strategic decision may be postponed and throws light upon the size and timing for new projects.

Although it is much more difficult to use, performance–risk gap analysis provides still more information to the planner because it draws attention to the rather neglected fact that it is often as important to alter the riskiness of a

D

company as it is to improve its profits. By analysing the performance–risk gap managers may be able to specify the required risk-profile for future projects and it will certainly help to decide whether a given company should search for the extra earnings it requires in a high or low risk area of business.

The technology of risk analysis and of forecasting are advancing at a rapid rate today and I believe it will not be long before those companies which now use single-figure gap analysis will turn to performance–risk gap analysis and those companies which now do long range planning will turn to very long range planning with horizons of decades rather than years. The rate of change is now such that, whereas in a previous era individual products become rapidly obsolete, the position now is that entire industries are becoming rapidly obsolete (see Part 2 page 226). If that is so then the correct horizon for any company's forecasts should be equal to the lead time to move out of one industry into another (perhaps quite different) without a discontinuity in the rate of growth or earnings record.

6 Collection of data for strategic decisions

Gap analysis brings together the targets and the forecasts to reveal the nature of the task that faces a company's strategists. It spells out the performance specification for the strategy. It does not, and is not intended to, tell them where to look for a strategy of the desired performance. This can be indicated only by a careful examination of the company's own abilities and disabilities and of the changes likely to occur in its environment over the relevant future – the relevant horizon will have been indicated during the process of gap analysis.

For many companies the area of search having the lowest risk is likely to be the company's existing business. A company aiming to make no change in its strategic structure is more likely to achieve its earnings forecast than one that launches into new fields. If that is so, a careful examination of some of the assumptions on which the F_0 forecast is made may prove to be revealing. It should be remembered that the F_0 forecast assumes that the company would make no changes in its current policy towards its existing business, it is assumed, for example, that all available cash flows, including depreciation, would be ploughed back into the current business, that no change would be made from current practice in the level of gearing or in marketing policy or in personnel policies and so on.

As a first step in the search for a strategy all the major assumptions that were made in drawing up this F_0 forecast would be examined for their gap-reducing potential. Thus Sparrow Engineering's management would certainly examine the list of assumptions (see page 79) to determine whether the gap could be closed by improving labour productivity, by obtaining bulk purchase discounts, by new design philosophies, and so on. It is highly questionable whether this enquiry could be said to be corporate planning; most of the measures that Sparrow would consider as a result of examining their existing business would be purely departmental in character. Labour productivity, work study, engineering design, and the introduction of new products are all the preserve of one or other specialist department. The only *corporate* decisions involved are (1) the decision to search for extra earnings in the existing business rather than elsewhere and (2) the act of confirming that any proposals made by these departments are, taken as a whole, in accordance with the performance–risk targets.

The search for more profits will probably begin therefore within the area of the existing business and, only if this fails to close the gaps sufficiently far ahead will the search be gradually widened until, in some cases, the only decision that will do is a complete diversification of the business amounting to the virtual elimination of all existing operations and their substitution with something totally different. While this approach – the philosophy of widening the search – is probably the one most commonly adopted it should be noted that if the gap analysis indicates that there is a low risk of failing to achieve the minimum target then the managers may be justified in adopting a relatively small but highly risky diversification instead of still further underwriting the performance of the existing business.

Whatever new strategies are adopted, whether they relate closely to the existing business or are a major diversification, they should only be selected after a thorough examination of the company's strengths and weaknesses and changes in its environment. I believe it necessary to emphasize that a strategic structure can only be determined after *all* these four categories of data have been collected; strengths and weaknesses *and* threats and opportunities. An internal appraisal *and* an external appraisal must both be performed before any conclusions as to a desirable strategy can be drawn. I emphasize this because, as Ewing (Ch. 4 and 5) points out, one school of thought suggests that a strategy may be selected solely or largely on the grounds that it exploits an opportunity and therefore that corporate planning consists largely of identifying opportunities to exploit (Ewing calls this the outside-in approach). The other school recommends companies to build on their strengths and this inside-out school emphasizes the search for strengths within the company as the most important aspect of corporate planning. I believe neither of these views on its own is correct. All four groups of fact have to be marshalled together before any strategic decision of any sort is made.

Internal appraisal

A great deal has been written on the subject of strengths and weaknesses synergy, capability profiles, management audits and so forth. Ansoff (Ch. 5 attempts to systematize the task of identifying strengths by his capability profile and competence grid techniques but appears to concentrate heavily on strengths as opposed to weaknesses and on the use of these techniques in identifying diversification strategies as opposed to identifying all strategies. I should always be borne in mind that corporate planning is not synonymous with marketing or product-market strategy or diversification policies. It is concerned with the total strategic structure of a company and this includes purchasing, finance, personnel and so forth, together with the interrelations between them. The sole purpose of identifying strengths and weaknesses is to ensure that they are fully taken into account when designing the new strategic structure.

Ansoff lists four main areas for examination; General Management and Finance, Research and Development, Marketing, and Operations. These, he suggests, may be examined in the light of facilities and equipment available, the personnel skills, organizational capabilities and management capabilities. There is no doubt that this is a useful approach; neither Steiner nor Ackoff deals with Internal Appraisal in such detail – indeed Ackoff barely mentions it. Ewing (Ch. 6) however, does consider this vital step in some detail, so do Hussey (Ch. 4) and Walley (Ch. 2)

It may be worth pointing out that in the case of very large companies the internal appraisal may yield a result identical to the 'what business are we in?' question. It might, for example, be valid for IBM to say that they are in the business of electronic business machinery. When we ask what outstanding strengths IBM has we may reply 'that they lead the field in electronic business machinery'; the two answers are similar if not identical. However in asking these questions of a smaller company the answer may be wholly different. A publishing company may find that its only significant strength is 'our computer- ized warehouse and distribution system'; this is not the same answer as the business they are in, which is 'publishing educational books'. There is every reason for suggesting that at least some of the business failures that occur every year are due to companies adopting bold imaginative strategies for the success- ful completion of which they have no relevant competence whatever. It is doubtful whether a strategic decision can properly be made without first making an internal appraisal of the sort that Ansoff and others have described.

I doubt if any check list can be devised that will include all the items that every company should consider in this internal appraisal. Ansoff's is rather brief; it may not adequately bring out the importance of financial strengths and weaknesses nor those relating to a company's buying position. The following list is now offered and examined below;

financial, productive, marketing and distribution, buying, research, employees, management, position in industry.

Financial

It may be that a company's profits fluctuate wildly over a given time cycle – annually perhaps, or over five years. Either this is debilitating or it is not. If it is then any proposed strategy must be designed to reduce the variation or render it less harmful in some way. This is the type of weakness that may be revealed in an internal appraisal and noted down as part of the specification for a satisfactory strategy. Another is the level of loan capital compared with equity, another is the cash flow. A strategy calling for massive capital expendi- ture when the company is already highly geared is almost certain to be in- appropriate; if the company's cash flow is also negative it is even less appropriate.

Other financial factors that often affect strategy are past dividend policies, the articles of association of the company, property values, stock levels, special tax advantages or disadvantages, selling terms, long term contracts, the extent of leasing or hire purchase agreements and so on.

Productive

Companies in service industries do not have production resources in the conventional sense of factories, mines, and so on. Nevertheless most companies do have offices, communications, data handling and transport services and so on. The efficiency, location and design of those facilities may be important elements in strategy formulation. The location of a shop in a High Street may be by far its most valuable asset – far exceeding the quality or range of its merchandise in importance.

In the case of manufacturing industry the quality of a company's production facilities is sometimes of overriding strategic importance. Thus one company's factory may be sited near the intersection of three motorways, another may contain the most up-to-date equipment in the country, another may still be using a batch process that its competitors have long since discarded.

The size, location, efficiency, degree of specialization and so on of a company's physical assets are clearly of significance in strategy formulation. Only a check list of almost infinite length could cover all the questions relevant to all companies; efficient mechanical handling is vital to one company, advanced optical precision technology to another.

Marketing and distribution

This is a major area which could legitimately be further broken down into Marketing, Products, Distribution and Transport.

In the marketing area, a company should consider whether it has too many customers or too few, whether customer loyalty is an important factor (as it is said to be for cars but not for cosmetics), whether its advertising and promotion is excellent or inadequate, whether its sales force is effective or supine, what image the company has with its customers, how valuable the after-sales service system is, how prompt is delivery and so on.

As to its products, the company should ask whether its range is too wide or narrow, how they compare with competitors' products, their price and contribution, their life cycle in each market, packaging and so on.

The items of possible strategic importance in distribution include both the system of distribution and the physical methods employed. Is the system dependent upon merchants, if so what are their strengths and weaknesses? If the company owns its own distribution network where are the weak links? Are the weaknesses geographical or do they lie in the margins and price structure obtaining through the network? On the physical side where are the warehouses? How many are there, are they automated, what is the distance between them?

It will be appreciated that for some companies some of these questions are of major importance, not for others. In the case of transport facilities, for example, the existence of good road and rail connections is vital for a cement manufacturer but not for a diamond merchant.

Buying

Except in the case of primary industries (agriculture, fishing, forestry, fossil fuels and so on) most companies purchase well over half the value of their turnover. Only in exceptional cases will buying not be an important element in a firm's strategic structure, therefore. Factors to be considered are the number and size-distribution of suppliers for each material, component, fuel and service, and the extent to which any one of the suppliers has the power to hold the company to ransom. The extent to which a high risk buying posture requires higher stocks, or justifies a lower purchase price has to be considered. The reputation of each major supplier may need to be considered together with his relevant strengths and weaknesses, including his susceptibility to being taken over by a competitor, his ability to control quality, his research effort and so on. The means by which materials are delivered from supplier to customer also needs to be considered. The level of reserves of certain materials (fossil fuels, for example) may be crucial.

Research

Research is usually taken to mean scientific research and development of new products and processes. Of course it can also include research into raw materials or into the end use of products. Some writers (Ansoff, for example) extend the meaning to cover non-scientific research such as market or consumer research. One of the key questions in any corporate planning study is the problem of how much research any given company should do itself and how much to leave to others. (An alternative to innovation is imitation – a fact sometimes overlooked.) The question is difficult to answer unless some evaluation is made of the company's strengths and weaknesses in this field. The existence of highly specialized research equipment, a history of successful innovation, a high reputation in the industry may be listed as strengths; product failures, poor facilities, an inefficient team may be weaknesses. It is important to identify just where the strengths or weaknesses lie within the total research effort; it would only be misleading to claim that the company is 'strong in R & D' if it is really only strong in process design.

Employees

In the assessment of strengths and weaknesses, the accumulated pool of skills, knowledge and attitudes of the employers is one major factor to be considered. The success of some companies, even quite large ones, can sometimes be traced to the inventive flair of just one or two key employees; sometimes it is the totality of relevant skills among large numbers of shop floor workers. A major source of weakness may spring from malevolent agitation by one or two employees or from a general and widespread feeling of alienation and antipathy towards the company as a whole.

Other human factors that may be of sufficient importance to be considered strategic include productivity per employee, the number of employees in the various categories of skill and knowledge, remuneration policy, motivation, their distribution by social background, their age distribution, training facilities and the various welfare, safety, pension and other personnel services. The local, national and sometimes international availability of each major category of employee may have to be considered.

Management

Management skills become critically important in companies employing more than a few hundred employees. Above that threshold management will certainly appear as one of the elements to be considered in the internal appraisal. It will, for example, almost certainly be necessary to alter the organization structure of the company over a period of several years and, as part of the corporate plan, some concept of how the company will be organized in five or ten years' time may be necessary.

Among possible strengths and weaknesses are financial management skills, the exercise of control and co-ordination of the company's many parts and activities, project management, systems design, the quality of planning and decision-making, data handling and information retrieval, business acumen and flair, cost control, opportunity identification and, not least, the management of human relationships.

Position in industry

The mere fact of size may be a significant strength or weakness. Clearly the larger a company the more bargaining power it may have with customers, suppliers, employees; but it may also be a weakness if it is so large that it cannot significantly increase its turnover without incurring government action. Small companies may have the advantage of flexibility. Reputation within an industry may be important.

Carrying out the internal appraisal

The proposal is that at this stage in the corporate planning process, before any strategy has been proposed, a thorough examination be made of the company's present strengths and weaknesses. It is assumed that any strategy based on a strength is more likely to be successful than one based on a weakness. If a company contains an impressive body of knowledge on the management of complex projects then any strategy devised for that company should call for a series of complex projects. If it has built up an exceptionally fine reputation for precision engineering then this skill should feature prominently in the strategy. Such statements may appear naive and obvious but the principle of synergy is not universally observed. Synergy (Ansoff Ch. 5) is a useful concept. Thus if a company already distributes Product A through a distribution channel it would make sense to use that channel for a new product B, as well, if B is similar to A. Again, if a company's management is skilled in the art of human relations then it should consider entering a new field of business that is labour-intensive rather than one that is capital-intensive. Many of the mergers that have taken place over the past decade have sought to exploit the idea of synergy in this way. Synergy may be found in selling and distribution, in production, in purchasing, investment and finance and in management; it may occur either in the starting up stage of an activity or in its operation. It should be noted, however, that synergy is unlikely to occur, or even to be negative, when a company attempts a new activity that is not related to a strength. A company with a *poor* distribution channel for Product A may court disaster by attempting to sell Product B through it as well. (Synergy is popularly described as the '2 + 2 = 5 effect'. This equation may be correct for strengths but for weaknesses it must be $-2-2--5$).

Synergy is gained through using strengths. The correct identification of strengths and weaknesses is therefore critical. Several techniques may be used to conduct this Internal Appraisal in which perhaps the most severe problem in practice is that those who know most about a company, its executives, are also the people whose opinion is likely to be biased. The more they know the more biased they may be. It is advisable, therefore, to conduct the Internal Appraisals in two areas; the executives should be invited to give their opinion as to where the company's main strengths and weaknesses lie but these opinions should be confirmed by a survey or opinion outside the company as well. Let us consider the executive survey methods first.

Executive surveys

Some companies use a formal printed questionnaire circulated to the relevant (senior) levels in the hierarchy of managers. Some companies make the survey less formal and conduct it by personal interview. Some use the Delphi method (see p. 227).

In other cases the top executives meet periodically away from their place of work and conduct an informal debate. Others adopt the same ploy but split the participants into several syndicates who each identify strengths and weaknesses independently, then report their findings to a plenary session which then debates the similarities and differences of each group's lists.

It will be appreciated that although the opinions expressed by each executive are subjective, the use of surveys and discussion may help to eliminate individual personal bias. Nevertheless certain myths survive in many companies long after their validity has evaporated. The strength of the personality of the head of a department may widely and profoundly influence opinion in the company as to the value of that department. It will also be appreciated that any survey of this sort could lead to severe personal disagreements among the executives involved since they are, in effect, being invited to criticize each other's departments – or they may believe that that is what they are being asked to do. Precisely which type of survey that any given company should use can be determined only by reference to its accepted style of management and its current state of morale.

Outside surveys

These consist of obtaining objective evidence either in the form of verifiable fact or of opinions expressed by people outside the company. In the first category facts can be obtained from other companies for comparison – an inter-firm comparison is one such formalized approach. It might be valid to conclude, for example, that if company X holds four month's stock where company Y holds only three, then Y is more expert at stock control than X. Unfortunately conclusions such as these are seldom so readily obtained. Perhaps of greater value is historical evidence; the introduction of several new products each of which has achieved a significant market share might well be taken as objective verification of a subjective opinion that launching new products is one of the company's major strengths.

Of greater value may be the opinion of outsiders. This is particularly useful when evaluating a product range where an opinion survey among customers, competitors, trade associations or consumer protection organizations can provide very full and accurate evidence. Outside opinion may also be useful for evaluating research, employees' skills and some aspects of management ability.

Taken together these two methods and their many variants allow companies to draw some very useful and specific conclusions as to their abilities and disabilities. It should be noted that some strengths and weaknesses are the result of years of careful cultivation while others may result from some accident of fate. Not every important fact about a company can be classified as a strength or weakness. Some are both. Some are neither or neutral but nevertheless important factors in strategic decisions.

One feature noted by Ewing (Ch. 6) is interesting. He observes that many of a company's strengths and weaknesses are fairly readily identified; it is not difficult to conclude that industrial relations are poor if the company has a history of strikes, nor that Rolls Royce make excellent engines. Some strengths and weaknesses may however be less easily identified; skill in negotiating with national governments may be a very important, but less obvious, strength in an oil company, for example.

Finally it must be clearly stated that these surveys are not intended to pinpoint every minute deficiency in the company or to list every ephemeral success it has achieved. It is a search for those strengths and weaknesses that make a company what it is. Very few companies are outstandingly capable in more than a very few areas of competence and any company outstandingly incompetent in many areas would have disappeared long ago. It is doubtful if any company will have more than half a dozen strengths or weaknesses of strategic significance. Many companies display only one strength of strategic importance, a few may have as many as three or four.

I give several typical examples in the case studies in Chapter 10.

External appraisal

That strategies should be based on strengths is generally recognized. They should also be centred around opportunities. There are, however, cases where a strategy should be designed more to correct a weakness than to employ a strength and more to avoid a threat than to exploit an opportunity. The External Appraisal should therefore be as much directed towards identifying Threats as Opportunties. Five areas of search are usually mentioned by authors; Competitors, Political, Economic, Social, Technological. Each of these may have to be considered at the local, national and international levels. This survey is intended to forecast what trends or events may affect the company's ability to achieve its targets over the planning period.

Competitors

The company will need to examine what actions its competitors might take over the relevant future that will affect it at the local, national or international level. Their actions may affect its market, its employees, its research, its suppliers and its position in the industry. Most companies face a very large number of competitors and it will seldom be possible to study them all. It is possible, however, to study a few of the most important ones and to place the others in categories by size or some other relevant classification. In most industries there are a few companies of national or international significance, a few dozen of moderate significance and thousands of small ones. In the vehicle building industry, for example, it may be possible to predict that virtually none of the thousands of truck and lorry manufacturers who employ less than ten people will enter the over 40-ton vehicle building market. Such generalizations serve to concentrate one's enquiries into those areas that are relevant to one's business.

Political

Here the company tries to determine whether any political changes at the local, national or international level will affect its business. Some of these are: anti-trust legislation, taxation, pollution and safety regulations, trade-union law, tariff and quota agreements, rising nationalism in developing nations, economic federation of nations, government sponsored research, nationalization, and so on. Such lists are endless; at the local level changes that may be significant include parking regulations, opening hours for shops, construction of roads and buildings, and so on. It must be remembered, however, that these studies are being conducted at a strategic level and that only those political changes that will materially affect the company over a period of years need to be considered.

A 'political change' is a change inspired by local, national or international governments or government controlled agencies.

Economic

At the local level economic changes affect remuneration rates, availability of labour, purchasing patterns and prices and so on. Clearly the smaller a company is relative to the local community, the more carefully it will have to predict local economic changes – a statement that is valid at the national level also. It should be noted that some companies operate only one very large factory but sell to international markets and local economic changes may therefore be highly significant for its costs but wholly insignificant for its prices.

The broad economic changes are well known; for example, primary and secondary industries are now growing rapidly in some of the developing nations while tertiary industries are growing more rapidly in the developed nations. It is well known that the size of companies in some industries is increasing while in other industries there may well be a revival of the small business.

Social

Changes in social attitudes, behaviour and composition are critically important to consumer-orientated industries; they are now becoming important to even the heavy end of industry as well for although consumer needs and buying patterns have an effect on the market for steel or coal only at second or third hand, certain social attitudes are beginning to affect many aspects of industry other than the market. In particular, attitudes to work are changing and these must be taken fully into account when designing the organizational elements of a strategic structure. Again, society is applying increasing pressure on all companies in respect of pollution, noise and environmental aesthetics generally, so that the design of factories, offices, products and equipment must take these changes into account.

Changes in education, wealth, life styles, attitudes to work, changes in the composition of a society and its attitude to race, colour, and religion are some of many areas that most companies need to consider, whether they are in consumer-orientated industries or not.

Technological

While social changes have to be forecast mainly to identify the changing needs of consumers, technological changes need to be forecast to identify how these needs might be met in the future. Technological changes can threaten a company in two main ways; a substitute product may appear or new methods of manufacture or distribution of the existing product may be discovered. In much the same way a company's technical knowledge can often be used to invade the markets or production methods of other industries. Technological changes do not only affect companies in areas of high technology; it is obvious that manufactured products and their processes are subject to technological change. It is perhaps less obvious that service industries are affected, and yet it can be argued that recent advances in computing and telecommunications have affected the banking industry at least as much as they have affected any manufacturing industry. Presumably the High Street retailing industry will feel the effects of 'television order' (i.e. a mail order service linked to television display and selection systems in the home) in the near future.

I describe many of the techniques of technological forecasting in Part 2.

Carrying out the external appraisal

The resources required to determine a company's strengths and weaknesses are very small compared with those required for the external appraisal. Few companies need to examine all five areas in great depth – a supermarket needs to look at technological change only superficially compared with an electronics company – but all companies have to study at least two or three of these areas in great detail. While the initial internal appraisal might take days or weeks the external will take months or years. The size of this task springs not from the depth of study required but from its wide range. Even if a company operates in a comparatively limited field of business the number of potential threats it faces are considerable and the number of alternative opportunities to be exploited are almost infinite. A multinational multiproduct company would, in theory need to try to predict every event in the history of the world over the relevant future if it was to claim that it had correctly carried out its external appraisal. Just as it was suggested on page 98 that only those strengths and weaknesses that were of strategic importance should be identified in the internal appraisal so, in the external appraisal, the company should limit its search to those trends and events that are likely to affect its earnings significantly over the relevant future. Two methods are again appropriate: Executive Surveys and Outside Surveys.

Executive surveys

This approach is particularly useful for small companies who cannot afford the advice of outside experts. Its value should not be underestimated for even the largest company, for few outside experts are likely to possess as much knowledge concerning its existing business area than that already residing within the company. Although corporate planning is carried out at the highest level in a company it is sometimes the case that a humble sales representative knows something significant about a competitor's product intentions or a research scientist knows something about the new technology of a related field of business. A Delphi study among the employees of the company, especially if conducted systematically, can yield useful forecasts in all five areas.

Outside surveys

Most companies will need to obtain forecasts from outside experts; consultants, market researchers, trade associations, universities and institutes. Where it is concluded that the company may have to move into a new field of business then outside experts will almost certainly have to be consulted.

The cruciform chart

It should be noted that all the separate studies so far described as part of the corporate planning process may be carried on concurrently; the ROSC performance–risk curve may be selected while the ethological targets are being chosen and, at the same time, the F_0 forecast can be made while the internal and external appraisals are made. In theory each of these tasks could be delegated to separate people or committees. Only when all this information is available, however, can a start be made on considering alternative strategic structures. Every one of these pieces of information goes into the strategic decisions and these cannot be made therefore in the absence of any.

I have pointed out that in most circumstances there will be no more than half a dozen strengths or weaknesses or threats of strategic importance to a company – very often there will be no more than two or three of each. Even so, in total there may well be a dozen or more items in these three categories and perhaps a dozen or more potential opportunities as well. At some stage during the corporate planning process it is essential to bring together all the items disclosed by the internal and external appraisals. This is certainly best done in writing where the precise nature of each item may be set out in some detail and accompanied by figures and supporting evidence.

Once this has been done it is possible for all those concerned with developing a strategy for the company to study, discuss, dispute and eventually agree the list of items. Once agreement has been reached it is necessary for the planners to stand back from the detail and attempt to see the data as a whole; to consider the interplay between the various strengths and opporunities, the threats and weaknesses, and to devise a strategy that will take them all into account. For this purpose it may be useful to present all these items in a more succinct form and for this a four-part display chart may be used. Examples of this Cruciform Chart are given in Exhibit 7·2 and in Chapter 10 (Cases 1 and 2).

If one of these charts is displayed at any meeting at which future strategy is being discussed those present can see at once whether any proposed strategy takes into account all the relevant data concerning the company, and can see at a glance whether, for example, a proposed strategy relies upon a strength which the company does not possess.

Summary of Chapter 6

If it is accepted that the coarse-grained strategic structure of a company should be designed, as opposed to be allowed to result from piecemeal strategic decisions, then I believe the design should take full account of the company's internal strengths and weaknesses and the threats and opportunities that it will encounter within the planning horizon.

Before any strategic decisions can be made, either for the strategic structure or for the individual strategies that may be deduced from it, a careful study of the company itself and its probable future environment should be made. Both the internal appraisal and the external are difficult to carry out; the internal because of the personal bias among those who know the company best; the external because of its wide range and because of the impossibility of forecasting the future.

Every company – at least every company that has survived for very long in a competitive field of business – must owe its survival to something; it may be the vigour of one man, a pool of knowledge among its specialists, an adjacent motorway, a chance discovery in its laboratories, or decades of quiet and careful salesmanship. Every company has its faults; its top managers may have failed to train a new generation of managers to succeed them, it may be subject to strikes, its products may be obsolescent. All companies are threatened by competition and by changes in social behaviour or in technology; or these changes may offer an opportunity for profitable exploitation. The object of this exercise – the internal and external appraisals – is to pinpoint the few strengths and weaknesses, threats and opportunities that may be of major strategic significance to the future of the company. All this data is then brought together in one document and perhaps summarized on a Cruciform Chart. Then, and only then, is the company in a position to determine its future strategic structure.

7 Evaluating alternative strategies

The revelation

At some stage towards the end of the appraisals the volume of opinions, facts, assumptions and possible strategic actions will rise to a level that becomes almost unmanageable. At that point those taking part in the corporate planning process will not be able to distinguish between facts and figures that are of strategic significance and those that are not; much of the data they are considering in their discussions will have been handed to them for no better reason than that it happened to be available in the company's records.

There comes a moment during the process, however, when through this fog of meaningless complexity, certain features begin to emerge with increasing clarity. Furthermore these features are often seen to be clearly interrelated in such a way that it may be said that a concept of the company emerges. Until that point none of the many strategic suggestions made by any of the participating planners or executives will appear to be more appropriate for the company than any other – they will just be good ideas that are no more relevant to their company than to any other company. After that point, however, not only will many of the proposals that they have been considering now be seen to be irrelevant to the company's strategic future, but the participating executives will from then on begin to propose larger numbers of new strategies that are relevant and fewer that are not. The previous jumble of facts and figures become quite sharply divisible into those that are manifestly of strategic importance and those that manifestly are not – a division that often allows the planners to direct any subsequent search for data towards those sources of information that are more likely to yield facts that are relevant and strategic rather than irrelevant or tactical.

I do not wish to exaggerate the importance of what one could describe as a revelation; it does not always occur; when it does, it does not take the form of a blinding flash of inspiration such as those reputed to occur to mystics, artists and inventors. It is mentioned in no textbook. Nevertheless, a well-known feature of the human mind is that it searches for patterns among the facts that are presented to it and it may not therefore be altogether surprising if a gestalt occurs during the corporate planning process.

Once the gestalt is revealed the planners may find that a highly appropriate strategic structure and many possible strategies suggest themselves. It becomes clear also that, for example, a market research study should be commissioned in this market rather than that, the next factory should be sited here rather than there, the company's scientists should research into this area rather than that. In other words it becomes possible to specify in general terms that, for example, the company should develop a P-like product in an M-like market, rather than adopt a policy of acquisition or merger or whatever.

I give two very detailed accounts of the revelation of a strategic structure and its associated strategies in Case Studies 1 and 2.

Some of the authors in this field mention the role of creative thought in corporate planning. Steiner (Ch. 12) deals extensively with it but it must be recorded that it is a seriously neglected feature in most of the literature which appears to concentrate attention upon the more quantitative and analytical aspects of planning technology.

Alternative strategic structures

I suggested on page 66 that one of the most severe problems in corporate planning is the large number of alternative structures that any company could adopt given a long enough planning horizon. Given an infinite horizon there are infinite structures. It is simply not possible to evaluate more than a very few of these alternatives and, I am suggesting, one way of reducing the number of alternatives to a manageable few is to eliminate all those that do not make use of the company's strengths or fail to correct weaknesses or fail to deal with threats or to exploit opportunities. These are four of the criteria; a fifth is that any proposed structure must be one in which the managers feel confidence – confidence that it is a practical proposition in the real world, confidence in its potential to meet the performance–risk curves for the company. Furthermore the managers must bear in mind that in the future the company may not be able to take many of the actions that it now takes because of the increasing severity of the constraints imposed upon it by society and reflected in its ethos.

There are then six criteria by which to test any proposed strategy:

1 Can it be shown that this strategy gives the company a performance–risk curve similar to the one selected by its shareholders (and managers, employees, etc.)?
2 Has the company the necessary competence to carry it out?
3 Does it eliminate or reduce the company's outstanding weaknesses?
4 Does it allow the company to exploit any opportunities that may occur in the future?
5 Does it sufficiently reduce any of the severe threats that may face the company?
6 Does it call for any action that is or may become objectionable on moral or social grounds?

These six criteria form the cloth of a sieve through which any proposed strategy may be passed – the greater the number of well-defined strands there are in the cloth the fewer will be the number of alternatives that pass through; ideally only one will do so but in practice several will and the final selection may well have to be made a matter of personal judgement by the managers.

Consider, for example, the number of alternative strategic structures that the Falcon Fertilizer Manufacturing Company might adopt:

1 continue to rely solely on making and selling fertilizers in its existing markets by increasing its share.
2 try to break into fertilizer markets abroad, concentrating on (a) neighbouring nations or (b) developing nations
3 gradually supplant the manufacture and sale of fertilizers with the sale of knowhow in fertilizer plant design in developing nations.
4 integrate forwards along the fertilizer distribution network.
5 integrate backwards into the mining and transport of fertilizer raw materials
6 merge with a competitor (a) at home
                      (b) in a neighbouring nation
                      (c) in a developing nation
7 introduce a non-fertilizer product in its home market.

The process of elimination

The list of alternatives is endless. However, let us now pass some of these strategies through the sieve. Assume that one of the strengths noted down by Falcon's managers during the internal appraisal is that 'Falcon is highly regarded in home agricultural circles and its name is well known'. That one fact is enough to suggest that strategies 1, 4 and 7 now look more promising than the others (except perhaps 6(a) in certain circumstances) because these others deny the use of this particular strength. Let us further assume that in the external appraisal Falcon's management noted that, 'the government pays 30% of the price of our products to farmers as a direct subsidy; no guarantee has been given that this subsidy will not be withdrawn'. Now this fact tends to favour strategies 2, 3 and 7. Some of the others, notably 1, 4, 5 and 6(a) look positively dangerous since they would make the company still more dependent upon the area of business which is under this threat. It is interesting to note that the three most promising strategies were, in the first list above, 1, 4 and 7 and in the second list numbers 2, 3 and 7. We now learn another fact about Falcon; 'Falcon has a 65% share of the home market'. Now this is both a strength (in that Falcon has considerable bargaining strength in the market) and a threat (in that Falcon's monopoly position may come under attack from the government) and seems to place strategies 4, 5 and 7 in a favourable light; it makes strategies 1 and 6 look rather doubtful.

I believe that even this obviously oversimple example illustrates a number of important general conclusions. Firstly it must be apparent that no company could examine all possible strategic structures – I listed only seven out of the hundreds that Falcon might have listed – and this implies that some method must be devised by which to eliminate most of the alternatives without giving them very much consideration. I believe that this process of elimination and the selection of a short-list is one of the key steps in corporate planning and it is the main purpose of the internal and external appraisals to collect the data upon which the selection is made. Secondly this example shows how the introduction of each new fact has the effect of favouring one or more strategies at the expense of others in the list. Although I only introduced three facts from Falcon's internal and external appraisal it was already becoming clear that strategy 7 was emerging as one that Falcon's managers would have to take very seriously. On the other hand strategy 6(a), namely a merger with a competitor, was beginning to look extremely unattractive and inappropriate. As the number of strengths, weaknesses, threats and opportunities that can be identified increase and as their nature becomes more precisely defined and quantified so the sieve that they form becomes more selective. It becomes possible to eliminate more strategies that ought not to be even considered and points progressively more decisively at one or two that should be considered very carefully.

A third general conclusion is that there is a strict limit to the number of strengths, weaknesses and threats (but perhaps not opportunities) that are truly significant at the strategic level of decision-making. I believe it can be said that an internal appraisal containing more than, say, half a dozen strengths and half a dozen weaknesses will be too detailed – it will contain items that are not strategic at the corporate level. Similarly, few companies will be faced with more than half a dozen threats of strategic significance to the company as a whole.

I simplified the Falcon Fertilizer case in two ways; I introduced only three facts from the appraisals and I offered a choice of only seven strategies. It will be appreciated that to reach a valid conclusion in real life demands a considerable creative effort on the part of the planners and managers who may be faced with a dozen or more facts in the appraisals and a nearly infinite list of strategies. I suspect that were it not for the revelation of a gestalt, mysterious and capricious though its appearance may be, the corporate planning task would be well-nigh impossible.

Evaluating the short list

Having reduced the number of alternative strategies to a manageable number by the use of this sieve, the management will need to determine whether any of the remainder are likely to have the performance–risk profile that the company requires. In other words the performance–risk profile of these strategic structures should be calculated and compared with that of the company. But clearly this calculation cannot be made until the precise nature of the proposed strategies have been determined. In other words the strategies have now to be quantified and an F_P forecast prepared for each of them and compared with the company's targets. (The F_P forecast, or planned projection as Ackoff calls it, shows the expected results of adopting a proposed new plan as opposed to the F_o which shows the expected results of continuing to run the company with current policies unchanged).

Almost every corporate plan will contain two main sections: it will involve proposals for modifying the existing business and proposals for entirely new activities. In order to quantify a corporate plan, therefore, figures have to be selected for both these areas which I will call respectively operational objectives (i.e. figures in the plan which, if approved, will be issued as targets to the operational departmental managers) and project specifications (i.e. figures which, if the plan is approved, will be issued to managers as targets for new projects).

It is at this stage in the corporate planning process that company models are particularly valuable. (See p. 274 for detailed descriptions and examples). It will be appreciated that a company may, at this stage, have as many as four or five significantly different strategic structures to evaluate, each of which may only be adequately represented by several hundred figures for each year of the planning horizon. Furthermore each has to be tested for risk which may mean that every figure for every year has to be varied within its probable limits. I should make two comments; firstly I suggested on page 26 that there is a strict rational limit to the volume of corporate planning that should be undertaken in any company; I suggested that the managers need only be confident that the strategy they were choosing was good enough to make it not worth searching for a better one. There is therefore a strict limit to the amount of detail that a plan must include in order to secure the management's confidence. The amount of detail will vary greatly depending upon circumstances but it can be said that the detail required to secure the management's approval is much less than the detail required in the subsequent action plans which have to be drawn up to give effect to the strategy. My second comment is that it is questionable whether *any* strategy can properly be evaluated without the use of a company model (although not necessarily one that is so complex and detailed that a computer has to be used).

A simple example

Dove Dishwashers Limited are a small well-established firm whose sole product is a dishwasher sold into their home market. The product has a very high reputation but sales and margins are under threat from the larger mass producers in the industry. Their F_0 forecast (Exhibit 7·1) shows that if they do nothing their profits in four years' time could easily be as high as $180,000 and the Board are confident that such a figure will be fully acceptable to shareholders. But the Board also feel that shareholders would like to see a 20% chance of achieving at least $120,000 and, as Exhibit 7·1 shows, there is in fact a 20% chance of profits falling to $40,000.

The company's appraisals are summarized in a Cruciform Chart shown in Exhibit 7·2. In view of the facts shown there the Board has rejected a large number of possible strategies including a merger, a major export effort and

Exhibit 7·1   The F_0 forecast for Dove Dishwashers

Results believed to be 50% probable:

Year	0	1	2	3	4
Turnover $000	1000	1100	1200	1300	1400
Margin %	40	40	40	40	40
Gross profit $000	400	440	480	520	560
Overheads $000	300	320	340	360	380
Profits $000	100	120	140	160	180

20% chance of results as bad as:

Year	0	1	2	3	4
Turnover $000	1000	1050	1100	1150	1200
Margin %	10	10	30	36	31
Gross profits $000	400	420	420	415	410
Overheads $000	300	320	350	360	370
Profits $000	100	100	70	55	40

Exhibit 7·2   Cruciform Chart for Dove Dishwashers

Strengths	**Weaknesses**
Well established company	Small company
Product of high repute	Single product in one market
$200 000 capital available	

Threats	**Opportunities**
Strong competition	Kitchen waste disposer

many others. But the Board is now split over two remaining possible strategies; Strategy A is to concentrate upon the existing product thus leaving the company's strategic structure as it is – a manufacturing company with a single product in a single market strategy B is to introduce a waste-disposal machine into the home market, thus altering the structure of the company. The capital required to modernize the production of the dishwasher is much the same as that required to set up the much smaller production line for the waste disposer.

Exhibit 7·3   Dove Dishwasher F_{PA} forecast

Results believed to be 50% probable:

Year	0	1	2	3	4
Turnover $000	1000	1100	1200	1300	1400
Margin %	40	41	42	44	46
Gross profits $000	400	450	500	570	650
Overheads $000	300	320	340	360	380
Profit $000	100	130	160	210	270

20% chance of results as bad as:

Year	0	1	2	3	4
Turnover $000	1000	1050	1100	1150	1200
Margin %	40	40	40	40	40
Gross profits $000	400	420	440	460	480
Overheads $000	300	320	350	360	370
Profits $000	100	100	90	100	110

Exhibit 7·4 Dove Dishwasher F$_{PB}$ forecast

Results believed to be 50% probable:

Year	0	1	2	3	4
Profits from dishwasher $000	100	120	140	160	180
Profits from waste disposer $000	0	0	20	80	140
Total $000	100	120	160	240	310

20% chance of results as bad as:

Year	0	1	2	3	4
Profits from dishwasher $000	100	100	70	55	40
Profits from waste disposer $000	0	−20	0	20	40
Total $000	100	80	70	75	80

In Exhibit 7·3 I show (grossly oversimplified) the consequences of Strategy A. Forecast F$_{PA}$ shows that margins could be so substantially improved that the minimum threshold target is very nearly attainable even if sales and margins come under severe pressure.

Exhibit 7·4 shows forecast F$_{PB}$ – the forecast for Strategy B – in which no attempt to support the dishwasher is to be made and all the available capital is spent on the new product. It is clear that while this strategy could be highly successful it could also place the company in severe difficulties if the project cost more than expected or was delayed for a year and came under severe competition. The Board, having made and studied these forecasts, agreed that neither Strategy A nor B was acceptable; B was too risky, A had the disadvantage that Dove Dishwashers would have to continue indefinitely to rely upon their single product. A mix of A and B would be a satisfactory solution but the company lacked the loan capacity to undertake both. They therefore considered Strategy C in which a foreign competitor's waste-disposal machine, made and sold in Italy would be licensed for sale in Dove's home market and, at the same time, Dove would adopt most of Strategy A. Forecast F$_{PC}$ is shown in Exhibit 7·5 and is seen to be much more satisfactory.

Exhibit 7·5 Dove Dishwasher F$_{PC}$ forecast

Results believed to be 50% probable:

Year	0	1	2	3	4
Profits from dishwasher $000	100	130	160	210	270
Profits from factoring $000	0	10	20	30	40
Total $000	100	140	180	240	320

20% chance of results as bad as

Year	0	1	2	3	4
Profits from dishwasher $000	100	100	90	100	110
Profits from factoring $000	0	0	5	10	15
Total $000	100	100	95	110	125

It is interesting to note that Strategies A and B represented two different possible strategic structures of which B was felt intuitively to be more in line with the facts revealed by the appraisals (Exhibit 7·2). The calculations in F$_{PB}$

failed to convince the directors that this particular strategy was right – the structure was right, the particular strategy was wrong. When a senior executive proposed Strategy C, however, it was seen not only to change the strategic structure in the direction in which it was felt it should be changed, (two products of which only one is manufactured) but the management felt sufficiently confident of the F_{PC} forecast to approve it. In my terminology F_{PC} then became F_A – the forecast representing the approved plan.

Giving instructions

Once a strategy is approved it only remains to fill out sufficient detail to allow unequivocal instructions to be given to the operational and project managers. Thus in the case of Dove Dishwashers:

1 A senior executive might be appointed to complete negotiations with the Italian waste-disposal machine manufacturers, arrange for distribution of the product, etc., all with the intention of launching the product in year 1 (or year 2 at the latest) to achieve a profit of not less than $5,000, $10,000 and $15,000 in years 2, 3 4 respectively but preferably, of course, reaching $20,000, $30,000 and $40,000.
2 The chief engineer would be invited to submit detailed proposals costing up to $200,000 showing how the dishwasher production line was to be modernized to produce at least $1·4m worth of dishwashers and to reduce the unit cost by 15% by year 4.
3 The finance director would have to consider how best to raise $200,000 capital required over years 1, 2 and 3.

And so on. One of the inevitable consequences of adopting the corporate planning approach to running a company is that many changes may have to be made to the organization structure of the company. These are described in detail on page 251 but the basic principles can be stated here. In those companies in which the overall view does not predominate there will be a tendency for new projects to be generated *within* each existing section of the company. Additional earnings will tend to come mainly from improving the way existing operations are carried out. Very few major *structural* changes in the shape of the company are made and, because the company tends to remain broadly the same shape, few changes in organization structure are required. As soon as the overall corporate view is adopted, however, structural changes will be more frequent and major changes in the organization structure may have to be made. But these consequential changes are not perhaps the most significant organizational alterations. Of greater importance is the need to set up several quite new sections whose task is to promote change itself; a mechanism of some sort must be formed by which new projects are sought out, designed, evaluated, approved, initiated, managed, monitored and finally absorbed by the operational managers of the company. The organization structure of the company has to be changed so that further changes may be facilitated – in other words, so that the company may become 'adaptive' (see Ackoff Ch. 1).

Summary of Chapter 7

In Chapter 6 I described a stage in the corporate planning process where analysis predominates. In this chapter I have described the process of synthesis, where all the relevant facts, opinions, forecasts, assumptions are gathered together, examined, considered and discussed. At some point in this rather confused stage of corporate planning, the participants will have to agree what would be the most appropriate coarse-grained strategic structure for their company over the next few years or decades. Of the thousands of alternatives only a very small number will be seen to be appropriate and, of these, only one will remain after the evaluation stage.

The detailed evaluation of a broad strategy becomes possible because of the following sequence; to move from the present strategic structure to a new proposed one it is necessary to make many physical changes to a company. Once it is known, even approximately, what the proposed new structure is to be, it becomes possible to specify more or less exactly what these physical changes must be, when they must occur, their scale, the resources required to bring them about, their consequences upon other parts of the company and so on. Once these have been determined and quantified it is possible for the management of the company to judge the level of their confidence in these physical changes being accomplished and hence judge the proposed structure.

A corporate plan, then, will specify both the strategic structure towards which the company is to move and the individual strategic actions that will bring it about. The depth of detail required in the corporate plan should be sufficient to allow the management to judge their confidence in it; if more than this depth of detail is present then the scope for opportunism and initiative by individual managers may be needlessly curtailed. Deciding how much to decide is an important part of all planning.

8 Monitoring confidence

I have so far described each of the steps in the corporate planning process more or less in the sequence in which a company would logically take them when introducing corporate planning for the first time. The final step comes when, having approved the corporate plan, the management issues the instructions that are required to put the plan into effect.

When a company has completed its first corporate plan, however, it is also necessary to set in motion a system for monitoring confidence on a *continuous* basis – any concept of corporate planning as a merely sequential process thus becomes inappropriate. In Exhibit 4·3 I showed the corporate planning process as three interlinked cycles; the activity that I call 'monitoring confidence' involves the management in a continuous movement through all these cycles, testing and questioning every forecast, fact, assumption and decision that they have made. In normal circumstances the management will need to move through the Purpose Cycle comparatively slowly and infrequently because the factors that affect a company's purpose are not normally subject to rapid change. They may have to move more frequently through the Ethos Cycle and almost continuously through the Strategy Cycle.

Review of purpose

The purpose of a company occasionally changes suddenly and dramatically as when a private company is sold or goes public or when a quoted company is nationalized or is taken over by a revolutionary group of employees or merges with another company. When these events occur there is seldom any doubt about who the new owners are although there may be considerable doubt as to what they want from the company. When one group of shareholders is simply replaced by another then it may merely result in a new return on shareholders' capital target or performance–risk curve being required. Where shareholders are replaced by the State or employees or the local community an entirely new set of targets may be required.

The purpose of a company may also change slowly and insidiously. If it is true that purpose is determined by those who have the power to decide it (as I suggested on page 41) then the management will need to consider whether any change in the power structure has occurred or is occurring. Equally insidious are the changes in the composition of the shareholders in a quoted company.

The proportion of shares held in Fisons (see page 48) by private shareholders, (as opposed to institutional shareholders) fell from 90% in 1931 to 45% in 1969, for example.

But regardless of whether the owners change or not, the performance–risk curve is certain to change over a period of years. The factors that affect such changes have therefore to be kept under review; these were listed on page 52 as including:

The attitude of the company's shareholders to risk.
The general level of return on risk and non-risk capital.
The general state of the world as this affects attitudes to risk.
The company's traditional performance–risk curve.
The anticipated level of inflation.
Society's attitude to what constitutes a reasonable return.

As shareholders become more sophisticated and as the capital markets of the world develop it is reasonable to anticipate two trends. The first is that standards and criteria will become more international so that whereas the shareholders in a food company in Holland might now expect a performance–risk curve from their company similar to one for other food companies in Holland, they will progressively come to judge their company by a generalized performance–risk curve applicable to all companies throughout the world. The second consequence is that the consensus of shareholder opinion throughout the world will become more sensitive to world financial changes and therefore more volatile. This implies that managements may have to take the pulse of shareholder opinion more frequently in future to ensure that the performance–risk targets for their company properly reflect the current views of their shareholders.

Whenever a change in the performance–risk curve becomes necessary it will inevitably affect the size or timing of the gap. Any significant change in this curve, therefore, demands that a new gap analysis exercise be undertaken.

It should be noted that the expected performance of a given company is not one of the factors that affect its shareholders' choice of performance–risk curve. If the outlook for a company is bleak this will be a signal to alter the strategy perhaps but not the targets.

Review of ethos

Society's attitude to companies is constantly changing; the top managers' opinions of how a company should behave changes, the top managers themselves are changed; the company's traditions change; new pressure groups spring up, have their say and disappear. In view of this flux it is necessary for a continuous review of the company's ethos to be maintained. Furthermore, as the nature of a company's operations changes the company will be brought into contact with new social or geographical areas in which the company's existing ethos may be unacceptable. Changes in society's attitude to companies normally takes place only rather slowly; it took perhaps a century, for example, for society to decide that women and young children should not work in the coal mines. But sometimes a change in attitude occurs within a matter of a few years as, for example, in the sudden change in attitude towards pollution; in the course of only two years (1970 to 1971) public opinion swung from an attitude of boredom and indifference on this matter to one of deep concern.

Companies therefore have to review their ethological objectives with increasing frequency today; not only do existing ethological targets have to be revised (usually upwards) but entirely new ones have to be added to the list.

Review of strategy

On page 72 I listed the factors that affect the choice of a strategy as follows:

> Purpose
> Ethos
> Strengths and Weaknesses
> Threats and Opportunities
> Expected Performance and Gap Analysis
> Risk

It will be appreciated that changes in purpose or ethos will be identified during the monitoring process that I described in the two sections above. If any significant changes do occur then the whole strategic structure may have to be reviewed. But it may also have to be reviewed if the management lose confidence in the validity of the list of strengths, weaknesses, threats and opportunities upon which their current strategy is based. These lists have to be reviewed continuously, therefore.

Review of Strengths and Weaknesses

A company's strengths and weaknesses may change for three reasons. Firstly it may be the intention of the management to change them – it is quite frequently an important aim of a strategic decision to correct a weakness or to build up an existing strength. If these are the intentions of a strategy then it would seem prudent to monitor whether the desired changes were in fact taking place.

Secondly, strengths and weaknesses may change unintentionally; a company whose strength lies in its research team will have to reconsider any strategy based on this strength if the team is broken up by retirement or resignation. Or perhaps one of the important strengths identified by a company is that no single customer has the power to hold it to ransom; it may be, however, that one of their customers grows so fast that it achieves just that power, thus destroying the validity of the original appraisal. Thirdly the original list of strengths and weaknesses may have been wrong. For example, a company may adopt a certain strategy in the belief that it has particular expertise in the launching of new products; a succession of failures should certainly provoke a re-examination of the findings of the original appraisal.

Review of threats and opportunities

Of all the factors that enter the strategic decisions none change more violently than these. Strategies have to be based on forecasts and assumptions; when these are invalidated they invariably provoke a change in the predicted performance of the company and a change in one or more individual strategies has to be made and even the entire strategic structure may have to be revised.

One of the justifications for any formal planning system is that the assumptions that underlie decisions are brought into the open. When a company introduces a new product, for example, the decision to do so may have been taken on the assumption that no change in technology would occur that would render the product obsolete during its intended lifetime. Now if this company had adopted a formal, systematic approach to planing one would expect to see an explicit statement somewhere in this company's external appraisal to the effect that, 'no significant technological change will affect our company's products before Year Y'. One would also expect that, as part of its monitoring activities, its research scientists would be carefully watching the progress of any relevant technology, and that they would report to the management if their confidence in this assumption was undermined. Again, if a strategy is based on the assumption that a certain market will expand by 20% over the next three years, it would be wise if the management maintained a careful watch for early indications that this assumption was not going to be invalidated.

Review of actual performance

It might have been supposed that the progress that a company is actually making towards its targets would be a valuable indicator by which managers could judge their confidence in their decisions. While this is the case in short term planning I believe it is not so in long range planning. There are two reasons for this view.

Firstly: that performance is above target for the first three years of a ten-year period does not justify as much confidence in achieving the ten-year targets as being above target for the first three days of a ten-day period justifies confidence in achieving the ten day targets. This is because the immediate past is a better guide to the immediate future than the distant past is for the distant future. In other words the fact that certain targets are achieved in the early stages of a long term plan does contribute to confidence, and early failures do contribute to lack of confidence but these actual results on their own are a poor criterion for confidence in the eventual outcome.

The second and more important reason why actual results are a poor guide to eventual success is that the results that are of particular interest in corporate planning are the overall performance indicators such as earnings per share, return on capital or stock market valuations. Now all these tend to suffer severe year-to-year variations; Exhibit 8·1 shows a typical series of five annual earnings per share figures for a well-known British company, together with the share value on the London Stock Market. It will be observed that the e.p.s. figure is perfectly capable of a 30% movement from one year to another (and

Exhibit 8·1   Key financial results for a major British company

	1966	1967	1968	1969	1970
Earnings per share (p)	16·4	14·8	19·4	22·8	14·3
Share price (p) high	178	256	348	402	371
low	119	148	215	217	194

the share price may double or halve in the course of a year). Now imagine that this company sets itself a growth target of 15% p.a. in earnings per share; even if its earnings per share *falls* by 15% in the first year this may mean nothing – nor is it significant if the earnings per share rises by 30%. Indeed it may take as many as three or four years before the managers of this company see any statistically significant results.

The conclusion I reach is somewhat ironic; it is that although one of the prime intentions of a company introducing corporate planning is to protect or improve its earnings per share record, it is almost impossible to use this measure as a criterion for success. This lack of verifiability is, as noted on page 28, one of the powerful reasons why so many senior executives are sceptical of the value of corporate planning.

Review of planned actions

One of the keys to confidence in a given plan is whether the physical actions called for in the plan are being taken. If the plan calls for the building of a new factory in Year 3 and if, by Year 2 it has not even been started, then clearly confidence in the plan will decline. There are today a large number of techniques for comparing actions with plans, such as Critical Path Analysis, Line of Balance and so on.

Failure to take planned actions may be due to incompetence, bad luck, or many other causes. However, when all the reasons have been explained and all excuses made, the fact that this failure has taken place at all must surely point in one direction; namely that the planning was at fault. It is easily predictable, for example, that the completion of a new factory might be delayed by a strike at a supplier's premises or by a contractor's labour force; a plan that fails to take account of this possibility is not a valid plan. Again, if the reason for an action not being taken as planned is lack of skill or energy by the company's management then the plan must have assumed a level of skill and energy that the management did not possess and the appraisal of strengths and weaknesses must have been at fault. The point I am making here is this; if an action is not taken according to a plan then (a) the plan may have to be revised; but more important and less self-evident, (b) the internal and external appraisals will also have to be revised in the light of this failure.

Review of expected performance

Confidence in an approved strategy, then, depends upon confidence in the continuing validity of the original assumptions, upon actions being taken as planned and, to a much lesser extent upon the results actually being achieved.

Thus even if the results in Years 1, 2 and 3 are exactly on target, a management's confidence in their strategy would be justifiably low if an event in Year 2 had invalidated one of the major assumptions upon which the strategy was based. Conversely their confidence for Years 4, 5 and 6 would be justifiably high if, *in spite* of poor results in Years 1, 2 and 3, none of their major assumptions had been invalidated.

All the factors affecting confidence may be brought together by preparing a new forecast every few months or so. As time passes it may be presumed that the performance that the managers can reasonably expect will depart progressively further from their original plans. At some point in time the gap between reality and hope will have widened to an extent that managers need to reconsider their strategy. Two forecasts are involved here, then. There is F_A, the forecast that represents the predicted outcome of the existing *approved* strategy and which, it must be presumed, coincides with the performance–risk curve of the company's shareholders (otherwise, it would not have been approved). There is also the new F_0 forecast, i.e. a forecast of what it is now predicted the company's performance will be assuming no change in the current approved strategy. We have thus come full circle; the first forecast in the corporate planning process was the F_0 (described in Chapter 5); this was followed by a number of experimental F_P forecasts to demonstrate the outcome of a number of alternative strategies; one of these gained the confidence of the management who approved it – this was the forecast I called the F_A. The F_A, since it was approved, must have had a performance–risk profile that was similar to the company's target performance at least for a number of years ahead. Logic demands that from time to time the management prepare a new F_0 forecast (which we could designate F_{01}) to reflect how they now feel the company will perform if they do not make any changes to the currently approved strategy. I show the sequence of forecasts used in the corporate planning process in Exhibit 8·2.

This new F_0 forecast, or F_{01} will be prepared as a result of new information that becomes available as time passes; it will be calculated as a result of;

Any new or changed strengths or weaknesses
Any new or changed threats or opportunities
Any results not consistent with F_A
Any actions taken not consistent with F_A.

As time passes the figures shown in F_{01} will diverge from those in F_A until eventually they become so different that the question must arise whether a new strategy is required. It should be noted that some of the figures in F_A are forecasts and some are targets; all the figures in F_{01} are forecasts. Thus an F_A forecast for a company may show that the total market is expected to rise from 1000 units in year 1 to 2000 units in year 5. This is a forecast. The same F_A may show the company's share of the market as a steady 10%. This is a target. As time passes however, the managers may lose confidence in both these figures; they may feel that the the total market in Year 5 will be nearer 2500 units but that the company's share will fall to 7%. Both these figures are forecasts, neither are

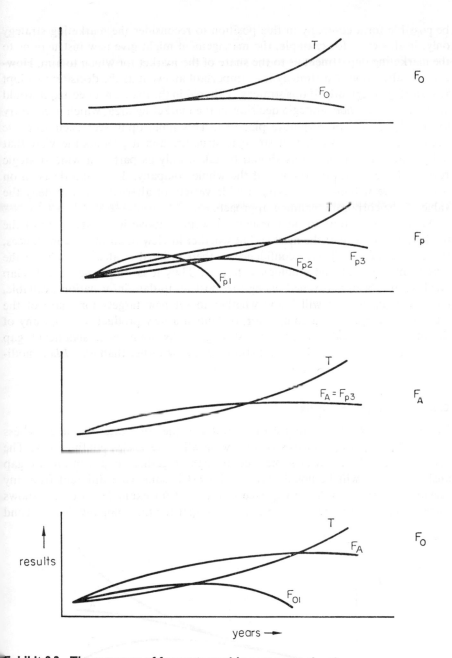

Exhibit 8·2   The sequence of forecasts used in corporate planning

targets. In this case the management are assumed to have believed originally that their marketing department could be expected to maintain the company's share of the market at 10%. Now, however, they recognize that this target was too optimistic. Their original strategy has lost credibility; the gap between F_A and F_{01} suggests that a new strategy is required. Now it would undoubtedly be possible for a company in this position to reconsider the marketing strategy only; in this case, for example, the management might give new instructions to the marketing department as to the share of the market for which to aim. However the alteration of a strategy is as important an event as the decision to adopt that strategy originally. If this strategy is altered in the manner suggested it would amount to an *ad hoc* strategic decision in the marketing area, which is contrary to the philosophy of corporate planning. This philosophy sees each strategic decision as part of a coherent strategic structure and it proffers the view that individual strategic decisions should be taken only as part of a wide strategic review of the strategic structure of the whole company. To take a decision on market share without considering a wide variety of alternatives is to deny the value of the corporate planning approach.

What really matters to the company described above is not its share of the market, nor the size of the market, but whether in view of *all* the circumstances, the management still have confidence in their original strategy to achieve the long term financial and ethological targets. Thus it is only when a full Gap Analysis has been performed, using the most up-to-date information available, that the management will know whether to set new targets for share of the market, or merge with a competitor, or launch a new product to adopt any of the other innumerable alternative strategies. As soon as a significant gap appears between F_A and F_{01} a full strategic review rather than an *ad hoc* modification to an individual strategy is required.

Continuous gap analysis

I have suggested that there are three cycles in the corporate planning process and that 'monitoring' consists of reviewing all these cycles continuously. The results of all three reviews may be brought together in a continuous gap analysis. But it will be noted that Exhibit 8·3 is somewhat different from my previous illustrations of the gap (see Exhibit 5·3 for example) in that it shows three curves. One represents the financial target for the company (T) a second

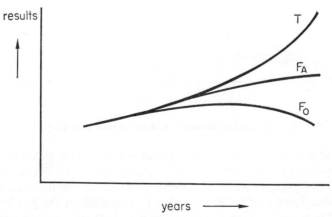

Exhibit 8·3

represents the results of adopting the current strategy as forecast at the time it was adopted (F_A) and the third represents the latest F_0 forecast – i.e. what the managers now believe is the likely outcome of their current strategy.

It will be observed that confidence in the current strategy will not only depend upon the size of the gap between F_A and F_0 but between F_A and T – so that if T changes (due to a change of opinion by shareholders, for example) that of itself may demand a change in strategy whether F_A equals F_0 or not. That is fairly obvious; less obvious is that an insignificant gap between F_A and F_0 does not demand a change in strategy, nor does an insignificant gap between T and F_A but taken together these two gaps may be significant as between T and F_0. Exhibit 8·4 shows a similar situation to Exhibit 8·3 but using performace–risk gap analysis.

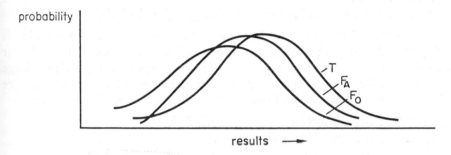

Exhibit 8·4

In theory it should be a simple matter to decide whether or not to embark upon a review of present strategy. The crucial question is whether the present strategy is more likely to achieve the financial and ethological targets than a new one, bearing in mind the cost of the search for a new one plus the cost of the dislocation caused by the change. In practice, calculations of this sort can seldom be made with sufficient accuracy to act as more than a general guide to the decision-makers. In many cases the management will be aware of a gradual rise or decline in their confidence in the present strategy. Provided they have constructed some form of monitoring system this will present to them a growing body of new facts and figures some of which will increase their confidence, others decrease it. Gradually a consensus of opinion will be formed and a decision to review or to postpone a review of the current strategy will emerge. The fact or event that finally convinces a management that a new strategy is required may be comparatively trivial but, taken with all the others, finally tips the balance.

Strategic review

A review of current strategy will follow exactly the same lines as the formation of the original strategy. The gap will be examined to determine the size of the task facing the company. A new list of Ethological Objectives, Strengths, Weaknesses, Threats, Opportunities will be prepared. Some idea of a new strategic structure will emerge. An imaginative search for new strategies will be conducted followed by their evaluation and the eventual selection of a sequence of appropriate strategic actions enshrined in a new F_A forecast.

A simple example

Consider the case of Finch Foods Ltd which two years ago decided to build a new factory to meet an expected increase in demand for its existing products. The salient facts that led to this decision were:

Strengths: *Largest company in the industry.*
Weaknesses: *None.*
Threats: *None.*
Opportunities: *Demand rising by 10% a year for the industry's products.*

Now assume that the factory has been partly constructed and everything is going according to plan when, to the surprise of the management, three of their largest competitors announce a merger to form a company that is twice as large as Finch Foods; they also announce plans to build a new factory twice the size of Finch's new factory. Finch Foods' appraisals will now read as follows:

Strengths: *Second largest company in the industry.*
Weaknesses: *A partially built factory.*
Threats: *Severe overcapacity in industry for at least 3 years.*
Opportunities: *Demand rising by 10% a year for the industry's products.*

Finch's management might now take one of three possible courses. Firstly they might do nothing. Secondly they might take an *ad hoc* decision such as to alter the completion date of the factory or recruit more salesmen to maintain their share of the market against increased competition. Thirdly they could undertake a full review of corporate strategy in the light of the new facts. If they were to do this and, unlike the *ad hoc* decision this would involve reconsidering the company's long term strategic structure – several new and far-reaching alternatives could come into view. They could decide upon a course of growth by acquisition of some of their remaining competitors. Or, perhaps more appropriately, acquire one of the industry's main suppliers or customers. Or, perhaps offer a massive increase in the discounts to their major customers. Or apply to join their merged rivals.

In this case Finch Foods had originally decided upon a long term strategic structure that was to remain largely unchanged – the decision to build the new factory was not merely a decision to build a new factory, it was implicitly a decision to continue doing more of the same things. As soon as they lost confidence in this strategy they had the options of either finding a new way to achieve the same long term structure (by recruiting more salesmen, for example) or by developing a whole new strategic structure (by acquiring a major supplier, for example, and thus adopting the structure of a vertically integrated company).

Summary of Chapter 8

A strategic plan is adopted by a management because they feel confident that it will close the gap between T and F_0. At the time of its adoption, therefore, $F_A = $ T. As time passes, however, any or all of the facts, figures, opinions, assumptions and forecasts upon which the adopted strategy was based may become invalid, and the financial targets, the ethological objectives, the strengths, weaknesses, threats, opportunities all have to be reviewed continuously. Any changes in these, together with actual performance figures as they become known, should be brought together in a continuous gap analysis.

A review of strategy is not required unless a significant gap appears between T and F_0 (or T and F_A or F_A and F_0) When a significant gap does appear then it may be more sensible to review the *entire strategic structure* rather than merely reconsider any one individual strategic decision. Thus a company's failure to achieve a market share target may or may not result in a significant gap. If it does not (due perhaps to compensating success somewhere) then no change in strategy is necessary. If it does then a change in the entire strategic structure may be necessary rather than merely a change in marketing strategy – whether this is so cannot be determined without a full review of all the factors that enter strategic decisions.

The confidence that managers feel in a given strategy is less dependent upon actual results than upon the company successfully taking those actions prescribed in the plan and on their confidence in the continuing validity of the assumptions, forecasts, opinions, etc., that went into their original strategic decision.

9 Organizing for corporate planning

Systematic decision-taking

The key distinction between a company that has adopted corporate planning and one that has not is that the one has a *system* for taking strategic decisions while the other has not.

A system for taking such decisions need be nothing more elaborate than a regular meeting among top managers to consider strategic questions or, almost as embryonic, a procedure in which managers are asked regularly to complete a five-year plan. Equally systematic, but at the other end of the scale, a huge department may supervise the whole strategic decision-making procedure throughout the company. Either of these extremes, or anywhere in between, is valid. What is required, after all, is merely some mechanism designed to invite a company's senior managers to take the following steps:

Decide Purpose and select a suitable ROSC target

List the major ethological targets and constraints

Carry out an Internal and External Appraisal

Decide the strategic structure

Select suitable operational objectives and project specifications

Set up a monitoring system.

Revise targets and strategy when necessary.

The minimum system

As stated on page 27 it is generally accepted that one of the major reasons why companies do not adopt a systematic approach to strategic decisions is that their senior executives are busy with short term matters. Unless a system or procedure has sufficient strength to turn their minds periodically to long term matters then that system will fail. This being so, it follows that where the senior managers are already fully aware of the need to consider strategic problems and where they are keen and able to give these matters sufficient thought, an embryonic system is all that is needed. The conditions under which this minimum system is required includes a very wide variety of companies. It certainly includes the very small company run by a chief executive who is keen to give strategic matters his attention but it also includes any very large company whose senior managers have become accustomed to taking strategic decisions. Thus the strength and formality of the planning procedure required needs to be related to the level of awareness of the importance of planning among the senior executives. Provided their attitude is favourable, then the minimum required is that those responsible for taking strategic decisions should draw up a time-table for the year and work to a schedule which includes the steps outlined on page 124. No corporate planner, no corporate planning department and no complicated forms or procedures are needed. The information required will be called for from the various parts of the company in just the same routine way as for any other discussion about the company.

It must be stressed that this system, or lack of it, is only appropriate where the strategic decision-makers can be relied upon to carry through the corporate planning process without having to be constantly prodded.

There can be little doubt that this arrangement is the ideal. Ackoff (Ch. 3) says that there is no profession of corporate planners, that no single man should be identified as 'a corporate planner' but that corporate planning should be done by line executives who call upon specialists when necessary. I believe this advice is entirely valid but, unfortunately, it is only valid where Warren's roadblocks have already been removed, i.e. where the senior executives already spend much of their time in strategic decision-making. Where this is not the case there most certainly *is* a need for a corporate planner, a vital part of whose task is that of encouraging the executives to think strategically; if he is successful in this his job will eventually become unnecessary.

A formal system

In the majority of companies a much more formal procedure will be required to ensure that corporate planning is carried out effectively. The more formal the procedure the more necessary is it to appoint someone to supervise its operation. This supervisor need not be a corporate planner; all that is required is someone to call upon the managers to take the steps of the corporate planning process in the right sequence, to ensure that any requests for information they make are met, that any forms required are well designed, properly completed and available for their consideration at the appropriate time.

Where the procedures are relatively simple this task can be carried out by an administrative officer; where they are complex it may be necessary to form a department specifically to administer the system. In this case the supervisor of the system will not be called upon to assist the managers with the content of the plans nor will he need to be expert in the field of planning. His task is purely administration: the content of the plans, the factors to be monitored, the targets to be set, etc. will be determined solely by the managers.

The corporate planner

In addition to the requirement for a supervisor for the system, many managements also feel the need for help and advice from a specialist in corporate planning. Unless those responsible for strategic decisions feel this need there is little hope of them taking much notice of a specialist were his appointment made and it might be preferable, in that case, not to appoint him at all but to be content with a systems supervisor.

Where a corporate planner is appointed, however, certain guidelines have now emerged concerning his position in the management team. Most of these rules are mentioned by most authors in the field. The most important is that the corporate planner should not be a line executive but an adviser – see Warren (Ch. 3), Hussey (Ch. 2). In other words it is not part of his job to reach conclusions or to take decisions and still less to give instructions but to help the management through the long and difficult process of corporate planning, to advise them on certain technical aspects (such as those considered in Part 2 of this book), perhaps to provide an objective, non-executive non-sectional viewpoint and to design and supervise the system. Most authors agree that if a corporate planner takes his job much further than this he will begin to usurp the functions of line management. At the extreme he will indulge in 'ivory tower planning' in which he alone prepares the corporate plan for the company, presents it to the management, and then hopefully expects them to carry it through with enthusiasm. While he should not do this, he should perhaps contribute to the discussion just as any other senior member of the management team would do.

The corporate planner's qualifications

If the corporate planner is materially to contribute to the development of an imaginative and practical strategy he must necessarily be of the same calibre as the other senior members of the management team. If his task is only to supervise the system and to offer advice on the technicalities of planning then his status may be that of a senior specialist or administrator. If he is to carry out both functions – and this is normally the case – then his qualifications should include the following attributes:

* Considerable practical experience in management preferably as an executive in one or more of the major functional departments of a company.
* Ability to discard all previously held sectional or specialist viewpoints, in favour of an overall corporate vision.
* Profound interest in and some knowledge of long term trends in a wide selection of areas including social, political, technical and economic.
* Knowledge of the techniques used in corporate planning.
* Personal characteristics consistent with advising and collaborating with very senior executives and advisers.

Of all the desirable qualifications, the one of greatest importance is the personality of the corporate planner. If his personality is too weak, he will be ignored; if too strong, he will provoke jealousies for, by the nature of his job, he is in a position to influence decisions concerning the long term future of major departments and sections of the firm. He has the ear of the chief executive. The opportunities for playing politics and empire building are endless. But on the other hand, a major part of his job is to convince his more sceptical colleagues of the value of planning and to show them how to do it – he should, then, be neither master nor servant of his colleagues but guide, philosopher and friend.

Opinion is divided as to who might make the best corporate planner; one school of thought believes that since corporate planning is largely concerned with profits, the corporate planner should have a financial background. Another school believes that marketing is the most appropriate. In fact it may not matter what specialist field the corporate planner comes from; what matters is whether he is capable of leaving behind him any narrow specialist viewpoints. It has been said that the corporate planner in a company involved in any advanced technology must understand that technology and while this may be true it does not imply that he must himself be a specialist in that technology – indeed there may already be an excessive emphasis on technology among the senior executives which could with advantage be diluted by a non-specialist viewpoint.

It has been suggested that the position of corporate planner should be treated as a temporary staging-post for managers on their way up the promotional ladder. A spell of, say, two years as his company's corporate planner might indeed be valuable experience for the general manager of a division on his way to another division or to general management (or perhaps chief executive). Some companies have invited their corporate planner to take charge of a major project which forms part of the plan he had helped to produce. There is only one objection to the staging-post idea; corporate planners have now to be familiar with several quite advanced techniques (see Part 2) and the job has become almost as complex technically as, say, the job of the accountant or the advertising manager. No one suggests that these jobs are particularly suitable as staging posts for future executives. However, where a company has set up a corporate planning department (see below) it may be assumed that the necessary knowledge of corporate planning techniques resides in that department and the post of head of the department could then change hands every few years without loss of efficiency; Warren (Ch. 3) suggests that it would be dangerous to mix executive development with *initiating* a corporate planning department – a cautionary comment with which one could hardly disagree.

The duties of the corporate planner

If all that is required is a systems administrator (i.e. if it has been decided that the content of the corporate plan is to be devised by the company's senior executives alone) then his duties can be simply described. They are to devise, maintain and administer a corporate planning procedure designed to facilitate the production of a corporate plan and to facilitate the flow of information required for monitoring. The administrator will be concerned only with providing the mechanism of planning, not with the contents of any plan.

Where the company appoints a corporate planner, as opposed to a systems administrator, his duties will, in addition to administering the mechanism, include the following:

1 Satisfy himself and his board that a clear consensus of opinion exists among the senior executives as to what is the fundamental purpose of the company.

2 Ensure that agreement exists among the senior executives and, where appropriate, with the company's financial advisers as to the shape of an appropriate performance–risk curve.

3 Set up a procedure by which the purpose and target is reconsidered at regular intervals.

4 Ensure agreement on the company's ethological objectives and targets with respect to all those areas considered to be of strategic importance.

5 Set up a procedure by which these may be regularly reviewed.

6 Co-ordinate and direct the F_0 forecasting exercise by regularly inviting the heads of all major parts of the company to forecast their contribution to profits. Supervise the consolidation of these.

7 Carry out a continuous gap analysis and submit to senior executives together with personal comments upon the targets, the forecasts and the situation revealed by the gap analysis.

8 Supervise the Internal Appraisal of strengths and weaknesses. Submit summary of these for approval by senior executives.

9 Supervise the External Appraisal of threats and opportunities. Submit summary of these for approval by senior executives.

10 Organize and co-ordinate the discussions on suitable strategic structures.

11 Act as focal point for suggested strategies, submitting them to senior executives for their comments.

12 Prepare F_P forecasts for the short-listed alternative strategies. Submit these for discussion and final decision.

13 Supervise preparation of action plans and draft instructions to executives (i.e. project specifications and operational objectives) to give effect to F_A forecast. Submit these for promulgation by senior executives.

14 Set up a procedure by which the F_A forecast is monitored. Monitor the continued validity of the Appraisals. Alert senior executives of any major changes since F_A was approved.

15 Advise executives on the technology of corporate planning.

It will be observed that the above summary of a corporate planner's duties suggests that his task is not to take a major part in the planning but to ensure that enough planning is done and that it is done well. He is not expected, for example, to suggest a more brilliant strategy than any other member of the management team. He is expected, however, to request the executives to submit a forecast by a certain date, for example, and to require these forecasts to be accompanied by an estimate of their accuracy. Again, he is not expected to propose dozens of imaginative projects; he is expected to insist that any project that is proposed is accompanied by a risk analysis calculation. He is also expected to alert the management to the need to take a certain planning decision within a given date, to advise on a suitable planning horizon and other technical matters.

Introducing corporate planning

The introduction of the corporate planning approach may not, of itself, require any major readjustments in the organization structure of a company. As emphasized above, it involves nothing more than a decision to give more attention to strategic problems and to do so more systematically. All that happens, then, is that those responsible for strategic decisions meet more formally, call for information more regularly, spend more time on these matters than they did before. Nor does the appointment or nomination of one man to supervise the system require a major change in organization structure or management style.

The appointment of a full corporate planner does call for a change in the organization structure at the top of the company. It is an appointment of as much significance as the introduction of any new department at board level; for a company which has no research department the decision to form a research department headed by a new research director with a seat on the board demands major consequential changes to be made in the duties of several of the existing departments and in the interrelations between them. So it is with the appointment of a corporate planner.

There are probably three stages of development through which corporate planning will pass in any company. Firstly the company will exist without a formal system. At that stage the executives will either not be making strategic decisions at all, or will be making them *ad hoc* whenever it becomes clear that a decision is required or they will have formed an informal procedure on a common sense basis. As the company grows or is faced with an impending strategic dilemma the second stage begins to emerge as the management recognize the need for a more formal system. At this stage they may either form a planning committee, or nominate a systems supervisor, or appoint a corporate planner or form a corporate planning department. In this stage the chief executive will play a major role in, and show close concern for, the corporate planning activities. This stage may last for a number of years. The third stage occurs when corporate planning becomes part and parcel of the way the company is managed. It then becomes informal again but ingrained and habitual among the senior executives.

In the first stage the organization structure of the senior executives may appear in the traditional pyramid form in Exhibit 9·1. In the second stage the corporate planner may appear in a prominent position as one of the very senior members of the management team. In Exhibit 9·2, for example, he appears as one of the directors reporting to and responsible to the chief executive. This is a very common configuration. In Exhibit 9·3 he appears as the head of a section inside one of the major departments. This is almost certainly less than satisfactory. A central feature of corporate planning is that it concerns planning for

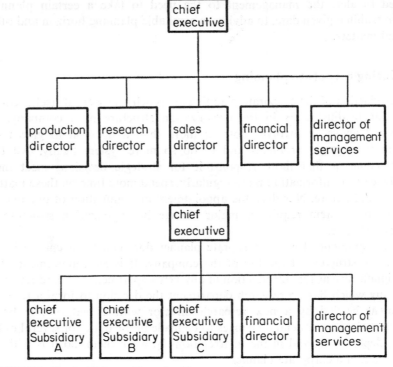

Exhibit 9·1 **Typical hierarchies of senior executives**

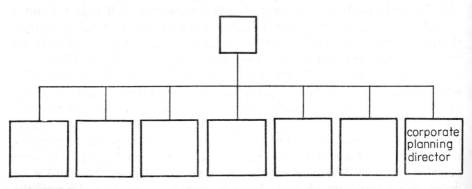

Exhibit 9·2

the corporate whole and it is unlikely that this can be done adequately where the corporate planner is responsible to an executive in charge of only a part of the whole. Whether this executive is head of a function (such as marketing) or of a specialist department (such as finance) or of a subsidiary company the same phenomenon is to be expected – the corporate planner's advice to the company will be biased and tinged with the specialism and the politics of that part of the whole. The organization chart in Exhibit 9·3 and variations on it invite unbalanced and inadequate corporate planning by placing the corporate planner in too lowly a position in the company hierarchy at this stage of introducing corporate planning. At this stage the chief executive must give sturdy backing to corporate planning and most authors agree that the corporate planner should report directly to the chief executive.

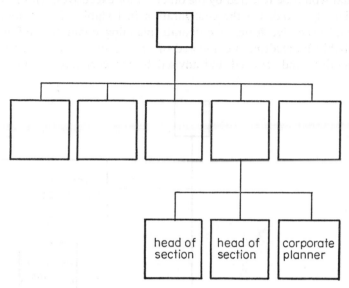

Exhibit 9·3

While Exhibit 9·3 shows the corporate planner in too weak and sectarian a position, Exhibit 9·4 shows him in an extremely strong position as a personal adviser to the chief executive. This configuration would be appropriate where the chief executive habitually takes the strategic decisions himself without consulting his senior executives. It could be appropriate also where it was agreed

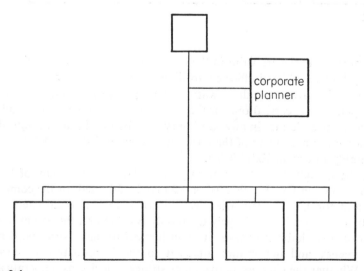

Exhibit 9·4

that the introduction of corporate planning was urgent and demanded the full attention of the chief executive. It would be appropriate in few other circumstances, however, for it would place the corporate planner in a position of privilege that would be resented by the other senior executives. This resentment would be largely avoided if the configuration in Exhibit 9·5 was adopted. In this the chief executive forms a corporate planning committee (of which he would probably be chairman) composed of an appropriate selection from the senior executives and serviced and advised by the corporate planner.

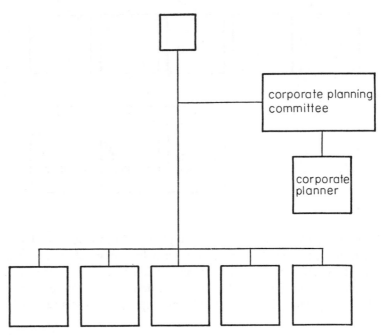

Exhibit 9·5

Very similar remarks are valid in the case of larger companies which consist essentially of a central head office controlling several subsidiary companies any of which may be large enough to warrant a corporate planner. Provided that corporate planning is carried out for the company as a whole at the head office then the corporate planner in any subsidiary may be fitted into the subsidiary's organization structure in any of the positions shown in Exhibits 9·2, 9·4, or 9·5. But preferably not as in Exhibit 9·3.

During the introductory stages of corporate planning then, any of the configurations shown in Exhibits 9·2, 9·4 or 9·5 may be adopted for the company as a whole and for large subsidiaries. Which configuration is adopted by any given company depends very largely upon only two factors; the extent to which the chief executive habitually takes it upon himself to make strategic decisions and the urgency and importance attached to the introduction of corporate planning. Whether the chief executive takes strategic decisions autocratically or not it is generally recognized that if he does not give his full personal backing to the introduction of corporate planning then it will be less than effective and will probably fail entirely.

If corporate planning is seen to be effective by the management, then, over a period of years it will become ingrained in the management style of the company. It will then no longer be necessary to employ a formal system designed to force management attention onto strategic questions. Indeed the senior executives may come to accept that strategic planning is their main task and will increasingly delegate short term management problems to carefully chosen subordinates. When that stage is reached, and few companies in the world had reached it by the early Seventies, it may be possible to eliminate the post of corporate planner and to abolish the corporate planning department. At least it may be desirable to move the corporate planner into a Management Services Department along with other specialists in operations research, behavioural science, commercial law, computing and so on (as proposed by Ackoff in Ch. 7); from there he will be available to advise on planning technicalities.

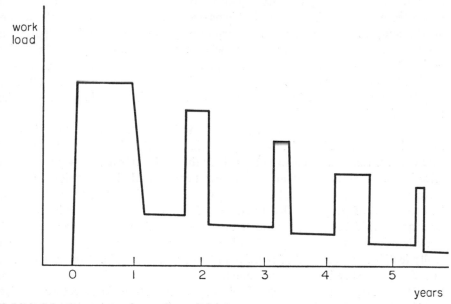

Exhibit 9·6   Corporate planner's work load

The work load on a corporate planner is naturally very heavy in the first few months while he is acting as a collecting-point for F_0 forecasts, internal and external appraisals, suggested strategic structures and individual projects. He will remain heavily engaged while he is helping to prepare the F_P forecasts and, after the approval of one of them, will probably assist the management to draw up some of the details of the action plan. At the same time he will be setting up the monitoring system. After that stage, however, his work load will decline rapidly to a comparatively low level – he will merely be supervising the monitoring system. From time to time, as the monitoring system reveals a new significant gap, he will become active again as changes in the original strategy are required. Gradually, as corporate planning becomes absorbed into the company's management system, his work load will decline. I show this work-load pattern, highly generalized, in Exhibit 9·6.

In view of the shape of this curve it may be argued that for all but the largest companies a part-time corporate planner is the most suitable once the intial stage is completed.

The corporate planning department

Very small companies may not be able to justify any form of corporate planning system – those that are run by an active entrepreneur almost certainly could not. But even quite small companies may be able to justify a part-time adviser or visiting consultant to supervise the system and, perhaps, to provide that often useful 'outside view'. In my opinion, it is a mistake to require a corporate planner to supervise any other activity at the same time as corporate planning. This is simply because urgent problems tend to take precedence over longer term but more important problems – a phenomenon noted by all authors on the subject. Thus a 'part-time corporate planner' should be a part-time employee or visiting adviser who is wholly engaged on corporate planning rather than a full-time employee engaged partly on corporate planning and partly on some other duties. Larger companies will employ one man full time, very large ones may need a department and companies with large subsidiaries may need a hierarchy of departments.

The size and number of departments, as well as their composition depends rather less on the size of the company than on the definition of the word 'strategic'. If this is defined so as to include the choice of every new product, the selection of a suitable layout for a new factory and the planning of every merger, then the corporate planning department may have to be very large and be composed of people skilled in these and many other specialist branches of management. If, however, the much narrower definition of strategic used in this book is adopted then it is questionable whether any company of any size can really justify a department of more than two or three people. Whatever the size of a company may be it requires much the same volume of work to determine the ROSC target, the ethological objectives, the strategic structure, project specifications and so on. If corporate planning is concerned only with the big questions then the number of big questions is not determined by the size of the company but by the definition of 'big'. The decision by a small company to merge with another small company is no more or less momentous or complex or time-consuming than the decision of a large company to merge with another large one. The decision by a small company to introduce a single new product is no less momentous than a large one deciding to introduce a whole range of new products. If, therefore, the corporate planner limits his attention to the momentous decisions he will be no more active in a large company than in a small one.

Of course, if the corporate planner is required to examine a detailed fifty-page report from each of four hundred subsidiary companies every year he will have a hundred times as much work to do – and need a department a hundred times as large – as if he receives a broad five-page report from forty groups of subsidiaries categorized by product or market or regions. Most corporate planning departments are in fact very small, consisting of no more than a dozen people even in the largest companies, indicating that most managements have understood the nature of corporate planning. However, some large companies employ as many as a hundred people in the corporate planning department; in some cases they have taken the view that a company selling several thousand products in several nations 'requires' such a department. Others believe that the ancillary services to corporate planning (operations reasearch, market research, computers, etc.) should be placed under the corporate planner.

In addition to the corporate planner himself, the department may be staffed on three different principles. It may be composed of other almost equally senior employees who act as his deputies – an arrangement that is useful where the planners are called upon to travel abroad, or where the company treats this department as a staging post in the promotion ladder. Where the corporate planner is expected to be more permanent his staff may be recruited from lower levels to act largely as his personal assistants to gather information, interpret results and so on. A third staffing policy is possible; it is to appoint several specialists in operations research, marketing, finance and so on, to advise the corporate planner in these fields. This may be a desirable arrangement if the company does not already employ such specialists. If it does it may be preferable for the corporate planner to seek such specialist advice as he needs from the existing specialist departments.

Multi-level corporate planning

Strictly interpreted, the word corporate precludes planning for any unit other than the entire company. Corporate planning cannot in theory take place in, or for, a part of a company even if that part is a profit-centre. But in practice large companies with large subsidiaries have set up corporate planning units in their subsidiary companies as well as at the centre. This is particularly the case in multinational companies.

The task of the planners at the centre, or group headquarters, is to determine the corporate objectives for the entire group as a corporate whole and to select a suitable strategic structure for the group as a whole. Neither of these tasks can be performed within any subsidiary company – they must be done at the centre. In deciding what the strategic structure should be, however, the central planners must decide what role each major part of the group must play within the group over the long term future; this implies that, when a proposed group structure has been approved, the central executive authority has to instruct each subsidiary company to take whatever actions are required to bring this structure about. But if that is the case it implies that part or all of the strategic structure of each subsidiary is determined at the centre. This may leave very little corporate planning to be done in each subsidiary.

For example, consider a multinational company, Pippit International Irrigation Pumps Inc. which manufactures in twenty-seven nations of the world. In 1962 this company decided to extend its business into the search for water in those nations in which it already operated. However, on the principle that any diversification is more risky than continuing in an existing field of business, Pippit's management decided not to invest any further capital in nations subject to political turbulence; they felt that the reduced political risks would very approximately balance the increased diversification risk, thus leaving the total riskiness of the company unchanged. But these decisions, which were taken at the centre on corporate grounds and which were intended to alter the group strategic structure, inevitably also altered the structure of each subsidiary company. Thus the Australian subsidiary rapidly become an irrigation and water search company – as intended. The Indian subsidiary, however, was closed down in 1970.

In this case then, although the two decisions taken at the centre contained an absolute minimum of detail they nevertheless determined the structure of each subsidiary down to considerable detail and for many years into their future. Of course there was a wealth of planning still to be done in each subsidiary including planning for production facilities, manpower, acquisitions and finance, but these are not corporate planning, they are facilities planning, manpower planning, acquisition planning.

Either one has to accept that the centre or head office or group board should decide the role of the parts or one argues that it should not. If one adopts the former view then corporate planning as defined in this book cannot be practised in the parts; if one adopts the latter view then one must accept that it leads directly to the true conglomerate.

Of course in practice a compromise between these two views is usually reached. The area of compromise stretches all the way from simply setting Return on Capital targets for the subsidiaries to deciding the details of their role within the group. At one extreme the centre will set the same ROC target for all the subsidiaries and leave it entirely to them to determine turnover, area of operation, nature of business, personnel policy, and so on. At the other extreme all these decisions will be centralized. Some companies encourage direct competition between their subsidiaries in the same products and markets; others rigidly delineate the boundaries to each subsidiary's products and markets.

However the problem now being discussed – how detailed should a corporate plan be – is no more acute for the large multinational company than for the company with a single profit-centre. The distinction is only one of degree, for in the one case the problem is how far the corporate plan should direct the sales department, research department or other parts of the whole and in the other case it so happens that the parts are profit centres. In both cases the question to be considered is the extent to which the company's broad strategic structure should be altered over the long term. The decision by a multinational to reduce the proportion of capital invested in India is no different in scale than the decision to close down a local warehouse to a smaller company. In each case, however, the way in which these strategic decisions are carried out must depend largely upon local conditions and traditions. Except in the case of a pure conglomerate, therefore, it will be more normal for the corporate plan of all companies (except true conglomerates), however many profit centres they may have, to state both the return on capital target for each susidiary *and* its long term role within the whole.

One other purely practical difficulty leads to this same conclusion. Acute difficulties exist in placing a figure upon the capital value of any given profit centre (see page 214 where the problem of setting financial targets to subsidiaries is discussed). For this reason alone it may be desirable for the central corporate plan to specify targets in other areas (such as turnover, labour productivity, etc.) in order to back up, cross-check and fill out the purely financial ones.

This conclusion suggests, then, that the central corporate plan will normally contain a fairly large number of decisions and preconditions handed down to the subsidiaries. This in turn implies that there will be less scope for corporate planning in those subsidiaries or, at best, that any corporate planning there is to do will have to be done within considerable constraints. It is unlikely, however, that all strategic decisions relating to each subsidiary will be made at the centre. Thus many ethological targets will have to be set locally especially in the case of foreign subsidiaries. Each subsidiary will have to draw up its own list of strengths and weaknesses and the threats and opportunities that are relevant to it. Although the broad strategic structure for the subsidiary may have been decided by the centre the process of corporate planning for a subsidiary is exactly the same as for the centre except that some of the strategic decisions will have already been made. I give a detailed example of multi-level corporate planning in Chapter 10.

Non-company corporate planning

Nearly all the very large companies in the world have now adopted corporate planning in some form; many other companies, some of them very small have either adopted this approach or recognize the need for it. However, the vast majority of companies have not yet taken any positive steps.

Although most of the literature on corporate planning is concerned with this form of planning within business organizations, my own opinion is that the greatest need for it lies in the non-company organization; in governments, in educational institutions, in professional bodies, in charities, in international agencies and so on. There are three reasons for this view. In the first place the size, number and social importance of these organizations is, I believe, growing much faster than business organizations now that so many nations are nearing the post-industrial phase. Secondly; while it is comparatively easy to identify the purpose of a company (i.e. to make a return on the shareholders' capital) and to set a target for it (in terms of a ROSC figure) it is much more difficult to state precisely what is the purpose of many non-profit-making organizations such as a national government, a professional organization, a school, a social club. It is even more difficult to place appropriate target figures on to these corporate objectives. The third reason is that, in recent years, certain techniques have been developed, such as cost benefit analysis, by means of which these objectives may be more readily quantified.

In other words these new techniques are beginning to appear just when it is becoming increasingly desirable that the standard of management in non-profit making organizations should be improved. If it becomes possible to state the corporate objectives of these organizations more precisely it will immediately become possible to select more appropriate strategies for them, to evaluate alternative strategies more precisely, to monitor confidence within closer limits, and generally to apply the many quantified management techniques to these organizations just as they have been applied for decades to business organizations. And, it need hardly be added, if companies are themselves to become social institutions then it will become increasingly important to be able to quantify their non-financial corporate objectives.

I see no reason why the system of corporate planning I have described should not be applicable to all types of organization. Their purpose has to be stated, target figures (or preferably performance–risk curves) have to be selected for the appropirate 'indicators' and their ethos defined just as for a company. Then follows an internal appraisal in which the strengths and weaknesses of the organization should be identified. An external appraisal would reveal the major threats and opportunities. A strategic structure would be selected and its viability tested by evaluating the projects implied by it. Confidence would then be monitored. It will be appreciated that if the corporate objectives of an organization cannot be stated with clarity and in terms that may be empirically verified, one cannot evaluate alternative strategies designed to achieve those objectives and, worse still, one cannot check what progress the organization is making towards them.

I think it would be widely accepted that the efficacy of many of our leading institutions – the processes of justice, for example, or urban government – is not yet being monitored with sufficient accuracy to allow their management to make changes in time to avert severe and often distressing failures. This lack is not due to incompetence or laziness, it is due to the difficulty of stating the purpose of these organizations with sufficient exactitude to allow progress to be monitored. Once the problem of quantifying their objectives is overcome, and I believe it will be progressively solved over the next two or three decades, then the managements of these organizations will gain access to such highly systematic methods of determining corporate strategy as I have been describing.

Summary of Chapter 9

Corporate planning is the systematic taking of corporate decisions. The extent to which corporate planning has to be formalized in any given company depends to some extent upon how systematically such decisions are currently taken. The minimum requirement is for some form of purely procedural device to be adopted as a result of which the management is encouraged to consider their company's long term strategy at regular intervals. In most companies, however, the pressure for short term results is such that an adequate response will only be achieved if someone is made responsible for the effective operation of the system. Under this arrangement the systems administrator would only be responsible for the mechanics of the system and would not be a corporate planner. A corporate planner would be expected to design and administer the system but would also be expected to take a more positive part in the planning process itself and it would be his responsibility to raise the level of the quality of the planning. In this duty his role includes that of communicator and even instructor in the techniques of planning. Some corporate planners are expected to contribute their own suggestions for strategies but this practice comes perilously close to the point where the corporate planner begins to usurp the functions of the company's line managers.

I believe the corporate planner's duties do include an obligation to comment on the quality of the plans but not to contribute any more to their content than would be expected of any other senior member of the management team. It would be useful if his background and experience allowed him to give an objective, practical, non-sectional viewpoint to the strategic discussions.

Corporate decisions – i.e. objectives and strategies – have to be taken by every company, indeed by every organization; there is no question about that; the question is how they are taken. I have suggested a step-by-step procedure consisting of three interrelated cycles which, simplified though it is, is nevertheless a complex procedure – one that is unlikely to be followed unless someone is responsible for supervising it. Whether a company leaves the running of its system entirely in the hands of a group of line managers or appoints a systems administrator or a corporate planner depends upon so many factors that no general statement is possible. Among the factors in this decision are the size of the organization, the severity of the strategic problems it faces, the rate of change, the style of management, the number of levels in the management hierarchy and the penalty for a faulty strategic decision.

10 Case studies

My aim in this chapter is to illustrate and illuminate the salient points made in the previous nine chapters. I think the best way to do this is to describe in great detail two real life case studies. Unfortunately I believe that it is essential to preserve the anonymity of the real companies and so I have elaborately disguised the firms, the people, the locations and markets; I have altered all the dates and figures; I have even altered the nature of the products – it would not be too difficult to identify the subject of Case 2, for example, if the real life company really did have 30% of the aperitif market in France!

One of the reasons I wish to preserve their anonymity is that all case studies are inevitably only simplified versions of what really happened and managements are often unavoidably made to appear to have behaved with unflattering naivety. A second reason is this; organizations are controlled by people. Usually they are controlled by only a few people at the top, sometimes by just one man. So a case study that is apparently about the Southtown Radio Company may very well be, in reality, a rather personal study of Mr Shine, the managing director. We must certainly remember that the facts presented to the reader of a case study may be less relevant to what happened in real life than how Mr Shine himself saw the facts. How a given company reacts to certain events may be less relevant than how certain senior executives react to each others reactions to these events! I do not mean to suggest that the senior executives of companies are forever locked in a kaleidescope of personal intrigue; this is not normally the case. What may be true, however, is that the decisions taken at this level of management – i.e. at the level of strategic decisions – are based more upon personal opinion than upon facts and figures (which may be a more important element in decisions taken lower in the management hierarchy). I have stressed (page 28) that the facts and figures available to strategic decision-makers are frequently unreliable or unobtainable and in these circumstances personal opinions and feelings become important. One of the major contributions that a corporate planning system can make is to bring these opinions and feelings into the open for rational discussion and perhaps quantification before being accepted as bases and assumptions for strategic decisions.

So if it appears that these case studies include as much detail about the people involved as about their companies, the reason is that I believe that this reflects the true ratio of importance as between opinion and fact in corporate planning as it occurs in real life. This is certainly true of family businesses, such as the one featured in Case Study 2, where the corporate objectives of the firm are virtually identical to the personal objectives of the family. It is possible that in these case studies I have placed only a slightly greater emphasis on the personal opinions of senior executives as a factor in corporate planning decisions than other authors in this field; Steiner and Denning both draw attention to 'values of top managers'; Ackoff introduces his 'stylistic objectives'; Warren emphasizes the importance of the personality of executives.

Case I—Davies Engineering

Background

The Southtown Radio and TV Co. Ltd was founded in 1949 as a family business and under the management of its proprietor had grown rapidly. The company went public in 1964 when its profits before tax exceeded £150,000. In 1965 the proprietor died and, being a bachelor, left his property, including his remaining 30% of the business, to a large number of relatives. There was, therefore, no longer any single shareholder with a significant proportion of the shares. The company was indebted to one of the major banks, however, and they appointed a Mr John Shine as Chairman and Managing Director together with three other professional managers as executive directors.

By 1968 the company's profits had risen to £180,000. Mr Shine discussed the position with his fellow directors at a routine board meeting in August 1968. As he described it the situation called for vigorous action because the company's performance over the past three years had not been good and, much more serious, he felt, and his colleagues agreed, that due to the rather depressed economic conditions in England, the future looked even worse. As he said to them, 'basically our company is a TV retailing organization. We own or rent several dozen retail shops in the High Streets of several dozen medium-sized towns in the South of England. We operate a TV leasing company and we do electrical repairs. That's about it'.

'What worries me', he went on, 'is that we are wholly dependent upon the consumer's standard of living continuing to rise rapidly and I don't think it will. I think it will be just about static for the next few years. But that's not all; we have considerable evidence that the black and white TV market is very nearly saturated in England – the radio market certainly is'.

One of the directors optimistically mentioned colour TV and stereo record players; they all agreed that these were coming – and when they came they would lift the company's profits like a surfboard on a tidal wave – but this would not occur until 1971 at the earliest and not then unless Britain's economic troubles were solved.

The conclusion they reached at this meeting was that the company should reduce its dependence upon the consumer by entering a new field of business, namely the manufacture of an industrial product.

Davies Engineering

Due to one of those coincidences that only occur in real life, Mr Shine received a telephone call one week after this meeting. The caller, Mr Davies, explained that he was looking for a buyer for his business, Davies Engineering of South-town, because, he, Mr Davies, wished to retire. Mr Shine visited Mr Davies at his company's premises and ascertained the following facts.

Mr Davies had built up the company over a period of thirty-five years. It had started as a small vehicle repair shop but was now essentially a vehicle building company, with a turnover of nearly £700,000. They purchased standard vehicle chassis from two of the very large British motor manufacturers and upon these constructed a wide variety of bodies. Some of these were general purpose vehicles, such as tipping lorries, box vans, flat platforms and some were built for individual customers for such special duties as waste disposal, servicing lamp posts, transporting bulk powders, and so on. Nearly one third of the output was exported – an important consideration in view of Mr Shine's pessimism over Britain's economic performance over the next few years. Davies Engineering had made profits of between £20,000 and £30,000 over the past ten years or so but in 1967 there was a loss of £5,000 and in 1968 the loss was £20,000; Mr Davies explained to Mr Shine that he was anxious to retire because, at the age of 71, it was all becoming too much for him.

Having consulted his colleagues and his financial advisers Mr Shine bought Davies Engineering for £140,000. Mr Davies retired in March 1969 a few weeks after a new managing director had been appointed.

The strategy

The new managing director of Davies Engineering was Mr Arthur Pepper who had been selected by Mr Shine from a short list of candidates proposed by a well-known firm of personnel selection consultants. He had held a senior executive position in one of Britain's largest engineering companies, was a qualified mechanical engineer and an expert on production engineering techniques. He was 33. It immediately became clear that Mr Pepper was providing the dynamic leadership that had been lacking over the past few years; the factory was painted, the floor areas cleared, scrap ratios fell, old stocks were cleared and morale soared.

Mr Shine felt he could well leave the day to day running of Davies Engineering to Mr Pepper but he did ask him to prepare a long term strategy for the company. Mr Pepper handed Mr Shine the following document in June 1969.

Five-year strategic plan for Davies Engineering

General policy

1.1   The Company will continue as a vehicle building business with financial objectives which compare well with other companies in the same industry.

.2 The targets for the next five years will be as follows:

Year	1969	1970	1971	1972	1973
Sales £000	1100	1500	2100	2650	3500
Profits £000	67	107	185	240	350
Return on capital employed %	14·3	18·1	26·4	28·5	35·2
Profit on sales %	6·1	7·2	8·8	9·0	10·0

.3 In addition to vehicle building the company will exploit other engineering •r associated markets if these can be integrated with our method of operation.

Marketing

.1 We will introduce more professional marketing techniques and offer our ustomers the optimum mix of quality, price, delivery, and after sales ervice.

.2 In view of the general economic climate in the home market, we will ·igorously expand our exports.

?.3 At home we will increase our share of the market for our existing ɔroducts from 3% to 12% by 1973 and widen our product range.

?.4 We will continue to expand sales of standard general-purpose vehicles on ↔ mass production basis but will also increase the output of specialized custom- ɔuilt vehicles.

?.5 The company will make full use of advertising and promotion techniques. t will be represented at international exhibitions.

Product Policy

·.1 The number of vehicles will rise from its current level of 500 a year to 700 a year by 1973.

?.2 It is expected that the company's share of the market in waste-disposal ·ehicles will rise from 3% to 12%.

?.3 We expect to increase our share of the tanker market from 7% to 25%.

?.4 We intend breaking into the market for road and pavement sweepers and ɔleaners.

?.5 We will extend our range of tankers into the larger size range especially in ɔulk powder and chemical markets.

·.6 We will not attempt to compete with the well-known tipper lorry manu- ·acturers but will concentrate on small non-standard tippers and develop a ·ange of very large tipper bodies made of reinforced fibre-glass.

·.7 Our range of box vans will be extended.

·.8 The company will break into the market for refrigerated vans, airport and ·ircraft service vehicles and highway construction.

3.9   The company will seek large orders of specialized vehicles for such government agencies as the Post Office, the armed services, British Rail. Sales will increase from the current level of £12,000 to £150,000 by 1973.

3.10   The number of special-purpose vehicles will increase but should not be allowed to exceed 10% of total turnover.

Export

4.1   Products for export will be generally those offered on the home market but modified for overseas use. New products for overseas markets will be of designs licensed abroad rather than designed by this company.

4.2   Most of our products are suitable for the developing nations. Where it is thought that our designs are sufficiently advanced technically they will be offered in developed nations.

4.3   In the main, sales overseas will be achieved through agents and distributors rather than by our own representatives in the field.

Service

5.1   The company will provide a highly efficient spares service based on new warehouses and more service engineers.

5.2   Profit margins on the sale of spare parts will be not less than 10%.

5.3   Great care will be taken in reducing stocks of spares held in service depots.

Design and Development

6.1   It is taking a progressively longer period to design a new product; it is necessary to anticipate market requirements further ahead and allow more time for design and development.

6.2   It is unlikely that any new products will be available before 1970; so any new designs required before then will have to be bought in.

6.3   New developments will include the use of new methods and materials to improve manufacturing efficiency.

6.4   The current emphasis on inspection will be placed in future on quality control.

Production Policy

7.1   It is proposed to rent a larger factory just outside Southtown and to close down and sell the existing premises.

7.2   In view of the company's policy of increasing share of the market by price competition the need for improved production efficiency is clear. We will therefore:

7.21   Manufacture more of the product than before and purchase less. Larger discounts will be obtained by bulk purchasing.

7.22   Batch sizes and production runs will increase.

7.23   Capital expenditure will be committed to equipping the new factory with a modern production line.

7.3   Value analysis, work study and other techniques will be employed.

7.4   Computer systems for stock and production planning will replace manual systems.

Five-Year Budgets

**Exhibit 101·1   Five Year Budget for Davies Engineering
The Trading Account**

£000	1969	1970	1971	1972	1973
Sales	1100	1500	2100	2650	3500
Direct labour	144	200	285	370	485
Direct materials	526	700	955	1165	1510
Total direct	670	900	1240	1535	1995
Gross margin	430	600	860	1115	1505
Overheads	354	485	685	890	1170
Net margin	76	115	175	225	335
Misc. income	10	10	15	15	15
Trading profit	86	125	190	240	350
Relocation cost	19	18	5	—	—
Net profit	67	107	185	240	350

**Exhibit 101·2   Five Year Budget for Davies Engineering
The Balance Sheets**

£000	1969	1970	1971	1972	1973
Freehold properties	123	78	—	—	
Plant and equipment	98	194	265	306	296
Fixed assets—total	221	272	265	306	296
Inventories	290	425	575	725	950
Debtors	156	214	298	367	503
Current assets—total	446	639	873	1092	1453
Creditors	195	265	365	460	605
Current taxation	8	53	73	95	150
Current liabilities—total	204	318	438	555	755
Capital employed—total	464	593	700	843	994

**Exhibit 101·3   Five Year Budget for Davies Engineering
Cash Flows**

£000	1969	1970	1971	1972	1973
Net profit	67	107	185	240	350
Depreciation	9	22	35	49	64
Government grants	7	15	20	20	20
Property sales	—	45	77	—	—
Increased creditors	22	70	100	95	145
Total cash inflow	105	259	417	404	579
Capital expenditure	68	133	125	110	75
Increased inventories	60	135	150	150	225
Increased debtors	37	58	84	69	236
Company taxation	10	7	53	73	95
Tax cash airflow	175	333	412	402	531
Net cash flow	−70	−75	+5	+2	+48

Exhibit 101·4   Five Year Budget for Davies Engineering Sales Mix

£000	1969	1970	1971	1972	1973
Home Market					
Local governments	400	550	740	900	1000
Businesses	300	400	600	800	1200
Total	700	950	1340	1700	2200
Export Markets					
Local governments	200	250	310	375	500
Businesses	100	175	300	400	600
Total	300	425	610	775	1100
Service & Spares	100	125	150	175	200
Total sales turnover	1100	1500	2100	2650	3500

Mr Shine's reaction

Two of the features of Mr Pepper's strategy worried Mr Shine. The first was the extreme optimism of the forecasts. Sales were expected to rise by well over thirty per cent each year after remaining more or less constant for the past five years. Trading profits were to rise by forty per cent a year. Mr Shine recognized that such a performance was possible in the real world; two of Davies Engineering's better-known competitors in the vehicle building industry had achieved it and so had many other quite large companies all over the world. But a return on capital of 35% could only be achieved, he felt, by companies possessing some quite unusual and outstanding feature and he was not sure what Davies had in that category.

The extent of the optimism in the forecasts could be seen more clearly if compared with the results of the past few years – see Exhibit 101·5.

Exhibit 101·5   Actual and forecast seen as a sequence

	Actual					*Forecast*				
	1964	1965	1966	1967	1968	1969	1970	1971	1972	1973
Sales £000	592	615	620	699	691	1100	1500	2100	2650	3500
Profit £000	26	21	30	−5	−20	67	107	185	240	350
Return on capital employed %	10·4	9·6	11·6	—	—	14·3	18·1	26·4	28·5	35·2
Profit on sales %	4·4	3·4	4·8	—	—	6·1	7·2	8·8	9·0	10·0

Mr Shine recognized that it was the forecast for 1969 that appeared to represent the largest and most optimistic leap in sales and profits. As it was already half way through the year he turned at once to examine the monthly reports from Davies Engineering to discover whether there was any evidence to confirm a rise in sales from the 1968 level to the forecast level for 1969. The monthly report for May was not available and sales up to April were only a little up on the same period of 1968. It was too early to come to any conclusion. Orders were being received at slightly above the 1969 level.

The second feature of the strategy that worried Mr Shine was the capital expenditure figures and the cash flows. Mr Pepper was expecting Mr Shine to sanction the expenditure of approximately half a million pounds over the five-year period in addition to the £140,000 his company had paid for the purchase of Davies Engineering. These sums represented almost the entire expected cash flow of Southtown Radio over this period.

The prospect of having to inject £145,000 as cash into Davies in the two years 1969 and 1970 (see Exhibit 101·3) did not deter him but the prospect of not receiving any cash out of Davies until 1973 did; if the expected colour-TV boom did come in 1971 this cash flow pattern could be very embarrassing.

Mr Shine was strongly tempted to reject the whole of Mr Pepper's document but he felt constrained not to do so by the fact that he had only appointed him a few months earlier, had given him a free hand, and, an important considera-tion, Mr Pepper was proving to be a dynamic and effective managing director. As a compromise Mr Shine accepted the document but rejected the move to the larger rented factory. He encouraged Mr Pepper to invest heavily in new equip-ment to modernize the existing factory as a matter of urgency. He resolved to watch the sales and orders received figures closely over the following months. At Mr Pepper's request he also approved the recruitment of a marketing director (to give effect to paragraph 2.1) and the purchase of a very small local company specializing in the manufacture of vehicle upholstery (in accordance with paragraph 1.3).

The events of 1969 and 1970

In addition to the five-year budget, Mr Pepper had also prepared a more detailed budget for 1969, the salient features of which are shown in Exhibit 101·6.

Exhibit 101·6   Summary of Davies Engineering Budget for 1969

£000	Jan	Feb	Mar	Apr	May	Jun	Jul	Aug	Sept	Oct	Nov	Dec	Total
Sales	55	55	60	70	80	100	170	60	120	120	140	120	1100
Direct cost	35	35	38	44	49	61	71	36	70	70	82	79	670
Gross margin	20	20	22	26	31	39	49	24	50	50	58	41	430
Overheads	25	25	28	28	28	30	30	30	32	32	32	34	354
Net margin	−5	−5	−6	−2	3	9	19	−6	18	18	26	7	76
Misc. income	0	1	1	1	1	1	0	1	1	1	1	1	10
Trading profit	−5	−4	−5	−1	4	10	20	−6	19	19	27	8	86

By the beginning of August, when the factory closed for a fortnight, sales had totalled £385,000 against the budget of £540,000, and instead of a cumula-tive profit of £19,000 there was a loss of £50,000. Sales in August, however, were just above target and in September they exceeded even the ambitious figure of £120,000. In November the results for October became known – sales were down to £61,000 against the target of £120,000. Mr Shine told Mr Pepper to cease recruitment but, almost immediately after this interview, Davies Engi-neering received an order for £200,000 from a new customer, which augured well for 1970. But the loss in 1969 came to £31,000.

In the first three months of 1970 sales were running well above the annual target level of £1,500,000 but orders declined sharply to a level of only £60,000 a month indicating that there would be another loss in 1970. In addition it had become clear towards the end of 1969 that there was something seriously at fault with the management accounting system which showed, for example, that in December sales of £65,000 had incurred direct costs of only £29,000 against the more normal percentage of direct cost to sales of approximately 60% (see Exhibit 101·7).

Exhibit 101·7   Actual Results for Davies Engineering in 1969

£000	Jan	Feb	Mar	Apr	May	Jun	Jul	Aug	Sept	Oct	Nov	Dec	Total
Sales	55	57	48	71	40	70	44	61	126	61	73	65	771
Direct costs	35	35	31	44	31	42	33	48	71	40	31	29	470
Gross margin	20	22	17	27	9	28	11	13	55	21	42	36	301
Overheads	25	25	28	28	28	28	28	31	31	31	31	31	342
Net margins	−5	−3	−11	−1	−19	0	−17	−15	24	−10	11	5	−41
Misc. income	0	1	1	1	1	1	1	0	1	1	1	1	10
Trading profit	−5	−2	−10	0	−18	1	−16	−15	25	−9	12	6	−31

Meanwhile in November, Mr Shine and his fellow directors on the board of Southtown Radio had come to the conclusion that their company was now large enough to warrant the appointment of a finance director who would also be responsible for corporate planning. Consequently a Mr Meaney joined the company in February 1970 just in time to take part in the discussions on the future of Davies Engineering. At a meeting the board of Southtown Radio made three decisions:

1 That Mr Meaney should immediately take a small task force of account-ants into Davies Engineering to ascertain the true short term profit posit-ion and to reorganize the system of management accounts.
2 That the strategy proposed by Mr Pepper be abandoned and that Mr Meaney should prepare a new corporate plan for Davies Engineering.
3 That the board of Southtown Radio should receive a weekly report of orders received by Davies Engineering.

By May 1970 it was clear from these weekly reports that Davies Engineering were obtaining orders at the annual rate of only £750,000 – i.e. much the same as in 1969 – but that overheads were running at an annual rate of £70,000 more than in the same period of 1969 indicating a possible loss for Davies Engineering of up to £100,000 for the full year. A strike at the factory of one of their chassis suppliers had begun to affect output and sales in April were down to £30,000 leading to a loss in that one month of nearly £25,000. At the same time it became clear that the business of Southtown Radio itself was in decline due to poor consumer demand and that their profit for the year might not exceed £100,000.

During June 1970, the board made a number of calculations designed to evaluate the alternatives of retrenchment, liquidation, closure or sale of Davies Engineering and decided to try to sell it as a going concern. In January 1971 they found a willing buyer at £5000. In addition to the initial purchase price of £140,000 this venture cost Southtown Radio £120,000 in losses during 1969 and 1970. Southtown Radio made a group profit of £7000 in 1970; fortunately the colour-TV and stereo boom began in 1971 and blossomed throughout 1972.

I believe the case of Davies Engineering is by no means exceptional and it might therefore be useful to spell out in some detail where the strategic plan put forward by Mr Pepper fell short of the system of corporate planning that I described in the first nine chapters of this book.

1 Project evaluation and project specification

It is questionable whether Mr Shine made an adequate evaluation of the project to purchase Davies Engineering; but whether he did or not is not the most important question. The most important question is whether this was the right sort of project – i.e. whether Davies Engineering was the piece of the jigsaw puzzle that was missing from the strategic structure of Southtown Radio. Let us consider each of these questions separately.

Mr Shine consulted several experts while evaluating Davies Engineering; engineers, property valuers, accountants and so on. The consensus of opinion was that the business was basically sound, that on a turnover of £700,000 and a (rather conservative) profit margin on sales of 5%, the company should generate an after tax profit of £21,000 a year. Given reasonably competent management, sales could be expanded at more than 3% p.a. A price-earnings ratio of 6 or 7 would be justified, making the purchase price of £140,000 quite a reasonable one. Mr Shine and his advisers believed they had properly evaluated this project; nor is it clear what evidence anyone could have produced, at the time the decision was made, that they had not. In other words, this project – the purchase of Davies Engineering – had been carefully and, I believe correctly evaluated, from the standpoint of its financial viability. But, as I remark on page 72, projects should always be evaluated against two criteria; one is the generally accepted one of financial validity, the other is whether the proposed project is in accordance with the proposed structure for the company.

The specification of this project took shape at the meeting of the directors of Southtown Radio in August 1968 (see page 141) when it was decided that the company should enter the industrial manufacturing business field. This decision was taken at a single meeting, without considering any alternative strategies and without analysing precisely what, if anything, was wrong with the present structure of Southtown Radio. It was not clearly stated, for example, whether their problem was the expected low level of consumer demand in Britain or that demand was liable to long term cyclical fluctuations or both. Some of the alternatives open to the company at that time were:

(a) to prepare for the colour-TV and stereo boom
(b) to expand their existing business abroad
(c) to diversify into industrial leasing
(d) to diversify into industrial TV or electronics manufacture
(e) to diversify into non-electronics manufacturing.

Of these they chose (e) without considering any of the others. Indeed it would not have been possible to state a preference for any of these other alternatives on a rational basis without a much more precise analysis of threats and opportunities than had been made. If the main threat to Southtown Radio was a low level of consumer demand in Britain then a diversification out of consumer retailing or outside Britain or both was indicated; if the threat was the cyclical nature of consumer demand then such a diversification was only one possible solution among several others – such as, for example concentrating on preparing for the next upswing.

To sum up, Mr Shine had prepared a project specification that was so general that almost any company that had been offered to him would have met the requirements; it was imprecise because no strategic structure had been selected for Southtown Radio and this had not been done because no internal or external appraisal had been carried out.

2 Mr Pepper's strategy

Mr Pepper's strategy was described by Mr Meaney as 'to lash out in all directions at once'. He pointed out that Mr Pepper intended to expand exports and share of the home market, reduce prices, improve service, enter other engineering or associated fields (including vehicle upholstery!), increase batch sizes but also increase output of custom-built vehicles, integrate backwards, break into several new markets, introduce new products and so on. He suggested that such a display of random and non-selective ideas should henceforth be termed Pepper-pot planning. He also pointed out that Mr Pepper had been given no long term objectives by Mr Shine and had made no internal or external appraisals – he felt that this was a serious lapse because Mr Pepper was a newcomer to vehicle building and should not have expected to be able to devise a long term strategy without learning a great deal about current conditions in the industry. He said that Mr Pepper's strategy was no more appropriate for Davies Engineering in 1969 than it might have been in 1939 or 1999 – in other words there was hardly any reference to the real world either inside or outside Davies Engineering.

It is difficult to disagree with Mr Meaney's comments. If Mr Pepper had asked Mr Shine to state the objectives for Davies Engineering within South town Radio he would have been able to do so, even if only after some further discussion with his colleagues on the Southdown Radio board. Their intentions in 1968 were only somewhat hazy but they clearly intended that profits earned by Southtown during the period of high consumer demand should be invested in Davies Engineering ready for the expansion of industrial and government expenditure that often follows the end of a period of high consumer demand in the economic cycle of a nation. In the same way the profits arising in Davies would be invested in Southtown in preparation for the next consumer demand upswing. It would have been possible to quantify this concept for the following few years; Southtown would invest a large part of its expected cash flows in 1969 and 1970 in Davies; Davies would hand over its 1971 and subsequent cash flows for investment in the colour-TV and stereo expansion. The figures involved might have been, say, £200,000 to be invested in Davies in 1969 and 1970 and then a cash flow of, say, £20,000 to £50,000 transferred from Davies to Southtown in each of the years 1971 to 1974.

The cash flow pattern suggested above, compared with the flow in the five-year plan proposed by Mr Pepper, is shown in the Exhibit 101·8. Even allowing for the possibility that the expected colour-TV boom may have been delayed the pattern proposed by Mr Pepper is clearly inappropriate. If the boom did come in 1971 or 1972 Southtown Radio would have had to meet the increased demand for capital to finance this extra business without any help from Davies Engineering.

Exhibit 101·8

£000	1969	1970	1971	1972	1973
Minimum cash flows required by Southtown Radio.	−200	0	+20	+30	+40
Cash flow pattern suggested in Davies Engineering's Five Year Budget.	−210	−75	+5	+2	+48

The F_0 forecast

Having been given no corporate objectives for Davies Engineering there would perhaps have been no point in Mr Pepper's preparing an F_0 forecast from which to make a gap analysis. If he had done so, however, Mr Meaney's opinion was that there would have been no gap at all. This view was based on the reports of the experts whom Mr Shine consulted before he purchased the company. Mr Meaney calculated that if £50,000 had been spent on modernizing the production facilities and if Mr Pepper had exercised his undoubted skills of leadership and engineering knowledge, then the profits from Davies Engineering would have returned to at least the level of 1966 (before Mr Davies had lost control due to advancing years). Mr Meaney's F_0 forecast on these assumptions is shown in Exhibit 101·9.

Exhibit 101·9

£000	1969	1970	1971	1972	1973
Capital expenditure	190	10	10	10	10
Turnover	720	740	760	780	800
Profit on sales %	4·5	5·0	5·5	5·5	5·5
Profit	32	38	42	43	44
Cash flow	−200	+12	+24	+28	+30
Return on capital employed %	10·6	10·8	11·2	11·4	11·7

Apart from the assumptions as to modernization and the change in the managing director this F_0 forecast assumed only that Mr Pepper would continue to run Davies Engineering as Mr Davies had done in the past – it was, in other words, a normal F_0 forecast, as defined on page 77.

Although this F_0 compares well with the minimum target requirements in Exhibit 101·8, it does not represent a very dramatic contribution to group profits and the return on capital employed is not impressive. Mr Shine certainly hoped for a better performance than this – he had in mind a return on capital employed of at least 15%, implying profits of approximately £50,000 to £60,000 by 1972.

Performance-risk gap analysis

It would have been possible in 1969 for Mr Shine to have presented Mr Pepper with a performance–risk target curve – albeit a very crude one. What he really wanted from Davies Engineering was a very high probability of achieving a positive cash flow of £20,000 by 1971 or 1972 at the latest and, at the same time, a fair chance of a cash flow of, say, £40,000 by 1972. It would have been possible for Mr Pepper to prepare an F_0 forecast from which it would have been observed that there was a very high probability of achieving the minimum Mr Shine required but a very low probability of achieving the higher figure, See Exhibit 101·10. The very high confidence in achieving £20,000 cash flow by 1972 (shown by the shape of the F_0 forecast) is due to the fact that Davies Engineering was considered to be a well-respected, long established company with a very stable range of well-known products.

What this Exhibit shows is that extra profits are certainly required but it also shows that a very stable profit base already existed. This implies that the

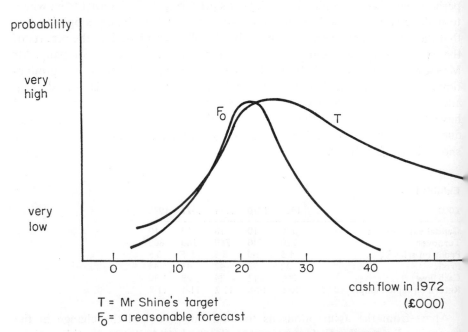

T = Mr Shine's target
F_0 = a reasonable forecast

Exhibit 101·10   A performance risk gap analysis for Davies Engineering

existing business should be allowed to continue almost unchanged but that some new activity would have to be found capable of producing an additional cash flow at least of £10,000 by 1972 (implying an additional profit of, say, £15,000) In order to identify what new activity might be most appropriate Mr Pepper should have carried out an internal and external appraisal.

The appraisals

When Mr Meaney was preparing his corporate plan for Davies Engineering in 1970 he made the following list of strengths and weaknesses, threats and opportunities – a list Mr Pepper could have made in 1969.

Davies Engineering

Internal Appraisal

In spite of its small size (it ranks 29th by turnover among Britain's vehicle builders) Davies Engineering is well known among urban and rural government authorities and amongst large commercial companies in the central part of Southern England. Its products are reputed to be well made, simple, reliable, robust. Two of its products have been exceptionally well received; one of these, a waste-disposal vehicle was introduced in 1965; the other, a highway servicing vehicle, in 1967. Both these technically advanced vehicles were designed by David Ducat who joined Davies Engineering in 1963 and is now aged 41. Mr Pepper is the other outstanding employee; he is ambitious, energetic and has a considerable knowledge of production engineering techniques.

The only major weakness of the company is that, over the past three years, it has been allowed to run down; morale was low, discipline was lax, the plant was obsolescent.

Its current problem is the great rise in the burden of overheads which was allowed to occur in anticipation of an enormous increase in sales which has not materialized.

External Appraisal

Competitors: In addition to the three very large British vehicle manufacturers there are approximately forty medium-sized builders all of whom specialize in a comparatively narrow range of products such as fire-engines, bulk liquid carriers, and so on. In addition, there are over four hundred small firms employing no more than a few dozen men. Competition in export markets is strong, especially from German manufacturers.

Political: There are no indications that the British government will sanction a higher level of expenditure by local government authorities over the next few years. There are indications that the government will assist any medium-sized firms to merge into larger groupings especially in fragmented industries such as vehicle building.

Economic: There are no indications that industrial investment will expand any

F

faster than consumer retail markets in the next few years. There are indications that exports will expand and that the British government will give assistance to exporters.

Social: The view is frequently expressed today that lorries must be made less slow, smelly and noisy; this will affect both the design of lorries and the provision of new highways. One social problem relevant to Davies products is the growing problem of waste disposal – in particular of packaging for consumer goods and of chemical wastes.

Technological: The industry (including Davies) is technologically extremely backward compared with, say, the United States and Germany. This is true both of product design and production methods. The trends are probably towards much larger and much smaller vehicles and towards special purpose vehicles.

It will be appreciated that at the same time Mr Meaney was preparing the new corporate plan for Davies Engineering there were growing doubts as to whether the company could continue in existence at all; were it not for this he would have been prepared to make the appraisals in greater depth. Nevertheless he had identified the major facts shown in the Cruciform Chart in Exhibit 101·11.

Exhibit 101·11   A Cruciform Chart for Davies Engineering

Strengths	Weaknesses
Solid reputation	Small company—29th in size in
Two outstanding products	industry
David Ducat	Excessive overheads
Mr. Pepper	Obsolescent equipment

Threats	Opportunities
Forty competitors in U.K.	Exports
Technologically backward	Waste disposal & highway
industry	vehicles
Static home markets	Fragmented industry
Legislation against lorries	New technology (as in U.S.A.)
	Very large or very small vehicles
	Special purpose vehicles

It is perhaps interesting to note that David Ducat, the designer, was a man of very retiring personality, whose personal relationship with Mr Davies had been excellent. He failed to impress Mr Pepper, however, who almost completely overlooked the significance of the two new products highlighted in Mr Meaney's report. (I discuss the problem of objectivity when identifying strengths and weaknesses on page 97.)

An Alternative Strategy

Mr Meaney believed that the gap analysis and the appraisals pointed with absolute clarity to a particular three-stage strategy for Davies. First; for Mr Pepper to use his undoubted skills to return the company to profitability based solely on the exisiting range of products – this, of course was a complete reversal of Mr Pepper's current strategy based on making major changes to almost every aspect of the business. Mr Meaney suggested that Mr Pepper should concentrate all his attention on production efficiency as a matter of urgency.

The second stage was to expand sales of the two new products in an attempt to bring them to real prominence in the home market and to expand sales of the other products in the developing nations where simplicity and robustness are often more appropriate qualities than advanced technology. The third stage was to give David Ducat the facilities he needed to design a new product to be developed in response to the needs of the market as shown by a market research exercise. Mr Meaney believed that Stage 1 should start at once and should include the reduction of overheads, many of which had only lately been incurred. Stage 2 could follow in a few months and Stage 3, the introduction of a new product, would not occur until 1974 athough Mr Ducat would start identifying market needs and preliminary design work immediately.

Although Mr Meaney obtained full approval for this outline strategy from Mr Shine, he failed to obtain Mr Pepper's approval, not unnaturally. It was, after all, Mr Pepper's strategy to expand Davies Engineering into a major producer of a wide range of relatively cheap, mass-produced vehicles while Mr Meaney saw the company's future as a relatively smaller producer with two categories of product; on the one hand a range of simple, robust vehicles suitable for heavy duty in those home and export areas where their reliability was a useful attribute and on the other hand a range of only two or three advanced, highly specialized, vehicles in two or three rapidly growing markets such as highway servicing and waste disposal.

Conclusions

Although Mr Meaney's strategy is incomplete, I personally believe that if it had been adopted in 1969 instead of Mr Pepper's there would have been a very different outcome; Davies Engineering might have become a useful part of the Southtown Radio Group in spite of the doubts there must always be as to whether Southtown Radio should ever have moved into vehicle building in the first place.

The following mistakes, many of which I believe to be common in strategic planning, were committed:

No corporate objectives were set for Southtown Radio; nor was a gap analysis performed so it was not known whether a new strategic structure was required.

No internal or external appraisal was carried out for Southtown Radio and no criteria were therefore available by which to adjudicate between alternative strategies. *Any* project, so long as it looked profitable, would have been acceptable.

No corporate objectives were set for Davies Engineering nor was a gap analysis performed so it was not known whether a new strategic structure was required.

No internal or external appraisal was carried out for Davies Engineering and no criteria were available by which to adjudicate between alternative strategies.

As soon as corporate objectives for Davies Engineering were determined it became possible to perform a gap analysis; this revealed that the chosen strategy *was* inappropriate.

It could be argued that Mr Pepper's plan took no cognizance whatever of the company's strengths nor was relevant to its position in its environment.

Mr Pepper's strategic document was well produced and contained more than enough detail from which Mr Shine could judge his confidence in it. It could be argued that there was far too much detail and not enough strategy. There was no 'gestalt'.

Mr Pepper's forecast of sales and profits were not rooted in the past. His sequence of five-year figures formed an unbelievable discontinuity with the previous five years.

Some of the figures in Mr Pepper's strategic document did not reflect the policy statement. (The target return on capital employed of 35·2% in 1973 was far above that of 'other companies in the industry'; compare paragraphs 1.1 and 1.2).

It only became apparent in paragraph 7.2 (in the section on Production Policy) that a major element in Mr Pepper's strategy was to increase market share by price competition.

Some of the statements in the policy document were capable of wide interpretation; the paragraph 1.3, for example, was used to justify the purchase of a vehicle upholstery business.

The problem of monitoring confidence in a strategy is well illustrated. It took approximately one year before Mr Shine became convinced that Davies Engineering would fail to achieve its targets. Even if he had been using the 'orders received' figure as the 'lead indicator' instead of 'sales turnover' (which he was used to using in Southtown Radio) the level of orders received varied so wildly from month to month that it would have been nine months before he would have lost confidence.

Finally, I believe this case study illustrates the point I made on page 138 that corporate planning is, in principle, the same for all companies – indeed for all organizations – whatever their size or type and regardless of whether they are composed of several levels of autonomous subsidiaries or one unit divided into functional activities. In this case a strategic structure had been determined for neither the parent company nor its new subsidiary; for neither company was it therefore possible to state a preference for one proposed action rather than some other. Instead of deciding an appropriate structure for Southtown Radio and then searching for a suitable acquisition, Mr Shine did the opposite – he bought Davies Engineering thus altering the structure. Instead of deciding the structure for Davies Engineering and then searching for suitable engineering and marketing projects Mr Pepper did the opposite – he embarked upon a number of projects thus altering the structure.

Case 2 – Delibes, Latour et Cie

Background

This company was founded in 1947 by three men: Louis Latour, Denis Delibes and Charles Cardine. The families of all three men had lived for several generations in the small town of Coulette in one of the lesser wine-growing areas of central France. Two of them, Louis and Denis had been to school together and all three had worked in the wine industry before the Second World War.

The company was formed as a result of an idea put forward by Denis to Louis; namely that there should be a good market for a cheap wine-based aperitif in post-war France. As neither Louis nor Denis on their own had sufficient capital resources they approached their mutual friend Charles Cardine who agreed to join them in their venture; each partner put up one third of the equity and Charles undertook to make loans available up to a certain maximum level – the amount is irrelevant for the business immediately became profitable and Charles' loan offer was never taken up. The company expanded rapidly; the aperitif itself was of a quality to cause much witty sarcasm among those who can afford the more expensive brands but, as Denis had anticipated, it was much appreciated by just that section of the population whose standard of living was about to rise as never before in the history of France. Furthermore Louis had carefully selected a bottle of distinctive shape, taken advertising space in precisely those journals read by that section of the community to whom they believed the product would appeal and had chosen the name – 'Le Duc' – with the same understanding of the psychology of their potential customers.

Charles, who was a decade older than Louis and Denis invited his two sons to join the company in 1949. When he died in 1950 they joined the board. By 1960 sales turnover of Le Duc had risen to an incredible Fr 60m (approximately $12m) with a profit before tax of Fr 15m. The product had become a household word and Louis and Denis had emerged as the leading personalities in the town of Coulette; indeed Denis, and to a lesser extent Pierre and Quentin, the two sons of Charles Cardine, began to live in considerable pomp and splendour and willingly accepted the honours that the local community showered upon them.

In 1963 Louis persuaded his partners to launch a new product, namely a cheap brandy called Le Baron. Denis, Pierre and Quentin were not enthusiastic over this project because they felt that if it failed it would not only damage the profit record of the company but might also reflect adversely upon their standing in the community. However Louis had been working on this project for two years with his sons François and Georges who had joined the company's marketing department in 1961 (aged then 22 and 19). They had made a very thorough study of the alcohol market in France and believed they had found a gap in the brandy market in the lower price range. They had obtained the services of a noted expert in the blending of alcoholic beverages, had studied the design of bottles, packs, labels, display materials; prepared an advertising campaign; calculated prices, agents' commissions, retailers' margins; discussed costs with the company's production managers. As may be seen from Exhibit 102·1 the launch was entirely successful, turnover rising to Fr 90m generating a profit of nearly Fr 20m by 1970.

Exhibit 102·1 Summary of results for Delibes, Latour et Cie 1960—1970

Fr. millions	1960	1961	1962	1963	1964	1965	1966	1967	1968	1969	1970
Size of national market											
aperitif	201·3	213·7	242·8	258·1	269·8	290·3	323·1	327·4	366·2	390·0	397·5
brandy	450·1	460·3	521·1	581·8	591·4	661·3	687·1	699·7	770·3	812·0	890·7
Le Duc											
Sales turnover	60·1	64·1	69·4	70·9	79·5	83·9	92·1	99·8	104·	110·6	115·2
Variable costs	30·1	32·7	34·8	35·9	40·0	42·6	45·1	49·6	53·0	56·0	55·1
Overheads allocated	3·3	3·4	3·7	4·1	4·4	4·7	5·1	5·2	5·9	6·3	6·7
Advertising	12·0	13·1	14·3	15·8	16·2	16·9	18·1	19·5	20·3	22·1	24·4
Profit	14·7	14·9	16·6	15·1	18·9	19·7	23·8	25·5	24·8	26·2	29·0
Tax at 50%	7·3	7·2	8·2	7·5	9·3	9·9	11·9	13·0	12·4	13·1	14·6
Le Baran											
Sales turnover					18·1	37·0	53·2	67·7	80·0	83·9	92·1
Variable costs					9·1	19·8	27·0	34·2	40·2	46·1	46·8
Overheads allocated					1·4	1·6	1·7	1·9	1·9	2·2	2·5
Advertising					12·1	13·2	14·2	17·1	20·4	21·3	23·1
Profit					—4·5	3·4	10·3	14·5	17·5	14·3	19·7
Tax at 50%					—	—	—	—	—	—	—
La Duchesse											
Sales turnover									14·3	22·9	29·1
Variable costs									6·1	10·3	13·1
Overheads allocated									2·0	2·6	3·1
Advertising									10·8	10·8	10·8
Profit									—4·5	—0·8	2·1
Tax at 50%									—	—	—
Sales of brandy in Spain						1·8	2·9	4·8	4·9	4·1	5·1
Profit						—0·8	0·0	0·1	0·4	—0·4	—0·1
Tax at 50%						—	—	—	—	—	—
Total profits after tax	7·4	7·7	8·4	7·6	5·1	12·4	22·2	27·1	29·9	27·2	36·1
Dividends paid out	3·4	3·8	4·0	4·0	4·0	6·0	10·5	15·0	15·0	20·0	20·0

In 1964 Louis proposed that the brandy should be launched into the Spanish Market and the board approved the appointment of his eldest son, François, as General Manager – Spain. However the board did not approve the whole of the proposed budget for this project and, as can be seen from Exhibit 102·1 it was not a success; Louis was convinced that the board's failure to give adequate financial backing was the main cause of this. In 1965 Denis proposed that Pierre Cardine be appointed general manager of Delibes, Latour et Cie. The reason for this proposal was plain; Denis, now aged 56, had no children to succeed him in the business but felt that his influence on the company would be severely weakened if he allowed Louis' sons on to the board before the question of management succession was settled. He certainly did not want either of Louis' sons to become general manager of the company; he considered them to be so adventurous as to threaten the stability of the company. Louis, being outvoted, had to accept Pierre as general manager together with the implication that this would lead to his appointment as managing director when Louis and Denis retired. Louis did not consider Pierre had the ability to run a company now employing 1000 people; he did feel that his own sons, whom he had carefully trained as business managers, could eventually run the company. The positions on the board in 1965 are shown in Exhibit 102·2.

Exhibit 102·2   Membership of the Board 1965

Board Member	Percentage of Shares held	Position
Louis Latour	33·3	Joint Managing Director
Denis Delibes	33·3	Joint Managing Director
Pierre Cardine	23·33	General Manager
Quentin Cardine	10·0	Production Manager

In 1966, Louis, again assisted by his two sons, began investigating a small gap in the aperitif market which they believed they had identified on the sweet side of the taste curve. (See Exhibit 102·3, showing the turnover of most of the major aperitif products plotted against their position on a taste scale). The

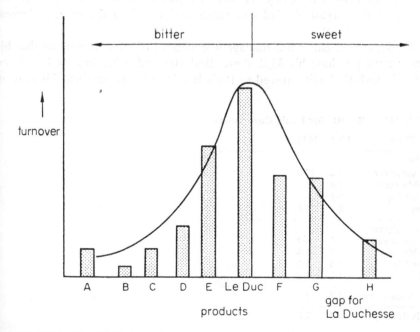

Exhibit 102·3   The 'Taste curve'

launch occurred, successfully, early in 1968 (see Exhibit 102·1) but, as predicted by Louis, La Duchesse would never achieve the turnover of Le Duc partly because the aperitif market in France was now rather crowded with products and partly because women, for whom La Duchesse was designed, consume less alcohol than men.

Later in 1968, Pierre and Quentin put up a proposal to build a large new factory just outside the town of Coulette at a cost of Fr 30m. Louis considered this to be ridiculous because in 1967 the French government had withdrawn the tax concession for companies in the development areas such as the area round Coulette. Since 1956 the government had allowed a complete 7 year tax holiday on the profits of all new projects (including new products) launched in these special development areas but this concession was now to be withdrawn on all projects not approved by the end of 1968.* There was not the slightest possibility of obtaining government approval for this factory by the deadline date and all profits arising from it would be taxed at the standard rate of 50%. The rift between Louis and the others, which had been growing for some years, now became open. Louis made it clear that unless the other directors widened their horizons and began running the company in a professional manner he could not continue as a director. They pointed to the company's past success, to the fact that none of them needed to work for their living and that they would prefer to enjoy their position of wealth and power in Coulette. Louis pointed to the dangers ahead; to the rioting in the streets of Paris which heralded major social and political changes in France, to the recent mergers among their competitors, to the possibility of an economic crisis by 1971 – all these must be considered even by a company the size of Delibes, Latour et Cie (which was now one of the largest alcohol companies and well into the top 200 largest companies in France).

Louis demanded either full management control of the company or that his partners must purchase his 33% share. Both demands were brusquely refused and Louis and his family moved to Paris late in 1968; he retained his seat on

Exhibit 102·4   Results for Louis Companies

Fr. millions	1969	1970
Paladin		
Sales turnover	3·0	14·8
Variable costs	1·8	8·0
Advertising	9·9	8·2
Losses	8·7	1·4
Ostienne Liqueur		
Sales turnover	2·1	4·9
Variable cost	1·0	2·6
Advertising	0·0	1·0
Profits	1·1	1·3
Paris office—cost	1·7	2·7
Totals (losses)	9·3	2·8

* I have, of course, grossly oversimplified the French regional development tax incentive system

the board of Delibes, Latour however, and appeared at the few formal meetings that were held. He and his sons lost no time in starting their own alcohol company; they launched a brandy, called Paladin, through a new network of agents – the brandy itself being manufactured and bottled by a competitor to Delibes, Latour with premises near Paris. They licensed a liqueur from the monks of Saint Ostienne which they also distributed through their agents to retailers. In order to finance their new company Louis sold an estate near Toulouse, purchased in 1964, for Fr 15m. Exhibit 102·4 shows the results of this activity for 1969 and 1970.

Financial objectives

During 1970 Louis and his sons began seriously to consider their long term objectives. Louis was now 62 years old; François and Georges were 31 and 28, both were married and had children. What were they trying to do? What did they want?

At first their discussions centred round the various possibilities for new products and for the acquisition of new companies. Later they realized that these were secondary to a number of more fundamental objectives, of which financial ones were not the least important. They concluded that they should aim to increase their capital wealth by 15% p.a. in money terms (or by, say 10–12% p.a. in real terms), over the next decade. But they also agreed that in their attempt to achieve this long term aim they should not jeopardize their existing wealth. However, as Georges pointed out, their wealth was already far in excess of any sum a reasonable man would need; he felt that there was a certain sum – he suggested 'an English million' (about Fr 12m) below which their wealth must certainly not fall.

Exhibit 102·5 Louis financial position in 1970

Asset	Market Value fr million	Annual Income
Apartment Block (Toulouse)	9	fr 100,000 (rents)
Equity Portfolio	1	fr 300,000 (dividends)
Private Home (Paris)	1	—
Paladin, Ostienne	1 (estimate)	—
33·33% Delibes, Latour	180 (assumes P/E =15)	Fr 6·7m (dividend)
Totals	192	Fr 7·1m
Personal expenditure, tax, charitable donations		Fr 3·7m
Surplus annual income		Fr 3·4m

They had thus determined three points on a performance–risk curve: a very low chance of losing their last £1,000,000; a very high probability of being at least as wealthy in 1980 as in 1970; a reasonable probability of being four times more wealthy in 1980 than in 1970. They calculated their present wealth on the assumption that if Delibes, Latour et Cie obtained a stock market quotation the price-earnings ratio would not be lower than 15, and that Louis' total wealth in 1970 therefore amounted to Fr 192m (see Exhibit 102·5). Exhibit 102·6 shows their performance–risk curve based on this figure.

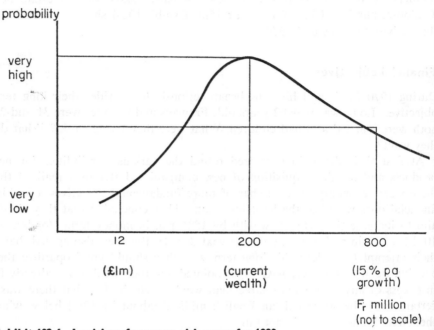

Exhibit 102·6   Louis' performance–risk curve for 1980

Ethological objectives

Discussion on ethological objectives was considerable. There was complete agreement among the three men that they wished to accept the challenge of building up a large, or very large, organization; by their standards, 'large' meant one of national or even international significance. To achieve this they recognized that their own capital resources, even including that tied up in Delibes, Latour et Cie, might be insufficient. They decided that they were prepared to admit new equity partners up to an equal share; later, however this decision was modified to allow equity partners a greater than equal share so long as they – the Latours – were allowed management control of the enterprise. This was again modified; the principle finally adopted was that they should have management control of the enterprise in which they also had a major – but not majority – shareholding but that, if they were at any time denied management control then they should be able to withdraw their share holding at the ruling market valuation.

They were a little startled by the implications of these objectives. If Louis' capital wealth was to rise to Fr 800m by 1980 and if this represented only, say, 25% of the total enterprise over which they had management control then the market value of that enterprise would exceed Fr 3000m. Assuming an annual sales turnover of approximately the same figure this would probably put them well into *Fortune's* Top Five Hundred companies outside America by 1980. They would have good reason to be very pleased with such a result, they thought. They also agreed that their considerable wealth should be used for a socially worthwhile purpose; where they did not agree was what 'socially worthwhile' really meant and, in particular, Georges questioned whether alcohol could really be considered socially worthwhile. François pointed out that they were not selling intoxicating liquor but 'atmosphere'. Georges retorted that this was typical of the deception and sleight of hand practised by the modern marketing executive. 'I would hate to think,' continued Georges, 'that a correlation might exist between our increasingly skilled use of marketing and advertising with the increase in the already murderous rate of accidents on the French roads'. François replied that any product or service could be misused – even education. After considerable and, at times, heated argument it was agreed that modern marketing techniques were legitimate if the product or service satisfied a socially worthwhile need and could not be misused unintentionally – even Georges agreed that they could not be held responsible for a consumer who *intentionally* put their products to ill purpose. But this did not exonerate alcohol which, being potentially addictive and insidious in its effects, could be unintentionally misused and harmful. It was agreed, therefore, that they would gradually diversify out of alcohol into a product or service which they could promote by using even the most potent modern marketing techniques with a clear conscience.

They next considered their attitude towards their employees. François voiced his distaste for the atmosphere at Delibes, Latour et Cie where he felt that the 'old fuddy duddies' at the top allowed the exercise of virtually no initiative by even the most senior executives. Total agreement was reached that their companies would not be run on feudal lines but that all employees would be given at least one chance to put their own ideas into operation. They all felt this was the key to success in the modern world; they would offer employees good pay and working conditions, of course, but these were of minute significance compared with providing the atmosphere within which their employees could develop their own abilities. They had, in fact, already adopted this attitude towards the staff in their Paris office; thus the first girl to be recruited as a telephonist was given sole responsibility for selecting and ordering a new switchboard for the offices.

They did not feel it necessary to identify any further ethological objectives; their concept of 'socially worthwhile' was, they believed, sufficiently general and unambiguous to be used as a criterion for any proposed activity. For a list of their corporate objectives see Exhibit 102·7.

Exhibit 102·7   Louis financial and ethological objectives

Financial
1   An almost zero possibility of losing his last £1m; i.e. his capital wealth must exceed Fr 12m in 1980.
2   A very high probability of retaining his existing wealth; i.e. his capital wealth in 1980 should be approximately Fr 200m.
3   A fair chance of quadrupling his wealth, i.e., a capital wealth of Fr 800 by 1980.

Ethological
4   To build a very large company.
5   Its management control to be in Latour hands.
6   Latour to have a major but not majority shareholding.
7   Must be able to realise market value of shareholding if management control passes out of Latour hands.
8   All activities to be socially worthwhile.
9   Powerful marketing techniques may only be used for products that cannot be unintentionally misused.
10   The company's dependence on alcohol will be reduced.
11   Employees will be encouraged to develop their own abilities.

The F_o forecast

François and Georges attempted to forecast their financial position in 1980 on the assumption that no further action would be taken other than to invest Louis' surplus income in an equity portfolio. Their calculations are shown in Exhibits 102·8 to 102·10 from which the following may be seen:

(a) Their total capital wealth in 1980 would amount to not more than Fr 322m compared with the top target figure of Fr 800m. There was thus a gap of enormous proportions at this level of target although the chances of achieving a modest increase in their total wealth were very good and their lowest target – the English million – looked very secure. See Exhibit 102·11 for the performance–risk gap analysis. These conclusions would probably still be valid even if the F_0 forecast had been prepared on less optimistic assumptions than those actually used and even if the accuracy of the forecast was extremely poor.

(b) Although Louis had warned his partners in Delibes, Latour of the importance of the effect of the tax holiday, even he had not realized, until he saw these calculations, just how severely the ending of the holiday would affect the company's earnings. and even more severely, its potential stock market valuation.

(c) These forecasts showed very clearly that the two companies recently launched by Louis in Paris were almost completely irrelevant to the financial targets that he had now accepted. It was almost inconceivable that any new products, any mergers, any projects on the scale of Paladin or Ostienne could significantly alter the size of the gap now revealed.

(d) The calculations in Exhibit 102·9 also suggest that these companies would show an unacceptably low return on investment; the capital injected so far amounted to Fr 12·1m and earnings of even Fr 0·5m were not expected before the year 1974. Clearly, if the return was to be brought to an acceptable level, a new product or some other highly profitable project would have to be launched as a matter of urgency.

Exhibit 102-8   F₀ forecast for Delibes, Latour 1970-1980

Fr million	1970	1971	1972	1973	1974	1975	1976	1977	1978	1979	1980	Assumptions
Size of market												
aperitif	397.5	425	455	487	525	562	600	642	687	735	790	Continued growth at 7% a year
brandy	890.7	952	1020	1090	1170	1250	1340	1430	1530	1640	1750	
Le Duc												
Market share	29	29	29	39	29	29	29	29	29	29	29	Market share
Sales turnover	115.2	123	132	142	152	163	174	186	198	214	229	profit margin and
Profit margin	24.4	24	24	24	24	24	24	24	24	24	24	tax at similar
Profit	29.0	29.5	31.5	34.0	36.5	39.0	42.0	44.5	47.5	51.5	55.0	levels to the
Tax	14.6	14.5	15.7	17.0	18.2	19.5	21.0	22.2	23.7	25.7	25.7	past decade
Le Baron												
Market share	10.5	10.5	10.5	10.5	10.5	10.5	10.5	10.5	10.5	10.5	10.5	As above
Sales turnover	92.1	100	107	114	122	131	140	150	161	172	184	but tax
Profit margin	21.4	21.5	21.5	21.5	21.5	21.5	21.5	21.5	21.5	21.5	21.5	holiday ends
Profit	19.7	21.5	23.0	24.5	26.2	28.0	30.0	32.2	34.5	37.0	39.5	in 1972
Tax	–	–	11.5	12.2	11.0	14.0	15.0	16.0	17.2	18.5	19.7	
La Duchesse												
Market share	3.2	3.4	3.6	3.7	3.7	3.8	3.8	3.9	3.9	4.0	4.0	Market share
Sales turnover	29.1	32.3	36.7	40	43	47	51	56	60	66	70	rises slowly to 4.0%
Profit margin	7.2	10	20	24	24	24	24	24	24	24	24	Profit margin rises
Profit	2.1	3.2	7.3	9.6	10.3	11.2	12.2	13.4	14.6	15.8	16.8	rapidly to 24%
Tax	–	–	–	–	–	–	–	–	5.5	7.9	8.4	Tax holiday ends in 1978
Total after tax profit	36.1	39.7	34.6	37.9	43.8	44.7	48.2	51.9	50.2	52.2	55.5	P/E ratio falls
Dividend	20	20	20	22	22	22	25	25	25	25	27	as earnings
Price/Earnings Ratio	15	13	12	12	12	12	11	10	10	11	11	level out due
Stock Market capitalization	540	515	415	450	515	535	525	520	500	570	610	to end of tax holidays
Dividend due to Louis	6.7	6.7	6.7	7.3	7.3	7.3	8.3	8.3	8.3	8.3	9.0	
Value of Louis shares	180	170	140	150	170	178	175	175	166	190	203	

Exhibit 102.9 F₀ forecast for Louis' companies 1970-1980

Fr million	1970	1971	1972	1973	1974	1975	1976	1977	1978	1979	1980	Assumptions
Paladin												
Turnover	14·8	17·0	18·0	19·5	21·0	22·5	24·0	26·0	27·5	29·5	32·0	Market share
Variable costs	8·0	10·0	10·7	11·7	12·6	13·5	14·5	15·5	16·5	17·5	19·0	rises to 4.0%
Advertising	8·2	5·0	5·0	5·3	5·5	6·0	6·0	6·5	7·0	7·5	8·0	
Profit	−1·4	2·0	2·3	2·5	2·9	3·0	3·5	4·0	4·0	4·5	5·0	
Ostienne												
Turnover	4·9	5·5	5·9	6·3	6·7	7·2	7·7	8·2	8·8	9·4	10·0	Sales
Variable costs	2·6	2·9	3·1	3·3	3·5	3·8	4·1	4·4	4·7	5·0	5·3	turnover
Advertising	1·0	1·0	1·1	1·2	1·3	1·3	1·4	1·4	1·5	1·5	1·6	rising by
Profit	1·3	1·6	1·7	1·8	1·9	2·1	2·2	2·4	2·6	2·9	3·1	7% p.a. from 1971
Paris office costs	2·7	3·7	4·0	4·2	4·4	4·6	4·8	5·1	5·4	5·7	6·0	Cost inflation at 5% and build up of staff in 1969-71
Total profit	−2·8	−0·1	0·0	0·1	0·4	0·5	0·9	1·3	1·2	1·7	2·1	Tax exemption
Tax	0	0	0	0	0	0	0	·1	·5	·8	1·0	in 1973-77
Earnings	−2·8	−0·1	0	0·1	0·4	0·5	0·9	1·2	0·7	0·9	1·1	after early losses
P/E ratio	0			5	5	5	5	5	7	7	7	
Stock market capitalization	1	1	1	0·5	2·0	2·5	4·5	5·0	5·0	6·0	7·7	

Exhibit 102·10   F₀ forecast of Louis' wealth 1970-1980

Fr millions	1970	1975	1980
Apartment block in Toulouse (assumes appreciation in value at 7% p.a.)	9	12·5	18
Equity Portfolio (assumes 7% growth in capital value plus investment of all Louis' annual surplus income—see Exhibit 102·5)	1	24	94
Private home	1	1·4	2
Paladin and Ostienne (see Exhibit 102·9)	1	2·5	7·7
Share of Delibes Latour (see Exhibit 102·8)	180	178	203
Totals (i.e. the F₀ forecast)	192	220	322

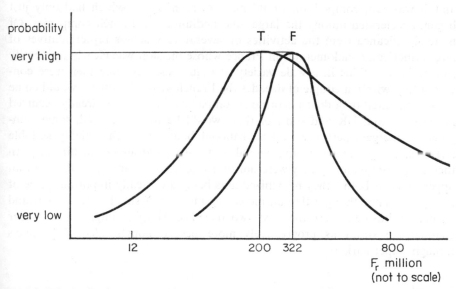

Exhibit 102·11   Performance–risk gap analysis for Louis in 1980

The internal appraisal

In listing their strengths and weaknesses they recognized that, except for one or two leading employees in the Paris office, the 'internal appraisal' referred to themselves and their own personal strengths and weaknesses as a team. The first fact on which they agreed was that, as an autonomous team they were untried as businessmen although there was more than enough evidence that they were a highly competent marketing team. Their knowledge of the alcohol market in France was possibly unrivalled. The family name was well known in the industry and in financial circles and they could count themselves as one of the most influential business families in France. But they totally lacked any detailed knowledge of production, transport, purchasing of raw materials or any of the physical side of a business. All their business knowledge was related to a large company (except for their experience in the past year); Louis had built up considerable knowledge of finance, François knew something of the alcohol market in Spain. Finally their existing company was very small but they had links, now rather tenuous and strained, with a very large company in which, of course, the vast bulk of their wealth was still invested.

The external appraisal

Competitors

There were thousands of small family businesses in the alcohol industry in France most of which were only of local significance. Of those operating nationally only a very few had really understood the marketing approach and most continued merely to sell. However there were signs that this was changing and, it was felt, competition would increase as mergers, which had only just begun, accelerated among the large and medium-sized French companies. Of more significance were the activities of several very senior representatives of large American conglomerates in France whose mission was clearly to identify suitable acquisitions in a wide variety of industries. All three men were convinced that within a couple of decades the French alcohol industry would come to be dominated by a dozen enormous companies, just as had already occurred in the USA and UK and some of these would be foreign owned, some composed of mergers across European national boundaries. One highly suitable target for merger or acquisition would be Delibes, Latour but at this stage in their corporate planning they were not sure whether this fact was a threat or an opportunity or both – they recognized it as being a critically important piece of the jigsaw. They thought that an increasing number of small companies would go out of business over the next two decades. Margins might come under considerable strain as progressively more people bought alcohol products through supermarkets.

Political

They believed that the political situation in France presented them with by far the most severe threat. A very large minority of the population regularly voted Communist and, they believed, the severe unrest of 1968 heralded a major swing towards the Left, or, to be more precise, away from capitalism. They considered that this threat existed throughout the world as evidenced by the increasing volume of legislation against companies, rising taxes on the wealthy, the pressure for redistribution of wealth as between both people and nations – and so on.

They assumed that alcohol would attract a growing burden of taxes and duties and become the subject of restrictive legislation on alcohol itself – the breathalyser would be introduced into France before long, they concluded – or on its advertisement or sale to young people.

Economic

Louis expected there would be a prolonged period of economic expansion in Europe but that this was certain to be punctuated by setbacks lasting for up to two or three years – the first of these, he felt, might well come in 1971. Over the long term, however, it was thought that living standards in France would continue to rise at 5% a year leading to a continually rising demand (probably growing at 7% a year) for high-margin wine products and a gradual decline in demand for low-margin wine products and cheap wine.

World trade would continue to grow faster than the economies of most nations were growing. Tariffs would decline in Europe and, more slowly, elsewhere but imports of wine into France (from Algeria, for example) would continue to be restricted.

Social

There would be a gradual but perceptible trend towards the internationalization of tastes and habits in Europe; the wine-drinking nations would drink more beer, the beer-drinking nations more wine. These trends were already evident, especially in the UK. The universal movement of population into towns, together with the increased stresses of urban living could well inflate demand for alcohol and tobacco to a level far above the 7% per annum growth rate; but, on the other hand demand for these traditional palliatives might fall if new ones, namely marijuana and others, became widely accepted. It was also conceivable, but only just, that social attitudes to alcohol might become positively hostile in France.

Technology

It was already technically possible to manufacture almost any alcoholic beverage almost entirely in the chemical laboratory. Louis believed that synthetic aperitifs were just around the corner but François pointed to the increasing pressure upon the Food and Drugs Administration in the USA and elsewhere to slow down the sale of synthetic materials for human consumption. Against that, argued Louis, the English chemical company, ICI was seriously proposing to market a synthetic tobacco – and, of course, many soft drinks made entirely synthetically had been on sale for years. François said that the French government, above all others in Europe, would protect the wine-growers against this threat – and, in any case, so long as they, the Latour family, kept away from heavy investment in production facilities, this threat was irrelevant.

There was general agreement that there would shortly be major advances in bulk liquid transport, in new types of bottle, more efficient bottling and handling plant and so on, but all these technical advances, while they might well affect the size, layout and location of factories and warehouses, were not of strategic significance.

The cruciform chart

The internal and external appraisals were summarized in the cruciform chart shown as Exhibit 102·12. The figures in brackets after each item represent an attempt by François to grade the items in order of strategic importance; thus (10) indicates an item of paramount significance which must be taken into full account by any proposed strategy – a strategy that failed to deal with the political threat to capitalism in France would be useless, for example. An item marked (1), however, was considered to be only bordering on the strategic and might be dealt with tactically or by some minor modification to the main strategy.

Exhibit 102·12   Cruciform Chart for Louis

Strengths	Weaknesses
Louis, Francois and Georges as a marketing team (8)	Louis, Francois and Georges untried as autonomous business team (3)
Their very considerable knowledge of the French alcohol market (8)	No knowledge of the physical side of business (6)
Well connected in financial circles (7)	No control over Fr 180m in Delibes, Latour (10)
Well known in alcohol industry (7)	Paladin and Ostienne very small (3)
Slight knowledge of alcohol industry in Spain (2)	Only Fr 10m available for investment (8)
Links with Delibes, Latour (9)	

Threats	Opportunities
Future domination by a few large companies (8)	Many family firms will disappear (6)
Increasing rate of mergers among competitors (6)	Only a few competitors really understand modern marketing methods (5)
Acquisitive American conglomerates (5)	Acquisitive American conglomerates (5)
Delibes, Latour as a merger victim (9)	Delibes, Latour as merger partner (9)
Profit margins under strain (7)	Prolonged period of economic growth in E.E.C. (6)
Anti-capitalist legislation (10)	Demand for high margin consumer products may grow by 7% p.a. (6)
Anti-alcohol taxes and legislation (6)	Ditto-may grow very much faster (3)
Economic and business cycle (5)	Exports (5)
Demand for alcohol reduced by drugs (1)	Internationaliaztion of tastes and drinking habits (7)
Synthetic alcohol products (4)	Reduction of tariffs and quotas (3)
All other technological changes (0)	
Imports (5)	
Reduction of tariff and quotas (3)	

The strategic structure

When Louis moved to Paris in 1969 and launched his new companies he had intended to build up an alcohol business of such a size that it might one day even rival the size of Delibes, Latour.

This plan was possibly impractical from the start but, more important, it led to a company the strategic structure of which would essentially have been *a very large French company manufacturing and selling alcohol products in France.*

At some stage during the appraisals it became increasingly clear that this structure was inappropriate and a quite different structure emerged as being far more suitable. The outstanding features of this structure would include (a) less reliance on alcohol, (b) more international, (c) very large indeed (d) marketing, as opposed to production, orientated. The factors leading to these conclusions were as follows:

(a) less reliance on alcohol
  1 Alcohol is not 'socially worthwhile'
  2 Profit margins will come under strain
  3 Anti-alcohol taxes and legislation
  4 Competition from drugs
  5 Synthetic alcohol products.
(b) more international
  1 Anti-capitalist legislation in France
  2 Economic and business cycle in France
  3 Import and export growth
  4 Internationalization of taste and habits
  5 Reduction of tariff and quota restrictions.
(c) very large indeed
  1 One of the ethological objectives
  2 Possibility of domination by a few huge companies
  3 Capital potentially available is very large
  4 Increasing rate of mergers.
(d) marketing, not production, orientated
  1 Their considerable skill in marketing
  2 Their weakness in production know-how
  3 Lack of competitors' knowledge of marketing
  4 Technological change may render production facilities obsolete
  5 Synthetic alcohol products.

The bare bones of the strategic structure of the proposed company were now becoming apparent as far as finance, management and activities were concerned; equally important, it was becoming clear that certain elements in the company's eventual structure need not be decided; one of these was their production facilities, another the distribution network, another was research and development – all of these, it was agreed, should only be determined at a much later stage. It was now necessary to fill out and quantify the financial, management and activity aspects of the very crude strategic structure shown in Exhibit 102·13.

The financial structure

It had to be assumed that Louis would be able by some means eventually to

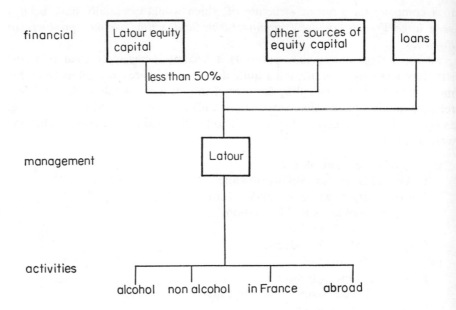

Exhibit 102·13   Proposed strategic structure

regain control over his capital invested in Delibes, Latour et Cie. Assuming he then controlled Fr 200m he could find another equity partner or group of partners to invest a further Fr 200m. This partner could be the Delibes and Cardine families, one of several other wealthy families (one of whom Louis had already approached), a French company, a foreign company, a bank. However, one of their objectives (No. 7 in Exhibit 102·7) called for marketability of their shareholding and this would be most readily obtained by a public subscription and quotation on a stock market – not necessarily on the French Bourse. They were advised that the public might well put up a further Fr 600m and possibly very much more if, at the time of the flotation, the proposed company could demonstrate a convincing record. A further Fr 200m would be forthcoming as long term loans from a bank.

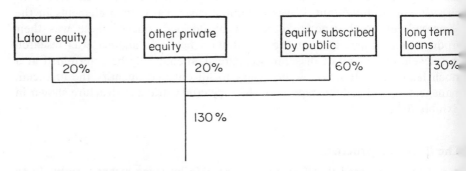

Exhibit 102·14 Proposed financial structure

This would leave Louis with a 20% share in the equity of the company and this, to judge by other similar companies in Europe would be enough to ensure his management control (perhaps through a cascade of holding companies) providing he showed reasonable competence. This financial structure is shown in Exhibit 102·14; it will be observed that the figures have been given as percentages of the total equity value of the company. This emphasizes Louis' belief that this financial structure was broadly correct *regardless of the eventual size of the company.*

The management structure

The board of the proposed company would be composed of shareholder representatives (including Louis) of which the Chairman would later be a distinguished independent industrialist. François and Georges would be joint managing directors, Louis himself taking the role of corporate planner (by the time a formal structure became necessary Louis would be near retirement). They resolved to maintain only a very small headquarters staff whose duties would consist only of searching for new projects, monitoring existing activities and

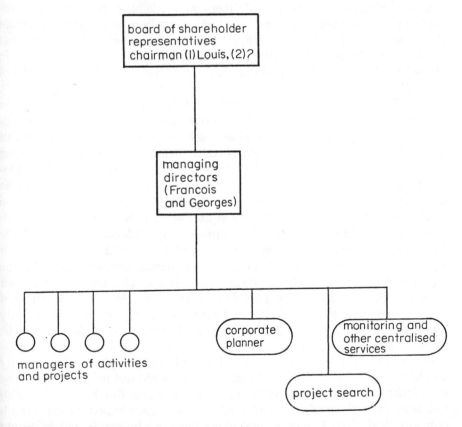

Exhibit 102·15   Proposed management structure

providing those very few specialist services that could only be provided by headquarters. Everything that could be delegated to the managing directors of the various activities would be delegated (in accordance with objective No. 11 Exhibit 102·7). These conclusions are shown in Exhibit 102·15; at this stage they considered that no detail other than that shown need be decided.

The structure of activities

They had decided that there were to be four main categories of activity; alcohol, non-alcohol, in France and abroad. It was necessary now to decide approximately in what proportion their capital should be invested in each category and also to spell out the nature of the non-alcohol products or services and to identify the non-French nations.

They first decided that by 1980 approximately 30% of their investment should be placed in non-alcohol products. This figure was felt to be appropriate because the threats to alcohol were not considered to be severe or immediate or even highly probable; indeed, were it not for George's quite strong feelings about alcohol they might well have selected a lower figure. However they would not have selected a figure lower than 10% in any case because this implied too limited a diversification to provide them with adequate experience of non-alcohol products if the need to move out of alcohol became pressing and urgent during the 1980s. In selecting this figure they also had in mind the decision that a comparatively small proportion of their capital assets would be tied up in alcohol production facilities and that they could therefore move out of alcohol relatively rapidly if the need arose.

They decided that not more than 40% of their capital should be invested in France at any time. The rationale behind this figure was as follows. If the anti-capitalist legislation that they feared so much was enacted it could take any of several forms, any of which could effectively result in their property being confiscated or subjected to a forced sale. While the probability of such legislation being enacted or even threatened was low, the consequences would be so severe that, Louis felt, it must be seriously considered now – to leave action until the threat actually materialized was useless since the slightest hint of such a possiblity would depress the value of property of all kinds in France. While the value of property owned by wealthy capitalists would fall in France, it would not fall abroad unless other nations were simultaneously confiscating the property of their wealthy classes. Furthermore, it would be much more difficult for a French government to confiscate property owned by a French citizen if the property was not physically in France – especially if certain perfectly legitimate and ethical legal devices were used such as ownership via trusts, bearer bonds, nominees and so on.

Louis argued that if it became the will of the French people that his property should be confiscated then, as a Frenchman, he would feel no resentment if he had to surrender 10% or 20% of his wealth to the nation. But, he felt, his wealth had been honestly made, he had made a valid contribution to the French economy, had given France several of its favourite beverages and he would resent it, very strongly, if he was asked to surrender more than 30% or 40% of his wealth to the nation. François and Georges were in total agreement – François adding that if France introduced confiscatory legislation of this sort Italy would not be far behind and that the 40% limit should apply to France and Italy together. This limitation also covered the threat from possible economic cycles in France; in spite of the gathering effect of the economic fusion of Europe within the Community each nation appeared to be still subject to individual business cycles and a policy of diversification among the nations of Europe was justified for this reason as well as an escape from possible confiscation. These decisions allowed the desired strategic structure to be further defined as shown in Exhibit 102·16. It is interesting to compare this with the present structure of Louis' wealth as shown in Exhibit 102·17.

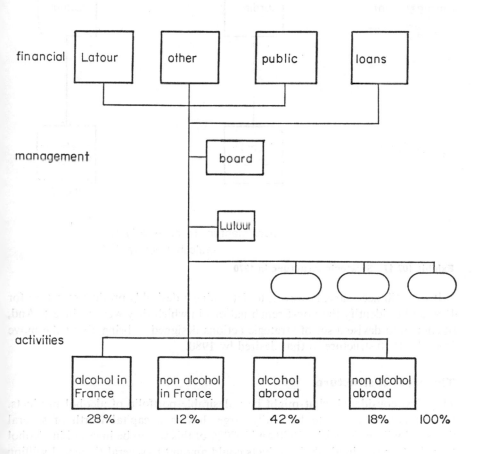

Exhibit 102·16 Further details of proposed strategic structure

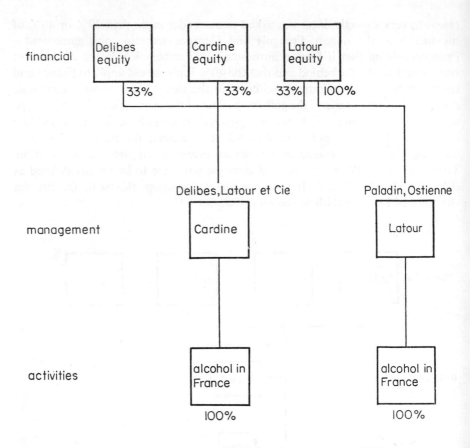

Exhibit 102·17   Strategic structure in 1970

It was still necessary, however, to determine a desirable product structure for 1980 and to identify the non-French nations in which they were to invest. And, of course, to devise a set of strategic actions designed to bring about the move from the 1970 structure to that desired by 1980.

The product structure

They first considered what might be a desirable portfolio of alcohol products. If their company was to be really large, having a capital worth of several thousand million francs by 1980 and if 70% of this was to be invested in alcohol then the turnover in alcohol products could amount to several thousand million francs – several times larger than the turnover of Fr 500m they had predicted for Delibes, Latour in 1980 (see Exhibit 102·8) and representing as much as 1% of the entire alcohol industry of the Common Market by 1980. While their portfolio of products would doubtless include a number of minor products, such as Ostienne, especially in the early years, they decided that it should consist mainly of products capable of selling at a turnover of several hundred million francs. They did not believe that the market could accommodate very many new products of this magnitude and this pointed to growth by merger – a conclusion confirmed by their relative lack of knowledge of the alcohol market outside France. It further indicated that, as a matter of policy, they should seek to acquire only fairly large, well-established companies having at least one major product line of national significance. Their managements should be capable of continuing to run these companies because they would retain considerable autonomy in accordance with Objective No. 11.

They decided to bear in mind the possibility of building up one of these products of national importance into one of international significance – the success of Martini, Cointreau, Drambuie and others was an object-lesson to them. One candidate for such treatment might well be Le Duc. They further decided to acquire only those alcohol products having a rate of gross margin similar to Le Duc, Le Baron and Paladin of approximately 40% or more and not to include cheap wines, low priced beers and so on in their portfolio. This decision was based on their strength in marketing such high-margin products; on the opportunity presented by rising standards of living; and on the consideration that these products, being in the higher price range, were less liable to 'unintentional misuse'. Finally they decided that they would be particularly interested to acquire any company selling a high-margin wine-based product in any beer-drinking nation or a high-margin beer in a wine-drinking nation. Thus they would search for a company selling lager, for example, in Spain (where consumption of beer was 30 litres per head per year and wine 60 litres) or in Italy (10 litres and 120 litres respectively) and for a company selling wine or wine products in England (consumption of beer 100 litres and wine only 3 litres) or in Germany (beer 130 litres and wine 20 litres). It should be noted that their accent was on companies selling these products, not necessarily producing them; merchants, distributors, retailers and importers were, they felt, even more legitimate targets for acquisition than manufacturers.

In summary their strategy for alcohol products was:
(a) only high-margin products;
(b) some wine or wine-based products in beer-drinking nations;
(c) some high-margin beers in wine-drinking nations;
(d) one or two products of national significance in each nation;
(e) One of these to be of potential international significance;
(f) growth mainly by acquisition of established importers, distributors etc.

Turning to non-alcoholic products and services, their outstanding strength in marketing suggested that any diversification should be into high-margin consumer goods selling to the same socio-economic sectors of the population as the alcohol products. The list of possible goods and services was almost endless and included cigars, delicatessen, cocktail snacks, cosmetics, antiques, education services, health farms, leisure and sports goods, proprietary pharmaceuticals, soft drinks, all forms of urban escape such as recreation parks, packaged holidays – and so on. Unfortunately, as there was no item in their list of strengths to indicate which of all these alternatives would be most appropriate, no criterion could be used to make the choice and their existing distribution network was an unsuitable vehicle for any of them. In view of the risks inherent in their ignorance, all these diversification options would be risky and should therefore (a) be on a small scale initially, (b) should be launched in France initially *not* abroad and (c) should be undertaken by means of acquiring companies already well established in any of these fields and not by launching new products. If one of these alternatives was more relevant than another it was that related to soft drinks which at least had something in common with alcoholic drinks.

The geographical structure

They felt that they ought only to invest capital in a nation if (1) that nation was unlikely to be hostile to private capital, (2) was likely to be politically stable (3) was likely to experience a prolonged consumer boom without severe intermittent down-turns (4) where the standard of living was already high (5) where television and other advertising media exists. At this stage all that was required to be decided was which nations were unsuitable so that a market research study could be mounted in the nations not eliminated. But first they briefly discussed whether any nations outside Europe should be considered.

They eliminated Africa, South America, the Middle East, the Far East and the communist bloc on grounds of political instability or distance. The United States was, they felt, ideal in all respects except that the art of marketing there surpassed their own skills. Australasia was ideal except only that it was too distant.

Turning to Europe they attempted to rank each nation according to how it measured up to the criteria listed above. On attitude to private capital they classified Sweden and Britain as hostile, with Switzerland, Luxemburg, Italy, Spain, Portugal, Turkey and Greece as favourable. They based this ranking on figures published in 1967 by the Statistical Office of the European Communities for the distribution of national income – see Exhibit 102·18. As for political

Exhibit 102·18

Country	Percentage of National Income going to private households from property and entrepreneurship
Sweden	15·5
U.K.	18·5
Switzerland	27·4
Luxemburg	29·7
Italy	37·5
Spain	36·1
Portugal	?
Turkey	?
Greece	?

stability, they considered that France, Italy, Greece and Spain were unstable, while Portugal, Finland, Turkey and Germany were potentially unstable over the next decade. As to economic growth they used the figures shown in Exhibit 102·19 to supplement their subjective opinion that, except Britain, virtually all

Exhibit 102·19

Country	Average annual growth of GNP at constant prices	
%	1956-6	1961-66
Germany	6·0	4·3
France	4·5	5·4·
Italy	6·4	4·9
Netherlands	4·1	4·9
Belgium	2·9	4·7
Greece	6·1	7·4
Turkey	3·5	6·6
U.K.	3·1	3·0
Norway	3·5	4·7
Sweden	3·9	4·4
Denmark	5·5	4·4
Switzerland	4·3	4·4
Austria	5·1	4·1
Portugal	4·7	6·3
Finland	5·2	4·1

the European nations would grow at 5% a year. They considered all the nations to have sufficiently high standards of living to provide useful mass markets for high-margin consumer goods except possibly Spain and Portugal and certainly Greece and Turkey, which not yet having broken through the subsistence level might become useful markets in the 1980s. As for advertising media, Exhibit 102·20 shows the number of television sets per head and suggests that only Portugal, Spain, Greece and Turkey are not ready to accept sophisticated advertising techniques.

Exhibit 102·20

Country	TV sets per 1000 population
Germany	212
France	150
Italy	130
Netherlands	189
Belgium	166
Luxemburg	109
Greece	—
Turkey	—
U.K.	256
Norway	152
Sweden	278
Denmark	239
Switzerland	128
Austria	115
Portugal	25
Finland	177
Spain	—

The nation to emerge best from this study was Switzerland with Norway, Austria, Belgium, Portugal and Germany coming high up on the list; lower down were Italy, Netherlands, Sweden, France and Denmark; at the bottom were Greece, Turkey, Spain, Britain and Finland. One of the implications of this list was that a market research study might be justified to search for opportunities in the top six nations but not in the bottom six. Another implication was that any project proposed for Italy or France would have to be carried out without committing any of Louis' capital and would therefore have to be a franchized or licensed operation. But it was appreciated that this exercise did not eliminate the bottom six nations entirely for some of them might well appear attractive for specific projects. Thus a project in Spain might provide a high return on capital but with a high risk, while one in Britain a low return and low risk. Judging from the performance-risk gap analysis (Exhibit 102·11) they were not looking for low risk projects because there was already a very good chance of achieving a modest increase in their wealth.

The missing piece

At this point Louis, François, and Georges agreed that the strategic structure in Exhibit 102·16 was broadly correct and that they were fully confident, even without any further study, that they could find a sufficient number of suitable companies to acquire having the desired range of products in suitable nations to achieve their long term aim of quadrupling their wealth by 1980. They happened to know of a company in Germany manufacturing soft drinks that was being offered for sale; they knew its turnover, profit margin, the quality of the managers and so on and it fitted well into their strategic structure. They also knew of an alcohol company in Portugal of just the right specification to fit into their plans. They were convinced that many such companies existed in Europe and that they could not only purchase them but successfully employ their marketing expertise to develop the sales of their product range. But none of these purchases could be made unless they somehow obtained control over Louis' capital in Delibes, Latour.

They had thought that there were two means by which this could be achieved; either to find some way of taking their capital out or to put enough additional capital in to gain full control. But both these strategies had severe disadvantages; nor was it at all clear how either could be achieved. The first alternative, that of extracting their money, had the disadvantage that they would then have no control over Delibes, Latour; even though he held only 33·3% of the company's shares Louis was still able to influence the activities of Denis and Pierre. Louis knew that Denis was unwilling to take any major decision without first obtaining Louis' approval and relations between the two men were still friendly if no longer close. But if Louis sold out, his control over the company would be wholly lost and Denis might then adopt a policy for Delibes, Latour that could damage Louis' business interests; he might decide, for example, to merge with a competitor thus providing powerful additional competition to Louis. Nor was it clear to whom Louis might sell his shares in

Delibes, Latour; Denis had specifically refused to buy them and a 33·3% share was not a particularly attractive proposition to a third party or to the public.

As to the second course, that of buying a controlling interest in Delibes, Latour, this was also fraught with difficulties. In theory it could be achieved if, having borrowed Fr 90m from his bank, Louis was then able to persuade Denis and the Cardine brothers to sell him the necessary additional 17% of the company. Louis had ascertained that the bank would be willing to lend him this sum but was quite sure that none of the shareholders would sell – in particular he was sure that Denis would not be willing to lose control of Delibes, Latour thus undermining his position in the local community. Nevertheless this alternative, that of obtaining control of Delibes, Latour was clearly more relevant to the strategic structure they had selected for 1980 than the other alternative, that of selling out. If they could obtain control this would, at one stroke, virtually complete the 'alcohol in France' segment of activities shown in Exhibit 102·16.

Because this alternative was apparently so attractive Louis and François considered what steps would be necessary to bring it about. They devised the following outline:

Step 1   Louis to borrow Fr 92m;
Step 2   Purchase an additional 17% of Delibes, Latour for Fr 92m making a total of 50·3% in Louis' hands;
Step 3   Claim management control;
Step 4   Offer 60% of the company to the public for Fr 324 m, of which Fr 163m would be due to Louis;
Step 5   Louis repays Fr 92m loan leaving him with a 20% share in the company worth Fr 109m and Fr 71m in cash;
Step 6   Invest this cash outside France, transfer all other assets outside France leaving only the 20% share in Delibes, Latour in France.

As a result of the transfers in Step 6 only Fr 109m out of Louis's total assets of Fr 192m would then remain in France, but even so this represents 57% of his assets still in France compared with the target of 40%. However, Louis was convinced that the solution to the problem of his share in Delibes, Latour lay somewhere along these lines even though this calculation showed that this particular strategy had severe disadvantages. These may be summarized as follows: firstly, although it left Louis with only a 20% shareholding, barely enough to give him management control, it still only allowed him to reduce the proportion of his assets in France to 57%. Secondly, it assumed that all six steps would be taken in 1970 – 1970 valuations having been used throughout the calculations – but it was more likely to take as much as two years to complete. If the value of the company fell between Louis obtaining the loan from the bank but before he could repay it from the sale of his shares then he could make a capital loss of tens of millions of francs. Of course the public flotation could be underwritten by a merchant bank but the premium would have been enormous and this would not eliminate the risk that anti-capitalist legislation in France might occur before Step 6 had been completed.

Louis and his sons made a large number of calculations to test the various alternative ways in which they might gain control of Delibes, Latour so as to place them in a position to achieve the network of objectives they had set themselves (in my terminology they made a number of F_P forecasts) but failed to find any sequence of actions that could be taken without incurring a severe and

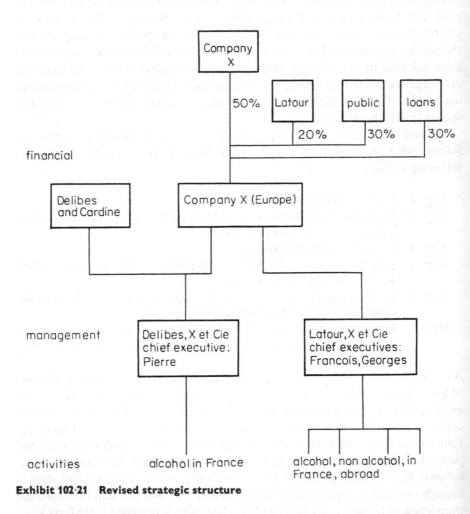

Exhibit 102·21   Revised strategic structure

unacceptable level of risk at some stage or other or one which would be acceptable to Denis and Pierre. As far as they could see there was only one event that might work in their favour, namely a severe economic turndown in 1971 leading to such difficulties that Denis would willingly sell out and Pierre would willingly relinquish management control. But neither was such an event very likely nor did Louis wish for it.

They then recognized that a third strategy might exist. Hitherto they had assumed that in order to obtain management control of their capital in Delibes, Latour, they must either extract their money to gain control or gain management control of the company and hence of their capital. It might be possible, they now argued, to achieve either of these by proxy; that is, by encouraging some third party to achieve these aims for them. If they could recognize Delibes, Latour as a valuable stepping stone towards the creation of a major international

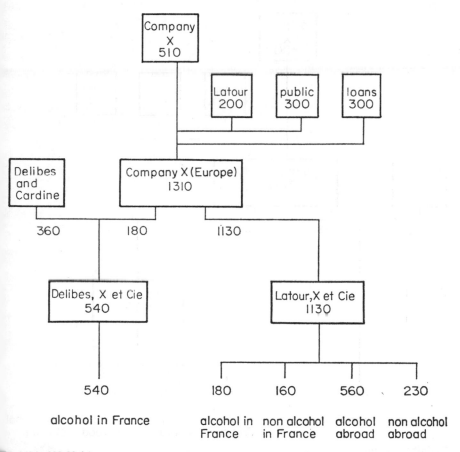

Exhibit 102·22 (a)
The figures show the proportion in which capital should be invested in the four groups of activity by Latour, X et Cie if Louis chosen proportions (see Exhibit 102.16) are to be achieved. Assumptions: (a) that Louis sells all his shares in Delibes, Latour to Company X for Fr 180m. (b) that he invests Fr 200m in Company X (Europe). (c) that the Delibes and Cardine families retain all their shares in Delibes, X et Cie. (d) that Company X takes 51% of the equity of Company X (Europe).
(All figures in Fr millions at 1970 market values)

ompany so, presumably, could anyone else with the same ambition. Furthermore, although Louis had left Delibes, Latour because he felt that it was not being managed with sufficient vigour or breadth of vision that criticism was valid only if it remained a single autonomous company; as part of a group, such as the one proposed for 1980 in Exhibit 102·16, it was already going to be almost large enough. The implication was that its existing management, who were determined to maintain the company's present structure, could be allowed to continue in office if it became part of a larger more diversified group. This also reduced, if not removed, one of the main barriers to any plan involving the acquisition of Delibes, Latour, namely the reluctance of Denis and Pierre to lose their positions of power in the company and the local community.

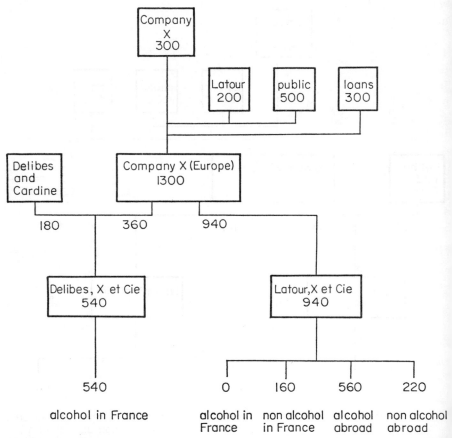

Exhibit 102·22 (b)
Assumptions as for 102·22 (a) except that Company X here takes only a 30% share in Company X (Europe) and the Delibes and Cardine families sell half their shares in Delibes, X et Cie. Under these assumptions Alphonse's chosen proportions can only be achieved if all the 'Alcohol in France' activity is carried out by Delibes, X et Cie.

The strategy that now occurred to Louis was as follows:

(a) Search for a company, either French or foreign, wishing to expand in the alcohol and high-margin consumer goods market in Europe.

(b) Suggest to this company, call it X, that it acquires a controlling interest in Delibes, Latour on the following terms: that Bertrand and Pierre sell approximately 20% of their holding to X and are appointed President and Managing Director respectively. That Louis sells his entire 33% holdings and resigns from all positions in the company. The company's name is changed to Delibes, X et Cie. That Denis and Pierre be allowed to continue to run the company as a stable, slowly growing source of profit from alcohol in France.

(c) that Louis takes a 20% share in a new company called Company X (Europe) with two wholly owned subsidiaries one of which will be Delibes, X et Cie and the other Latour, X et Cie.

(d) that Louis and his sons have management control of Latour, X et Cie with responsibility to carry through a programme of expansion in Europe to achieve approximately the structure shown in Exhibit 102·16.

The proposed strategic structure of X (Europe) is shown in Exhibit 102·21. It will be seen that although it differs somewhat from Exhibit 102·16, the differences are not significant – except that Louis is shown as having less than full management control because he would be answerable to the management of Company X; however he argued that unless he retained a fifty per cent holding in a company of which he was a manager he would be liable to control by other shareholders whether they exercised this control direct – as in Exhibit 102·16 or through the hierarchy of managers in a very large company as in Exhibit 102·21. This Exhibit shows the financial, management and activity structure of Company X (Europe).

Louis was now convinced that a strategic structure, sufficiently similar to Exhibit 102·16 to be satisfactory, was obtainable by these means. He calculated that the desired proportion of his wealth to be invested in the various activities could be achieved, regardless of whether Company X obtained a majority holding in Company X (Europe) or in Delibes, X et Cie or not. Exhibits 102·22(a) and (b) show that the desired proportions could be achieved in spite of a wide variation of shareholding ratios as between Company X and its various proposed subsidiaries in Europe. It was, of course, important for him to know the range within which the ratio of shareholdings was critical to the achievement of his objectives, because he was not in a position to know the opinion of either Denis or Company X as to their shareholding requirements nor even whether either of them would demand a clear majority.

The strategic action plan

Louis now felt that he should summarize all their decisions so far in an Action Plan which could then be evaluated against their agreed objectives and checked against the list of items in their internal and external appraisals.

The sequence of strategic actions now selected to bring about the proposed strategic structure was as follows:

1 To transfer all immediately available capital assets outside France and reinvest abroad through trusts or other legal means.

2 To search for a new product to sell through the existing network of agents selling Paladin; this product not necessarily to be an alcoholic beverage; it could well be a high-margin soft drink licensed from a manufacturer.

3 To search for a large company, preferably not French, willing to join Louis and his sons in acquiring Delibes, Latour and diversifying in Europe.

4 Continue searching for acquisition targets in Europe and developing the details of a corporate plan to put forward as a basis for discussion with Company X. This plan to contain four main sections:

(a) the various alternative detailed financial structures that would all be broadly similar to that shown in Exhibits 102·21 and 102·22.

(b) the various routes by which Delibes, Latour et Cie might be acquired including details of how Denis and Pierre could best be approached.

(c) the various detailed alternative organization structures including especially the voting strengths of the various shareholder representatives on the Board of Company X (Europe).

(d) a list of suitable acquisition targets in Europe according to the chart shown in Exhibit 102·23. In view of the suggested specification of some of these target companies (i.e. that they be fairly large, well established companies having at least one product line of national significance) it was assumed that many of them would be large family firms with earnings in the range Fr 5–20m.

Exhibit 102·23

Key

C=nations where operations may be financed by investing capital in fixed assets, land, property, offices, etc.
L=nations where operations must be financed largely by leasing licensing, factoring, etc.
P=postpone any operations for some years

Country	High margin wine based alcohol products	High margin non-wine alcohol products	High margin non-alcohol consumer products,
Sweden	—	—	—
U.K.	—	—	—
Norway	C	C	C
Netherlands	C	C	C
Denmark	C	C	C
Germany	L	—	L
Finland	L	L	L
Italy	—	L	L
Turkey	—	P	P
Austria	C	C	C
Belgium	C	C	C
France	—	—	L
Greece	—	P	P
Portugal	—	P	P
Switzerland	C	C	C
Luxemburg	C	C	C
Spain	—	P	P

Evaluation of proposed strategy

François and Georges did not consider that any further evaluation was necessary; they had sufficient confidence that the proposed strategic structure was both desirable and practical that no further formal or detailed calculations (or in my terminology F_P forecasts) were necessary. Louis agreed. They did, how ever, check through the lists of objectives and the items in the cruciform chart to ensure that the strategy took everything of importance into account. They concluded that the strategy did rely heavily upon their strengths and not on any known weaknesses which, on the contrary, it tended to correct and buttress. All the threats had been taken into account and they had made full use of the outstanding opportunities.* They felt that they now knew what they were trying to achieve and with considerable accuracy, where to look for the means.

Comment

It might be objected that this case is exceptional in two respects: firstly that its central feature is a dispute between two rival factions in what is virtually a family business, and secondly that it concerns an individual, Louis, starting a business from scratch with Fr 200m. Most companies, it may be said, do not have such problems. In my opinion these features are common, although they do not always occur in such an obvious form. Most companies have found themselves, at one time or another, at a strategic cross-roads with one group of executives urging one path and another group urging the opposite. Sometimes the board splits openly as in the above case, sometimes a compromise is possible. But in many such board-room rows the question before the company is a strategic one such as that faced by Delibes, Latour in 1969.

As to the second point – that companies do not normally start from scratch as Alphonse did – this is true but irrelevant. The central strategic problem facing any company is where to direct its cash flow and other resources such as top management skills. This was Louis's problem and the fact that his corporate plan consisted almost exclusively of new project specifications as opposed to project specifications plus operational objectives is merely one of proportion.

I should make some further comments. It is noteworthy that in this case Louis set up an alcohol company in Paris before deciding his objectives; having decided these he then saw that this company was not relevant to his objectives; much the same sequence was evident in Case 1 where Mr Pepper devised a strategy for Davies Engineering which was later seen to be irrelevant to the objectives that Mr Shine eventually formulated. I draw attention to this because one of the continuing debates among corporate planners concerns precisely this question: whether corporate objectives should be determined first and then a strategy devised to achieve them or whether this procedure should be reversed (see page 32 in Chapter 2) as recommended by some authorities such as the Stanford Research Institute. I hope it is clear why I disagree so strongly with this view.

It is also interesting to note that most of the information available to Louis and his sons was unreliable and unquantified. Few companies have the resources to gather reliable data on the scale required for their strategic decisions and therefore these decisions have to be taken in the knowledge that the

* In fact, they used a rather crude form of Pay-Off Table—see page 273—to do this evaluation.

data is unreliable. Thus Louis would have liked to know the rate at which the alcohol market in all the nations of Europe might grow over the next decade; he could have called for a detailed survey but the cost would have been prohibitive and the conclusions could have been invalidated by the eruption of some new unforeseen change in social attitudes or whatever. Thus the strategic structure for which he was searching, and which he believed he had found, was one that had to be robust against errors in his assumptions.

I believe this case also illustrates the folly of attempting to strive for ever-greater accuracy in setting targets and making forecasts. One of the aims that Louis and his sons set themselves was to quadruple their wealth in a decade; they fully recognized, however, that this objective was subjective, that although a figure had been attached to their ambitions it was not sacrosanct. Their aim was not to mulitply their wealth by 4·000 but by a factor of three or four or five – or even two or six. They were not even sure of Louis' current wealth; the figure of Fr 192m was known to be liable to an error of several tens of millions of francs. Nor was there any value in attempting to forecast the earnings for Delibes, Latour for 1980 to any greater degree of accuracy than that shown in Exhibit 102·8; this forecast could have been made with much greater attention to detail but all this would have shown was that Alphonse would not be able to achieve his target by this means – a fact fully illustrated by the relatively crude method of forecasting in Exhibit 102·8. (In much the same way Mr Meaney's forecast in Case 1 (see Exhibit 101·9), crude though it was, was perfectly adequate to show that Mr Shine's targets *could* have been achieved by this means). As Ewing says (Ch. 4), strategic planning is more qualitative than quantitative in nature.

I believe this case also illustrates how a strategic structure emerges with rapidly increasing clarity as the number of items in the appraisals rises. The bare bones of a possible structure were visible on page 171 when less than two dozen items were known and the details as to financial structure, product structure and geographical structure required no more than another dozen or so additional statements. And yet it is also clear that the structure as shown in Exhibit 102·16 is sufficiently detailed to allow Alphonse to decide that it is not worth looking for a better one; one should not, I believe, attempt to devise a corporate plan in any more detail than is required to make this important decision (see page 27). And yet there is certainly enough detail in this structure to show any senior executives working for Louis what proposed activities do and do not fit into the concept of the company. More than enough scope is thus allowed to the executives in which to exercise their initiative and to take advantage of any new opportunities as they may present themselves.

PART TWO

PART TWO

11 Target setting

Introduction

I believe all authors would agree that at some stage in the corporate planning process one must determine corporate objectives and set targets. Not all of them agree with my belief that corporate objectives should be set first, nor do they all agree with the distinction I make between an objective as being a purely qualitative statement while a target is the quantification of an objective. I think there is general agreement that a target must (a) unequivocally represent the wishes or requirements of the target setter so that those to whom the target is set know what results he wants them to achieve and (b) it must be capable of empirical verification so that all concerned may agree whether the target has or has not been achieved.

There are two unsolved problems here; one reflects the fact that very few people know what they want and, in particular, as discussed at length in Chapter 3, there is currently a major question mark over what people want companies to do for them. So there is this profound philosophical hurdle to clear first – but this cannot be discussed again in this chapter. Secondly there is the purely technical difficulty of selecting a figure or set of figures that unequivocally and verifiably reflect whatever it is that people do want from companies – and this will be discussed in this chapter.

In this chapter, then, I shall list and discuss a number of methods of quantifying corporate objectives; I shall deal with both financial and ethological target setting for corporate bodies and also with several methods of setting targets to subsidiary companies. I must again make it quite clear that in my opinion there is a massive logical distinction between corporate objectives and objectives for subsidiaries or parts of corporate bodies. Corporate objectives are the starting point in corporate planning; objectives for subsidiaries can only be set when the strategic structure of the corporate body has been determined – corporate objectives and targets are the starting point; objectives and targets for parts or subsidiaries are the end point in corporate planning.

This chapter is in three parts, then; financial targets for companies as corporate bodies, ethological targets for corporate bodies and targets for parts of corporate bodies.

1 Corporate financial targets

In this section I consider most of the better-known indicators used to measure overall company performance.

Return on capital employed

Return on Capital Employed (ROCE) has been used as the top financial objective for companies throughout the world for many decades. Its use has, however, declined very considerably over the past two or three decades and it has been largely superseded by other more specifically financial, as opposed to accountancy, measures. Because it is still used by some companies it may be worth while listing some of the difficulties associated with it. ROCE may be defined as the profit before tax made by a company during a given period expressed as a percentage of the capital employed at the end of that period. Thus if a company makes a profit of $274,128 in 1973 and if the capital employed on 31 December 1973 (i.e. the date on which its financial year ends) amounts to $2,993,071 then the ROCE for that year would have been approximately 9·2%.

The difficulties associated with ROCE include the following:

1 Because the capital employed is calculated for one instant of time, chance variations in stock levels, for example, may inflate or deflate the figure. This may not normally be of great consequence except in highly cyclical industries; thus if two retail organizations wish to compare their ROCE they may be unable to do so meaningfully if the financial year of one of them ends in June and the other in January.

2 No definition of either profit or capital employed has been universally agreed even within the accountancy profession of one nation let alone internationally. This means that when a company is aiming to achieve the average ROCE for its industry (a very common corporate objective – see Payne Ch. 3) great difficulty is encountered in estimating what this average may be.

3 Even if these definitions were agreed each company may wish to pursue different policies as regards depreciation, leasing and so on. This makes it difficult to relate ROCE between companies pursuing different policies and difficult to relate ROCE of the same company over a period of years during which changes in policy have been made.

4 It is questionable whether any measure of success for a company that neglects the effect of taxation is meaningful in an era when tax on profits is as much as 50%.

5 It could be argued that when a company revalues its assets upwards the company is somehow better off than if it had to revalue downwards; and yet an upwards revaluation often results in a decline in ROCE.

6 Even if these technical problems could be solved – and the accountancy professions in several nations are making efforts to harmonize definitions, etc. – there is still the problem of selecting a suitable target figure for a company. Should one select a target ROCE for the next, say, five years which is an

average of the company's past five years ROCE? Or average out the ROCE for the company's competitors? If the latter, how does one identify which competitors are relevant – for most companies today operate in more than one field of business and in more than one segment of a market?

7 Of the companies that do use ROCE as the prime or sole corporate target, some aim to achieve the average ROCE for their industry, others aim to improve ROCE over a period of years. Where their ROCE is low this latter may well be a useful aim; so far as I know, however, no company has ever adopted the aim of reducing ROCE – not even companies whose ROCE is already as high as 40% or more. Figures as high as this may indicate either that the company is extremely profitable – in which case one strategy would be to expand its activities rapidly, probably using loan capital to finance this – or that the assets are undervalued or heavily written down due to obsolescence and in this case a possible strategy would be to renew these assets. But all these entirely sensible actions would result in the decline of the company's ROCE. One difficulty, then, is that although there is general agreement that a company's ROCE can be too low, there is much less recognition that it can also be too high and no agreement at all as to what figure represents the optimum.

8 Some companies use ROCE as the prime corporate target jointly with a rate of growth target. Two problems are associated with this common device. Firstly it is difficult to see by what criteria any pair of figures may be selected: is a ROCE of 15% with a growth target of 15% 'better' than, say, a ROCE target of 20% coupled with a growth target of 10%? Is 15% and 10% better than 10% and 15%?

The second problem is the question of mathematical compatibility. Take a company with a capital employed of $1000 and assume a 20% ROCE; its profits before tax will therefore be $200 per annum. Taxation will reduce this to $100, say, and dividends of, say, $70 will be paid out. Only $30 will be retained for growth and all things being equal, growth will therefore amount to 3% per annum. Thus, in this case, a ROCE of 20% is compatible only with a growth of 3%. Now suppose this company wishes to achieve a ROCE target of 20% coupled with a growth target of 10%; with the ratios assumed above (tax at 50%, dividend ratio at 70%) these targets are incompatible. They could be made compatible by altering one or more of these ratios or by accepting some loan capital. In other words ROCE is linked to growth via tax, dividends, gearing and so on and to render ROCE and growth targets compatible a sequence of other decisions may have to be made. But which decision is the prime one – the ROCE target, the growth target, the dividend policy, gearing? Are they all equal in priority or is there some other corporate objective, not included in these calculations, that is more fundamental than all of them?

To conclude: ROCE is essentially a short term management ratio – and as such its value is unquestionable, in spite of the technical difficulties associated with its accurate estimation. What is in question, however, is whether it can be said to represent the really fundamental long term corporate aim of any company. In my opinion, it is questionable whether it should ever be used as a starting point (or joint starting point) in any corporate target setting exercise.

Multiple targets

Some companies make it a practice to set a number of targets to represent the corporate objective. Typically these include profits, sales, dividends, margin on sales and other salient management ratios – in one case I know, no less than seventeen such ratios were used. There is one particular difficulty with multiple targets.

Every figure selected as a target represents a decision. Now the corporate planning process is nothing if it is not a system for taking strategic decisions. The greater the number of targets set as aims to be achieved by the corporate plan the fewer are the decisions that remain to be made by and within the planning process itself and the greater the extent to which its strategic decision-making system is preempted and redundant. (I am here merely re-stating the point made on page 37 relating to the words 'corporate objectives' being used as means and aims and the confusion that results therefrom).

Consider a company which has adopted the set of objectives in Exhibit 11·1.

Exhibit 11·1

1	2	3	4	5
Year	Sales Turnover $	Maximum Profit Goal $	Stockholders' Equity $	Dividend Payment $
0	24·0m	751000	9150000	500000
1	26·5m	937000	9777000	460000
2	29·0m	1172000	10374000	480000
3	31·6m	1466000	11038000	510000
4	34·0m	1813000	11791000	530000
5	36·0m	2219000	12549000	560000

I have taken these figures from Payne (Ch. 3); Payne says of these figures that 'this is the beginning of one company's long range plan. Everything that follows (in the plan) is a statement of corporate moves that will enable the company to meet its goals by the target date'. Now the figures in columns 4 and 5 may well represent the wishes of the shareholders and these may therefore be entirely legitimate inputs to the corporate planning process. In order to achieve these targets it may well have been necessary to achieve the profit figures in column 3; it should be noted, however, that while the dividends are required to rise by only ten per cent over the entire period, profits are required to more than double. Is this declining pay-out ratio a strategic decision or not? If it is, as I believe it to be, should it appear as an input to the corporate planning process or be decided by the process? It will also be observed that while profits are scheduled to grow at over 20% p.a., sales turnover is to rise at only 10%. Where should the decision be made to increase margins on sales by this 15% p.a. – before the corporate planning process, as apparently in this case, or during it? One is entitled to ask whether any consideration was given by this company to the alternative strategies of increasing turnover by 20% p.a. and leaving margins unchanged – or of increasing turnover by 15% and margins by 10%, or any other combination. By selecting this particular pattern of sales and margin targets this company appears to have precluded any high-volume low-margin marketing strategy.

The greater the number of targets used to specify what the corporate plan is to achieve the more is the corporate planning process constrained. In the case of the company that used seventeen ratios there was virtually nothing left to be decided. The targets employed were as shown in Exhibit 11·2.

Exhibit 11·2

operating profit as a percentage of operating assets
operating profit   ,,   ,,   ,,   sales
sales   ,,   ,,   ,,   ,, operating assets
production cost of sales   ,,   ,, sales
research costs as a percentage of sales
distribution costs   ,,   ,,   ,, sales
administrative costs   ,,   ,, sales
materials costs as a   ,,   ,, sales value of production
works labour costs ,,   ,,   ,, sales value of production
other production costs as a percentage of sales value of production
work subcontracted   ,,   ,, ,, sales value of production
current assets   ,,   ,, ,, sales
fixed assets   ,,   ,, ,, sales
land and buildings   ,,   ,, ,, sales
plant and machinery   ,,   ,, ,, sales
vehicles   ,,   ,, ,, sales
materials stock   ,,   ,, ,, sales
work in progress   ,,   ,, ,, sales
finished goods stock   ,,   ,, ,, sales
debtors   ,,   ,, ,, sales

Clearly, to set such a network of targets involves taking a large number of decisions, many of them strategic in nature, before the corporate planning process starts.

The question being raised here is whether such targets are inputs or outputs of the corporate planning process. If they are inputs, how are they determined, what criteria are used in their selection? I am suggesting that it may be dangerous to develop a corporate plan which is designed to achieve multiple targets – the more targets there are the more dangerous it is. As outputs from the corporate plan, multiple targets are not only useful and valid but, almost invariably, unavoidable; but, of course, as outputs they are targets to parts of the company, not corporate targets to the company as a whole.

Management ratios

Many companies use management ratios as corporate targets, ROCE (see above) being the most usual but, as illustrated in Exhibit 11·2 other management ratios appear, often in some profusion.

It is perhaps not surprising that management ratios are not satisfactory as long term corporate targets since their value lies in the function for which they have traditionally been used, namely as short term target and control tools for use by managers. In this role their value is unquestionable. Thus if a company's margin on sales is 10% and if it has been decided that no change shall be made in this ratio, then this figure may be set as a target to the relevant sales managers and their performance can be judged by making the necessary simple calculations at regular intervals. Providing that the strategic decision has been made not to alter the marketing strategy over the next x years then this same figure could be set as a long term target for x years ahead. The problem arises when the no-change decision cannot be made for then a new target figure has to be selected. On what basis should this new figure be determined? There are probably three methods in common use:

(a) A new figure may be chosen on the basis of hunch or experience or the personal opinion of a senior executive. If this occurs then the managers to whom the target is set will have to alter their strategy to achieve the target. As suggested above (see ROCE and Multiple Targets) this is tantamount to by-passing the corporate planning process.

(b) A new strategy may be devised in the light of the data collected during the internal and external appraisals and then a new target ratio selected to reflect the change. In this case the new ratio is used as a target to managers and their progress towards it may be monitored. But, in this usage it is not only the manager's progress that is being monitored but the progress towards the new strategy as well. In my opinion this is the correct role of management ratios in corporate planning – i.e. as indicators of the progress that managers are making towards the carrying out of a stategic decision.

(c) A third method of selecting management ratios as targets is to use some form of inter-firm comparison. Severe difficulties attend this method. One is the purely technical one of ensuring compatibility as between one company and another. One of the reasons that meaningful compatibility is so difficult to attain is that each company uses different accounting definitions – the same problem that bedevils the use of ROCE. Another reason is that no two companies *should* exhibit the same ratios. Thus a company that is growing rapidly will employ more people in its projects departments, its personnel departments, its marketing departments than a similar company not growing rapidly. Their relevant ratios will be different.

A further difficulty associated with selecting a management ratio as a target is this: Company X has a ratio of 7% for plant maintenance costs to sales turnover (i.e. it spends $7 on maintenance for every $100 sales) while all its competitors have a ratio of less than 5%. Does that necessarily imply that Company X should take the strategic decision to cut maintenance costs? I suggest that this is a wholly inadequate reason for making a strategic decision of this sort – or, indeed, any sort. (This example does, however, illustrate one of the valid uses of management ratios, namely in provoking enquiry as to why one's company's ratios differ from other companies.) Company X may be pursuing a policy of competition on quality while its competitors are competing on price in which case high plant maintenance costs ratios may merely indicate that this policy is being pursued. Such decisions should be made in the light of the appraisals rather than an inter-firm comparison exercise.

Even if the technical problem of comparability can be overcome, therefore, it is highly questionable whether management ratios should be used to set corporate objectives. Their usefulness as targets to managers, especially those in charge of parts of companies, is unquestioned, as is their value as indicators of progress and control. (See also page 222 for their role in cross-checking forecasts).

Profits

A number of authors (Ansoff (Ch. 3) and Ackoff (Ch. 2)) have pointed to the deficiencies inherent in using profits as the sole or even main criteria of financial progress or as the sole or main corporate target. I believe that most managers today recognize that among the deficiencies of profit as a target are these:

(a) the difficulty of defining the word;
(b) the existence of an increasing number of companies, especially those in the property development field, who do not make conventional annual 'trading profits' at all but who rely on intermittent capital gains;
(c) the comparative irrelevance of profit before tax when taxation is of the order of 50%;
(d) the effects of inflation and the revaluation of assets and depreciation rates that this necessitates intermittently.

In spite of these well-known difficulties, the fact remains that profits are by far the simplest and most widely understood criterion of progress used by managers (although not by financial specialists) and I believe that profits do have a role to play as corporate targets for this reason. Their role is a secondary one, however. The sequence in which I believe corporate targets should be set are (1) a financial target in terms of earnings, earnings per share, capitalization or whatever (see sections below) is determined and then (2) expressed as profit targets for the benefit of those managers who are more accustomed to this measure than to the financial ones. In order to move from (1) to (2) it will normally be necessary to make a number of calculations and, very often, to make several strategic decisions as to gearing, dividend policy and so on.

Return on shareholders' Capital

ROSC differs in several fundamental respects from ROCE. Although they both measure return on capital the 'return' and the 'capital' are quite different. ROCE takes profit before tax as return while for ROSC the definition is the actual cash flow that the shareholder receives from his shares. ROCE takes book values as the definition of capital employed while in ROSC it is the cash value of the shareholders' original equity holding. Thus while ROCE is a nominal ratio whose value depends heavily upon accountancy conventions, ROSC measures what has actually happened in terms of hard cash.

Thus if a shareholder buys $100 worth of shares in a company in Year 0, receives a dividend of $3 in Year 1 and sells his shares in Year 2 for $118 then these figures form the data upon which the calculation of this return is made. Before considering the three severe disadvantages of this method, consider its advantages:

1 The figures are cash; there can be no argument as to whether or not the shareholder really received $3 through his letter-box. Compare this with the arguments that occur over what profit a company has made – the well-known case of Pergamon being an extreme example perhaps, where, of two firms of auditors one was able to certify a profit while the other certified a large loss for the same financial year. Nor can there be any argument over the fact that if the shareholder sold his shares for $118 then he would actually receive $118 in cash.

2 The calculation is simple; to determine the return on the shareholders' capital one merely carries out a normal discounting calculation (Exhibit 11·3).

Exhibit 11·3

Year	Cash flow $	Discount factor at 10%	Discounted Cash flow
0	−100	0·0	−100·0
1	+3	0·909	+2·7
2	+118	0·826	+97·5
			0·0 (approx.)

Therefore ROSC=10%

3 There is therefore no difficulty in establishing what return a shareholder has obtained in the past; whether that helps to establish a target for the future is discussed below, but once a target figure for future performance has been selected and provided the current value of the shareholders' shares is known a simple calculation is all that is needed to derive the earnings per share target figure for as far into the future as is required.

4 All forms of cash receipts that a shareholder receives from his company may be brought into the calculation. Thus a bonus issue of shares, a special dividend, a deferred dividend may all be included as may the shareholder's purchase of further shares at any time.

5 Whether the shareholder actually sells his shares or not makes no difference to one's ability to make these calculations at any moment during a year because, of course, the share price of most public companies are quoted daily; ROCE is usually only calculated once a year.

6 A signal advantage of this method is that it allows one to suspend judgement on a company's performance until a number of years have passed thus evening out the fluctuations in performance to which most companies are subject. ROCE tends to concentrate the mind upon one year's performance because there is no accepted way in which a single ROCE figure may be derived to cover a period of more than one year.

7 The artificial and increasingly unpopular distinction between capital and income or revenue is dispensed with in the ROSC method. It has by now become widely recognized that what really matters in financial affairs is not whether money is paid out in a lump sum and returned in a stream but the timing of positive and negative payments of cash. Thus the traditional distinction between dividends and capital gains becomes less important, and, more significantly, a target set in terms of ROSC does not preempt the essentially strategic decision as to rates of growth. Thus a target of 15% ROSC may be achieved by any combination of growth and dividend yield that gives 15% – 10% growth and 5% yield or 5% and 10% or 0% and 15% or even minus 10% growth and 25% yield. Thus the ROSC method forces managements carefully to select which growth rate they, or the shareholders, prefer rather than merely accepting whatever rate may currently be in fashion for other companies.

8 A further advantage of the ROSC method is that it makes the dilemma between short term and long term profits more amenable to rational analysis. This is because the ROSC method depends for its validity upon the discounted cash flow technique and this technique enables one to establish comparability between the earnings (or profits) in one year with another. Thus, for example, if earnings fall short of target by $100 in Year 1 and if the ROSC target figure is 15% then profits in Year 2 must exceed the target by $115 if the long term ROSC target is to be achieved. This may be particularly useful where a company's profit record follows a cyclical pattern.

Unfortunately the ROSC method has several disadvantages, some of them severe:

1 There is no general agreement as to whether the cash flows experienced by the shareholder should be calculated before or after his personal taxation. One argument rests on the statement that a company cannot be held responsible for the changes that a government may make in personal taxation and, therefore, that the return on a shareholder's capital should be shown before his personal taxes (but, of course, after all company taxation – there is no disagreement on that point). This means that the shareholder who received $3 gross dividend and $18 capital gains could correctly be said to have received 10% return on his capital as calculated above in Exhibit 11·3. The other argument claims that companies may not be responsible for tax changes but that they should certainly take cognizance of them. This implies that where taxes on dividends and on capital gains are not levied at the same rates companies should tailor their dividend and retention policies for the greater after-tax benefit of shareholders. If this is accepted then, taking personal taxes as 33% for both dividend income and capital gains, the return in Exhibit 11·3 would only have been 7% approximately. In my opinion companies should certainly take cognizance of changes in personal taxation when deciding dividend policy but that, in general, it is still preferable to make these ROSC calculations before personal taxation if only because this facilitates international comparisons of ROSC (the alternative being to take ROSC after personal taxes and adjust for the differences in taxation between the relevant nations).

2 Where the shares of a company are quoted on a stock market it is possible to establish ROSC to almost infinite accuracy. If they are not quoted then some other means of valuing the company's market capitailzation must be employed. To put the matter bluntly, there is no way of doing this with any accuracy. To take the capital employed figure as shown in the company's accounts is almost certainly incorrect – the figure may be shown to the nearest penny but it will reflect book values rather than market values. The most logical method is to estimate what the shares would be worth if the company went public or if it was the subject of a merger or acquisition. While this can certainly be done for any company at any moment in time the fact that the estimate is untested in the market must reduce confidence in its accuracy. The question of accuracy is considered below.

3 Even where a company's shares are quoted on a stock market the share price may fluctuate wildly due both to the inevitable fluctuations in fortune attending all companies but also due to rises and falls in the general level of stock market prices. These can be severe – see Exhibit 8·1 – and the accuracy of ROSC calculations may be severely eroded. To obtain an indication of the effect of stock market gyrations on ROSC calculations, consider the following example. Exhibit 11·4 shows the end-year share price and dividend record for the Corncrake Carpet Company.

Exhibit 11·4

Year	Share price $	Dividend per share $
0	100	
1	110	3
2	120	3
3	130	5

The ROSC may be calculated as having been 12% over this four year period. However in Year 4 the stock market suffered a severe decline and although Corncrake Carpets maintained their growing earnings and held the dividend at $5 per share the price fell to $100 per share instead of rising to perhaps $140 as one would have expected. Now the ROSC for the five years becomes only 4%. Clearly this latter figure does not accurately reflect the actual performance of this company and one is faced with two alternatives. Either one may ignore the stock market valuation of the company's shares in Year 5 and attempt to estimate what the value should have been (but all estimates are unreliable and one cannot be entirely confident in any conclusions based upon them), or one can ignore share values entirely. This means rejecting ROSC and using some other indicator of performance such as earnings per share or price earnings ratio (see below).

It may be thought that if one cannot estimate what return a company has achieved on equity capital over the past (either because its shares are not quoted or because, if they are, their value is so subject to fluctuation) then it would be even more difficult to use ROSC as a target for future performance. I question whether this is so.

On page 52 I listed the factors that I believe affect the level of performance selected as targets. One of these is the past performance of the company in question and there is no doubt that if a company has performed well over the past then a somewhat more ambitious target may be set than if it had performed badly. However I believe that of greater significance in the decision is the general levels of return expected by shareholders from companies in their nation or, increasingly, throughout the world. If this is so then the choice of a ROSC target becomes virtually identical to the choice of a suitable cost of capital figure to use in discounted cash flow calculations.

Unfortunately there appears to be no more agreement as to what cost of capital figure should be chosen than on what ROCE figure is desirable. In my opinion this debate is largely spurious or at least irrelevant to the task of setting corporate financial targets. While it would be more satisfactory to be able to state categorically that all financial experts agree on one figure correct to several places of decimals, it is more realistic to recognize that accuracy is unobtainable in any of the figures handled by corporate planners. It is because of this that I placed considerable emphasis in Chapter 3 upon the necessity of regularly reviewing all figures set as corporate targets (both the financial ones and the ethological) and upon the use of performance–risk curves which, in part at least, take account of the risk that the chosen figure may be incorrect. Furthermore I doubt whether the difference in opinion as between any two financial advisers would be very great in any given circumstances; I doubt if many advisers at the time of writing (1972) would recommend a *minimum* ROSC target of less than 12% and more than 14% for the average quoted company in Britain. (These figures are based on the knowledge that yields to redemption on long dated government stocks are currently nearly 10%.) The implication of this two-point divergence of opinion would be that if 12% was selected as a target for a company whose 1972 earnings were £1,000,000 and whose dividend yield was 3% then its minimum target earnings for 1982 would be £2,370,000 while if it had adopted 14% its minimum earnings by 1982 would have to be £2,840,000. I suggest that over such a long period this difference of £470,000 is not significant – and, to repeat the point, no company would set a ten-year target and not review it at some point during the period.

To summarize the position of ROSC as an overall financial target; it may be a significantly more appropriate indicator of shareholders' wishes than any other measure that has so far been proposed. I believe that it *is* possible to select a meaningful ROSC target figure for any company.

Earnings per share

Earnings per share has probably now emerged as the most widely used financial indicator of all. It has the great merit of simplicity, it is closely related to profits, which all managers understand, it is net of company taxes so d.c.f.

calculations can be performed on it. Perhaps its greatest advantage is that it is unaffected by stock market fluctuations and therefore more closely reflects the changing fortunes of the company and therefore the skill of its managers.

Its chief significant disadvantage springs directly from its isolation from the stock market – it fails to take account of share values. The plain fact is that the stock market does move violently up and down, that the value of a given company, whether quoted on a stock exchange or not, does vary independently of earnings per share and, from the shareholders' viewpoint any indicator that does not take account of capital values is inadequate.

Share values are linked to earnings per share through the Price-Earnings Ratio. Thus a company whose earnings are $100m and whose P/E is 10 will have a total market capitalization of $1000m; assuming one million equity shares have been issued then the earnings per share are $100 and they will be quoted on the stock market at $1000 each. The P/E ratio, however, depends upon the level of confidence that investors have in the future of the company so that two companies with the same earnings may have widely differing P/E ratios – as widely different as 5 and 50, perhaps, depending upon the expected rate of growth of earnings per share.

It is clear that if earnings multiplied by P/E ratio determines the market value of a company and if the P/E ratio itself is determined by the expected growth in earnings per share then this one parameter – rate of growth in earnings per share – is the key determinant of all the salient measures. This accounts for its growing use all over the world as the most suitable single corporate financial target.

In my opinion its disadvantages should not be minimized; namely (a) that it does, by definition, ignore stock market fluctuations and (b) that when selecting a growth target managers tend to be unduly influenced by current fashions in growth and may neglect the other constituents of return on capital such as dividend yield, bonuses and so on.

Price-earnings ratio

It has been suggested that the key corporate financial target should not be growth in earnings per share but a P/E ratio of not less than 20. This argument (which is put forward in D. R. C. Halford's book *Business Planning*) is based on calculations which suggest that P/E ratios of less than this could result in the shareholders' dividends not rising even as fast as inflation. While this may well be the case it can also be argued that a more direct approach would be to set a growth target for earnings per share that is greater than the anticipated rate of inflation. Because P/E and growth in e.p.s. are two sides of the same coin it may not matter which is used – but in that case it might be preferable to use the one which most people understand.

Growth

That growth should be a fundamental aim for companies has become axiomatic. Two questions should be settled, however, before setting targets in terms of growth.

1 The technical question that must be asked is 'growth of what'? Some managements answer 'growth of everything' and this is sometimes called balanced growth; while it may have validity in the short term it is unlikely to have any in the long term. Thus in the short term a company aiming to grow at 10% may well wish to see sales turnover, profits, research expenditure, number of employees, and so on all rising at 10%. In the long term few companies would adopt a strategy of balanced growth. If growth is not to be 'balanced' then decisions have to be made as to which elements are to grow faster than others and each of these decisions is, in my opinion, a strategic decision to be decided within and as a result of the corporate planning process – i.e. these are not corporate objectives but targets to be set for parts or subsidiaries.

2 If growth is accepted as axiomatic then the long term consequences must be faced – i.e. the problems of size have to be recognized. There may now be a significant number of companies that are 'too big' either for the well-being of the shareholders, the managers, the employees or the community in which they operate. When that point is reached then serious consideration must be given to alternative targets. As pointed out on page 50 one of these is zero growth. This may be attained by a dividend payout ratio of 100%. Negative growth may be achieved by a payout in excess of 100%, i.e. the shareholder's capital is returned to him in annual instalments – or, of course, it may be returned in lump sums following the disposal of parts of the company or at any other time.

The point I am making is simply that unless shareholders have specifically stated a preference for a particular rate of growth, then any figure that is selected should be chosen either on ethological grounds or as part of the strategy. If a company selects a rate of growth of say 7% it will do so either because it is known that shareholders prefer 7% rather than some other rate, or that there is some ethological reason for this figure or because a 7% growth rate gives the best chance of achieving the ROSC target.

Hussey (Ch. 3) suggests that a declining profit target is hardly likely to appeal to the owners of a business. Perhaps not; but a shareholder who invests $100 in Year 0 would earn a much better return from a company that was declared bankrupt in Year 4 after paying annual dividends of $80, $50, $20 than from most of the companies he could find to invest in today (this d.c.f. return is about 30% compared with an average of approximately 15%).

Nationalized companies

Overall corporate objectives for nationalized companies are almost invariably set in terms of ROCE. The same problems occur in its use in this context as reviewed above in the context of companies – plus two more. The first concerns a further difficulty in defining the word profit, for most nationalized corporations are expected to contribute something other than profits to the community. Thus branch line railways are not closed down, even though they may be hopelessly uneconomic, for fear of the damage this might do to the communities they serve, and uneconomic coal mines are retained in operation to prevent pockets of unacceptably high unemployment. In theory – and probably in practice also – it is not difficult to calculate the cost of these decisions and nor is it difficult in theory for an equivalent subsidy to be paid to the undertaking concerned by the government. The difficulties here are political, not technical, because the granting of any subsidy is a political act.

Assume that the profits of a nationalized railway would be $10m if the branch line to a certain village was closed and $9m if it was left open. The political decision that has to be made depends upon whether $1m worth of social injury will be done to the village if the line is closed. The decision may be made subjectively or it may be made using a cost-benefit technique. If this technique can be used, however, an alternative method of setting targets to nationalized undertakings may be adopted. This involves estimating the social benefits provided by the undertaking, adding these to the conventional profits earned and expressing the total as a return on capital. Thus the two methods of estimating return on capital are (1) conventional profits plus subsidies as a percentage of capital or (2) conventional profits plus social profits as calculated by cost-benefit techniques expressed as a percentage of capital.

For the target setter, then, the first problem is to discover whether nationalized industries are supposed to make a return on capital or not and if so how profits are to be defined and in particular whether these are deemed to include subsidies or social profits or neither. The second problem is to define what is meant by capital. As indicated earlier 'capital' may be taken to mean either shareholders' capital or capital employed. The latter, which is almost invariably the definition used when target setting for nationalized companies, is, as seen earlier, so severely affected by the looseness of accountancy conventions as to render it almost useless for companies. It is probably useless for nationalized companies also – for the same reasons plus one other: this is the tendency for governments to allow nationalized companies to write off large portions of government loan which, quite arbitrarily, reduces the capital employed figure.

The alternative to using ROCE is to use ROSC. It may be objected that since nationalized companies have no shareholders the ROSC method cannot be used. However two methods of estimating the current market capitalization of a nationalized company suggest themselves. One is to estimate what capital sum the company would realize if it was denationalized. The other is to express as net present value all the moneys injected by the government into the company (including the original purchase price) less any dividends paid to the government by the company. The discount factor to be used would be the historic costs of capital, of course. In these ways I believe the current capitalization of the company may be established; as for the return required, that may be taken as the prospective cost of capital to the government – a figure that may be considerably less difficult to determine than the figure for the prospective return on equity risk capital.

Performance-risk curves

In Chapter 3 I explained why I thought it was misleading for a company to set itself a single figure target whether it used ROCE or ROSC or profits or P/E ratio or whatever. Briefly my reasons were (a) that shareholders have a range of expectations and (b) that none of the indicators could be accurately established or predicted. To aim for a profit of $1,073,421 by Year 10 is patently absurd; but even to aim for one of $1m is nearly as absurd for it is common knowledge (a) that shareholders would prefer that company to have aimed for $2m and (b) over such time spans an outcome could not be controlled to within many hundreds of thousands of dollars. To overcome these difficulties I suggested (1) that targets be frequently reviewed and (2) that they be set as a bracket rather than a single figure. But in addition I suggested that, because risk is fundamental to business, it should be reflected in the target-setting procedure.

To meet all these points I suggested adopting the performance–risk method which, I believe, may be used with any of the indicators reviewed above. That is to say one could set targets in terms of ROCE-risk or ROSC-risk or e.p.s.-risk; one could for example, set a corporate target as 'We will aim for a 50% chance of achieving a ROCE of 17 and a 10% chance of achieving more than 10% or less than 25%'. However, since I believe that ROCE, profits, P/E, e.p.s. are all derivatives of ROSC, the prime indicator of shareholders' wishes, it follows that I would recommend using a ROSC-risk curve.

Unfortunately I doubt if many shareholders could state their ROSC-risk curve – most private shareholders are somewhat naive about financial matters

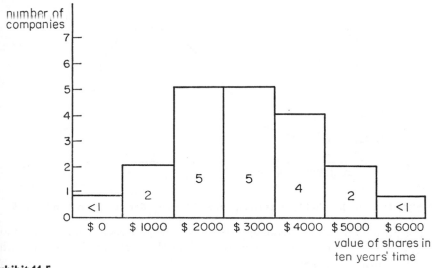

Exhibit 11·5

In the opinion of this shareholder four of the twenty companies in which he holds a $1000 share will quadruple their share price over the next decade, five will double it, and so on. He thinks he will lose his entire investment in less than one of these twenty companies.

and few know their expectations in terms of figures; fewer still could attach probability estimates to various ROSC levels. I doubt if even many of the sophisticated institutional shareholders could either. What I believe they could do is to state what rate of growth in capital appreciation they expect to see (assuming a constant dividend yield) from the constituents of their portfolio. Thus shareholders could answer this question; 'Assume you have $1000 invested in each of twenty companies. Assume dividends are the same from each (say 3% yield). How many of your holdings would you expect to have doubled, trebled, quadrupled by Year 10?' Their answers would form a histogram as in Exhibit 11·5.

Crude and indirect though this approach may be I believe it is adequate. It is crude and indirect because (a) it would only show what shareholders expect from 20 companies, not from one, (b) it does not directly measure ROSC which would have to be calculated using d.c.f. from the expectations of dividend and growth. However this calculation is simple and this approach does have the merit of showing how shareholders feel about risk. Thus the histogram in Exhibit 11·5 may be translated into the ROSC-risk curve shown in Exhibit 11·6, where, for example, the fact that Exhibit 11·5 indicates that this shareholder thought that two companies in 20 would give a return of over 20% (a growth factor of 5 times in ten years, i.e. 17% p.a. plus 3% dividend yield) allows us to place a probability of 0·10 on a 20% return in Exhibit 11·6.

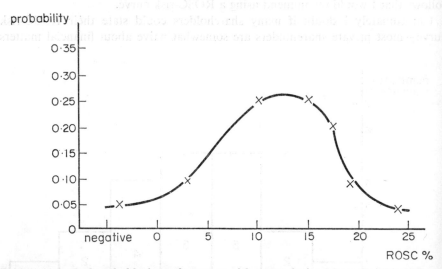

Exhibit 11·6   A shareholder's performance–risk curve derived from Exhibit 11·5

For all its obvious disadvantages I believe this approach would give a more useful and accurate answer than asking shareholders simply to state what ROSC return they expect.

Shareholder surveys

Very few companies have formally invited their shareholders to state their expectations. Those that have – see page 48 – have sometimes uncovered some surprises such as the extent to which shareholders are concerned about the means their company employs to achieve their aims. In fact, while more surveys should doubtless be conducted, especially by companies who are in some way out of the ordinary in respect of growth, stability, dividends, etc. it is questionable whether there is merit in every company conducting such surveys. The business world is now so minutely studied and documented, the statistics so profuse, the experts in financial analysis so numerous, that most companies can probably select a financial target that is appropriate for its circumstances without recourse to a formal survey.

It need hardly be said but, if a survey is to be carried out, great care has to be exercised in the choice of the questions and in the manner in which they are phrased. (I need not repeat my contention that shareholders have a range of expectations but I doubt if any survey has been phrased so as to give them a chance to express these. Nor, so far as I know have shareholders been asked if they would prefer to take their 15% return as a 15% dividend rather than the traditional combination of 3–5% yield and 12–10 growth.)

Financial targets – a summary

I doubt if any indicator exists that will reflect shareholders' financial aspirations to within an error of less than 10% or even 20%. This is partly because shareholders do not know what they should expect, and partly because of the difficulty of measuring it even if they did. Of the various indicators proposed, I have discussed:

ROSC which I believe to be the best of the bunch because (a) it measures what the shareholders want directly, namely return on their capital and (b) because it can be measured extremely accurately from the past records.

ROSC-risk has the additional advantage that risk is brought into the planning process right at the start. Also the fact that shareholder expectations cannot be determined accurately is taken into account.

ROCE has the disadvantage that it is an accounting ratio more useful for short term management control than as a long term target.

Earnings per share has the advantage of being independent of stock market gyrations but the disadvantage that it begs the questions of dividend strategy and what growth rate to aim for. By definition it ignores stock market values.

Profits are measured pre-tax and suffer from the same problems of accountancy definitions as ROCE.

P/E ratio could be said to be a derivative of growth in e.p.s.

Growth targets in terms of anything other than earnings per share, (e.g. growth in turnover, etc.) beg strategic questions and are thus *wholly* inappropriate as *corporate* aims. Even growth in e.p.s. may be an ethological or strategic decision rather than a corporate objective.

All management ratios beg strategic questions.

All multiple targets beg strategic questions except when it is known that shareholders expect their return to take some particular form, such as a specific dividend yield or rate of growth.

Shareholder surveys may be required to establish shareholder preferences when these are thought to be different to the general consensus as shown by financial statistics.

To conclude: as a general rule a ROSC or ROSC-risk target should be selected first and all other corporate financial targets derived from it; each figure that is derived represents a strategic decision.

II Corporate ethological targets

In this section I consider some of the methods of measuring some of the ethological objectives commonly adopted by companies and other organizations. So wide and numerous are the social, moral, aesthetic and personal aims attributed to organizations that no list can be exhaustive.

Shareholders

In addition to return on their capital some shareholders look for other benefits from their company. This is especially so in the case of privately owned companies, of course.

In Denning (Ch. 19) Tilles and Contas point out that among the objectives for all companies such targets as return on capital, growth, and profitability are general, but that in the family firm a number of other objectives are usually found: whether the chief executive must be a member of the family, for example, or whether the family wishes to retain control. Tilles and Contas remark that although family firms usually accept a number of extremely important obligations – to the younger generation, to employees, to the local community – these are seldom made explicit. They do have important implications for strategy formulation however.

It seems to me that where only one or two members of a family are concerned in a firm – and especially if they are also its most senior executives – there is less need for such personal aims to be made explicit or be quantified. The greater the number of members involved, however, and the greater the influence of non-family executives, the more important it is formally to discuss and agree ethological objectives. Thus if one of the objectives is 'to remain independent' there should be some agreement as to the circumstances under which this objective would be discarded; an exceptionally generous bid for their company? How generous? Would this objective be reconsidered if the company was approaching bankruptcy? Any figures that might emerge from these discussions would necessarily be very approximate and, like all objectives, subject to continued revision as circumstances and opinions changed.

As Tilles and Contas point out these non-financial objectives are often highly personal and individual in character and although some may be quantifiable (see Case 2 in Chapter 10 for examples) most will remain qualitative.

Employees

Many companies today recognize that they have moral obligations towards their employees and these are regarded as being something distinct from the way in which employees are motivated. There are thus two possible reasons why a particular company treats its employees in a particular manner; either because the company believes that this will improve its long term profits (a strategic decision) or because this is how that company believes employees *should* be treated (an ethological decision). Sometimes the two arguments are convergent, sometimes divergent; that is to say, a company may provide good working conditions both because this improves productivity and because it is 'the right thing to do'; on the other hand to declare men redundant may be good for profits but may be considered unethical.

Unfortunately there is no single indicator that reflects the happiness of employees. If there was – and perhaps there may be eventually – it would only be necessary for a company to decide where on the scale they felt morally obliged to aim and that would end the problem. In fact a large number of indicators must be used. It is probably necessary to cover four areas; earnings, security, conditions and job satisfaction.

Earnings

Targets may have to be set for the minimum earnings considered acceptable, for stability of earnings, for differentials as between skills, for a target growth in take-home pay per annum. Although each of these is easily measured it is not so easy to see what rational criteria may be used to select one figure rather than some other. Should a company select as a minimum wage for its employees the minimum ruling in its local community, or in its industry, or in its nation? Or attempt to calculate what an employee must be paid to raise him above subsistence levels? Once this ethical choice is made, quantification is not difficult.

Security

In some nations, Japan, for example and to some extent in Italy, it is almost unthinkable for a company to dismiss an employee. In other nations job security is regulated by well established tradition or by law – but even where this is the case individual management may wish to improve job security for their employees beyond the national norm. Long term targets may readily be set for redundancy, sickness benefits, and so on.

Conditions

Most of the physical conditions in which employees work are easily quantifiable in terms of temperature, noise, dirt and so on. Many of these are regulated by law, so companies have target levels already suggested for them; some companies set long term targets for improvement in physical working conditions well beyond these legal minima. It is not difficult to set a long term target, over say five years, for reducing accident rates, for example. The non-physical or psychological conditions of work are much more difficult to quantify; indicators that may be useful include the number of disputes per unit time reaching each level of management, absenteeism, productivity, strikes, accident rates and so on. Attitude surveys among employees may also be used.

Job Satisfaction

A number of techniques now exist by which the level of satisfaction may be measured. Most of these are based on the work of Herzberg, and a growing number of companies are coming to the belief that they have an obligation to create working conditions in which every employee may develop his own abilities. As the number of firms using job satisfaction indices grows a norm for 'job satisfaction' on a standard index may emerge and it may then become practical for individual companies to decide where on the index they should aim for over a long term.

In setting all these targets I believe that a bracket of figures or a performance –risk curve, or a minimum threshhold should be set rather than a point-target (see page 44).

Management

Some companies express one of their aims as 'to provide an atmosphere of challenge and opportunity' to their managers. I am not sure how this worthy aim could be quantified; nor am I sure that this aim, and others like it referring specifically to managers, is qualitatively very different from the aims described in the above section for employees generally. If it is morally right to provide opportunities for advancement for managers it is presumably right to offer the same for non-managers (in terms of job enrichment if not necessarily promotion). In other words I would have thought that the bundle of targets that a company sets for its employees could be applied, *mutatis mutandis*, for its managers and therefore that no separate or distinctive bundle of targets is needed for the managers.

Customers

Many companies state, as part of their moral creed, that they wish to serve the interests of the consumer. Steiner (Ch. 6) quotes several typical examples along the lines, 'best possible products at reasonable prices', and other somewhat unverifiable phrases. As Steiner says, vagueness in language is typical at this level of setting objectives and he claims that this has its advantages; these statements are intended only to set the tone for the firm – to get too specific could detract from the value of these statements by stifling creativity. However I suggest that the role of creativity lies in devising means of achieving corporate objectives and the more precisely stated these are the more ingenuity is required to achieve them. Whether any meaningful target or group of targets can be found to reflect a management's attitude to its customers I am not certain but I believe that each management knows with considerable accuracy how many complaints from customers represents an acceptable level. It is, I suggest, the volume and severity of complaints (and compliments) from customers, consumer organizations, government inspectorates and so on per unit time or volume of output that is the best indicator – because it measures customer attitudes directly – rather than a group of targets for quality, delivery, service and so on.

Suppliers

Although many companies explicitly recognize their moral obligations to employees and customers very few recognize similar obligations to their suppliers. Presumably a blanket indicator that could be used would be the volume and severity of complaints made by suppliers to the company.

Society

Many of the obligations that companies have towards society may be quantified – certainly most of those relating to pollution by effluent, noise, smell – and long term targets may readily be set. Some of these targets are suggested by legislation, of course.

Unfortunately many social obligations cannot be quantified; a company may feel it has an obligation to society not to display misleading or offensive advertising material, for example, but it is difficult to see what indicator one would use to set this target and monitor progress towards it. It seems to me that the best way of measuring whether a company is living up to its aim 'to be a good citizen' is to record and study the volume and severity of complaints and compliments received from individual citizens and the innumerable bodies that now exist to protect their interests.

Ethological targets – a summary

Society is imposing increasing pressures upon companies to be of good behaviour. Managements are increasingly having to decide formally and explicitly how far they feel their company should bow towards this trend, whether to resist it as far as possible or to take a lead in it. It is too easy merely to state that one's company will try to be a good citizen; subordinate managers will not know precisely what this means and neither they nor anyone else will be able to monitor the company's behaviour unless this aim is spelt out in some detail. While many aspects of good citizenship may not yet be quantifiable many aspects can readily be expressed in figures. New methods of quantification appear at an accelerating rate – job satisfaction indices, for example were unknown until the late Sixties and attitude surveys are now increasingly being used. Norms of corporate behaviour are becoming established and embodied in legislation, thus providing managements with appropriate levels on which to base targets for their companies.

III Targets for subsidiaries and departments

So far in this chapter I have been discussing only targets set to corporate bodies at the start of the corporate planning process. I shall now consider the setting of targets to subsidiary companies, departments and parts of corporate wholes.

Ethological targets

Many of the ethological targets selected for the corporate body may be applied without change to all parts of it. If one such target is to achieve a safety record of no more than one lost time accident per 100,000 man hours then that target may be appropriate to all the company's factories. On the other hand they may not be universally applicable especially in companies having widely diverse interests. We return to the age-old dilemma; if the corporate management do not set targets then the management of the parts may misunderstand their intentions while if they do set targets some of them may be inappropriate to some of the parts. I believe that the performance–risk approach might offer a solution; i.e. if the corporate management declared that '2 accidents per 100,000 man hours is intolerable in any of our factories; 1 accident per 100,000 man hours is tolerable once in every 10 periods' – or whatever, then the tone is set for the whole company while local variations are permissible. Even the declaration of a threshold figure is better than no figure at all – for example, 'more than one prosecution per three year period for giving short weight is intolerable for any of our subsidiaries'.

The hierarchy of targets

The targets set to companies as corporate wholes are almost exclusively finan-

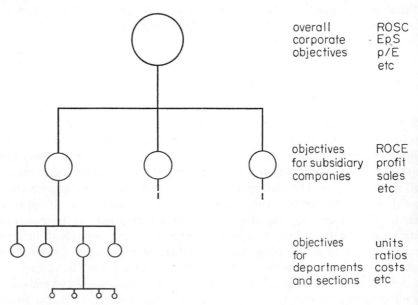

overall corporate objectives	ROSC EpS p/E etc
objectives for subsidiary companies	ROCE profit sales etc
objectives for departments and sections	units ratios costs etc

Exhibit 11·7

cial in nature – ROSC, earnings per share and so on. The targets set to a subsidiary company are largely accountancy based – ROCE, profits, costs and so on – and sometimes physical – units of sales, number of employees and so on. The targets set to parts of companies and subsidiaries are usually physical with some accountancy targets. This generalization is shown in Exhibit 11·7. The lower down the hierarchy of management the more one finds physical targets and the less one finds financial ones.

Because strategic decisions are those taken at the top of the management hierarchy one would expect, as a general rule, that the objectives set to the decision-makers would be mainly in financial terms while their decisions would be expressed mainly in accountancy or physical terms – mainly physical if the decisions refer to departments, more accountancy if to subsidiaries.

Targets for departments

Consider the simplest possible case, that of a small single product company. Assume it has a target growth of 10% per annum in earnings per share and that its strategy is balanced growth. All that the chief executive need do is to set the same target to all his departmental managers – 10% growth of everything; see Exhibit 11·8. This example is intended to illustrate only one point; that

Exhibit 11·8 Balanced growth

$000	year 0	1	2	3
Earnings	50	55	60	66
Sales	2000	2200	2400	2640
Margin %	10	10	10	10
Contribution	200	220	240	264
Overheads	100	110	120	132
Profits	100	110	120	132
Tax	50	55	60	66

targets set to departmental managers are nothing more than quantified instructions to them which describe the role their departments are to play in the company's future. In this case they are all expected to contribute equally.

Exhibit 11·9 A budget is a set of instructions to the parts of a whole

$000	year 0	1	2	3
Earnings	50	55	60	70
Sales of existing product	2000	2200	2200	2200
Margin %	10	10	10	10
Contribution	200	220	220	220
Sales of new product	—	—	1000	1800
Margin %	—	—	15	16
Contribution	—	—	150	290
Total contribution	200	220	370	410
Overheads (includes loan interest)	100	110	250	270
Profits	100	110	120	140
Tax	50	55	60	70
Capital expenditure	—	300	700	—

Now assume that this same company, having the same growth target, has carefully considered its strategic situation and has decided to introduce a new product. What is required now is for the chief executive to draw up a similar set of quantified instructions to the departmental heads – but this time the situation is far more complex. It will be seen from Exhibit 11·9, for example, that the sales manager is not to attempt to increase sales of the existing product after Year 1 but to concentrate on the new one. The production department have to install new plant, the finance manager will have to raise $1,000,000 additional loan capital – and so on.

Exhibits 11·8 and 11·9 are, in fact, no more or less than simple examples of a Budget.

Budgets

A budget is a most valuable integrating tool – I use the word integrating in two senses. Firstly a budget brings together all the decisions made by a company's executives into one comprehensive document where each figure reflects a decision as to future action. Secondly a budget contains some figures that have been determined by the senior managers (top-down mangement) and some that have been determined by managers of parts of the company (bottom-up management) and the budget shows whether there is a conflict between them – if there is a conflict the figures will not cross-check. In addition, of course, the budget figures may be compared with actual results and any divergences spark off control activities.

A budget is a detailed formal statement of what Ackoff (Ch. 2) calls a Planned Projection and what I called an Approved Forecast or F_A in Chapter 7. It is a detailed set of instructions to the managers of parts of the company showing what role they are expected to play in the whole and how their efforts add up to the achievement of the company's overall aims. It is a quantified statement of decisions taken in the planning process, however, not a means of taking decisions.

Targets to subsidiaries

The difference between a company that is divided into functional departments and one that is divided into subsidiary companies is partly organizational and partly an accounting distinction. The operations of one functional department must be closely harmonized with the others – production with sales, production with buying, sales with invoicing, research with marketing and so on – and this is one reason why a budget is so useful a tool in departmentalized companies; it shows how the aims of each department are integrated with and related to the others. But the operations of one subsidiary company do not normally have to be integrated closely with the others – indeed many subsidiaries behave almost autonomously. As for the accountancy difference, most departments are cost centres while most subsidiaries are profit centres.

These differences suggest (a) that the detailed budget which is so useful for departments may be less useful to subsidiary companies and (b) that accountancy tools (and even financial tools) may be more useful for setting targets to sub-sidiaries rather than the physical measures that are so useful for departments.

In fact where a subsidiary is given total autonomy by the parent the only target that need be set is return on capital but this implies that the parent is indifferent as to all other decisions made within the subsidiary. Consider a company having two subsidiaries as in Exhibit 11·10. Now assume that the

Exhibit 11·10   Group and subsidiaries results for year 0

	Subsidiary A	Subsidiary B	The Group
Profits $000	100	40	140
Capital Employed $000	1000	100	1100
ROCE %	10	40	12.7

parent company sets both companies the same target – 25% ROCE. What will happen? Presumably Subsidiary A will strive to improve the efficiency with which it uses its existing resources including perhaps disposing of unprofitable activities while Subsidiary B will seek to expand by investing capital at 25% in new projects until its average ROCE becomes 25%. Provided that the parent company is indifferent as to these relative contractions and expansions – see Exhibit 11·11 for one possible outcome – then no problems arise (and the

Exhibit 11·11   Group and subsidiaries results for year X

	Subsidiary A	Subsidiary B	The Group
Profits $000	200	200	400
Capital employed $000	800	800	1600
ROCE %	25	25	25

group tends to become a true conglomerate). But if the parent is not indifferent then it will have to reduce the number of degrees of freedom for these sub-sidiaries by setting at least one other target – such as sales turnover or growth of profits – alongside the ROCE target.

So let us now assume that this parent company, having completed its appraisals, decides that the best strategic structure for the future is where the profits from A continue to be approximately twice that of B (because B operates in a high risk market, or whatever) then it will set such targets to A and B that will bring about this result and no other. Thus if the strategic structure for the group demands that one subsidiary should act as a very large low risk base-load profit generator then the targets to be set must include (a) a low ROCE and (b) a turnover growth target. If the strategic structure demands that no competition between subsidiaries is to be allowed then the targets must include (a) a ROCE target and (b) a definition of the boundaries of each subsidiary's markets.

In Denning (Ch. 18) Millard H. Pryor suggests that the headquarters of a multinational group should set different ROCE targets to each subsidiary according to the riskiness of that subsidiary. Thus while a 12% ROCE may be valid for a US subsidiary of a US group, a target of 25% should be set to one operating in a nation of high political risk while perhaps 18% is appropriate for one subject to currency risk. This may well be a useful approach so long as it is recognized that, other things being equal, the US subsidiary will grow very much faster than the others – projects yielding 12% being more numerous than ones yielding 18%. Provided that this company's strategic structure also demands that the US subsidiary grows faster than the others no incompatibility is present; if it does not then either this method of target setting is invalid or the strategic structure is inappropriate or an attempt to reconcile the two will have to be made by altering the risk structure of the company.

The basic principle in setting targets to subsidiaries, then, is this; having determined what role each subsidiary is to play in the group strategic structure targets are set to each subsidiary in such a way that in achieving the targets they cannot but act their role. Care has to be taken to guard against three problems; the first is that the targets set do in fact lead to the desired outcome and no other, the second is that the targets do not unintentionally constrain the management of the subsidiary in areas not covered by the strategic decisions of the group and the third is that the bundle of targets set to the subsidiaries are mathematically compatible (a) within each subsidiary (b) between the various subsidiaries and (c) with the overall group objectives. I believe that the only way to make sure that none of these problems has been overlooked is to build a model of the relevant structure of the company and test the effects of the proposed bundle of targets on paper before they are finally promulgated. (Company models are described on page 274).

Accuracy and Reality

I firmly believe that a figure that approximately represents reality is far more useful than one that accurately reflects a fiction.

I have already suggested that a company's ROCE can be stated to several places of decimals but that it measures an accountancy fiction composed of 'written down' assets, stocks at cost, and other unreal conventions. The ROCE figure for a subsidiary within a group can also be stated to several places of decimals but is even more fictional than for a company. It is common practice for example, for trade between two subsidiaries of a group to be conducted at a notional transfer price, for the group headquarters to charge notional fees for management services and for loan interest to be borne solely by the group and charged out to subsidiaries on a fictional basis such as in proportion to their assets employed or turnover.

It is not uncommon for one subsidiary to show a ROCE of 4% while another shows 40%; on the face of it the group management should close down the former and invest heavily in the latter. But, of course, the figures are distorted by inter-subsidiary accounting fictions. I believe that corporate planning cannot even begin unless the figures being discussed by decision-makers reflect reality even if they do so only approximately.

Early in the planning process, therefore, (probably before the forecasts are prepared by the subsidiary companies) some attempt must be made to establish the true market value of each subsidiary and its true profitability. The market value of a subsidiary may be established (approximately) by the same two methods I described for the nationalized industries (see page 203) – a nationalized company is, after all, a subsidiary of the national government. The two methods were (1) to express as a net present value all the funds invested by the group in the subsidiary (using the cost of risk capital ruling at the time of each tranche) less the present value of dividends paid to the group, or (2) the capital value that each subsidiary would command if it was sold to a third party. The profitability of each subsidiary may be established either by taking transfer prices at the true market value of the goods or services or by estimating the opportunity cost of elminating the subsidiary – i.e. the contribution of a subsidiary to a group is the effect on total group profits of not having that subsidiary as a member of the group.

As a simple illustration take a subsidiary company where the book value is $10m and profits are $400,000. The ROCE is 4%. But the group directors estimate that this subsidiary could be sold to a competitor for $8m and that, if it was sold, group profits would fall by $1·2m. The real profitability of *this* subsidiary to *this* group is therefore 15%. It can be argued that all this group's corporate forecasts and strategic decisions should be based on this figure and that this is the figure that should be used as the base for all future targets to be set to this subsidiary.

Hard and soft areas

It will be appreciated that in the system of corporate planning described in this book there will inevitably be a considerable period of delay between the setting of corporate objectives and the setting of partial objectives – i.e. those to subsidiary companies within a group or to departments within a company. In this system corporate objectives are the input and partial objectives the output – between them lies the entire planning process which, in a large complex company may take two years to complete.

It may be intolerable for the managers of the parts of the company to have to wait for months or years before agreement is reached as to their future role in the corporate whole. This delay may be substantially reduced if it was possible, as often it is, for the corporate management to identify those parts of the company whose future role is virtually assured and those whose role must remain in doubt until the corporate plan has been devised. I call these the hard and soft areas of a company respectively. If this classification can be made, the corporate management will then be in a position to indicate to the managers of the parts which category their part is considered to be in and those in hard areas may confidently put forward ambitious ideas for expansion while those in soft areas may expect to have their ideas treated with reserve until their place in the stratgeic structure has been determined. (My 'hard' and 'soft' areas are not the same as Cannon's 'known' and 'unknown' areas (Ch. 11).

12 Techniques of forecasting

Introduction

Vanity and optimism are two of the reasons why forecasters so seldom admit that their forecasts might be wrong. It is an extraordinary fact but, time after time and against all evidence to the contrary, those who make forecasts manage to persuade themselves that *this time* they will get it right and they therefore need not reveal how wrong it might be.

But vanity and optimism are only two of the reasons why forecasters are so shy to admit the possible width of the range of errors. There is another: if a sales manager informs his production management colleague that demand next week will be 1017 units then the production manager is faced with no problem – he simply plans to produce 1017 units. But if the sales manager had informed him that sales next week could be anywhere between 800 and 1200 units the production manager would have to make the infinitely more difficult decision whether to manufacture 800 units and face the wrath of the customers if demand turns out to be 1200 or to make 1200 units and face the wrath of the finance manager if 400 units are left in stock.

In long range planning the errors in the forecasts rise to absurd levels – forecasts can be 50% wrong, 200% wrong; the opposite to what was predicted may happen.* It seems to me, therefore, that although one ought to use advanced

---

* Steiner (Ch. 8) gives some interesting figures. He quotes Carlson who reports that errors of 15% were common in a study he made of firms forecasting sales one year ahead. Sord and Welsch mention 25% for errors in sales forecasts for specific products. 25% is mentioned in an AMA study. Steiner himself suggests 15% for a five-year forecast.

In my opinion the scale of errors in long range forecasting is better reflected in the estimates made by Ford of Britain and the National Economic Development Office in 1964 for demand for new cars in 1970 in the UK. Ford suggested that the 1970 demand would be 1·7 million. NEDO suggested 1·8 million. In fact it was 1·0 million. I am not suggesting that all five-year forecasts are as wrong as this, merely that some are and, since one does not know in advance which of them will be so wrong, one has to assume any of them will be.

As for very long range forecasting, consider the various attempts by the British Government to forecast the population of the UK in 1990. In 1952 the forecast for 1990 was 46 million,

in 1957 it was 49m	in 1969 it was 56m	in 1972 it was 60m
in 1962 it was 57m	in 1971 it was 62m	

The spread of estimates reaches from 46 to 62m (approximately 30% spread) in spite of the fact that national population statistics have probably been subjected to more scrutiny by demographers than any other statistic, that the UK government is certainly no less competent than most forecasters and that these statistics are as voluminous and reliable for UK as for any other nation in the world.

To be frank, then, I am always surprised if any long range forecast turns out to be only 15 to 25% wrong.

techniques of forecasting and although forecasting specialists should certainly continue to devise new methods of forecasting, what really matters to the corporate planner is (a) to reduce the errors in his forecasts as far as possible but (b) to recognize that enormous errors will even so exist, to recognize this uncomfortable fact explicitly and to take full account of it in his planning.

In this chapter I will describe some of the techniques now in use in long range forecasting but, in recognition of (a) above I will also suggest a number of ways in which errors may be reduced (and in Chapter 14 I will describe methods of taking account of errors in recognition of (b)).

The Sources of Error

Errors enter the forecasting process at five main points.

The simplest form of forecast is the extrapolation (not to be confused with 'projection' which may or may not be an extrapolation). I shall refer to extrapolations as F_{00} forecasts; the double subscript is intended to draw attention to the fact that extrapolation implies that the future will be identical to the past; nothing in the company's environment will change, nor will the company act to change anything. Thus if wage rates have risen by 10% per annum in the past, an F_{00} forecast will show them rising at 10% per annum in the future. But notice that, except in quite exceptional circumstances, even the F_{00} forecast is bound to be inaccurate due to variations in the past.

Now consider the next most elementary forecast, the F_0. This single subscript indicates that this forecast assumes the company does not intend to act to change anything but that changes in the environment are recognized. Thus while an F_{00} forecast assumed that wages rates would rise at 10% in the future as in the past, an F_0 forecast might see them rising at 15% due to an increase in union militancy. Clearly two more uncertainties have now been revealed – the occurrence of an event and the effect of that event upon the subject being forecast (in this case the effect of militancy on wage rates).

Now consider the final stage of forecasting; the Budget or F_P as I call it or Planned Projection as Ackoff calls it. This is based on the assumptions that both the environment and the company's policy will change. Thus, to continue my example, the company might decide to recruit a Labour Relations Director and their F_P forecast will show the effect of doing so. But two more sources of uncertainty have appeared; there may be some unforeseen difficulty in carrying out this planned appointment and the effect this new official will have on wage rates is uncertain in the extreme. There are, then, at least five different sources of error in the three different types of forecast. Some of the techniques I describe below are particularly useful in reducing particular types of error and I should mention the following;

At the F_{00} forecast some of the worst errors of extrapolation may be reduced by using Curve Fitting, Trend Analysis, Time Series and other mathematical techniques.

At the F_0 forecast it may be possible to use such techniques as Delphi, Projection to Absurdity and Life Cycle Analysis to predict events and the use

Scenario, Models and Correlation Analysis to predict how an event will affect a trend.

At the F_P forecast it may be possible to reduce errors by using such techniques as Management Ratios, Verification Sessions and Prudent Manager Forecasts to estimate the effect of a proposed plan.

Although it may be a little arbitrary to do so I propose to divide this chapter into two parts; that concerned with methods of reducing errors in forecasts and that concerned with specific techniques of forecasting.

I Error reduction

Standardized Assumptions

Most of the forecasting exercises that are carried out in the corporate planning process are of a fairly complex nature. A company's F_0 forecast, its forecast of markets, its budgets (or F_P forecasts) are all very complex and, very often, a number of different managers have to take part in the exercise, each contributing figures from his own area of specialist knowledge. If each manager makes different assumptions as to the future then, inevitably, the consolidated forecast will be invalid. If the sales manager assumes that no international agreement on tariff barriers will be reached until Year Y while the buying manager assumes it will be Year X, the consolidated profit forecast may be nonsense. If the managers in Subsidiary A make their forecast on the assumption of 5% real growth in the size of their market while Subsidiary B assumes theirs as 9% in money terms then the consolidated profit forecast of the group will be invalid.

It is simple enough to suggest, as I did on page 79, that all assumptions should be written down before making a forecast; the difficulty is that, in practice, a very large number of these may have to be agreed and recorded before any forecasting at all may begin. However, if this is not done, there is a high risk of the forecasts containing wholly unnecessary inconsistencies.

Internal Crosschecks

Complex forecasts, such as the F_0, are built up piece by piece. The market size is forecast, then the company's projected share of that market, then the price structure – and so on through direct costs, fixed costs, capital expenditure, cash flows, and so on. Even where all the assumptions have been conscientiously agreed among the forecasters inconsistencies may still appear. It is often possible to reduce or eliminate these by crosschecking one item with any other that may be relevant. Thus a forecast that wage rates will rise by 12% a year is not, on its own, very extraordinary. But if the same F_0 forecast contains a prediction that salaries will rise by 8% a year one is bound to ask whether these two forecasts can both be correct. Again, if the cost of manufacturing a component is shown as rising by 5% a year and in the same forecasting excercise the cost of bought-in-components is shown at a constant price over the same period this must raise the question as to whether these two statements can be compat ible. In such cases either there is a rational explanation for these anomalies – in which case both forecasts may well be correct – or there is not, in which case an error exists in one or the other or both.

External Crosschecks

Internal crosschecks are useful for ensuring consistency as between figures within a forecast. External crosschecks are used to attain consistency as between a forecast and some relevant fact outside it. Thus if a forecast shows that a company's share of a market is expected to increase this must imply that its competitors' share will decrease. It may be useful to examine which of these competitors will lose share, why, and what response they might make – unless a convincing scenario can be envisioned doubt must be thrown upon the credibility of the increased share shown in the forecast. (In Case 1, page 143, for example, the forecast saw an increase in share from 3% to 12% in five years. It was calculated that, because the market itself was not expanding, at least two of Davies Engineering's major competitors would go out of business if this share was obtained. No one believed that this was likely to happen.)

Multiple Technique Crosscheck

Where it is vital to narrow down the range of errors in a forecast several forecasts may be made each based on a different technique. In view of the cost of forecasting this cannot be done for all forecasts but, where it is really vital to reduce the area of error one forecast can be made using Delphi, for example, another using Trend Analysis, a third by the Scenario Method and so on. The same event may thus be predicted by using several different methods and the difference in results analysed and compared.

Projection to Absurdity

The price of material M was $30 in 1955, $26 in 1960, $19 in 1965 and $14 in 1970. If this trend is projected for only five more years it will suggest that the price of M in 1975 will be down to $10. In another five years it will be $5 and by 1985 the price will be zero. Either this is an absurd result or it is not. It is not absurd if material M is in fact likely to disappear from the market by 1985 due perhaps to the appearance of a better substitute. But if that is not likely to happen then the trend does become absurd; furthermore it may be possible to pinpoint *when* it becomes absurd and hence the moment in time when the falling trend *must* be halted or reversed.

This useful method of reducing forecasting errors may also be used as follows; take all the items in, say, a five-year forecast and project them for a further five or ten years. Carry out an internal and an external crosscheck on the tenth or fifteenth year; this may reveal, for example that by the eighth year research costs will form an absurd proportion of revenue or that shop floor wages will exceed the salary of the senior managers or whatever. Thus although there may have been no obvious absurdities within the five year period of the forecast some of the trends assumed there may lead to absurdities in the period immediately following it and this may cast suspicion upon the figures in the period.

This method, then, may be used to test the validity of a forecast of a single item on its own or of a set of items such as those in an F_0 forecast. The nearer in time does the absurdity appear, the sooner or the more violently must the trend be changed.

Management Ratio Checks

It is almost impossible for a manager not to introduce an element of optimism or pessimism into any forecast he makes. Where the element of bias is large it will be readily apparent to his colleagues but where it is only marginal each figure in his forecast may appear to be acceptable. However it may be possible to detect bias by using a battery of management ratios. Thus a sales manager's forecast of unit sales may be marginally optimistic, so may his forecast of unit prices, so may be his forecast of profit margins; these may each be undetectably optimistic on their own. However these three minor elements of optimism may be detectable in the aggregate. This could be revealed by calculating the profit per unit ratio for each year of the forecast and judging whether its rate of improvement represented an unbelievably optimistic trend.

The greater the number of ratios calculated across the elements in a complex forecast the more likely is one to detect anomalies and bias. It is theoretically desirable to express each figure as a ratio of every other figure in a forecast thus obtaining a five or ten-year sequence of ratios for sales turnover to loan capital, for example, or creditors to work-in-progress; while many of these may be meaningless some at least will provoke further inquiry and, perhaps, the location of an otherwise undetected error.

Overall ratios, such as ROCE can be particularly useful in evaluating overall bias in a complex forecasting exercise such as the F_0 or F_P.

Verification Sessions

Another technique for eliminating needless errors in a complex forecast is to submit the draft forecast for discussion at a meeting. The figures are thrown open to challenge both by the managers who contributed to the forecast and by others who did not. This approach may be particularly useful to group managers when receiving F_0 and F_P forecasts from a number of subsidiary companies; the forecasters from each subsidiary have to justify their forecasts at a meeting composed of group managers and senior managers from other subsidiaries.

Multi-stage forecasting

Most managers draw up their plans and budgets (i.e. their F_P forecasts) in one large, complex and prolonged exercise, often carried out towards the end of each financial year. If these F_P forecasts are prepared in this way, i.e. in one major exercise, managers may not be able to isolate and control the five types of error described on page 219. It may help to reduce the size of these errors – or at least it may serve to bring the errors into the open for discussion – if managers make their forecasts showing the three stages – F_{00}, F_0 and F_P – separately. Thus as an initial stage in the preparation of an F_0 forecast the manager may make an F_{00} forecast – i.e. a forecast based on the assumption that past trends will continue entirely unchanged into the future. To do this the manager must clearly identify what these trends are, of course. He will then state explicitly (a) what events he believes will affect these trends and (b) how they will affect them. Finally he will show these conclusions as an F_0 forecast.

Again, when moving from an F_0 forecast to an F_P it may be beneficial if each stage is shown separately and explicitly. Thus the manager will show (a) what actions are to be taken by the company and (b) how these are expected to affect the F_0 forecast. For example if a manager has shown demand for product P rising at 7% p.a. in his F_0 forecast but at 10% in his F_P forecast he should justify this by showing (a) what action he proposes to take to bring about this change and (b) how this proposed action will have this effect. It is possible that systematic procedures for showing these steps may be used including perhaps the 'Forecast Amendment Matrix' method proposed by S. Jeckovich (*L.R.P.* Vol. 4 No. 1 Sept. 1971).

Rooting a Forecast in the Past

There are three reasons why a forecast should be made only after a study of the past has been made. The first is that the past is the only guide to the future that we have; it is an unreliable guide but it is all there is. For this reason it is prudent always to show a forecast as part of a continuous series with the past. In Case 1 (page 146) the forecast prepared by Mr Pepper showed only the five future years; it was only necessary to insert the past three years' figures to show that the eight years together could not possibly form a realistic series and therefore that the forecast was probably wildly optimistic.

Ideally, a forecast that looks five years into the future should be seen to be consistent with the past ten years and a ten-year forecast consistent with the past twenty. To forecast ahead five years on the evidence of the past three years, say, may be to risk basing the full five years upon only one half of the most recent national economic cycle for example.

The second justification for showing the past and future as a continuous series rests on a purely practical consideration. The accounting systems of most companies are reorganized and revised almost continuously; in one such revision the basis on which loan interest is charged out to a subsidiary may be altered, in another the definition of fixed and variable costs may be altered, in another the method of valuing stock or work in progress is changed. Sometimes the definition of a product or market is changed in the official government statistics, sometimes a geographical boundary is altered thus changing the basis on which statistics are collected. In order to ensure that a forecast of profits or costs or market shares – or whatever – is on the same basis as past figures it is desirable to show past and present as part of a continuous consistent series.

The third justification for basing a forecast on the careful examination of the past is that this examination may remind the forecaster of the scale of the changes that occur over such long periods of time as five or ten years – I made this point on page 78.

II Forecasting techniques

Until recently nearly all the highly sophisticated forecasting techniques were to be found in the field of short term forecasting; exponential smoothing, regression analysis, input/output matrices and so on. A large number of techniques now exist in the long range field, however, and some of these are briefly described below. I cannot claim that they are listed in any particular sequence. I do claim to have selected them for their usefulness to planners in the next decade or so.

Forecasts are required at no less than four stages in the planning process. The first is where a target (or performance–risk curve) is being selected and when the managers have to try to predict what ROSC shareholders are likely to require over the planning period and what ethological targets will satisfy employees and others. The second is where the F_0 forecasts are being made to determine whether any change in the company's strategic structure is required. The third is when threats and opportunities are being examined where managers will need to predict changes in technology, in social attitudes, in economic prospects and so forth.* The fourth is when the F_P forecasts are made; these, it will be recalled, are intended to show how successful each alternative strategy may be in achieving the long term objectives – i.e. these forecasts show the effect of the company's proposed responses to the threats and opportunities. Forecasting in all four roles is required during the monitoring process, of course.

Futurology and Forecasting

I know of no generally accepted definition of futurology and am not certain how it differs from mere forecasting. A forecast may be of two kinds; it may represent a prediction as to what might happen to one particular item of interest such as the price of gold next year or in five years' time; or it may be a prediction as to the future of a much more complex entity such as an economy or a company. In the first case a single figure, such as $80 per ounce, is the final output of the forecast; in the second case the forecast must contain a battery of figures forming a fairly complete description of the state of the entity at the forecast date including, for example; GDP, balance of trade, money supply etc.

---

* In much of the literature pride of place is given to technological forecasting. Techniques such as Delphi and Conditional Demand Analysis are listed under technological forecasting. cannot understand why such emphasis is placed on this area. Social, economic and political changes are arguably more important than technological ones—or equal in importance at the least—and nearly all the techniques used to forecast technology may be used to forecast other types of change.

in the case of an economy and turnover, loan capital, number of employees, etc. in the case of the company. Both these types, the single and the complex, may be made over the short term (weeks and months) or the long (years and decades). Futurology, as I understand it, not only relates to forecast horizons extending over decades or generations but is concerned with a number of broad aspects of life in the future. Thus to forecast the state of the British economy in AD 2000 is economic forecasting, not futurology; to forecast the state of space research in 1990 is technological forecasting, not futurology. But to forecast the social, political, economic *and* technological conditions in Europe in 1990 *is* futurology.

Kahn and Wiener, for example, in their book *Toward the Year 2000* cover virtually the whole range of human activity on a global scale. Their forecasts range from 'programmed dreams' and 'non-harmful methods of over-indulging' to 'permanent manned satellites' and 'a per capita income of $5000 to $15,000 a year in the USA.' Cannon (Ch. 16) forecasts the appearance of new markets, new technologies, new strategies and so on. Again, the Hudson Institute, in its study of the Corporation and its Environment 1975–85 forecasts some reaction against mass-consumption values, an enormous increase in tourism, computer-ized buying and payments systems, and so on – a very wide-ranging exercise. The well-known MIT study, described in *The Limits to Growth* by Denis L. Meadows is another example of futurology, as opposed to mere forecasting, for it not only looks ahead many decades but covers demographic, technological, economic trends and their interactions. Futurology, then, is very long term (decades) interdisciplinary forecasting. I would add two comments.

The first is to repeat the point made on page 84 where I suggested that, due to the apparently relentless increase in lead-times, the corporate planner will have to plan further and further ahead. A planning horizon of a decade is now commonplace in large companies and I believe that many will soon be looking two or three decades ahead. But there are other relevant trends; the tendency for companies to become social institutions, the rise in the size and number of multinational and international companies, the trend towards diversification – all these suggest that a corporate plan cannot be adequately prepared unless it takes account of political *and* social *and* economic *and* technical changes *and* their interactions on a world wide canvas. In other words the corporate planner will increasingly need to rely on very long range interdisciplinary futurology rather than on separate technological forecasts, economic forecasts, social forecasts. These will continue to be valid in such partial planning areas as research planning, finance planning, manpower planning and so on. Futur-ology is, of course, highly relevant to the growing number of governments and government agencies who are now beginning to adopt the corporate planning philosophy.

The second point I should make relates to the tendency of most futurologists to concentrate upon the positive aspects of the future. Most of them seem to be more concerned to predict phenomena that will appear – such as new products, new industries, new social patterns – rather than to predict which of the features of our present world will disappear. It is as important, it seems to me, to try to predict the consequences of the long term decline of coal-mining in Europe as it is to predict the consequences of the rise of nuclear power. I happen to believe the Building Societies (Savings and Loans Associations as they are called in the USA) will cease to exist (as we know them today) within a few decades – if I am right this could have social consequences that are at least as interesting as the social consequences of, say, new methods of urban transport. I also believe that the mechanical engineering industry will soon enter a decline that will lead to its virtual extinction within five decades – a prediction that is at least as interesting as the more familiar futurological statements about the growth of electronics. In other words, I believe that corporate planners should carefully ensure that the futurology on which their plans are based contains negative as well as positive predictions.

One final point: most of the long range forecasting techniques I am about to describe (including Futurology) are of such recent origin that no one can yet say how accurate any of them are. Few have been in use for more than a decade and therefore many of the predictions made by them are still to be verified. I can only say that, in my experience, long term trends seem to establish themselves for a long enough period to allow one to observe that they exist; then they change.

Sensitivity and Key Factor Analysis

A very large proportion of the time devoted to corporate planning is spent on forecasting. It is prudent, therefore, to forecast only those items that are really going to have a major impact upon the decisions to be made.

At an early stage in the planning process, therefore, an attempt should be made to identify what the key factors are likely to be. When building a model, for example, it may be possible to show that the results are not sensitive to even large changes in one particular variable; it may then be possible to simplify that model by treating this variable as a constant or by leaving it out altogether.

It is important to know, when making assumptions, just how critically these assumptions are going to affect later decisions; Steiner (Ch. 8) refers to High and Low Impact Premises. Part of the art of planning is knowing what not to forecast.

The Delphi Method

I have the impression that this technique is emerging as the most popular of all the newer long range forecasting methods, partly perhaps because it is basically simple and partly because it is not essentially mathematical.

There are two stages. In the first a questionnaire is sent to a number of experts in the field relevant to the event that is to be forecast. Thus if the event to be forecast is, say, the eradication of brucellosis in cattle, a carefully phrased question will be put to a number of veterinary experts inviting them to say when this disease will affect only an insignificant percentage of cattle in a given nation. Their replies are grouped as in Exhibit 12·1, from which it will be seen that there is a considerable span of opinion. In the second stage, those

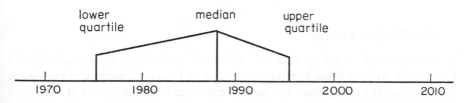

Exhibit 12·1   A typical Delphi result. Stage I, a wide spread of opinion

experts whose estimates differ substantially from the mean are invited to explain why they were so optimistic (or pessimistic) and these explanations are submitted for comment to those who were pessimistic (or optimistic) and to those in the mean. As a result there will be a revision of consensus which may be revised again as the argument runs its course; hopefully the end result will be close to Exhibit 12·2. No communication between the experts takes place in

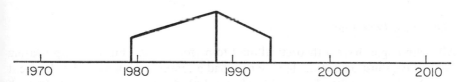

Exhibit 12·2   A typical Delphi result Stage II, expert opinion now less diverse.

the first stage to ensure that the full span of independent opinion is represented; the interaction between these views takes place in the second stage. Variations on this two stage procedure are many and varied (see, for example the articles by George Teeling-Smith in *L.R.P.* Vol. 3 No. 4, June 1971 and by Ole Lachmann in Vol. 5 No. 2 June 1972).

One of the reasons why the Delphi Method has become so popular is that its use is not confined to forecasting. It is essentially a device for obtaining a consensus of opinion; the opinions sought may be those of a group of experts as to some future event but they might just as well be the opinions of a company's top managers as to the strengths and weaknesses of their company. In this case the procedure is very much as described above; the senior managers are asked to list the company's most important strengths and weaknesses. Then, and only then, these differing views are brought together usually at a face-to-face meeting between all the participants and a consensus emerges, often with great clarity, from the discussion. I have no doubt that the Delphi method could be used to set company objectives by forming a consensus as to suitable performance–risk curves for shareholders, managers, customers and so on.

Gordon Wills gives several examples of the use of this technique, together with a specimen questionnaire (*L.R.P.* Vol. 2 No. 3 March 1970).

Prudent Manager Forecasts

One method of forecasting used in Lockheed Aircraft Corporation according to Ewing (Ch. 6) is to bring together a number of Lockheed managers and invite them to play the role of the managers in customer companies who are about to decide what orders to place with Lockheed. In this way Lockheed believe they obtain a useful idea as to the likely demand for any given product.

Steiner (Ch. 8) describes a method known as the Jury of Executive Opinion used in Cooper-Bessemer Corporation. The sales manager makes his forecast of sales and hands it to another manager who comments and passes it to another. Thus a blend of opinion is built up.

Most companies, I think, are aware of the fund of knowledge within their own company, their suppliers, their customers, their advisers, their trade associations, trade embassies and so on whose advice and opinion may be culled in various ways. Nor should one forget to mention the Think Tanks and 'wild men' who may contribute much to a long term forecast.

Theoretical Potentials

All technologies have a theoretical limit to performance. Thus the reciprocating internal combustion engine, having now had a century of intensive development behind it is believed to be capable of very little further improvement. In such circumstances it is reasonable to predict that either progress in automotive engine performance will slow down and eventually cease altogether or that some new form of propulsion will appear (or perhaps, that there is a third alternative the nature of which is unknown at present). Assuming progress is in the nature of man, it must come as no surprise to witness the intense interest today in turbine, rotary, electric, steam, and other vehicle propulsion systems each jockeying for the throne that is about to be vacated by the internal combustion engine.

This succession of technologies is so well established in so many fields – piston, turbine, ram-jet, rockets for aircraft; candles, oil lamps, filaments, tubes for lighting and so on, that technological progress must be considered one of the most reliable features of our society. This being so, if one can establish what is the theoretical limit of potential of any given technology then, if one also knows how far away that limit is, one can predict when a new successor technology will begin to appear.

Establishing theoretical potentials is obviously a job for experts. I should make three points. Firstly this is one of the techniques that is always listed under 'technological forecasting' but its use may extend far beyond technology – the theoretical potential of a nation's capacity to support a given population, the potential of a given system (of traffic control, of documentation, of anything) can often be usefully established and used for predicting change.

Secondly I should warn against the well-known 'sailing-ship effect', when the threat of the appearance of a new technology stimulates new ideas in the old technology thus extending its supposed potential. This occurred when the steamship appeared and, by provoking new designs in sailing ships prolonged the economic battle between them far beyond expectations. It happened more recently when the appearance of nuclear electricity generators provoked improvements in the design of conventional power generation.

Thirdly one must beware of 'technological backlash'. Nearly all new technologies carry unfortunate side-effects; some sections of society are becoming less tolerant to these side-effects and, at the same time, are beginning to value the benefits of technology less highly. The life of some obsolescent technologies may well be prolonged by 'backlash' if not by the sailing-ship effect.

Life Cycle Analysis

Virtually all things display a life cycle pattern commonly known as the S-curve; it is valid for most products, markets, economies, companies, technologies, fashions, social systems and even civilizations. The stages are; birth, rapid growth, moderate growth or stabilitly, decline and extinction. So all-pervasive is this S-curve pattern that it must be highly valued as a predictive tool.

In his article in (*L.R.P.* Vol. 5 No. 1, March 1972), I. C. Hendry describes a Three Parameter Approach for using the S-curve phenomenon. The forecaster has first to judge whether the data he has available best fits a logistic or a Gompertz curve (two varieties of S-Curve); usually, technological changes are best reflected in the logistic curve which has a somewhat longer initial growth phase than the Gompertz. Hendry suggests that the forecaster then needs to estimate three parameters – the initial value, the ultimate value (or Theoretical Potential – see p. 228) and the lifetime for the adoption process – and the life cycle may then be predicted using the standard logistic or Gompertz equations.

Hendry's article is well illustrated with examples and calculations; a brief description of life cycle analysis appears in Denning (Ch. 8 by M. J. Cetron and D. N. Dick) but for a more detailed and mathematical treatment the student will have to turn to mathematical textbooks.

One caution is in order. To be able to predict the second part of a life cycle, knowing the first part, is extremely useful in itself; it would be still more useful if one could predict the nature of the product or technology that was to succeed the existing one – indeed this is frequently why S-curve analysis is performed as Walley (Ch. 6) says. Consider an example, however. It is clear that, some time in the early Eighties the proportion of homes in the USA having colour TV will approach saturation. It is perfectly reasonable to assume that something new will emerge at that point just as, in the Sixties, colour TV emerged to supersede mono. But it would be dangerous to assume that one single new device will emerge, such as 3-D colour TV; it is just as likely that several TV-related devices will appear or that the successor will not be TV-related at all. In dentistry, for example, the drilling of cavities was performed first manually, then by electric motor, then by turbine, now by laser; the next step may be another method of drilling or several different methods of drilling or treatment with no drilling at all. In other words, to predict the end of technology does not imply the start of another *similar* technology. It may imply the start of several new technologies, or something else quite unexpected.

Morphological Analysis

This technique depends on the fact that any object (or concept) may be classified along a number of dimensions; by colour, shape, function, method of construction, and so on. Consider, for example, a common brick; it is oblong, made of clay, opaque. But in theory its shape could be spherical, square, interlocking; it could be made of plastic, metal, wood, fly-ash; and so on. It may be possible, by permutating these alternatives to predict possible new products or even whole technologies; several examples are given in Gordon Wills' article (*L.R.P.* Vol. 2 No. 3, March 1970).

Trend Analysis

Trend Analysis is the collective term for several of the techniques described here including Time Series, Correlation, and Life Cycle Analysis.

Correlation Analysis

It can sometimes be established that a correlation exists between the item to be forecast and some other item. It was widely held, at one time in Britain, that the rate of growth in the demand for new cars was $2\frac{1}{2}$ times the rate of rise in per capita income. Thus if it was forecast that per capita incomes would rise by 3% p.a over the next few years then, according to this supposed correlation, the demand for cars would rise by $7\frac{1}{2}$%. The value of this correlation was (a) that even the least sophisticated motor dealer could forecast future demand for cars from the official government projections as to growth in the UK economy and (b) the more sophisticated companies in the motor industry could crosscheck their independent forecasts of demand against this.

A suspected correlation may be established by the use of several statistical techniques which may also allow one to determine how reliable the correlation is as a predictive aid. The danger, of course, is that the co-relationship may break down without warning. Steiner (Ch. 8) gives several interesting examples of the use of correlation and mentions some of the mathematical techniques used – regression analysis, least squares, etc.

Input-Output Analysis

This technique, invented by Leontieff in the Forties, is now being used extensively as a predictive instrument for national economies. Its use as a tool by individual companies is limited by the cost. The principle employed is simple; the raw materials of one industry in an economy are the finished products of others so that if a forecast of some aspects of economic activity can be made then the level of activity of other parts may be deduced. These inputs and outputs may be formed into a self-balancing matrix and simulation exercises performed using a computer. The potential predictive value of this technique is realized only if changes in productivity, materials usage efficiencies, advances in technology and many other relationships can be forecast.

Time Series Analysis

The fluctuations in sales turnover experienced by any company are due to three main causes; seasonal variations, the business cycle and long term growth trends. Regression analysis, curve fitting and analysis of variance are some of the mathematical techniques that may be used to separate out one from another. Where they can be used it is usually possible to calculate 'confidence limits' – an extremely useful thing to be able to do. To be able to state that 'there is a 95% chance that sales will be between 800 and 1200 in Year X' is considerably more useful than the statement 'sales will be between 800 and 1200 in Year X' for one may then employ mathematical decision analysis techniques – see page 270.

Diffusion Analysis

This is the name given to any systematic attempt to estimate how rapidly a new technology will spread into new fields. A number of uses have already been found for the laser for example; how soon will lasers be used in the building industry, in photography, and so on? Clearly such forecasts can only be made by specialists.

Scenarios

A technique that is particularly useful when quantification is difficult, for example when predicting discrete events as opposed to trends.

A company may wish to know how the technology on which its industry is based will develop over the next two decades. A specialist in that technology will write a detailed account of the changes he foresees; thus ... 'by Year 10 rising fuel costs will demand the introduction of forced draught, oxygen enriched burners. ...' and so on. The scenario is then subjected to discussion and amendment until the management are satisfied that it is a coherent and feasible story.

Scenarios are used extensively to make social and political forecasts; the possible outcomes of the Arab-Israeli dispute, the circumstances under which a conventional war in Europe might develop, or how social patterns might change in America and so on. The key to a good scenario is that it should describe a *feasible* sequence of events that are consistent with each other and with the relevant features of the real world.

Functional Weakness Analysis

It may be possible to predict change by analysing weaknesses in current products, technologies, social patterns. It is widely accepted, for example, that the lead/acid battery is heavy and messy, that jet engines are noisy, that international currency arrangements are inadequate; it is reasonable to assume that major improvements in these areas may come soon. By a careful and systematic analysis of one's own company's products or services and of those of one's competitors, it may be possible to identify weaknesses that, sooner or later, are bound to be corrected.

Conditional Demand Analysis

This is a systematic study of the conditions in which new sources of demand for products, services, technologies and so on would emerge. For example, the demand for weapons for personal defence in Britain is currently extremely small; the conditions in which demand might increase are obvious – they have existed for years in many other nations – and while the probability of these conditions coming about may be low a gunsmith might find it worth while to analyse how and when they could come about. (Not, one hopes, with the aim bringing them about.)

Again, if the Catholic church altered its policy, demand for contraceptives in Italy would rise; how and when this condition might come about could be subjected to systematic study. A whole new field of technology based on the laser would appear if . . . Demand for sulphuric acid would fall dramatically if . . .

Opportunity Identification

This is the name given to the deliberate, systematic search for future opportunities, usually within an area limited by prior discussion. Thus a plastics manufacturer may have decided, on strategic grounds, to move into the building industry. He would then send out teams of employees to make a detailed systematic study of building materials to identify which of those currently used could be replaced by his plastics; wood, metal, clay, glass? In the doors, the walls, the washbasins, the water pipes, the windows? How, where, when? As part of the exercise the teams would have to specify what technical and design changes would have to be made to the company's existing product to take advantage of any opportunity and show how its cost effectiveness could be made better than the existing materials.

Models

Forecasts can be made by means of two rather different types of calculation. In the one type the past performance of the item to be forecast is analysed and its future behaviour predicted from this single set of past figures. Thus, essentially, regression analysis, curve fitting, time series are designed to analyse one series of figures, namely the past behaviour of the item itself; sales of product P were

92, 93, 94, 95, ... , over the past four years and will therefore be 96, 97, ... , over the next two. Some of the mathematics is complex but essentially this is all that this type of forecasting is intended to do and no attempt is made to analyse *why* each year's figures for product P were as they were. The second type of calculation is concerned with analysing the forces behind the item to be forecast.

Unfortunately the factors affecting the behaviour of any item are complex; sales of product P are affected by its price, quality, population trends, disposable income and so on endlessly. Clearly, if one could forecast these causal factors, then, knowing the extent to which they affect sales of P, one could forecast sales of P. So complex are such calculations, however, that it was only when the calculating capacity of the computer became available that it became worthwhile to build 'models'. A model is a set of mathematical equations describing how several factors are interrelated.

Models for short term forecasting are used extensively in government and industry. For example, a nation's GNP is defined as Consumption + Investment + (Exports – Imports) or

$$Y = C + I + (X - M)$$

But we know that consumption is a function of prices and incomes and that investment is a function of income and profits; or

$$C = f \text{ (Income; prices)}$$
$$I = f \text{ (Income; profits)}$$

and that exports and imports . . . and so on. Provided that the data can be obtained for current levels of income, prices and so on, and provided that the relationships between them are known, then if one forecasts what all these variables and coefficients will be in a year's time one can calculate what Y will be. But, more important, one may make a large number of calculations to show what Y will be under a variety of assumptions as to the behaviour of the variables. Unfortunately, in practice, (a) most of the data available to a government is several months out of date (b) taxation decisions take several months to affect consumption and investment decisions even longer, (c) there are a number of exogenous variables over which even governments have no control and cannot forecast accurately and finally (d) a small error in one sensitive variable can cause very large errors in the result and this may render this type of model unsuitable for long range forecasting.*

A manufacturer supplying retail outlets may forecast future demand in period p as:

$$D_p = S_p + I_c$$

where S_p is the retailers' estimate of sales in that period plus any change they

---

* I heard of one model where an error of only 0·01 % in one variable caused the computer to show a very severe dis-stability in the forecast for the year 1984. Of course, it could be right.

make in their inventory levels (I_c). S_p itself may be estimated as sales in the current period (S_{p-1}) adjusted by the growth rate of the market (g) or;

$$S_p = g\,S_{p-1}$$

The retailers' inventory level in period p will depend on its current level, on delivery dates, on their view of future demand in period $p+1$—and so on – all of which may be expressed mathematically. In this way the equations are built up step by step, the model is tested against past trends to verify its accuracy and then used to make forecasts.

There are a number of models now in use for short term forecasting; confidence in them for a long range forecasting is not very high, I believe. Their value in either role is much enhanced if, rather than making one calculation to establish a point forecast, a large number of calculations are made on different assumptions as to both variables and coefficients to establish a range forecast. This approach, often termed Simulation, is generally well understood today.

Social Forecasting

The various methods of trend analysis are used in social forecasting as in any other area; forecasts of population, employment, occupation, marriage, divorce, housing and so on may all be forecast by reference to past trends.

However, while these quantitative forecasts are valuable for themselves, it is the qualitative implication of these trends and their interactions within the total social system that are often of major significance. It may be possible to predict, for example, that the distribution of wealth in, say, Italy will continue to become more unequal; but, important though that may be in itself for forecasting sales of goods in the various price brackets, it may be of more importance to forecast if and when this trend will cause severe social tensions.

In view of the importance of making qualitative forecasts sociologists now use three methods of forecasting that deserve particular mention; analysis of changes in social attitudes, life style analysis and social analogies. As to changes in social attitudes; considerable study has been given to such well-known changes as: the marked rise in consumerism, a reaction against the business ethic, an increase in permissiveness in individual behaviour (but the reverse in corporate behaviour), a reaction against efficiency and against inequality. None of these may be readily quantified but their impact upon companies is considerable. Attitudes to work, for example, appear to be forming up into two very distinct camps; on the one hand it is believed that work should be rewarding and enjoyable (this leads to job enrichment strategies) while on the other hand it is held that work is merely a means of earning a richer life outside work (leading to the extremely high pay and short hours of the American motor industries).

As to life style analysis; one trend that appears to have been established for many decades is the general upgrading of occupations. Assuming that this will continue it may be legitimate to predict a decline in working class life styles together with the implications this has on housing needs, leisure pursuits, savings patterns, insurance requirements, consumption patterns and so on.

As to the argument by analogy with trends in other similar societies, the difficulty is to identify which of the trends in other nations are relevant to one's own. Will British companies accept the German system of Supervisory boards? Will the infrastructure of European cities break down to the extent it has in New York? Will any of the European nations follow the Californian life style patterns?

13 The gamut of strategies

Introduction

I drew attention on page 15 to the fact that it was not possible to distinguish clearly between a 'strategic decision' and a 'tactical decision'. But I also suggested that the most relevant feature of a strategic decision was that it was intended to bring about a major change in the structure of the company as a whole. A strategic decision is usually worthy of inclusion in the chairman's annual report to shareholders; it is a decision that may be remembered and discussed years after it has been put into effect.

And yet, if my view of corporate planning is correct, a strategic decision is located only at the third level of importance in the hierarchy of decisions. At the first level is the determination of the corporate objectives (both financial and ethological). At the second level there is the decision as to the long term coarse-grained strategic structure. Only at the third level does one select a portfolio of individual strategies that are specifically chosen to bring about the desired structure. Thus the structure largely limits the area of choice among the gamut of strategies that lie before one. This is just as well for the range of possible strategies is almost infinite.

Not all strategies are selected with the strategic structure in mind, however. I suggested on page 69 that a good rule of thumb in planning is to take as few decisions as possible; the strategic structure should be as skeletal as possible, it should contain only those elements that really have to be specified years ahead and should not include any features of the future company that do not have to be determined. This usually means that only some of the financial structure, some of the product and market structure, some of the organizational structure need be specified and very little else. Thus the strategic structure, once determined, will often only constrain the choice of strategy in the financial, in the product and market and in the organizational areas. Many of the other areas – buying, research, or production – need not be so specified and the selection of individual strategies in these areas will be made on the grounds that they marry up with the strategies chosen in the finance, marketing and organizational areas. For some companies, however, the buying strategy, and for others the production strategy, will be specified by the strategic structure and the marketing or the organizational strategies will be selected to marry with them. It might be helpful to classify strategies in two categories, then: primary strategies which are selected because they lead to a desired change in the strategic structure and secondary strategies which are selected because they follow rationally from a primary strategy. (Cannon (Ch. 2) prefers three categories; results strategies, action strategies and commitment strategies).

To illustrate: a company currently sells two products into twenty different markets. The management decides, following an analysis of their performance-risk gap and the data in their cruciform chart, that this structure should be changed to four products into seven markets. This is the chosen strategic structure. They would then select two new products to launch into a selected seven of their existing markets and gradually withdraw the existing two products from thirteen markets – these are all primary strategies because they are demanded by the structure. They also decide to build two factories, one in market area 5 and another in area 7 and to appoint four new project managers. These are secondary strategies because they follow from the primary strategies; they do not follow directly from the strategic structure which was silent as to the production and organizational areas of the company.

In this chapter I shall list or classify some of the common strategies and types of strategies that companies adopt. No list can ever include all possible strategies (although Cannon's list must come close to it) let alone include all possible combinations and permutations. I happen to believe that for each company at any given moment in time there is one portfolio of strategies that will be more appropriate than any other but that it is impossible in practice to identify it. But the converse is also true, namely that there are countless thousands of strategies that are very definitely *not* appropriate to any given company and that the corporate planning process is a practical and efficient means of ensuring that no company will choose one of these.

Growth strategies

Apart from the Non-growth strategies, which are briefly described below, and those specifically concerned with Risk-reduction, all strategies are growth strategies. With these two exceptions, then, a diversification strategy, or a product pricing strategy, or an R & D strategy – *any* strategy – is designed to facilitate the growth of earnings or share price or turnover or size or whatever.

Non-growth strategies

As I suggested on page 50 it is not inconceivable that in the coming decades more firms will adopt non-growth strategies. There are a number of reasons why this may be so; some companies, IBM for example, are constantly under attack on the grounds of their virtual world monopoly position; some on the grounds that their influence in a given local community is disproportionate; some on the grounds of their supposed inefficiency due to their 'unmanageable size'. Other firms may simply prefer to remain below the critical size (probably around the level of a few hundred employees) where the management problems of human relations, financial control and so on become suddenly severe. The two alternatives to growth are zero growth and de-growth.

A zero-growth objective simply means that the company chooses an earnings growth of nil; it does not imply a ROSC target of nil, of course. A ROSC target of 15% with nil growth may be achieved by a 15% dividend yield, one of 25% by a 25% dividend yield. Nor does a zero-growth earnings target necessarily imply a zero-growth turnover target, nor that new products do not have to be introduced. If margins are falling, turnover will have to rise to maintain earnings; if products become obsolescent new ones will have to be introduced. To achieve a zero-growth earnings target, then, the firm continues to act in the same way as one aiming at growth but the rate of change demanded is that much lower. If margins are falling by 5% a year then to achieve zero growth the company must increase turnover by 5% instead of, say, by 15% to achieve a 10% growth target.

Clearly to achieve zero growth calls for a much lower level of activity from the management; far fewer project proposals will be required, fewer evaluations are required; fewer project managers, fewer market researchers are needed and so on. There is less innovation and less risk. The quality of management required is lower and their remuneration and recruitment costs are lower. It is not inconceivable, therefore, that with a zero-growth strategy the achievement of a given level of ROSC would be easier and some shareholders might conceivably prefer the 'jam today' of high dividend yields rather than the 'jam tomorrow' promise of future capital gains.

A de-growth strategy is one designed to meet a dividend pay-out ratio that is in excess of 100% of earnings. Thus a ROSC of 15% may be achieved by a dividend yield of 25% declining at 10 %p.a., i.e., the reserves of the company are intentionally depleted in order to return some of their capital to the shareholders each year. This could be achieved by a strategy of divestment; this does not imply management neglect or that the efficiency of the company's remaining activities are allowed to decay. It merely implies that the capital realized by divestment exceeds the capital invested in the remaining activities and the surplus is returned to the shareholder.

It is important to distinguish between a declining or decaying company and one pursuing a strategy of de-growth. In the first case the shareholder receives a declining level of *ROSC* while in the second he may receive a declining level of *dividend* – but, since the capital remaining invested in the company is declining his ROSC remains constant or may even rise. (It may well rise if the company disposes of its activities in the right sequence, i.e. starting with the least profitable and leaving the most profitable to the last).

Risk-reducing strategies

All companies face the possibility that an event E (or combination of events) will occur with severe consequences to that company's ability to achieve its targets. Three broad categories of strategy may be adopted; (a) to prevent or postpone or modify the occurrence of E itself, (b) to mitigate its effects on the company before it occurs or (c) to mitigate its effects when it occurs.

(a) Prevention, Postponement or Modification

Where a company has sufficient political influence it may be able to prevent or modify legislation that will harm its business interests – a ploy said to be used by the American Rifle Association to foil attempts to legislate against the freedom of American citizens to purchase weapons. Where a company fears a savage price war among its competitors it may propose a cartel; where it is very dependent upon one customer (or supplier) it may enter into a long term contract, reduce the price of its product to that customer (or allow the supplier to raise the price) or introduce penalty clauses into contracts and so on. It may purchase the patent rights to a rival invention, it may dump goods in a foreign competitor's market as a warning – the list of such strategies is endless, but it must be added, there is increasing pressure from public opinion against many of these risk-prevention strategies.

(b) Mitigation

The most popular risk-mitigation strategy is diversification. If the threat comes from possible changes in the market, one seeks new and different markets, if the threat is to one's product one seeks different products, if the threat is from suppliers in one nation one seeks suppliers in different nations. If the threat is from the economic cycle one seeks a new business area that is counter-cyclical.

Other mitigation strategies are possible, however. One possibility is to prepare to meet the threat head-on; thus a company may build up its liquidity in property, trade investments, stocks and so on during the upswing of a business cycle against the possibility of a downswing. Again, a company pro-posing to build a plant in a politically unstable nation will mitigate the risk of sequestration by raising much of the capital in the host nation.

It is often stated that plans should be 'flexible' so that the company may be left room for a mitigating manoeuvre should a threat (or opportunity) appear. I have suggested that decisions should not be made before they have to be made and that plans should never be more detailed than they have to be (page 69) but it is in the nature of the business situation that once a 1000 ton sulphuric acid plant has been built it becomes a somewhat inflexible object; once taken, the decision to market a range of products in Brazil becomes somewhat limited in flexibility – one cannot easily switch the decision to Peru. Flexibility may not often be a practical risk mitigation strategy.

(c) Contingency

Mitigation strategies will normally be used where the threat posed by event E is very great and when E is thought very likely to occur; a contingency plan will normally be used when the occurrence of event E is thought to be highly improbable but of such importance that it must be allowed for. A mitigation strategy will normally form an integral part of a corporate plan; a contingency plan will normally consist of an alternative sub-plan to be put into action if the event E occurs.

In his article in *L.R.P.* Vol. 3 No. 3 April 1971 Michael J. Clay lists some of the contingencies that many companies may wish to plan against; they include a take-over bid, an accident incapacitating the board, an epidemic, destruction of company records, 'scare' rumours concerning one's product in the popular press and so on. Clay suggests that when such events occur it may be possible to use the Decision Tree technique (see page 287) to identify the most appropriate response.

Because risk is so crucial an element in the business situation I must add that I cannot believe that a corporate plan can be valid in the real world unless it contains some form of risk reduction strategy. If a corporate plan contains strategies that are designed merely to increase profits, then, in my opinion it is incomplete. Unless the planner can point to at least one element in his plan which is designed to prevent or mitigate a threat or deal with a contingency I would suggest that it is basically misconceived.

Some of the techniques described in Chapter 15 are particularly relevant to risk reducing strategies; games theory may be used in developing risk-prevention strategies, decision theory in risk-mitigation and so on. However the most important strategic decision is which of the three different types of risk reducing strategy to adopt in any given circumstances; I believe this can best be determined by reference to the performance–risk gap analysis (which indicates the nature of the company's risk position) and to the data in the cruciform chart.

Acquisition and merger strategies

There does not appear to be a standard definition of either of these terms. In general in an acquisition the acquiring company is much larger than the acquired and the acquired is neutral or hostile to the bid; there is no obvious advantage to the acquired in joining the acquirer, other than the eventually agreed terms of the bid. In a merger the companies are of more equal size and there are clear mutual advantages to both companies. Thus a French company A, wishing to market its products in Turkey will either *acquire* the Turkish company B by offering such terms that B's objections are overcome or it will *merge* with Turkish company C which happens to be thinking of marketing its products in France. Many mergers and acquisitions occur because one or both companies wish to diversify; some – especially in the case of mergers – occur to strengthen the partners in their existing business area.

Mergers or acquisitions are not ends in themselves; they are means of achieving a given strategic structure. Any given structure may be achieved either by gradual internal change or by the more drastic device of a merger or acquisition. Deciding which route is best is a typical make or buy decision; the key primary variables which influence the choice are, says Ansoff (Ch. 9), start-up costs and timing – to which Steiner (Ch. 21) would add risk, (rightly I believe). Thus an acquisition strategy would be adopted if (a) the cost of buying into a new business area was less than developing into it, (b) if this diversification was considered urgent and (c) if the risk of developing into it was greater than buying into it. While it is relatively easy to make such general statements it is by no means easy to make the calculations that these statements imply can be made.

Among the reasons Steiner lists for companies wishing to make acquisitions are; to grow, to reduce dependence on one product, to obtain greater stability, to obtain needed technical abilities, to cut costs by economy of scale or synergy, break into new markets, acquire tax write-offs. Companies are willing to be acquired because of the owner's need to pay inheritance tax, or he wishes to retire or needs additional cash. Steiner also lists several warnings, for it must be said that a number of mergers have failed sadly and few have been entirely successful; even the new, rather tentative form of semi-merger between Fiat and Renault and Dunlop and Pirelli have been disappointing and there was no lack of careful consideration before these were consummated. Among Steiner's warnings are: do not acquire a company in distress, use the services of reputable experts (for acquisitions raise very complex issues), make use of a high P/E ratio to acquire a lower one and, very important, the chief executive must be heavily involved. Ansoff suggests that acquisitions that have been thoroughly planned are often the more successful (*L.R.P.* Vol. 3 No. 2 Dec. 1970) – an assertion echoed by most authors.

Hussey (Ch. 7) adds other reasons for a policy of acquisition; it may serve to reduce competition or, alternatively, to reorganize a fragmented industry. Stemp (Ch. 11) introduces another factor into the internal versus external (or make or buy) dilemma; the choice depends to some extent upon management style he says, thus reminding us of the importance of what Ackoff calls stylistic objectives. Stemp also casts severe doubt on the validity of a merger as a means of taking up slack in idle capacity. He questions whether we yet know enough about the management of diverse enterprises to make acquisition a fully valid strategy for its own sake. Acquisitions are just one alternative route to growth – one amongst many.

Walley (Ch. 11) believes that, in spite of the large number of failures, mergers can be successful if (a) the acquiring company is well managed and can realize the full potential of the acquired company and (b) if there is an appropriate strategy, including a strategy for the bid itself. He then summarizes a method of determining an acquisition strategy which, I believe, is very similar to the procedure outlined in this book. Thus he lists the company's objectives and determines the gap, examines the company's strengths and weaknesses and threats and opportunities. He declares that the necessity for an acquisition may stem from the formulation of general company strategies or, perhaps, as a contingency strategy. Walley seems to consider risk separately, however, while I attempt to consider it together with performance in performance–risk analysis.

Diversification strategies

Ansof (Ch. 7) lists four reasons why firms diversify; (1) when their objectives can no longer be met by merely expanding within their existing product-market, (2) because the retained cash exceeds the investment demand for mere expansion (3) if there are greater profit opportunities than in its present product market, (4) firms may explore diversification possibilities if the information available does not permit a conclusive comparison between expansion and diversification. Steiner adds a few more; to avoid dependence on one product line, to achieve greater stability of profits, to make greater use of an existing distribution system and to acquire new know-how – but here, and elsewhere in Ch. 21, Steiner is discussing acquisition and merger strategies in the same breath as diversification strategies. (Diversification can be attained without acquisition and an acquisition can be made that does not lead to diversification, of course).

Ansoff lists four types of diversification: horizontal, vertical, concentric and conglomerate. Other authors use almost an identical classification of alternatives although, for example, in Dr Bruno Hako's article, concentric and conglomerate are combined in 'lateral' (*L.R.P.* Vol. 5 No. 2 June 1972). Most authors deal at length with the subject of diversification and my impression is that there is an extremely wide measure of agreement on (a) the various types of diversification (b) why firms diversify and (c) the advantages, disadvantages and pitfalls of each of the types of diversification. I shall try to summarize these briefly.

Horizontal diversification

When a company widens its range of products (by which I mean goods or services) to its current markets it is said to be diversifying horizontally. Examples of this type are given by Ansoff; a motor manufacturer offering motor cycles or lawnmowers to its traditional customers or, and this involves a technological departure, offering them electrical home appliances. Steiner quotes BVD Co. Inc., an underwear manufacturer which achieved horizontal diversification by acquiring several firms making knitwear, lingerie, men's clothing. Hako quotes Unilever which moved outwards from food and soap to other consumer goods and services.

The advantages of a horizontal diversification are (a) the firm continues to sell into a market which it knows and understands – or, in Ansoff's terms it may take advantage of marketing synergy by continuing to sell through its existing distribution channels; (b) it allows greater specialization in one area of knowledge (the market) and may allow spare manufacturing capacity to be usefully taken up. But the disadvantages are (a) that the company will be moving deeper into an existing business area and, clearly, it has to be very sure of the long term future for the area; (b) if it is sure of this, so perhaps will its competitors be and they may also decide upon a horizontal diversification as occurred when, according to Hako, Unilever, Motta, Nestlé, Lyons all diversified into similar areas simultaneously; (c) a large firm may eventually come to dominate one market thus provoking anti-trust legislation.

Vertical diversification

A vertical diversification (sometimes called vertical integration) takes place when a company begins to manufacture its own components (or to win its own raw materials). This is a backwards integration as exemplified by Ansoff in the case of a motor manufacturer making its own engines, wheels, or I should add, steel. Hako quotes ICI integrating forwards into the manufacture of textiles from its own synthetic fibres.

The advantages of a vertical integration are (a) the firm may obtain much better control over the flow of materials, reduction in stock holdings and other reduced costs; (b) it may reap advantages in specialization within the framework of one industry (c) it may lead to a strengthening of its position with customers. The disadvantages may be very severe especially in an era of rapid change for (a) by diversifying vertically it is placing still more eggs in the same end-product basket (as Ansoff puts it); (b) there may be little or no similarity between, say, making components and assembling them – as Henry Ford discovered when, according to Ansoff, he found that he was unable to sell his surplus components to his competitors; (c) there may be no technical similarities between the new and the old business and technological synergy may even be negative. Hako points out that a raw materials supplier could integrate forwards by starting to manufacture the goods from which the materials are made, but, if he does he will be competing with his own customers. He suggests a very interesting alternative – to offer an applications service to this customers instead. Hako draws particular attention to the danger, inherent in a vertical diversification, that one's customers may resent competition from their erstwhile suppliers.

Concentric diversification

Ansoff's example of Concentric is of the motor manufacturer who decides also to manufacture farm machinery; the new customers are only somewhat similar to the old, the new product and its technology is only somewhat similar to a car and yet a car and a pea-harvester are not wholly dissimilar – there is some commonality and hence some scope for positive synergy. Cannon describes this type of diversification as composite.

I do not believe it is possible to generalize as to the advantages and disadvantages of concentric diversification; this is because a move in this direction is almost invariably made for quite specific reasons. An oil company having close relations with an Arab government might, for example, become a general import-export dealer for that nation; this diversification is neither vertical nor horizontal and is validated solely by one important strength. The machine tool company, quoted by Ackoff (Ch. 1), which diversified into earthmoving equipment did so solely because the latter was countercyclical to the former – i.e. it was justified by one important weakness. A firm may diversify concentrically solely because one of the directors happens also to be an expert in that area.

Conglomerate diversification

A true conglomerate is a company active in several business areas of which none has any intentional relationship or similarly with any other. There is no synergy at all other than the management skills required to make a conglomerate function. Ansoff properly notes the difference between a company having no strategy at all and one that has deliberately adopted the strategy of conglomerate diversification. Conglomerates include Ling-Temco-Vought, Textron, ITT.

The advantages of a conglomerate company are (a) better access to capital due partly to size and partly to the stability that comes from a wide portfolio of activities, (b) the company may move quickly, usually by acquisition, into any area seen to be profitable (c) anti-trust legislation and other penalties of market dominance are avoided or postponed. But the disadvantages are (a) they appear to be more severely affected by economic recessions than other companies, (b) in such a recession their earnings multiple may fall, thus severely limiting their ability to acquire new companies – as this is the main plank on which their growth is built the consequences may be severe; (c) as they grow larger the fewer are the companies suitable for acquisition – in the ultimate there are none; (d) there being no synergy there is, in theory, no reason to believe that a conglomerate can be more profitable than the sum of its separate parts; however this is only true if one ignores the key to conglomerate success, namely the quality of the management and financial ability at their headquarters.

Multinational strategies

David P. Rutenburg, in his article in *LR.P.* (Vol. 2 No. 2 Dec. 1969) suggests that the headquarters of a multinational company should plan the movements of products, ideas, money and people so that the synergistic benefits of multi-national co-ordination exceed the behavioural costs of intervening in the affairs of the subsidiaries. He then analyses where such synergy may be found: by introducing a product sequentially, nation by nation, for example, instead of simultaneously; by assigning all commercially risky orders to a plant that is located in a particular nation not on grounds of low production costs but because that nation offers commercial insurance for exports; by the use of tax havens; by dispersing sub-assembly or component factories (such as producing oil in Venezuela, refining in Curaçao, marketing in Brazil). He suggests that a number of operational research techniques (such as mathematical programming) may be used to make such decisions which should be made by reference to the base case, namely the case where headquarters makes no decisions at all.

In a wide ranging survey of international business published in *The Economist* (Jan. 22nd 1972) Norman Macrae suggests a number of multinational strategies. Because of the potential power of computerized learning techniques Macrae suggests that it will be both possible and desirable for the industrial multinationals progressively to site more of their productive capacity in the developing world – by the time this trend becomes of major significance, in a few decades, inter-continental communications will have become cheap and easy. The successful multinational, he suggests, will be the one which knows how to use local labour more skilfully than the local company, rather than the one which identifies and exploits a foreign market. The article suggests that the days of the multinational are numbered; international trade unions and their own internal bureaucracy being their main threats.

Payne (Ch. 11) emphasizes the need for a multinational company to plan the introduction of its products into a nation in strict accordance with the phase of developement attained by that nation. He cites Rostow's five stages of national development (which, incidentally, do not include the post-industrial phase) and comments that there would be little merit in introducing a highly sophisticated new product into a nation that was still in the early stages of agriculture for neither the demand nor the capital nor the skill nor the distribution channels would exist. While that may be obvious, less obvious is the point that a very large number of these conditions have to be right for a successful introduction. One other condition is important; 'your company has to be *first* into the market,' (a view that appears to be at variance with Macrae's).

In Stemp (Ch. 10) Leslie F. Murphy draws particular attention to the problems of international financing. He describes some of the legal snares: the regulations as to capital movements, the repatriation of dividends to parent companies, tariffs and quotas, Eurodollars and bonds. Cannon (Ch. 6) draws particular attention to this problem area. I would venture this suggestion: most multinational companies are large enough to be fully capable of designing a suitable strategic structure, of investigating suitable markets, of researching new products, of raising new capital, of recruiting good managers; but there is one rock on which many of their plans may founder – international trade legislation. This is now so complex and so subject to detailed change that only a team of international legal and financial experts can sometimes unravel the true position. Those managements who are at home in its complexities have a signal advantage over those who are not.

In Denning (Ch. 18) Millard H. Pryor suggests that three common strategic mistakes are made when planning a world wide business. The first is for headquarters to decide too much of the detail for the subsidiaries – a point that echoes Rutenburg's base case concept. (It should be noted, however, that the only multinational to emerge unscathed from the 1968–72 world recession was ITT, reputed to be the most centralized multinational of them all!) Secondly Pryor suggests that multinationals tend to make plans in a regional rather than national framework. Thus Canada is not similar to the US as the Singer Company, which treated them as a single North American region, soon discovered. The third mistake, says Pryor, is to underestimate the importance of local politics, (but perhaps this is merely a special case of the first mistake).

Pryor suggests that the major functions of a multinational corporate plan should be (1) to set and monitor financial objectives, (2) to prepare a world wide supply strategy and (3) to plan the hiring and training of key managers. Marketing, he suggests, is almost certainly not one of the functions that may be planned at headquarters.

On the other hand Cannon (Ch. 6) seems to see marketing strategy as one of the key areas in multinational planning. He suggests that there are three broad types of marketing strategy; one based on world wide exports from the parent's base, one based on geographic decentralization of semi-autonomous subsidiaries in which manufacturing and other facilities are set up in foreign nations and one he calls global functional operation with a matrix form of organization (see page 254). He lists some of the major advantages and disadvantages of each and states that the global strategic structure will become increasingly valid. (Macrae seems to be predicting that the geographic decentralization style will predominate). James Leontiades seems to share Cannon's view; in his article (*L.R.P.* Vol. 3 No. 2 Dec. 1970), he suggests that while some multinationals do well by adapting their marketing approach to local national conditions, others do well by simply transferring their products and marketing techniques unaltered to the foreign markets. Which is the best strategy must surely be decided at headquarters: and if so then perhaps the matrix technique described by Leontiades could prove useful in identifying patterns of similarity and dissimilarity between the many markets of the world. The article describes some interesting patterns in international markets.

Steiner (Ch. 23) makes an important statement; he believes that the principles of corporate planning apply to international business in almost exactly the same way as they apply to any other organization. But there are some important dissimilarities which include: (a) the alternatives open are on a world wide scale, (b) local variations, being national rather than merely international, are sometimes extremely wide so that responsibility for strategy may be centralized while operational control may not, (c) the mode of entry to a new market is different (the sequence: export – licence a foreign producer – local manufacture, being a common one), (d) data on conditions abroad is difficult to obtain, (e) decisions by several host governments must be taken into account, (f) there may be more conflicts between national and company objectives, (g) international currency crises and changes frequently occur, (h) local nationalism may demand that unsuitable local employees are recruited.

I do not know how to summarize this section; the various views I have summarized are often contradictory. My view is expressed on page 136 where I said that corporate planning in a huge multinational is no different in principle to planning in a small firm; corporate planning is concerned with the big questions, so the crux is the definition of 'big'. I define big as the strategic structure – the corporate plan of all companies, large or small, must specify at least some aspects of this, and which aspects are and which are not specified is itself an important decision. In order to devise a strategic structure it is seldom necessary to delve into detail – the cruciform chart, for example, need contain very little detail – but, unlike those in other companies, international corporate planners do have to examine one area in minute and painstaking detail. This is the complex web of international trade and financial legislation and practice. All other details may be left to decision by local managements who know the local conditions; what they may not know and what the central management may not know either are the regulations governing trade *between* the various nations in which the multinational proposes to operate. I believe this *international* problem to be the sole difference in principle between planning for the international company and planning for a national company. The problem will, to some extent, be ameliorated by the more extensive use of computer models in which the great burden of calculating the effect of international financial regulations will be taken over by the computer. A start in this direction is foreshadowed in James B. Boulden's article in *L.R.P.* (Vol. 5, No. 3 Sep. 1972).

Product strategies

Cannon (Ch. 4) classifies product strategies into six categories and gives many examples of each. In the first of these, 'primary versus selective demand' he examines the multi-million dollar programme adopted by RCA to develop consumer demand for their colour-TV process. This contained elements of primary and selective demand product strategies; primary because RCA were attempting to develop an entirely new market for a new product, selective because they were trying to steer the customer towards RCA products selectively. A primary strategy is one designed to expand demand for a new or an established product and frequently involves finding new uses for the product; a selective strategy is rather more defensive in that it rests not on expanding demand but on obtaining an increased share.

Cannon clearly relates each type of strategy to the results required – i.e. to the company's chosen objectives and strategic structure; thus, for example, to reduce cyclical declines one would tend to choose a primary strategy for an established product. His second category is termed 'breadth of line' and is concerned with diversification and simplification of the product portfolio. The third is 'product overlap'; he cites Proctor and Gamble as one well-known illustration of the strategy of competing with oneself; another version of this strategy is the private label so common in the food industries. A fourth category is 'product customerization' – i.e. the careful design of a product to suit a section of the total customer population which leads to segmentation of markets, to the production of several grades of products, to the modification of existing products, and to custom-built production.

Cannon's fifth category is the product-system strategy. Typical of these are the supply of an entire defence system to a government – as opposed to the company merely supplying a number of tanks, rockets, radars. Product pricing strategies come in his sixth category; these include leasing, warranties and guarantees, expendables (i.e. design the product so that parts of it are expendable thus encouraging a continued demand) and 'iceberg' pricing (i.e.

pricing the product so as to cover its future servicing by the supplying company).

In his article in *L.R.P.* (Vol. 2 No. 4 June 1970), Reginald May draws attention to the critical importance of pricing policy within a corporate strategy. He emphasizes the disadvantages of absorption costing (which is still used by a large number of companies, I believe), and describes the difficulty of using marginal costing. He suggests (a) that one should price a product in accordance with its value to the customer and (b) that a pricing strategy must be related to other strategies.

Walley (Ch. 9) also emphasizes the importance of integrating a pricing strategy with other marketing strategies; his attitude to absorption and marginal costing is similar to May's and adds that games and decision theory (see page 286) may be used in pricing decisions. Hussey (Ch. 11) particularly emphasizes the concept of product life cycle as a factor in deciding product strategies – indeed one sufficient justification for long range planning is the identification of the point when the company has to act to extend the life cycle of a product. Payne (Ch. 6) concentrates less on existing products than on new ones. He emphasizes that new product ideas should be evaluated, not only against purely financial criteria, but by asking whether the company has the necessary competences to exploit the idea, whether it enhances the company's reputation and whether the company is willing and able to devote the resources necessary to market it. He lists the sources of product ideas that companies may tap. In this context it is interesting to learn from Ronald S. Wishart in Stemp (Ch. 7) that most new product ideas come from outside the company; it is a company's ability to develop these ideas that really counts.

Steiner (Ch. 10) reminds managers of the rate of product failures. Of one hundred bright ideas that are considered only one will be a commercial success – in the pharmaceutical industry the ratio may be as low as one in 6000. The keys to success are (a) bright ideas (b) the ability to develop them (c) planning – i.e. a systematic procedure and a carefully designed organization devoted to the generation, screening and implementation of product ideas.

D. W. Foster, (*L.R.P.* Vol. 2 No. 3 March 1970) described multi-product strategies in some detail. The essence of this article is that a company should define a product-market strategy in terms of a correct definition of its business and then build up an integrated portfolio of products in that business. Thus a product-market strategy defined as 'providing amenities for human living' would suggest a whole portfolio of products that would include furniture, domestic heating and ventilation, pharmaceuticals and aerosols, servicing machines and vehicles, home electronics.

Market strategies

Cannon (Ch. 5) lists three broad types of market strategy; Industry, Customer Application. The first includes (a) across-the-board strategies, i.e. where a product line is offered to industrial consumers in all types of industry as IBM does, for example; (b) selective industry strategies where a company identifies one or two industries only as its marketing target, exemplified by International Computers Limited who have decided not to try to compete with IBM over the whole field but have selected certain industries only; and (c) a 'beachhead' strategy which is of particular relevance for a company launching a new product and wishing to use one selected industry as a beachhead.

Among customer strategies are (a) those which deliberately exclude sales to small customers, poor credit risk customers, or other marginal groups – Cannon calls these 'exclusion of marginal accounts' strategies; (b) key account strategies, i.e. those designed to concentrate sales through very large customers, or customers of high repute or customers with international connections or whatever; (c) small business strategies such as providing an extra specific service for certain customers or tailoring the products specifically to small customers. He lists the following application strategies; (a) penetration and saturation of established applications (i.e. increasing one's share of the market in those areas where the product is already used); (b) development of new uses for established products; (c) invading established applications through product substitution and (d) finding new applications through technological refinements.

Cannon suggests that companies traditionally define their business in terms of products but for every product strategy there is a matching market strategy – a statement that accords well with Ansoff's product-market strategic concept. Cannon also classifies a number of geographic strategies (Ch. 6) and distribution channel strategies (Ch. 7); in the former he describes local, national and international market strategies and the location of facilities and in the latter he describes direct sales, retailing, wholesaling and mail order strategies.

While Cannon repeatedly stresses that strategies should be selected for the results the company wishes to achieve, Walley starts with aims and then classifies strategies. Among strategic aims relevant to marketing strategies he lists the desire to take share from a competitor, to protect ones own share, to create new markets for existing products, to launch a new product, etc. Among the key marketing decisions are those related to choice of markets which Walley classifies as (1) capable of being expanded, (2) saturated, (3) contracting, (4) volatile (i.e. open to price cutting) and (5) static. Within these divisions are many others – the market may be defined by the customer's age, sex, income, education, religion or by its geographical location and so on. Among market strategies he lists (1) Undifferentiated – i.e. every possible market segment is covered by the company in what is sometimes called 'the shotgun' approach; (2) Differentiated – i.e. where the full range of products are offered only to a segment or selected segments of the market and (3) Concentrated where a limited number of products are offered to a segment or segments.

Financial strategies

Considerable confusion surrounds this area because in business all strategies are financial in the sense that business is about money. However I believe there are some strategies that are purely or largely financial.

One of them is dividend policy. The manner in which a company makes payment of interest on shareholders' capital depends partly on shareholders' specific wishes, partly on tradition and partly on the management. If the shareholders specifically state their preference for a particular pay-out ratio then, presumably, this must be accepted as a corporate objective. If the shareholders have not stated their preference then the pay-out ratio may be considered a strategic decision to be decided in the light of tradition, taxation, legislation and other relevant factors – one of which may be the company's target rate of growth. Some controversy exists as to the relative strategic advantages of high and low pay-out ratios. A low pay-out leaves more retained profits for reinvestment for the company's growth – this is the strategy adopted by nearly every company in industrial nations today. Some experts argue that society would be better served if pay-out ratios were very high, for then it would be the shareholder who decides whether to reinvest his income in the same company or in another company. It is partly this thinking that is behind the trend in Europe to adopt the imputation tax system for, it is argued, the shareholder (through the stock market and other financial mechanisms) is better placed to spot opportunities than the managers in a single company. Furthermore if a company wishes to grow in size then the capital it requires will have to be raised in the market-place where its record of management may be openly discussed – a discussion that may not take place when a company grows by retaining earnings.

A second area of financial strategy is gearing (or leverage). The gearing decision is essentially one of balancing the profit improvement obtained by borrowing money more cheaply against the risk of not being able to cover the dividend. Thus a company with no loan capital and a traditional pay-out ratio of 50% could suffer a 50% fall in after-tax profits in any one year without having to cut the dividend. The same company with 50% gearing could have to cut the dividend (see Exhibit 13·1).

Liquidity reserves are another strategic area. The extent to which a company builds up reserves in property, stocks or trade investment as an insurance against a fall in profits is closely related to other financial and non-financial risk reducing strategies.

A further financial strategic area is the choice of long term capital resources capital for growth may be obtained from new issues of equity (voting, non voting, conditional voting, deferred, convertible, etc) or by long term loan (debenture, preference, subordinated,) or a succession of short term loans (leasing, hire purchase, factoring, delayed payment to creditors). A public flotation of a private company, the acquisition of a company with liquid reserves or tax losses are yet more examples of the innumerable alternative methods of raising finance.

Another strategic area is the company's financial image; for although companies should be judged by their results this is often extremely difficult to do due to the fluctuations to which all company results are subject. Shareholder and the financial institutions are therefore significantly influenced by appearances as well as realities; the company which strategically pursues a policy of conservatism and moderation in the preparation of its annual accounts may be able to borrow money the more advantageously. But, balanced against that must be the danger that the company's share values may be lower than justified by their true results and the company may be disadvantageously placed in a merger. Most companies will do all they can to achieve a high P/E ratio and to have themselves placed in the highest categories of such credit rating systems as Moody's and Standard and Poor's.

Exhibit 13·1

A. Company with no loan capital

		$
1. In a normal year:	Profits before tax	240
	Profits after tax	120
	Dividend	60
	Retain	60
2. When profits fall by 50%:	Profits before tax	120
	Profits after tax	60
	Dividend	60
	Retain	nil

B. Company with loan capital

1. In a normal year:	Profits before tax	
	and interest	280
	Loan interest	40
	Profits before tax	240
	Profits after tax	120
	Dividend	60
	Retain	60
2. When profits fall by 50%:	Profits before tax	
	and interest	140
	Loan interest	40
	Profits before tax	100
	Profits after tax	50
	Dividend	50
	Retain	nil

The complexity of financial strategic decisions rises to daunting levels as the size of a company grows past the merely national boundaries. The total lack of international agreement in legal, financial, commercial and monetary fields makes the raising, servicing and expenditure of capital on an international scale an area strictly for specialists.

Hussey (Ch. 8), Walley (Ch. 12), Payne (Ch. 10) and Steiner (Ch. 20) all devote a full chapter to financial planning. I would particularly draw attention to the chapter by Harry A. Lund in Stemp (Ch. 9) and, for a discussion on international financing, to the chapter by Leslie F. Murphy also in Stemp (Ch. 10).

Organization strategies

I believe that, at the strategic level, two main factors affect the design of

I*

organization structures. These are (1) the activities that the company has decided to include in the strategic structure and (2) the style of management to be adopted. Thus, consider 'the four basic organizational concepts' listed by Payne (Ch. 9); Functional, Product, Market and Geographical (Exhibit 13·2). I believe that Payne is correct in saying that the geographical concept is likely to be used by a company that is (or intends to be) geographically diversified, that the market concept is best when the company operates in several markets – and so on. However, what if the company clearly faces a period of danger – does that not affect the choice of organization structure? I believe it does and should because the management style it will adopt will probably be more centralized and autocratic than in a period of calm. (See Exhibit 13·3.) While Payne's four types may be the most common they are not by any means the only manifestation of the pyramid organization; a company whose business is project management may be organized into project managers, for example.

Nor is the pyramid the only type of organization structure. A number of trends suggest that the hierarchy concept is being joined by several entirely different organizational concepts that do not involve a hierarchy at all. One of these is the matrix (Exhibit 13·4), another is the Cell or autonomous work group (Exhibit 13·5) and another is the Ladder which may be a particularly appropriate form of organization for management services departments (see Exhibit 13·6). Quite clearly the Cell would not be appropriate to organizations whose style of management is autocratic, while the Ladder is consistent with a centralized company.

If the strategic structure calls for a major and rapid rate of expansion involving the launching of many new projects then it may be that a Matrix structure and a Ladder are required together. (See Exhibit 13·7).

Organization strategies, then, are strategies relating to the long term changes required in the organization structure and are selected by reference to the proposed activities of the company and to its proposed style of management. Once the scale of the organizational changes required are known it will be necessary to decide how they are to be brought about (whether in one or two major reorganizations in Year X and Y perhaps, or gradually over a number of years as favoured by Walley (Ch. 15)). Once this is known, the number and quality of employees can be determined together with the training they may require – thus a manpower plan (see page 289) may be developed.

Ackoff (Ch. 5) suggests that the design of organization structures takes place in five stages: (1) decision-flow analysis, (2) modelling, (3) information requirements, (4) design of jobs, (5) development of performance measurements, making and using these measurements and developing incentive systems. He emphasizes that organizational planning should be directed towards identifying the tasks required to accomplish organizational objectives.

Cannon (Ch. 10) also emphasizes these objectives but says that organizational design is essentially about the unification and division of work. Thus, recognizing the increasing need for specialization today, he stresses the need to unify this diversity in the design of the structure; this implies that the flow of communication and authority must be facilitated.

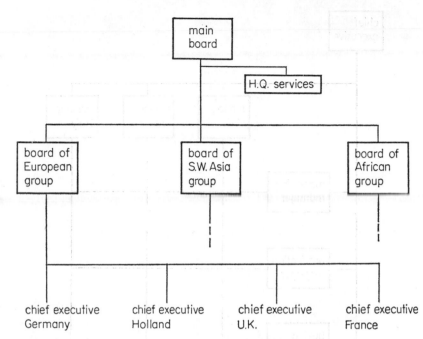

Exhibit 13·2 Outline organization chart for a decentralized geographically diverse company.

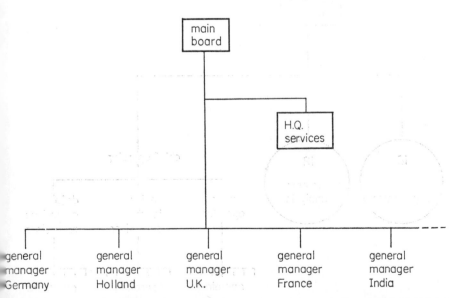

Exhibit 13·3 Outline organization chart for a heavily centralized geographically diverse company.

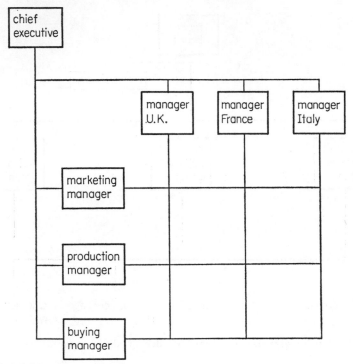

Exhibit 13·4 A Matrix organization structure.

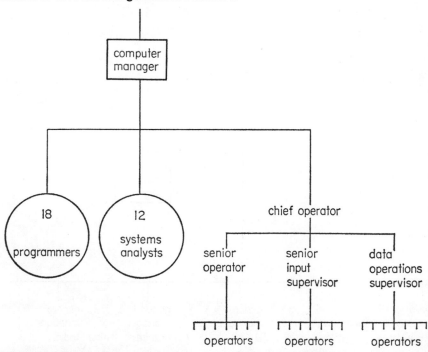

Exhibit 13·5 Two cells (or autonomous work groups) alongside a conventional pyramid in a computer department.

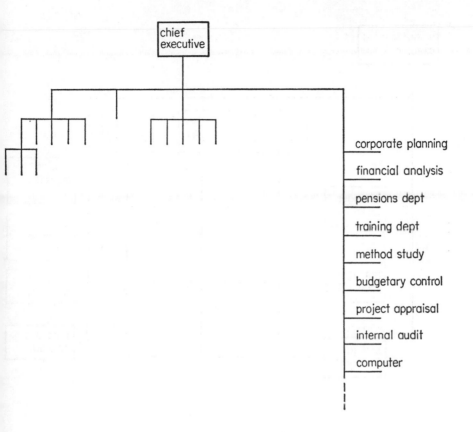

Exhibit 13·6 A conventional pyramid with a management services department ladder.

He divides the basic forms of organization into functional, geographic, product and project concepts. I believe his six guidelines for organizational design in the growing company are of considerable strategic interest. They are:

1 Organize by market – i.e. of all the various ways in which one might divide the company into areas of responsibility among its managers the most appropriate is the market or customer-group division.
2 Decentralize operations and strategic planning for established types of business – i.e. delegate very fully to what I call the Hard Areas and what Cannon calls the Known Areas.
3 Centralize measurement – i.e. collect all historical data at headquarters (but do not necessarily use it to control the decentralized sectors of the company).

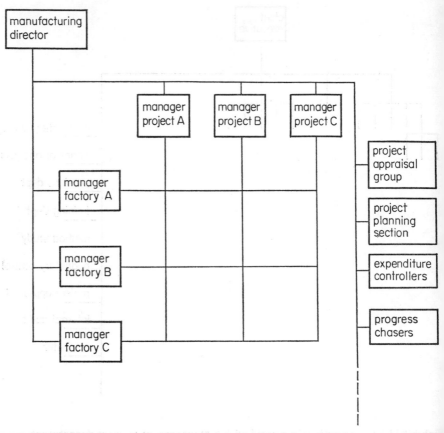

Exhibit 13·7 A matrix and a ladder in a company which is undertaking a number of major projects.

4 Centralize strategic planning for the Unknown Areas – i.e. the chief executive and headquarters staff should plan major departures from the traditional business, (and for what I call the Soft Areas).

5 Emphasize line rather than staff – i.e. place authority squarely in the hands of managers, not in the hands of advisers.

6 Emphasize results rather than profits-centred decentralization – i.e. rather than divide responsibilities into the occasionally somewhat arbitrary Subsidiary Company, divide it into results categories.

While I believe his principles are correct under normal circumstances, they would not be correct if the management style adopted by a company was more autocratic or more entrepreneurial than implied by Cannon; a company facing a major threat might temporarily reverse or reject his item 2 while an entrepreneurial company, such as a true conglomerate or one that encouraged venture management, would largely ignore item 4. His item 5 might be affected by a trend towards company decisions being made in public as many decisions in government are made.

I wish now to examine a completely different part of a company's organization structure, one which neither Cannon nor any other writer ever mentions.

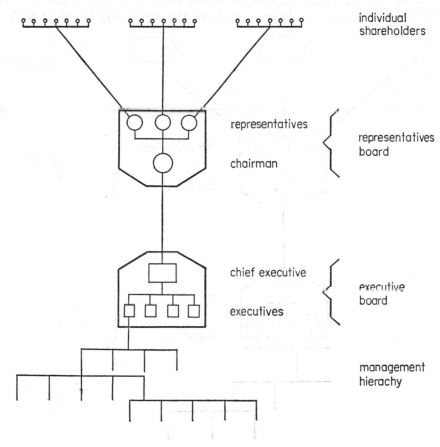

individual
shareholders

representatives

chairman

representatives
board

chief executive

executives

executive
board

management
hierachy

Exhibit 13·8 Personal representation, i.e. where each shareholder is in direct personal contact with a member of the Representatives Board.

On page 40 I drew attention to the vigorous debate that is still in progress as to the true objectives of a company. The two schools are, on the one hand the Shareholder school which states that the sole purpose of a company is to earn a return on shareholders' capital. On the other hand is the Stakeholder theory which suggests that employees, customers, the community also have a stake in the company. Now whichever school is valid there should surely be some formal structure by which these intended beneficiaries may make their views known to the executives. There should, in other words, be two hierarchies, one for the beneficiaries and their representatives and another, the traditional one, for managers. I propose to deal briefly with these questions here (briefly because the area is almost unexplored) for three reasons: (1) because the debate as to objectives is of major social importance, (2) because the role of the supervisory board is hotly debated in Europe and such boards are unknown in Britain and (3) because while the corporate planner is currently assumed to be properly responsible to the chief executive, a case can be argued for him to be partly responsible to the supervisory board as well.

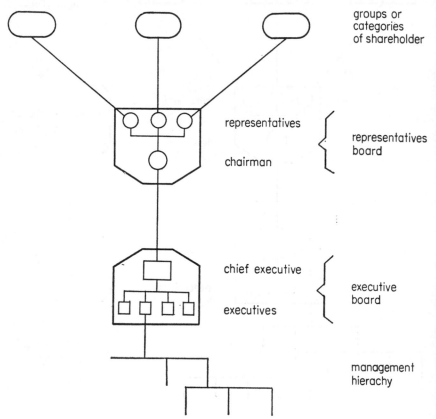

Exhibit 13·9 Group Representation, i.e. where each representative is responsible for communicating the views of groups of shareholders to the Representatives Board.

Let us first assume that the shareholder is the sole intended beneficiary; how may he make his views known to the chief executive? Clearly if there is only one shareholder, or only a few, or one who holds the vast majority of shares, his views can be expressed by personal contact with the chief executive. If there are more than a few, however, some form of representation is necessary. I suggest some of these in Exhibits 13·8 to 13·10. But what should be the nature of the information that passes between the shareholder and the executive? I believe shareholders should – i.e. have a right and probably a duty to – express their views as to the following:

1 the shape of the performance–risk curve that they have in mind for their company. I suggested on page 49 that managers also have a performance–risk curve for their company in their minds, that theirs is probably different to that of the shareholders and that, although they have no mandate to do so, their views will predominate unless the shareholders make their views known.

2 the competence, or lack of it, shown by the executives. The shareholders should decide whether the chief executive (and perhaps some of his senior colleagues) should be exceptionally well rewarded for his effort or replaced for lack of it.

3 the ethological objectives. Shareholders in some companies would be horrified, I believe, at some of the actions their managers take to earn a return on their capital.

4 strategic decisions. Some shareholders undoubtedly believe they have the right to determine strategy. (My personal view is that they do not).

It seems to me that if this list is accepted, then, when the corporate planner is clarifying corporate objectives', he should report to the chairman (as chief shareholder representative) – and when 'monitoring progress'. But he should assist the chief executive when it comes to strategic decision-making – unless item 4 is accepted, in which case he should properly report to the chairman (not the chief executive) in all corporate planning matters.

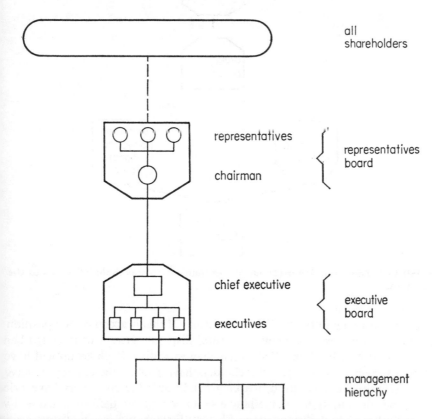

Exhibit 13·10 Indirect Representation, i.e. where the representatives as a board attempt to reflect a concensus of the views of the shareholders as a whole.

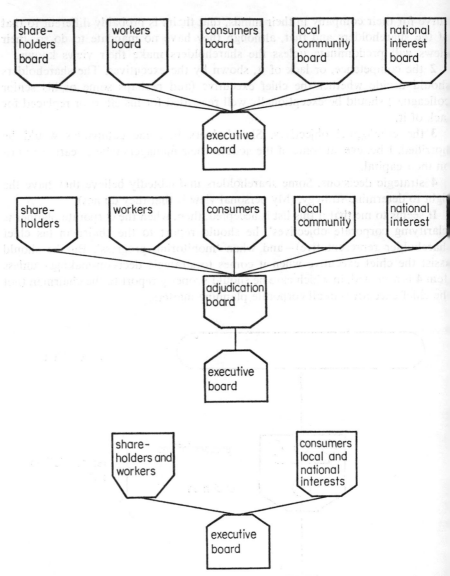

Exhibit 13·11 Some untried methods of communicating stakeholders' views to the executive.

Let me turn now to the Stakeholder theory. If this is accepted the position vastly more complex. The views of several disparate groups of intended ben ficiaries must now be channelled to the chief executive. Each group will have different benefit in mind – the shareholders have ROSC; the employees have mix of security, remuneration, working conditions; the customers have pric utility; the community has something else not yet clearly defined. Each will v with the other as to the proportion of benefit they should receive. Some grou will refuse to recognize the claims of other groups. Before any instructions ca be given to the chief executive, therefore, all these representatives must come to agreement amongst themselves. (I assume they would not wish to leave this argument to be decided by the chief executive himself).

I wish to distinguish between the two types of board that these two theories imply. In the case of the shareholders the board has two main functions: (a) to agree among themselves as to suitable ROSC and ethological objectives and (b) to supervise the work of the executive. The first function of these directors, then, is to represent the views of the shareholders and, because they are a relatively homogeneous group, this is but a small part of their task; the second function is supervisory. In the case of the stakeholders, however, the first task, that of agreeing among themselves, is exceedingly difficult and would form a major part of their duties. In the first case the board is mainly a supervisory body and in the second mainly a representative body. It is the design of this latter type that presents such severe difficulties. The German Co-determination scheme calls for one third of the members of such boards to represent the employees and two thirds are shareholders, local dignitaries, academics. So far as I am aware the German pattern is the only formal one yet tried in practice. No other proportion of representatives has been attempted nor has any attempt been made to put into practice any of the alternatives such as shown in Exhibit 13·11

I firmly believe that unless an organization has been set clear objectives it rapidly becomes a limp, bureaucratic, self-perpetuating, institutionalized drain on the resources of society. The larger the organization, the worse the drain – and we now have some very large limp organizations among us. I cannot see how corporate planners can even begin their valuable work if the problem of representatives and supervisory boards is not tackled with vigour; prehaps the corporate planner is as well placed as anyone to tackle it.

Research strategies

A fundamental change of attitude towards research has taken place over the past few decades. At one time research was conducted in the hope of making some new and potentially commercial discovery; the research budget was allocated in accordance with the current affluence of the company; the department was staffed by those with the highest academic qualifications and judged by the technical excellence of its work; no attempt was made to direct the work of these savants lest this damaged their creative zeal. With few exceptions (see below) this approach has been completely reversed so that now R & D is almost wholly subservient to needs of the marketing or some other department. The quality of the R & D department is judged by results and its budget allocated according to what it needs to complete a carefully defined set of results.

Even within this new philosophy there is room for a wide range of R & D strategies. Steiner (Ch. 22) describes one of the most common as 'innovate to order' where the design specification is well defined, the technology is generally well known and the application is rigidly supervised. In this case there is virtually no R & D planning at all – the R & D activity is a derivative of the plans of the marketing department who are planning a new product or the production department who require a new process or whatever.

Steiner also describes 'advanced technology-dominated' R & D planning where R & D plays the dominant role in the success of the company as, for instance, in the military and space industries. Even here, however, the research is results-orientated; the difference is that the product specification is ill-defined and the technology largely unknown and the performance and even the specification of the product depends overwhelmingly upon the R & D effort. In between these two extremes, Steiner places the technically motivated companies such as Du Pont, Union Carbide and others. These seek expansion through new products researched in their own departments and use modern technology whenever it can be to their advantage. In addition to 'innovation to order' R & D these companies deliberately search for new products – 'technology-push' Steiner calls it, and gives several examples. He adds one other strategy, that of purchasing R & D; many companies, not only small ones, prefer to buy their R & D from universities, trade research institutes and so on.

Cannon (Ch. 13) lists fifteen different levels of R & D activity ranging from making a minor improvement to a product right through to 'work producing only knowledge for its own sake'. Cannon's spectrum, though wider than Steiner's, follows a very similar pattern. Cannon also classifies R & D strategies as Maintenance, Expansion and Exploratory – the first two being described as Defensive and Offensive respectively by George L. Bata in Stemp (Ch. 8) and by B. C. Twiss (see below). Maintenance or Defensive R & D being the R & D effort required merely to ensure that the products and processes the company needs to maintain its profits are developed as current products and process become obsolete. Expansion or Offensive R & D being the level required to overtake the natural rate of obsolescence thus adding extra momentum to company growth at the expense of competitors. A very similar classification is used by Melvin E. Salveson in Denning (Ch. 16). Exploratory R & D covers what used to be known as pure science and is today conducted mainly in universities, think tanks and very large technology-based companies. Those who do exploratory research do so in the expectation that something fundamentally new and commercially viable will emerge – this class of R & D is not mainly results-orientated therefore. K. M. Hill suggests that there is a more down-to-earth justification for basic research; in L.R.P. (Vol. 1 No. 3 March 1969) he and others suggest that the presence of a group of scientists working in basic research results in a measurable improvement in the results-orientated research going on elsewhere in the R & D department. The authors claim to be able to measure this improvement in financial terms and, using the current cost of capital, can therefore calculate how much basic research expenditure is justified. They conclude 'the major benefit to be expected from a program of basic or underlying research was not the long term benefit of the occasional scientific discovery but rather the current benefit from the enrichment of the quality of applied research'.

While I am sure that it is useful to be able to list, classify and categorize the various R & D strategies as reviewed above, it would be still more useful to describe how a given company may determine which type of R & D strategy it should adopt. I believe the most succinct description of such a procedure is that of Brian C. Twiss in his article in *L.R.P.* (Vol. 3, No. 1, Sep. 1970). He points out, for example, that it makes little sense for a company to try to exploit a technical success if its marketing or production facilities are inadequate; it makes little sense to strive for a major technological breakthrough (i.e. to adopt high-risk research project) if the company's overall risk situation is already high; it makes little sense to introduce an advanced new product if one's competitors are about to do the same thing better. In other words Twiss is saying that a research strategy may only be selected by reference to *all* the relevant facts surrounding the company – its strengths, weaknesses, competitive position, financial status, risk structure and all the other items that, in my terminology, are contained in the performance–risk gap analysis and the cruciform chart.

Supplies strategies

Only Ackoff (Ch. 4), Payne (Ch. 8), Weinwurm (Ch. 10) and Cannon (Ch. 3) mention supplies strategies and then only very briefly. In theory this lack of interest in the purchasing function is surprising; most companies purchase at least 50% of their turnover. And should there not be as many purchasing strategies as there are marketing strategies, for buying and selling are two sides of the same coin?

Consider also the strategic supply position of some well-known industries. Oil, for example is the root of an enormous range of products and yet this material is threatened both by the growing nationalism of the producing nations and by natural depletion within a few decades. So crucial is oil to most national economies that wars are fought over it. Reserves of many vital metals may be depleted within a few decades. The price of some commodities can rise or fall by 50% in a single year. Many companies purchasing abroad have experienced the effect of international currency crises. Key suppliers go into liquidation just as disastrously as key customers – as Lockheed Aircraft must know. Suppliers are subject to strikes which may be equally as damaging as a strike at a customer's premises. But, in spite of all this, supply is a neglected strategic area.

Among supply strategies one may list the following:

The make or buy decision (which I discussed on page 243 under the heading of Vertical Integration);

Strategies to reduce prices, such as entering bulk buying agreements, opportunist shopping around or quality trade-offs;

Strategies to reduce price fluctuations, such as long term contracts, maintaining buffer stocks or such devices for restraining competition as the formation of cartels;

Strategies for promoting competition among suppliers such as widespread tendering;

Strategies for improving co-operation and closer relations with supplier such as would be achieved by a minority mutual share exchange or a premium price;

Mixed strategies such as purchasing 80% of one's requirements from on supplier to obtain bulk discounts on a guaranteed off-take and 20% from othe suppliers who are not given any guarantee as to off-take;

Strategies designed to reduce one's dependence upon key suppliers such a redesigning the product to eliminate that part or developing substitute part or materials.

I do not hesitate to emphasize that, for some companies, the supplies strateg; may be quite as important as its market strategy – a statement that man; managers would agree with but which is not reflected in the literature.

Facilities strategies

By facilities I mean physical facilities such as factories, offices, warehouses.

Walley (Ch. 14) draws attention to a number of problem areas: the reductio of the complexity of manufacturing operations either by simplifying th products themselves or their design or the processes by which they are made the improvement of production control; the reduction of manufacturing costs project control; the make or buy decision; customer service; trade unions location. Some of these may well be of sufficient importance to warran inclusion in a corporate plan. Steiner (Ch. 23) presents a somewhat differen classification: tooling, plant facilities and location, personnel, production plan ning and control, maintenance, health and safety of employees, manufacturing research and development, waste control and organization.

Cannon (Ch. 13) considers the make or buy decision in some detail and list the strategic advantages of each course. He also draws attention to technique of modular production and to the advantages of process modernization. Payn (Ch. 8) and Weinwurm (Ch. 10) deal briefly with facilities planning.

The extremely perfunctory manner in which most authors deal with facilitie strategies is a sign of the times. In a Europe ravaged by war and plagued b; scarcities it was reasonable two decades ago to treat facilities planning as th pivot of company planning. Today the pivot is marketing and, so radically ha the economic background changed in two decades, companies order the con struction of huge production facilities almost as a tailpiece of the marketin; plan. I believe that the balance of relative importance may now swing bac; significantly, but perhaps not overwhelmingly, towards facilities planning. will put forward two reasons for this view.

The first is the current concern with the environment. Until recently th location of a factory could be determined by a study of transport costs, th infrastructure of the locality (i.e. roads, harbours, etc.) and all the wel documented traditional factors that affect the location of industries. One c these factors has always been concern with the environment – chemical com panies have had to take account of the laws relating to air and river pollutio for decades. However this factor has now become so significant that, in certai areas of some highly populated nations, *no* site can be found for certain factories. It may be therefore that some companies will have to diversify out of their traditional business, not because their market is threatened but because they cannot produce their product. While this may be an extreme case, it is clear that facilities strategy may soon become relatively more important than in recent years.

The second pointer in this direction concerns the changing attitude to work. In the extreme case it may become *impossible* to persuade any employee to operate some processes or make some products; some companies may therefore have to cease production entirely, not because demand does not exist but because no one is prepared to make the products for an economic wage or under conditions that are economic. Again, this may be an extreme case but it suggests that the manufacturing function may now be returning to strategic eminence. This is exemplified in the motor industry today where a strategic decision of major importance faces the manufacturers: whether to continue building cars on an assembly line or to make the switch to methods of production depending upon Group Technology, Autonomous Work Groups, and so on. Some companies may deliberately have to build several small factories rather than one large one in order to avoid the alienation of employees that so often afflicts employees in the large factory.

Ackoff makes the point that the theories and techniques for facilities planning are very well developed; he reminds us of mathematical programming, PERT, replacement theory, model building and so on. He suggests that these be used to solve such strategic questions as the optimum size and location of plant, the date of commencement of construction, the production orders to be assigned to each plant, the sources of supply, and the linking of warehouses, offices and so on.

14 Techniques of evaluation

Introduction

During the corporate planning process the step known as evaluation occurs at two main levels. The various alternative strategic structures have to be evaluated and each individual strategy has to be evaluated.

Essentially 'evaluation' means testing a decision or proposed decision against a set of criteria; selecting the criteria is not usually considered part of the evaluation process, but clearly the outcome of an evaluation depends heavily upon what criteria are chosen. Using one set of criteria the evaluation will result in three alternatives being ranked A, B, C; another set could rank them C, B, A. The criteria for evaluating strategic structures are slightly different to those for evaluating individual strategies. I shall first consider these and then describe a number of techniques of evaluation.

Criteria for evaluating strategic structures

The purpose of any proposed strategic structure is to ensure that the company's total portfolio of strategies is so devised as to yield a performance–risk curve similar to the one chosen for it by its shareholders. But this portfolio is unlikely to be effective unless (a) use is made of the company's strengths, (b) the company's weaknesses are reduced or at least not called upon (c) opportunities are exploited and (d) threats are avoided. But the structure must also allow the company's ethological objectives to be achieved and must not infringe any of the ethological constraints. Finally the managers must have confidence that the structure does not call for any action that will prove to be impracticable.

The criteria for testing the validity of a proposed strategic structure, then, are these:

1 Is this structure likely to result in the target performance–risk curve being achieved for (a) the financial and (b) the ethological objectives,
2 Does it make use of the company's corporate strengths and does it do anything to reinforce these strengths?
3 Does it rely upon a corporate weakness and does it do anything to reduce these weaknesses?
4 Are all the major threats avoided, reduced or mitigated? If not are there adequate contingency plans?

5 What major opportunities are exploited?
6 Are any ethological constraints infringed?
7 Are the strategies called for or implied really capable of being carried out in practice?

It is this last criterion that may lead to the next level of evaluation, i.e. the evaluation of individual strategies. It is entirely possible for managers to feel complete and justifiable confidence in a given strategic structure for their company even if no individual strategies have yet been proposed. Thus a company with impressive strengths in marketing new products in a given market area might justifiably accept a proposed structure that calls for more new products in that area or in one closely related to it; the management might, in this case, be fully justified in feeling complete confidence in such a structure even before they had specified the nature of the products, their costs, their turnover, their margins.

The further a proposed strategic structure departs from the company's present structure the less confidence will managers feel in their ability to put it into practice in the real world. Thus a structure that does not make full use of their strengths (such as a diversification), or does not avoid a major threat, or incurs risks which may exceed those in the target performance–risk curve, will be treated with suspicion and will be less likely to pass the seventh of the tests listed above. The only way to restore confidence in such a strategic structure is to show that the individual strategies that it implies are capable of being put into practice. The lower the confidence the more detailed does the definition of the individual strategies have to be. It is only by showing that each strategy is practicable that one can show that the strategic structure itself is practicable.

Criteria for evaluating individual strategies

The purpose of many proposed strategies is to bring about the proposed strategic structure (I called these 'primary strategies' on page 237) and, clearly, the extent to which they do this is one criterion to be used in their evaluation. Other strategies, which I called secondary, are designed to supplement primary strategies (such as a research program designed to create a new product to a specification prepared by the marketing department) and the relevant criterion here is whether the secondary does contribute to the primary.

Just as the strategic structure must be tested against the target ROSC so individual strategies must be tested against the company's financial criteria (usually ROI – see page 43) and its riskiness must be examined (see the techniques below). Just as the strategic structure must accord with the strengths, weaknesses, threats and opportunities at the corporate level so must individual strategies at the strategic level. Thus a marketing strategy must be based on marketing strengths, a research strategy must take account of opportunities in technology, a supplies strategy must not be based upon a weakness in the company's bargaining power with a supplier. Nor must any individual strategy breach the company's moral code. Each individual strategy must not only be consistent with the strategic structure but must be consistent with other primary and secondary strategies. Finally it must inspire the managers with confidence in their ability to put it into practical effect in the real world; if it does not then either it is faulty and should be rejected or further detailed study is required to demonstrate that it is in fact worthy of their confidence.

The list of criteria for evaluating individual strategies is then a little different and a little longer than the list for the strategic structure. It may be summarized as follows:

1 Does it contribute to the proposed strategic structure or to a proposed primary strategy?
2 Is it likely to show a return on investment that exceeds the company's cut-off rate?
3 Is its risk profile acceptable?
4 Does it make use of or reinforce strategic strengths?
5 Does it rely on weaknesses or do anything to reduce them?
6 Does it exploit major opportunities?
7 Does it avoid, reduce or mitigate the major threats? If not are there adequate contingency plans?
8 Does it accord with company morals?
9 Is it consistent with other primary or secondary strategies?
10 Are the managers fully confident that this strategy is capable of being carried out in the real practical world?

This list is not dissimilar to that shown by Walley (Ch. 15) and that suggested by Tilles in Denning (Ch. 7) who adds 'appropriate time horizon' which I have subsumed in items (1) and (9). I also subsume 'resources', listed separately by Walley and Tilles, under (2) and (3) which relate to financial resources and (4) and (5) which relate to resources of skill, management and so on.

While it is possible to apply most of these tests only qualitatively it is often possible to use quantitative techniques especially in the case of ROI, risk, and consistency with other strategies and the strategic structure. The remainder of this chapter is concerned with these techniques. In my opinion by far the most important of these techniques is model building because it allows one not only to test the ROI and the risk profile of many alternative individual strategies but to make these tests within the context of a proposed strategic structure. Testing the strategies also tests the structure; before the development of the art of model-building it was possible only to test one strategy at a time and on its own out of the context of the structure, as one does when using any of the more traditional methods of project evaluation such as risk analysis and others described briefly below. I think I would go so far as to say that a corporate plan cannot be really adequately evaluated without the use of a model of some sort.

Sensitivity tests

This technique is so well known that only a very brief description is needed here.

A company is about to build a factory for $1m in the belief that the return will be $0·25m p.a., i.e. 25% ROI (d.c.f. is not used here in the interests of simplicity) based on the calculations in Exhibit 14·1. But the management recognize that all these assumptions could be invalid – most of them, they think, could be wrong by as much as 10% and the unit sales forecast itself could be 20% in error. The calculations in Exhibit 14·2 show what the return might be if each of the assumptions was invalid by these amounts. This is a sensitivity test. It shows how sensitive the return on investment is to possible errors in each of the key assumptions that underly a proposed project.

Exhibit 14·1 The essentials of a Capital Expenditure Proposal for 'Project P'

forecast cost of factory	$1,000,000
forecast sales	2000 units p.a.
forecast selling price of product	$1000 per unit
Therefore sales turnover	$2,000,000 p.a.
forecast variable costs	$500 per unit
Therefore contribution	$1,000,000 p.a.
forecast fixed costs	$750,000 p.a.
Therefore profit	$250,000 p.a.
ROI of project	25%

Exhibit 14·2 A sensitivity test on the Capital Expenditure Proposal for 'Project P'

If the capital cost of the factory is between	$0·8m and $1·2m (a 20% error)	then the ROI will be between	31·4 and 20·8%
If unit sales per annum are between	1600 and 2400 (a 20% error)	„	5 and 45%
If the unit selling price is between	$900 and $1100 (a 10% error)	„	5 and 45%
If variable costs per unit are between	$450 and $550 (a 10% error)	„	35 and 15%
If fixed costs are between	$675,000 and $825,000 (a 10% error)	„	32·5 and 17·5%

Note that the proposal is highly sensitive to an error of 10% in the selling price of the product. It is relatively insensitive to a 10% error in the fixed costs.

The main advantages of sensitivity testing are:

1 it shows which are the most important assumptions underlying any proposed project;

2 it indicates just how bad (or good) the project could be if the worst (or best) happens – i.e. how low (or high) the ROI might be;

3 it does not rely for its efficacy on any estimates of probability. Some of the most difficult estimates to make are those relating to probability; sensitivity testing answers the question 'what would happen if X occurs?' without reference to the likelihood of X occurring. (Probability estimates are not barred from this technique, of course, see Steiner (Ch. 15), but they are not essential).

A signal disadvantage of sensitivity testing is that one may only test the effect of one parameter at a time. In the above example it is possible to see that a 10% rise in variable costs would reduce the ROI to 15% or that a 10% fall in selling prices would reduce the ROI to 5%. But this reveals nothing of the effect of both these occurring simultaneously. Of course one can easily calculate the effect of a 10% fall in selling prices occurring at the same time as a 10% rise in variable costs – ROI would be *minus* 5% – but this is such a pessimistic assumption as to be almost meaningless. It would be meaningful if one knew how likely such a combination of errors was – but this is moving us away from the simplicity of sensitivity testing into the complexities of probability estimation.

Walley (Ch. 7) gives a very simple example of this technique while a complex – and rather more realistic – example is given by L. M. Sneddon in *L.R.P.* Vol. 3 No. 1 Sep. 1970.

Risk analysis

Provided that one can estimate the probability of an event occurring (see Estimating Probabilities on page 280) one can use this very important technique. Its importance resides in the way a risk analysis calculation may be tied in with performance–risk curves; the statement 'this project has a 50% chance of attaining a profit of $2m p.a. and only a 5% chance of making a loss of $500,000 p.a.' is obviously one that can be linked with the performance–risk concept for either the company is searching for a project with this risk profile or it is not. If not then, however profitable the project may be, whatever the ROI, it may be the wrong sort of project for the company in its current circumstances.

To illustrate risk analysis consider the example shown in Exhibit 14·1 which I used to illustrate Sensitivity Tests. Now let us assume that the managers believe that there is only a ten to one chance of the factory being built for less than $0·8m but a five to one chance of it costing $1·2m or more. Let us assume, then:

Probability of factory costing less than $0·8m. = 0·10
Probability of its costing more than $1·2m. = 0·20

Now we know that the ROI of this project would be 31·4% if the factory did cost $0·8m and 20·8% if it cost $1·2m; so we can draw the curve in Exhibit 14·3. But, of course, the cost of the factory was only one item; we should now try to estimate the probability of variable costs being above $500, $600, $700 per unit and below $500, $400, $300 per unit and so on across the whole list of variables. But we now have to face a further problem.

Either these variables are independent of each other or they are related. Thus the cost of the factory is probably dependent upon factors wholly unrelated to the selling price of the product; they are wholly independent. On the other hand volume and price are closely related through the price elasticity curve. In order to generate a risk curve for this project which takes account of all the probabilities, then, a very complex set of calculations will have to be made. The independent variables may be dealt with by using some form of randoming device (by throwing dice, or by random number tables or a random number generator in a computer), so that a risk curve may be calculated which displays, on one simple graph, the total effect of all the probabilities of all the variables, independent and correlated, that enter into the project decision. Exhibit 14·4 shows such a graph for two alternative projects from which it can be seen that project A has a high-risk high-return profile while B is much less exciting.

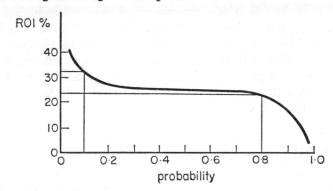

Exhibit 14·3

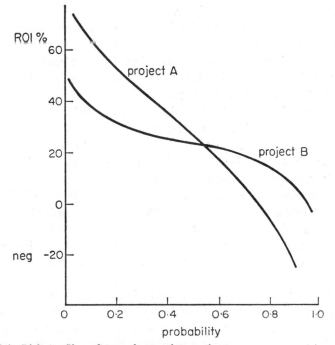

Exhibit 14·4   Risk profiles of two alternative projects

It is sometimes suggested that the disadvantage of Risk Analysis is that all the probability estimates are subjective and therefore unreliable. This is true but all decisions are based on estimates and opinions as well as hard facts. One may as well get these estimates down on paper for discussion and make the calculations explicitly instead of privately and intuitively in the mind. I cannot see how such an examination can be a disadvantage; I certainly can see one disadvantage in Risk Analysis and that is the massive number of tedious calculations that have to be made if one does not use a computer.

Steiner (Ch. 15), Walley (Ch. 7) and Hussey (Ch. 5) also describe this technique. But Dr D. H. Allen (*L.R.P.* Vol. 2 No. 5 June 1972) believes that the assessment of probability is so difficult, especially when one is dealing with entirely new projects such as a programme in basic research, that 'credibility' should be used rather than probability. The advantage is simple; either a forecast is credible or it is not. He further points out that the credibility of one prediction is unaffected by the credibility of any others and that the credibility of a combination of predictions is equal to the credibility of the least credible prediction – both these qualities render credibility calculations simpler than probablity calculations.

Outcome matrix

The Pay-Off Tables (or Outcome Matrix) comes half-way between sensitivity tests and risk analysis in terms of complexity and difficulty in use. The Outcome Matrix can be especially useful in evaluating alternative strategies qualitatively as well as quantitatively.

Imagine a British company which wishes to advance into Europe with a new product and is considering three alternative strategies. It wishes to evaluate these against the criteria suggested on page 268. It may already have used Risk Analysis to evaluate ROI and risk but now it wishes to formalize the evaluation of each strategy against the list of Threats and Opportunities identified during the External Appraisal (i.e. against criteria 6 and 7 on page 268). Let us list the three strategies down the matrix and the threats and opportunities across it and attempt to evaluate the consequences to the company of each combination as in Exhibit 14·5. It will be seen that an attempt has been made to rank each strategy under each of the threats and opportunities. Thus under the 'vigorous response by competitors' threat, strategy B is ranked No. 1 (see the figure in the small box), C is No. 2 and A is third. It will also be seen that strategy C is the only one that is not ranked last against any threat so this is the one that is most robust. Strategy A comes out very badly against two rather serious threats while B comes out badly against two other threats – but not very badly.

All sorts of ranking systems may be used of course, but the value of this Pay-Off Table technique lies not as a highly sensitive fine-tooth comb, which it is not, but as an invitation to managers to write down exactly why a supposed threat is real, exactly what the consequences of its occurrence might be, exactly how the company could respond to it, and, in short, why they prefer one strategy rather than another.

Exhibit 14·5 An Outcome Matrix or Pay-Off Table
(Strategy C is the most robust)

	Threats and Opportunities			
Alternative strategies	Vigorous response by competitors	Devaluation of £	Severe labour unrest in UK factories	Severe labour unrest in Europe
A Set up factory in Southern France and gradually develop market over 10 years	Could result in failure of project. But could sell factory for £1m.	This would improve U.K. profits.	Not affected	Could be serious in view of our inexperience of European labour.
Total cost £4m	3	1	1	3
B Joint project with very large competitor to make product in U.K. and sell in Europe through their outlets.	Should be able to withstand almost any attack.	Partner would object to change of transfer price.	Partner would be irritated by unreliability	Probably no direct effect
Total cost £2m	1	3	3	1
C Acquire a small European competitor expand his factory and launch product through his outlets	Profitability of project does not depend on new products	Could improve U.K. profits.	not affected	Not as severe as A because of labour know-how inherited from acquired competitor.
Total cost £6m	1	1	1	2

Discounted cash flow

The nub of a business decision is the act of spending money today in the expectation of a return tomorrow. In long range planning tomorrow is, by definition, many years away. It is inconceivable, to my mind, that strategic decisions could ever be made without taking account of the time value of money. Steiner (Ch. 13) emphasizes discounting, so does Hussey (Ch. 12); on the other hand there are still a very large number of companies who do not use d.c.f. or NPV or IRR as Weinwurm (Ch. 8) notes ('The majority of companies surveyed (in USA in 1968) have not yet taken advantage of these techniques!') and a number of authors level severe criticisms at these techniques. One of these is Walley (Ch. 8) who suggests that, 'by itself, d.c.f. is a highly suspect method of evaluating competitive projects'. He points out that the data on which d.c.f. operations are performed are often inaccurate; this is true but the same data would be used in all ROI calculations whether d.c.f. or pay-back or ROCE was used. One can hardly blame the data.

He further suggests that data for the distant years of a forecast are treated as seriously as the earlier years in spite of the fact that the former are manifestly less reliable than the latter; but surely, as Hussey points out, the fact that the discount factor applied to the later years is much smaller than for the early years does reduce the weight of the latter compared with the former? In my opinion one of the signal advantages of the d.c.f. method is that it forces managers to collect certain highly relevant items of data that they would not collect when using traditional methods of evaluation – residual values, for example, which are not demanded by the pay-back method but are by the d.c.f. methods. Or trends in company taxation, or future rates of inflation, both required by d.c.f. but not by other methods.

Another popular criticism is that it is difficult to determine which cost of capital figure to use in d.c.f. calculations. This is true; but it is equally difficult to determine a cut-off rate for a traditional ROI calculation. Nor is it clear on what grounds a manager may select three years as the maximum acceptable pay-off period rather than two years or four.

Even if d.c.f. does not give the right answers, I am convinced that its use at least ensures that managers ask the right questions.

Models and simulation

Model building is the central tool of the systems analyst. The systems analyst holds the view that to understand how a system works is the key to forecasting, to planning and to control. One cannot make a forecast of a nation's GNP in five years' time, for example, or plan to achieve a given GNP, or control a national economy, say the systems analysts, unless one understands how a national economy works. This means, in practice, that one must know not only whether the money supply and labour productivity, for example, are factors that determine GNP but also how they are linked to GNP, to each other and to many other variables. Now corporate planning is similar to government planning for a nation's economy in that it is concerned with the totality of the company rather than with parts or sections of it. To be able to build a model that simulates the working of the entire company, showing how profits, share values, turnover, labour productivity, return on investment, factory capacity, taxation, research expenditure, etc., etc. are related to each other would open up a remarkable prospect. It would mean firstly that one understands how the company works, what are the key factors affecting performance, how sensitive the key results are likely to be to each proposed decision. Secondly it would mean that one could examine each proposal, not only on its own merits, but on its simulated effects upon the entire company. This is what *corporate* planning is all about.

There are, however, severe difficulties in using models. The prime problem is their complexity. Clearly, the value of a model is proportional to the complexity of the system it describes – faced with a simple system one would not need to build a model at all. To some extent the problem of their complexity is reduced by 'putting the model on the computer' but the data and the equations still have to be prepared by human beings – a point repeatedly overlooked by computer enthusiasts. There are other severe disadvantages in using computer models. Their very speed of operation allows one to build more and more detail into a model without suffering much additional delay in obtaining results but with the potentially more serious disadvantage of loss of intelligibility and 'feel' for the model. Again, computer models are inflexible and the effort required to adapt a model designed for one purpose to another purpose is almost as great as the effort required to build a new model.

Exhibit 14·6

$	year	0	1	2
Turnover		10000	11000	12100
Profit		1000	1100	1210
Capital Employed		4000	4400	4840
ROCE %		25	25	25

Having made these points, however, the alternative to using a computer model is to use a manual model and perhaps the best way to illustrate the limitation of manual models is to demonstrate one in use. First consider Exhibit 14·6 which shows a brief summary of the current year's results for a company together with a forecast of the following two years. Turnover is expected to rise by 10% each year and so are profits and capital employed. ROCE will remain at 25%.

Exhibit 14·7

$	year	0	1	2
Turnover		10000	10000	10000
Profit		1000	1000	1000
Capital Employed		4000	4000	4000
ROCE %		25	25	25

Exhibit 14·6 is not a model, it is merely a sequence of annual results similar to the budgets that most companies produce and, although it may not be obvious at first glance, the figures are quite meaningless for they are not mathematically compatible from one year to the next. To show that this is so let us simplify these 'budgets' even further by eliminating growth. See Exhibit 14·7. It is now possible to see why Exhibit 14·6 was unsatisfactory – the profits were not carried forward from one year to the next – or, if they were, the figures failed to show how the cash flow was used. A model would have to show this; Exhibit 14·8 shows that, with company tax at 50% and dividends at 70% of earnings, there is a positive cash flow of $150,000 to be carried forward to the next year. Notice, however, that in order to show this fact the model now contains 7 rows where before there were 4, and even this is quite inadequate to show how the cash flow is used in Year 1. A further four rows are needed to show that the cash flow has been invested in a project (the nature of which has not been revealed to us but which will yield the same ROI as this company expects from investments in its existing business), see Exhibit 14·9 which contains 12 rows. But this calculation is still grossly oversimplified;

Exhibit 14·8

$	year 0	1	2
a Turnover	10000	10000	
b Profit (0·1 x a)	1000	1000	
c Earnings (0·5 x b)	500	?	
d Dividend (0·7 x c)	350		
e Retained (0·3 x c)	150		
f Capital Employed	4000		
g ROCE % (100 x b ÷ f)	25		

In a model the mathematical relationships are known. In this case some are known but the equation linking profits retained in one year with the earnings in the following year is not known; we cannot therefore complete year 1.

Exhibit 14·9

$	year 0	1	2
Turnover	10000	10000	10000
Profits	1000	1000	1000
Retained profits invested in a project	—	150	155·6
Cumulative investment in these projects	—	150	305·6
ROI on these projects %	—	25	25
Profits from these projects	—	37·5	76·4
Total Profits	1000	1037·5	1076·4
Earnings	500	518·75	538·2
Dividends	350	363·125	376·7
Profits retained for investment next year	150	155·625	161·5
Capital Employed	4000	4155·6	4317·0
ROCE %	25	25	25

The model is developed to show how retained profits are used in the following year.

for one thing it assumes no growth in the existing business. To cater for this the model has to be extended again by another two rows to show how much cash is required to finance the expanded levels of inventory demanded by the higher turnover in Years 1 and 2. The model now contains 14 rows. But whether it now accurately reflects the mechanism by which this company makes its profits is open to doubt because of the rapidly rising ROCE figure – there is no obvious reason why this ratio should improve, unless it is that the 10% annual growth in turnover can be achieved without further investment in fixed plant. If this spare capacity does not exist then further rows are required to show what capital is to be spent on extending the company's fixed assets. The model in 14·11, which shows this also shows certain limited loan facilities being taken up in Years 1 and 2; but the model now contains 19 rows! Even that is not enough to explain convincingly the fall in ROCE in Year 2

Exhibit 14·10

$	year 0	1	2
Turnover	10000	11000	12100
Profit	1000	1100	1210
Investment in projects during year	—	150	70·6
Cumulative investment in projects	—	150	220·6
ROI %	—	25	25
Profit from projects	—	37·5	55·1
Total profits	1000	1137·5	1265·1
Earnings	500	568·7	632·5
Dividends	350	398·1	442·8
Retained	150	170·6	189·6
Capital employed	4000	4170·6	4360·2
Increase in net current assets	—	100	110
Cash available for investment in projects next year	150	70·7	79·6
ROCE %	25	27	29

Further development of the model is required if growth is to be accommodated. Here the relationship between increased turnover and increases in net current assets is established.

Exhibit 14·11

$	year 0	1	2
Turnover	10000	11000	12100
Profit	1000	1100	1210
Investment in projects during year	—	650	81·8
Cumulative investment in projects	—	650	731·8
ROI %	—	25	25
Profits from projects	—	162	183
Total Profits	1000	1262	1393
Long term loans	—	500	1000
Interest rate on loans %	—	10	10
Interest paid on loans	—	50	100
Total profits after interest	1000	1212	1293
Earnings	500	606	641·5
Dividends	350	424·2	449
Retained	150	181·8	192
Capital employed	4000	4681·8	5373
Increases in net current assets	—	100	110
Extension of existing fixed assets	—	—	500
Cash available for investment in projects next year	150	81·8	82
ROCE %	25	27	26

I think this series of Exhibits demonstrates the following facts about model building:

1 It can be an extremely tedious and complex task.
2 A model containing fewer than approximately two dozen items is unlikely to be of much practical value.
3 Once the model has been built its value as a planning tool increases rapidly as its complexity increases. Models containing several dozen variables can be of very great practical value.

4 Even these complex models may be operated by hand. Although tedious, the calculations are simple and a junior accounts clerk can be 'programmed' to make the calculations more easily than a computer. One manual 'run' through a 30-item model need take only an hour or so for each 'year'.

5 Manual models have the advantage that they are flexible. It would have been a simple matter, for example, to test the effect of altering the dividend payout ratio from 70% to 60% in Exhibit 14·11. Or to add a couple more variables to test the effect of an improvement in labour productivity or whatever.

6 Beyond a certain point it becomes sensible to use a computer to make the calculations.

7 The process of building a model is almost identical to the process of learning.

Computer models

Walley (Ch. 5) suggests that there are four types of model: the static and the dynamic, the stochastic and the deterministic. Because static models take no account of time their value in corporate planning is somewhat limited and, in my opinion, the value of optimizing models is also somewhat limited in corporate planning (but see page 288). The true and valid function of a model is not to select 'the best' strategy for the decision-maker but to allow the decision-maker more easily to examine the probable consequences of alternatives. Some interesting examples of their use in this role may be quoted.

James L. McKenney, for example, describes one firm's long, arduous but extremely rewarding attempts to build a model. The firm was planning to enter the European market – its first venture outside the US – and decided to allocate $70,000 a year for three years to develop a simulation model of production and marketing activities in Europe in order to test alternative methods of launch into alternative market segments. The article (*L.R.P.* Vol. 2 No. 3 March 1970) describes clearly how the building of the model helped the company's executives to learn about the market, how their key assumptions affected the model's behaviour, how some assumptions that they thought were important were in fact relatively unimportant and vice versa. One reason for the success of this model may have been the company's policy of not allowing the model to be built solely by specialists but by the executives themselves aided by specialists.

Probably the best known standard financial computer model is the one developed by RTZ Consultants in London. This is briefly described by W. R. V. Archer in *L.R.P.* (Vol. 3 No. 4 June 1971). This particular model is relatively flexible and the user may select his choice of calculations from a wide range of facilities – he may select from eighteen different types of financial report, for example. There are facilities for accumulating values through time, spreading values over several years, reading values off curves and step functions and testing against limits and, of course, d.c.f. calculations may readily be made. There are also facilities for sensitivity testing; the user states the base case and specifies which variations from it are of particular interest to him and the computer calculates the effect of these variations from the base case. Several different tax systems may be incorporated; thus a multinational company may model the taxation legislation pertaining to subsidiary companies in several different nations – including such difficulties as withholding taxes and double-taxation reliefs.

A rather similar model has been used in Cunard Steamship Co. Ltd. This is described by Jonathan P. L. Packer in an article in *L.R.P.* (Vol. 3 No 3 April 1971). The program was written especially for the Cunard company which had adopted an overall corporate objective of *x* per cent per annum growth in dividends per share subject to certain constraints. This target was written into the computer program so that the model automatically assumed the required dividend payments as a standard condition; it was the purpose of the model to show what would be the consequences on the company of adopting this target and pursuing certain alternative strategies. This model, then, was used as a gap analysis tool.

In point of fact nearly all the computer models developed over the past decade are very similar in principle; some are more flexible than others, some have this facility but not that, some are a little more appropriate for this company than for that. J. C. Higgins and D. Whitaker in their article in *The Computer Bulletin* of September 1972 suggest there are really two types of computer model; the computer model proper which usually has but one specialized purpose or which may be used to study one particular analysis and computer modelling systems which are much more flexible because the user has to state the relationships within the model. As the authors also say, this is a somewhat arbitrary distinction but some models are clearly computer models (the Cunard model, for example), while others are clearly modelling systems (the Prosper model, for example – see page 302).

Some models have become extremely complex; thus most of the early models allowed the user only to input forecasts via the input variables of the model – the user himself having had to make the forecasts prior to feeding them into the model. Modern computer systems allow forecasts to be made inside the model using time series, multiple regression, exponential smoothing and so on. Again, modern models allow the consolidation of several individual sub-models, representing subsidiary companies into group models. Risk analysis is possible with many models; automatic sensitivity testing is a common facility; some now allow 'backward iteration' by which the user may ask the computer to show what input variables have to be changed to achieve a given target. Nearly all modern models have facilities for making d.c.f. calculations. Most modelling systems now allow output in the form of graphs and histograms.

A list of computer models is given on page 302.

15 Other planning techniques

Introduction

I have repeatedly suggested that understanding the philosophy of corporate planning is of far greater importance than the technology. If an executive was to misunderstand or misuse either the philosophy or the technology I would hope it would be the latter. Nevertheless I have to admit that I doubt whether a really professional and thorough job can be made of a corporate plan unless at least some of the techniques of setting targets, of forecasting and evaluation, such as those described in Chapter 11, 12 and 14, are employed. In addition there are certain other techniques which I believe corporate planners may occasionally find extremely useful and I propose to describe these briefly in this chapter. They appear in no particular rank or order of merit.

Estimating subjective probabilities

One of the main reasons why advanced mathematical techniques are so seldom used in the real business world is that the data upon which the calculations should be performed is not available. This is particularly so in the case of probabilities; risk analysis and other techniques are potentially of enormous value – if only executives could bring themselves to place probabilities upon their estimates.

That this is possible more often than most executives will admit is one of my enduring beliefs. Both Steiner (Ch. 15) and Walley (Ch. 7) give examples of how several knowledgeable executives might be asked to estimate their company's sales of Product P in a given period. Suppose their answers are as shown in Exhibit 15·1 where one executive estimates sales at 10,000 units, two believe sales will be 11,000 units and so on. Now this does not mean that there is, for example, a 0·4 chance of sales reaching 12,000 units. It only means that four executives out of 10 *believe* that sales will reach 12,000; but at least that is *something*! It may well be worth using this probability distribution in a risk analysis calculation.

It may be worth noting that book-makers and other professional risk-takers, including insurance underwriters, very often feel able to back their probability estimates with their own money. Is it too much to ask senior executives to go at east part of the way towards that? It may be the case that many of the events on which executives are called upon to make judgements have never taken place before: the launch of a new product, research into some new phenomenon, the construction of some new pilot plant, are all, by definition, unique. And yet they are not perhaps so unique that no guidance as to their probable outcome may be found from other not too dissimilar new product launches, other not too dissimilar research programs.

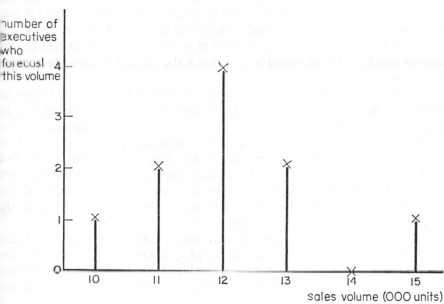

Exhibit 13.1

Quantifying executive opinion

There are today two important reasons why an effort to quantify opinion should be made. The first is that the attempt itself may serve to clarify the opinion being expressed – this reason has been valid for all time, of course. The second arises because of the growing importance of the computer model as an aid to decision-making. If an executive's opinion can be quantified then the opinion can, in effect, be accepted by a computer as part of a program and the computer becomes able to 'think like an executive'.

Take the following statement, 'sales will fall catastrophically if we increase the price of our product'. Now it might be possible to quantify this proposition by asking the executive to state how many units of sales he thinks would be lost if the product price was raised by $1, $2, $5, $10. And how many extra units would be sold if the price was lowered by $10, $5, $2, $1? The executive's replies should fall into the well-known price elasticity curve that is common to many products and his replies should be fairly similar to the replies given by other knowledgeable executives. Perhaps there is some historical evidence describing what actually happened when the product price was last altered.

In other words, it ought to be possible, for most statements of opinion of strategic importance, to find some way of quantifying opinions and of verifying that the figures so obtained are not wildly inappropriate.

Cost benefit analysis

Great confusion reigns over the terms cost-benefit analysis, cost-effectiveness, planning-programming-budgeting (PPB) and cost-utility analysis – see Steiner (Ch. 14). Cost-effectiveness is, as I understand it, a systematic study to determine which is the cheapest method of achieving a stated effect. This is closely related to program budgets (see below) but not closely related to cost-benefit analysis which, as I understand it, is a systematic attempt to quantify benefits that are not normally quantifiable.

The most important example, in Europe, of the use of CBA (also known as Social Cost Benefit) is the report on the location of the third London airport. In this study an attempt was made to quantify, in terms of pounds sterling, the benefits and disbenefits to the people of England of siting the proposed airport at a number of possible sites. In addition to taking into account the cost of building the physical facilities and the communication links – all of which are normally included in this sort of study – the commission also calculated the costs of such disbenefits as loss of amenity, noise nuisance and other previously unquantified 'value judgements' such as an ancient church, a fine view.

The key to making such estimates is to invite answers to the question 'what would you pay to obtain this benefit or what would you pay to make this nuisance or disbenefit go away?' Thus the value of not having close neighbours is presumably the difference in price between a semi-detached and a detached house of otherwise identical design and location.

Now the importance of CBA to corporate planners is this: society is showing greater interest in corporate behaviour and, at the same time, many social institutions, such as government agencies, charities and so on are showing greater interest in corporate planning. It seems highly probable that in evaluating strategic plans, much more emphasis will have to be placed upon the non-economic criteria – which, at present are less readily quantifiable than the traditional ROSC and risk criteria. I have little doubt also that CBA will have to be used to establish many of the corporate ethological objectives mentioned on pages 208–211.

Utility theory

In principle Utility Theory should be of very considerable value in corporate planning. It is well known that the failure of a million dollar project spells disaster to some companies but would pass unnoticed in others and that, in other words, a million dollars is of greater utility to some companies than to others. To be able to establish the utility of a sum of money would seem, on the face of it, to be a useful thing to be able to do. So far as I know, no company has ever used Utility Theory or Preference Curves.

I believe its use will come into vogue during the next decade or so. The concept is still unfamiliar to many managers and very few indeed have any experience of quantifying utilities. And yet an interest rate is a measure of the time utility of money and far more executives are at home with interest rates, discount tables and so on today than a decade ago.

Creativity

Strictly speaking creativity means the ability to create something entirely new; the meaning of the word has become somewhat devalued from over-use so that it may now mean ingenuity. Ingenuity itself is a rare quality in management and one that requires deliberate fertilization if it is to flourish. The place of ingenuity and creativity in the planning process is open to debate; my view is that, having determined an objective and having identified the ethological constraints – neither of which activities require any creative ability at all – creativity and ingenuity will be required to devise the best method of achieving the objective without infringing the constraints. The more challenging the target, the more constricting the constraints, the greater will be the ingenuity that is required to find a suitable means.

Steiner lists six ways in which management may encourage creativity within the organization: (1) top management should set an example; (2) the planning system should be designed to force and command managers to be creative; (3) creativity should be rewarded; (4) selection and recruitment criteria should include creativity; (5) management should deliberately provide occasions for the use of creativity techniques such as brainstorming; (6) there must be some procedure by which bright ideas have a proper airing and evaluation. I do not think I can improve upon this list except to emphasize the importance of item (2); and I believe that the system described in this book makes creativity unavoidable at the stage, described in Chapter 7, which I called the 'Revelation'.

A number of systematic techniques now exist and are, I believe, well known if not yet well tried. They include Brainstorming, Lateral Thinking, Logical Trees, Morphological Analysis (see page 230). Think Tanks and the employment of 'wild men'.

Program budgets and PPB

There is considerable confusion as to the various names and meanings of these techniques. I believe the least confusing view is given by David Novick in Denning (Ch. 11).

PPB contributes to the planning process in two important ways: firstly it shows the linkages between an organization's objectives and its resources and secondly it allows the consequences of a decision to be seen in terms of costs and benefits. Novick distinguishes betwen objectives, programs and resources; objectives are the organization's raison d'être, programs are the sets of activities undertaken to achieve the objectives and resources are consumed by these activities. What PPB does is to show all three together and this is in marked contradistinction to the traditional method of budgeting where expenditure is shown but what the expenditure is for is not shown. Novick relies heavily upon the concept of effectiveness – i.e. the extent to which a program yields the benefit it is intended to yield – which is not the same thing as efficiency. Indeed the whole concept of PPB rests on recognizing the need to identify objectives and gear the organization to achieving these; a budgeting system that does not specifically help to do this is ill-designed for its task. Instead of allocating resources, departmentally, therefore, PPB shows the allocation of resources by program; these allocations may cut across departmental boundaries. I attempt to illustrate the crucial difference between traditional budgeting, in Exhibit 15·2 and Program Budgets in 15·3. I see no reason why the two methods should not be combined into a Matrix Budget, see Exhibit 15·4. This certainly has the merit of being precisely the form in which target and control information is needed by those companies who adopt the Matrix form of organization briefly described on page 252.

Exhibit 15·2   A Traditional Budget

	$
Chemistry Laboratory	70000
Physics Section	30000
Biology Section	40000
Experimental Station	250000
Administration	60000
Total	450000

Shows *where* the money is to be spent

Exhibit 15·3   A Program Budget

	$
Bio-plastic project	60000
Cryo-genetic project	240000
Electrocardiac design	150000
Total	450000

Shows *what* the money is to be spent on

Exhibit 15·4   A Matrix Budget

$	Bio-plastic project	Cryogenetic project	Electrocardiac design	Totals
Chemistry laboratory	10000	40000	20000	70000
Physics section	—	20000	10000	30000
Biology section	10000	—	30000	40000
Experimental station	30000	140000	80000	250000
Administration	10000	40000	10000	60000
Totals	60000	240000	150000	450000

I do not think that many companies or governments have yet understood the full significance of the difference between the traditional departmental method of management and the new results-orientated approach to the management of organizations characterized by corporate planning, PPB, management by objecives, systems analysis. Part of the reason for the lack of understanding is due, I am convinced, to the failure to realize that 'objective' must be properly defined – see Chapter 3. One of the signal merits of PPB is that it draws attention to achieving objectives instead of to the use of resources.

However it must be stated that very few companies have adopted PPB and while it is reported in the press from time to time that one government agency or another has started to use PPB, reports also appear that some agencies have ceased to use it. I believe these difficulties are due less to the disadvantages inherent in PPB than to the difficulty that many people have in accepting a radically new way of thinking.

Management information systems

Information may reach a manager either because he goes out and seeks the information, or because someone happens to pass the information to him or because there is a carefully designed system by which any information he needs is deliberately placed before him. Now a 'management information system' may mean either of two things: it may describe the last of the three situations above where the manager is served by a system that has been designed to help him to do his job or it may mean a particular computer-based information technique. This latter consists of a Data Base, i.e. a bank of raw facts and figures about sales, customer accounts, employees and so on, and the 'MIS' which, by means of a computer which performs calculations on the data in the data base, gives each manager just the information he needs when he needs it in the form in which he needs it. We can ignore this second, technical use of this phrase because it has very little relevance to corporate planning; computer-based information systems will certainly be necessary for day to day control but hardly appropriate to corporate planning time cycles.

Regardless of the time cycle involved, all managers at all levels would appreciate being served by an efficient management information system. But the data required by those who take strategic decisions is very different from that used at tactical and operational levels and is so non-routine in character that one would be forgiven for doubting whether it could be worth-while developing an information system for this level of management. According to John F. Green (*L.R.P.* Vol. 2 No 4 June 1970) it is extremely doubtful whether a management information system is desirable at this level. He makes the interesting point that, at the strategic level, a few clerks collecting and collating press cuttings on competitors, technology and so on may be worth far more to a strategist than any sophisticated computerized MIS.

On the other hand R. N. Kashyap sees the possibility of drawing up a fairly comprehensive list of information required at the strategic level and then putting into effect a systematic scanning process. This is the purpose of his Information Requirements Matrix described in *L.R.P.* Vol. 5 No. 2 June 1972 which includes such items as competitor intelligence, market information, technological forecasts, social trends and so on.

I certainly hold the view that once a company has been through the corporate planning process, by which time it will know what are the key informational factors, it should set up a routine formal monitoring system which, as described in Chapter 8, must include the routine scanning of relevant information sources and the routine preparation of technological forecasts, market forecasts and so on.

In other words a management information system must be established; at the tactical, operational level this system may well be capable of full computerization; at the strategic level I believe it has to be systematic only in the sense that the strategist must systematically ask himself what information he should be searching for.

Decision analysis

The term Decision Analysis now embraces a large number of individual techniques designed to improve the quality of decision-making. These include Sensitivity Tests, Risk Analysis and Outcome Matrices which I described in Chapter 14; I consider that these three are by far the most useful of the DA tools. But there are others that are worthy of mention in this chapter. I am sure that Games Theory is worthy of more than a very brief mention. In principle it should have much to offer the strategist but I know of no case when it has been successfully used in real-life strategic situations. But we should distinguish between Mathematical Games Theory, with its 'saddlepoint' and sophisticated equations and the use of Games in analysing decisions. I do not think that the playing of games is normally considered part of DA, however.

Games were first used by military strategists – 'war games' have become well known to the general public – but are increasingly being used to examine possible outcomes of alternative competitive strategies. An interesting example is provided by R. H. R. Armstrong and Margaret Holsan in their article in *L.R.P* (Vol. 5 No 1 March 1972). They describe how a local government authority wishing to predict what problems they would face if they designated an area as a new town development, invited certain 'players' to take the role of the various relevant interest groups. A similar game is played by some companies before entering negotiations with trade unions, suppliers, customers and so on.

Decision trees frequently appear in the literature; see Walley (Ch. 7) and Steiner (Ch. 15). Consider the problem of whether to build a large factory now or a small one now followed by another factory later on, if demand justifies it. If one can estimate the probable demand then the calculation becomes relatively simple in principle – see Exhibit 15·5 – where it is assumed that the cost of the factories, their probabilities and other data are all available, as well as the probabilities of the various levels of demand. In practice two severe problems attend the use of decision trees; the first is the obvious one that the required data are very seldom available. The second is a much more serious one; it is that decisions in real life are seldom made as between two alternatives but between at least half a dozen. In real life the number of branches in the decision tree becomes unmanageable. Furthermore the number of alternative outcomes is usually more than two or three, so again the branches brachiate

nintelligibly. I doubt if decision trees have much practical value in strategic
lanning except as a device for clarifying the alternatives that lie before one.

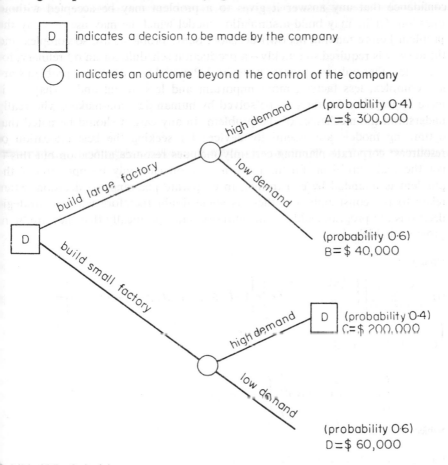

$\boxed{\text{D}}$ indicates a decision to be made by the company

◯   indicates an outcome beyond the control of the company

high demand — (probability 0·4) A = \$ 300,000

build large factory

low demand (probability 0·6) B = \$ 40,000

$\boxed{\text{D}}$

build small factory

high demand $\boxed{\text{D}}$ (probability 0·4) C = \$ 200,000

low demand (probability 0·6) D = \$ 60,000

Exhibit 15·5   A decision tree

Assume that the NPV of Branch A is \$300,000 then, since its probability is 0·4, its probable NPV
is \$120,000 The probable NPV of building a large factory (branches A and B together) is
thus \$144,000. The probable NPV for the small factory alternative is only \$116,000.

Optimizing models

suggested on page 278 that optimizing models are of less value to corporate
lanners than simulation models. This does not imply that optimizing models
are of no value at all – they are used in corporate planning – but, in my
pinion, they do have the severe disadvantage that they are designed to reach
he optimum solution thus leaving no choice to the manager.

It may be objected that the manager does have a choice – he can reject the
ptimum solution – but I am not certain that he does. Very often the problems
olved by such optimizing techniques as Linear Programming are so complex
hat no human mind can understand how the computer has arrived at the
optimum conclusion and where this is so the manager who rejects the computer

solution cannot be acting rationally. I believe that the model-using decision maker has two choices: he can build an optimizing model in which he has such confidence that any answer it gives to a problem may be accepted without question. Or he may build a simulation model which he may use to study the problem before making his own decision. Some problems are so complex and the answer is required so quickly – a production schedule for an oil refinery, for example – that only a computer using an LP model will do; other problems are less complex, less factual, more important and less urgent and perhaps it is more appropriate for these to be solved by human decision-makers who really understand the mechanics of the problem. In any case it should be noted that optimizing models are essentially devices for seeking the best allocation of resources; corporate planning certainly includes resource allocation but this is not the main problem. Furthermore a solution can only be optimum if the problem is bounded by constraints; in corporate planning the decisions often relate to the constraints and there is some doubt therefore whether strategic decisions are programmable; some authors state specifically that they are 'non programmable'.

Optimize:

$$(1) \quad \sum_{k=1}^{2e} \sum_{i=1}^{7} \sum_{j=1}^{e_7} \left[\left(\frac{n_{i,k}}{\sum_{i=1}^{7} n_{i,k}} * \frac{Y_{i,k-1}}{(1+\delta^k)^j} \right) * \left\{ 1 - (-5_1 + 5_2) + .F_{i,k}(-5_1 + 5_2) + \lambda_i.\mathrm{M} \right\} - \right.$$

$$\left\{ (n_{i,k-1}) * (\phi_{i,k-1}) + Q_k \right.$$

$$\left. \left. * \left(\frac{n_{i,k-1}}{\sum_{i=1}^{7} n_{i,k-1}} * \frac{Y_{i,k-2}}{(1+\delta^k \mathrm{E}^1)^j} \right) * \left\{ 1 - (-5_1 + 5_2) + .F_{i,k-1}(-5_1 + 5_2) + \lambda_i. \right\} \right\} \right]$$

Subject to:

$$(2) \quad \sum_{}^{7} n_{i,k} = \sum_{}^{7} n_{i,k-1} 6 (1 + K_k + I_{i,k} - E_{i,k})$$

$$(3) \quad n_{i,k} \ldots n^j \mathrm{E}^1 (1 + I_{i,k} - E_{i,k}); \qquad i = 2,3 \ldots 7; \qquad j = 2 \ldots R_i$$

$$(4) \quad n_{i,k} = n^j \mathrm{E}^1 (1 + I_{i,k} - E_{i,k}); \qquad i = 2,3 \ldots 7; \qquad j = R_i + 1, \ldots 47$$

$$(5) \quad \phi_{i,k} \mathrm{Tg}_i = \frac{n_{i,k}}{\sum_{i=1}^{} n_{i,k}} 6 (\phi_{i,k}) 6 (1 + \lambda_i)$$

Where:

$\phi_{i,k}$ = Unit cost of activity i in generation k.
$n_{i,k}$ = Number of individual engaged in activity i in generation k.
$Y_{i,k}$ = Income from activity i in generation k in year j.
δ^k = Discount rate for activity i in generation k.
R_i = Last year of non-zero costs in activity i.
$F_{i,k}$ = Fiscal dividend for activity i in generation k.
λ_i = Feedback multiplier for activity i.
Q_k = Proportion of regional income added to education budget in generation k.
$5_1, 5_2$ = Tax rates.
K_k = Population growth rate in generation k.
$I_{i,k}$ = Immigration in activity i in generation k in year j.
$E_{i,k}$ = Emigration from activity i in generation k in year j.

Exhibit 15·6. Dynamic Program model of a nation's education system.

Linear programming has been used to determine the optimum mix of financial resources for a company as well as the many well-known uses for locating physical resources. Certain other types of non-linear programming may have a corporate planning application; among these other types of mathematical programming often mentioned (see Walley (Ch. 7) for example) are integer programming, dynamic programming and separable programming. An example of dynamic programming appears in the article by Duncan Bailey and Charles Schotta in *L.R.P.* (Vol. 4 No. 1 Sept. 1971). The equations described there and reproduced in Exhibit 15·6 illustrate well the point I made above about leaving a decision to a machine without the decision-maker understanding why it has made a given decision.

One particular type of optimizing model may prove useful when more experience has been gained of its use; this is Portfolio Selection. In theory this technique is precisely what the corporate planner requires to help him determine the best strategic structure for his company. The Portfolio Selection technique, as originally conceived by Markovitz, was designed to select a portfolio of shares for a shareholder such that the return and risk were optimum. This meant that the shares had to be selected by reference to (a) their individual return and riskiness and (b) the total return and riskiness of the portfolio as a whole. This latter criterion meant that the interrelatedness of any share to any other had to be taken into account by the model. I know of no successful practical applications so far in corporate planning.

Manpower planning

Few planners doubt the necessity for financial planning, facilities planning, product planning; some corporate planners do question whether manpower planning is necessary, and both Stemp (Ch. 5) and Weinwurm (Ch. 8) suggest that many companies overlook it. I have no doubt that it is necessary but I do consider that it is a less well-developed branch of planning than these other specialist branches and that is why it appears in this chapter rather than in chapter 13.

Part of the problem with manpower planning is that it is very much a secondary strategy – the future manpower needs of a company are wholly dependent upon what activities the company will be carrying out. Part of the problem is that manpower planning is essentially about people and people are even less predictable and controllable than other resources. Ideally it should be possible to make the following calculation; a company employs 1,000 men of whom 10 are skilled spot welders. In ten years' time turnover will, it is hoped, be three times as great as today, and labour productivity will have doubled. Therefore in ten years' time the company will need 1,500 employees of whom 15 will be spot welders. But, in practice, (a) turnover might be between one and six times today's level, (b) productivity might be between one and four times as great and (c) spot welding might be obsolete. Thus the number of employees required in ten years' time might be between 250 and 6,000 and the number of spot welders could be between 0 and 60. In spite of such wide margins of error

inherent in secondary strategic decision-making, I believe manpower plannin
does have a role in corporate planning.

Hussey (Ch. 9) makes the point that most companies have to decide how the
are to meet their future manpower needs including, in particular, the
management needs. Should it be through recruitment, by interdepartment;
transfers, by the training and development of suitable employees? How f;
ahead do such plans have to be laid? To answer these questions it is necessar
to gather such statistics as an analysis of employee numbers by job categor
and location, by age, sex, skill, nationality, wage rates, working hours and s
on. Then predictions have to be made as to these statistics in future year
bearing in mind changes in productivity, technology, attitudes to work, workir
methods, density of supervision, holidays, retirement age and so on. Then or
can identify possible deficits and surpluses or, and this is often just as in
portant, one may identify on what scale facilities will be needed for selectio
training and other personnel services.

John R. Hinricks in Stemp (Ch. 5) points out that manpower planning
particularly important for the rapidly growing company – particularly manag
ment manpower. He suggests that the systematic identification of potenti
managerial talent is one vital element in manpower planning.

The chapter by Johnston and Meredith in Denning (Ch. 10) identifies tw
elements in a manpower plan. The first is the identification of strengths ar
weaknesses in human resources, both qualitative and quantitative, in relatic
to possible future needs and the second is the action plan to put right any lac
of balance between them. They quote the case of a company employing 4,0(
people which would need over 5,000 new employees within a five-year peric
necessitating over 10,000 internal personnel moves. This suggested a level
activity far beyond the current capacity of the personnel services departmen
They quote another company, which, having grown rapidly by acquisitio
found the distribution of skill wholly out of balance as between the centre ar
the various parts of the organization. The chapter describes the manpower pla
ning process in some detail.

Charts, profiles, matrices etc.

Many of the techniques used in planning are, in principle, nothing more than
systematic or methodical version of common sense. Corporate planning itself
nothing more than a systematic, methodical way of doing what entrepreneu
and far-sighted business men have been doing since the dawn of history.
check-list is, in principle, nothing more sophisticated than a housewife's sho
ping list – not even if it is called 'situation audit' or 'resource profile'. The val
of charts, profiles, matrices, check-lists, tables, graphs and grids lies in the w;
information is presented to the manager so that he can see at a glance how tl
is related to that, or how, if he decides this, that will happen or if he decid
that, this will happen. A useful rule, I suggest, is: when the mind is confuse
draw up a matrix.

Ansoff (Ch. 5) is well known for his Capability Profile, Competence Grid ar

Competitive Profile. He devised the Product-Mission Matrix (Ch. 7). Denning (Ch. 14) shows a 'profile' of responsibilities of several planning departments in different organizations while Weinwurm (in his Exhibit 9) uses exactly the same form of presentation to show the contents of various plans.

The Program Budget is little more than the presentation of budget data shown allocated to missions instead of being shown allocated to the traditional departmental hierarchies. A Decision Tree is little more than a chart representing a sequence of decisions; Morphological Analysis is little more than a matrix of qualities – and so on.

The point I am making is simply this: the volume of data required in the process of corporate planning is considerable. I doubt, however, whether it is so vast as to demand the incessant use of computers, automated data banks, multi-scan data terminals. It is of sufficient volume, however, to warrant the use of a large number of very simple, very elegant, well-tried mental aids such as lists, charts, matrices, and so on.

16 Education and training

Introduction

I would like to repeat my contention that corporate planning represents a fundamental change in approach away from the traditional departmental institutionalized method of running an organization. It is the same change of approach that has brought systems analysis and program budgets into prominence in management at the expense of the traditional accountancy budget, for example, and has produced quite new forms of organization structure at the expense of the traditional hierarchy. I do not believe that such a profound change of philosophy can be made to a company overnight; I do not think that it can be made in less than a few years; I do not think it can be made to all the major companies in a nation in less than several decades. And this takes me back to what I said in the introduction to this book – that the spread of corporate planning throughout the companies of the world is proceeding only very slowly. That is the speed that I would expect. What we have here is not the mere introduction of some new technique but part of a whole ground-swell of change.

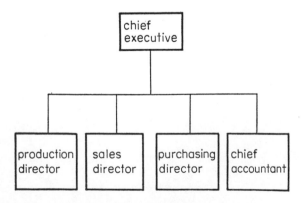

Exhibit 16·1

Let me give one more example of how these new philosophies differ from the old. There was once a company organized into a hierarchy as in Exhibit 16·1. As it grew in size more and more top managers and directors were appointed until the organization chart appeared as Exhibit 16·2. Clearly the company was

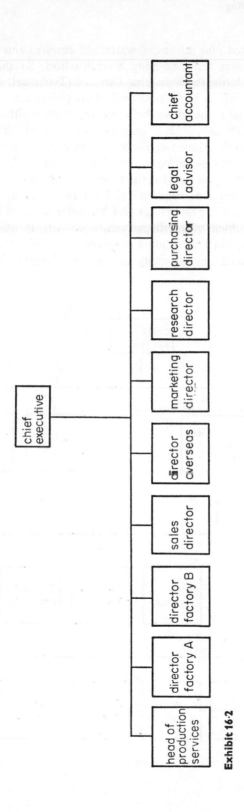

Exhibit 16-2

becoming fragmented into dozens of watertight empires and what was neede
was some mechanism for improving co-ordination. So the chief executi
appointed two overlords; the Managing Director (Technical) and the Managi
Director (Commercial) as in Exhibit 16·3. Two points are noteworthy in th
arrangement; the first is that it will be a failure, because although a mechanis
is provided by which, say, R & D may be co-ordinated with factory A – th
would be the task of the Managing Director (Technical) – no mechanism exis
to co-ordinate decisions as between, say, R & D and marketing, or factory
and Sales. The second point is that the Overlord solution is cast in exactly tl
same mould as the previous solution – Exhibit 16·3 is identical in principle
16·2 which is identical in principle to 16·1. A better solution to this company
problem, i.e. the problem of interdepartmental co-ordination, is the adoption
corporate planning, but this solution requires a radical break from the hie
archical way in which this company has always thought about its organiz
tional problems.

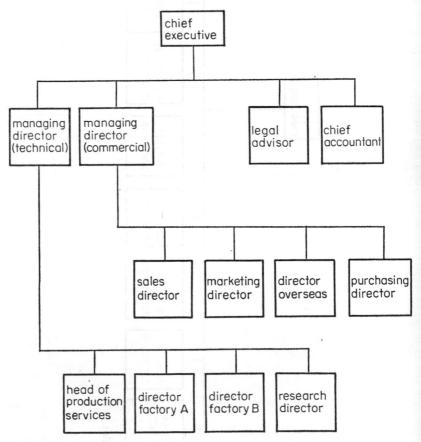

Exhibit 16·3

Corporate planning, then, is as much a change in attitude as a technique and as such it cannot be introduced into an organization overnight. Its introduction is as much a *process of education* as anything. In this chapter, therefore, I will consider the educational and training aspects of corporate planning.

Educating the company

Once it has been decided 'to introduce corporate planning' into a company two actions will be required. The first is to set up some procedure or system for the processing of corporate and strategic decisions. The second is to reform the company so as to be able to accept new methods of management.

I dealt at some length with the first of these actions in Chapter 9 where I suggested that someone should be made responsible for the corporate planning process. As a minimum this official would act as a secretary to the executive or group of executives who were to make the strategic decisions; he would take notes at meetings, search for information, ensure the arrival of reports for their next meeting, and so on. Or this official could be a fully-fledged corporate planner who would be able to supervise the quality of the planning and even perhaps contribute strategic ideas. As part of this action – i.e. the introduction of corporate planning – the management will naturally include the training of the corporate planner, the training of those executives who will be responsible for strategic decision-making and also for any very senior employees who may not be taking an active part in corporate planning. I suggest a syllabus for courses specifically designed for each of the three categories of people on pages 296–300.

But this leaves the second action to be tackled – the re-education of those of the company's managers who are not directly involved in making strategic decisions but whose knowledge contributes to the decisions and whose work is affected by them. I can only deal here with methods of informing these employees about corporate planning; I must, however, add the point that if informing them of the corporate planning is the only action the company takes to re-educate its managers then it may be doomed to failure. Corporate planning is only one symptom of the management revolution that is going on all the time; in addition to corporate planning, systems analysis and other ideas I have mentioned before, managers also need to know of such concepts as job enrichment and so on. Corporate planning, then is only one subject among many about which managers need to be kept up to date.

I believe the most effective way is to hold a briefing meeting for all senior managers approximately six months after the decision to introduce corporate planning has been made. By this date there will be some progress to report to the managers but not so much that the managers will have already been drawn into the process. The agenda for such meetings might follow these lines:

Session 1 Chief Executive explains why it was felt necessary to introduce corporate planning.

Session 2 Corporate Planner explains what corporate planning is, what it should achieve and describes the steps in the process.

Session 3 Senior member of the planning body describes progress so far and explains what part the assembled managers will be asked to play in the process over the next 12 months.

Session 4 General Discussion. Or: a discussion of the strengths and weaknesses of the company or the possible threats and opportunities; or an explanation as to what assumptions managers are to make in their forecasts; or managers are shown how to make the forecasts needed by the planning body.

Session 5 Conclusions. Chief Executive sums up.

Naturally each company will approach such a meeting differently. Some will ask the speakers to reinforce their lectures with written notes, others will invite outside speakers to describe the planning process, some chief executives will take this opportunity to announce the company's long term profit target or to reveal the broad lines of a new company policy.

The point being made here is this: corporate planning will result in major changes being made to the company over the next few years; either one believes that it is prudent to advise managers of such a prospect or one does not. If one does then a meeting of the sort described may be useful.

Training the planners

Some of the managers who attend the briefing meetings suggested above may require training in specific planning techniques in addition to the more general and educative information given to them at the briefing. Some companies extend the briefing meetings beyond the normal single day to provide training in forecasting or whatever. Thus a company may wish to ensure that its research staff are familiar with certain technological forecasting techniques if they are going to be asked to contribute such forecasts to the corporate plan and these men would attend a short course on this particular subject. Or perhaps a short course on five-year budgets is considered necessary for those managers who have so far only had to make one-year budgets.

Providing training for these managers in some specific planning techniques may be necessary, then. But two other groups of planners will certainly need to be trained. These are (1) the corporate planner himself and his staff, if any, and (2) the very senior managers who are going to be responsible for making strategic decisions and this will certainly include the Chief Executive together with any of his colleagues whom he invites to join him on the strategic decision-making body. These people require a course of training lasting not less than two days as suggested in the section below; if possible they should be given much more than two days if they are not going to have the services of a fully trained corporate planner to guide them through the long process. If they are, two days should be quite sufficient.

Syllabus for corporate planning courses

I A one-day appreciation course

This course is designed for the very senior employees of a company that is about to introduce corporate planning but who will not be responsible for making the strategic decisions. It is, in other words designed for the colleagues and immediate subordinates of the company's strategic planners. I suggest that four sessions each of $1\frac{1}{2}$ hours is a useful norm.

Session 1	Introduction
	What Corporate Planning is
	Why it is necessary
	Who should do it
	How it is done: 1 Objectives and Targets
Session 2	How it is done: 2 F_o forecast and gap
	3 Internal and External Appraisal
	4 Strategic Structure
	5 Evaluating Strategies
	6 Monitoring
	Summary and Discussion
Session 3	Case Study – Discussion
	The participants break into syndicate groups to discuss a suitable case study*
Session 4	Case Study – Report
	The syndicates report their findings to the full meeting.
	Conclusion.

*Note to course organizer – It is absolutely essential that this case study is designed to bring out the difference between corporate and all other types of planning. This means that the syndicates must be forced, by the way in which the case is presented to them, to consider *corporate* objectives and to discuss the *strategic structure*.

II A short course for company planners

This course is designed for the managers who are responsible for making the corporate and strategic plans. These may be a group of a dozen very senior executives, or only the two or three top men in the company or, in many cases just the Chief Executive. I suggest ten sessions each of $1\frac{1}{2}$ hours which can be accommodated in two days if the work is continued in the evening, or in three days.

Session 1	Introduction
	Systematic corporate planning
	A system described
Session 2	Setting Objectives and Targets
	F_o forecasts and Gap Analysis

Session 3 Internal and External Appraisal
Strategic Structure
Session 4 Evaluating Strategies
Action Plans
Monitoring
Session 5 Case Study and Discussion*
Session 6 Case Study – Reports*
Session 7 Forecasting Techniques
Reduction of Errors
Session 8 Evaluation Techniques
The Use of Models
Session 9 The problems and pitfalls of introducing corporate planning
Session 10 Discussion of each Participant's practical problems
Conclusion

* See 'Notes to course organizer' on page 297

III A one-week course for corporate planners

This course is designed for those who are to be employed as professional
corporate planners and whose job therefore will consist largely of helping very
senior executives through the planning process. I have assumed that those
who attend a course such as this will have had considerable experience of
management and will have attained an educational standard approaching
that of graduate status. I suggest 30 sessions of $1\frac{1}{2}$ hours. I have assumed that
only a course organizer of the very highest competence would attempt to offer
a course of this calibre.

Session 1 Introduction
Why corporate planning is necessary
Who should do it
How it is done – the process described.
Session 2 The three types of objective: purpose, ethos and means
The three theories on company purpose: shareholder, stakeholder
and concensus
Discussion and conclusions.
Session 3 Corporate financial targets – I
Participants break into syndicates; one half tries to determine a
suitable point target for a company and the other half tries to
determine a performance–risk curve. Participants then re-form to
compare difficulties associated with each.
Session 4 Corporate financial Targets – II
The argument in favour of each financial indicator – ROCE, e.p.s.
etc. Participants each build a model to show how ROCE, ROSC,
P/E ratios etc. are interlinked.
Session 5 Corporate Ethological Targets. Each syndicate challenges another
to devise suitable indicators for use as ethological targets. For

example: 'devise a battery of target indicators to show that your company is discharging its obligations to the community'.

Sessions 6 and 7 F_o forecasts

Each syndicate is asked to make an F_o forecast from the same past data (such as that in the Exercise Q 5.3 below). They should each indicate the range of errors. Participants compare notes in full session and discuss the various methods of reducing errors in an F_o or F_P forecast.

These forecasts are compared to an appropriate point target and a gap analysis made, and to a performance–risk curve and a gap analysis made with that.

Session 8 Identifying strengths and weaknesses – I

Lecturer describes the various methods with case illustrations.

Session 9 Identifying strengths and weaknesses – II

Participants break into syndicates. Each syndicate is visited in turn by several senior executives from a well-known company. Each syndicate attempts to draw up a list of that company's strengths and weaknesses. They compare results in full session.

Session 10 Identifying Threats and Opportunities

Speaker from well-known company describes the threats and opportunities facing his company over 10 to 20 years.

Session 11 Technological Forecasting – I

Participants to prepare their own individual forecast of technological change in their own industry.

Session 12 Technological forecasting – II

Each participant studies an article on morphological analysis (see *L.R.P.* March 1972 for example) and carries out a study on his company's products.

Session 13 Technological forecasting – III

Discussion between participants on their work in Sessions 11 and 12. Course leader to obtain agreed summary and conclusions, if possible, on the feasibility of technological forecasting.

Session 14 Strategic structure – I

Each syndicate to write out a case study designed to demonstrate the importance of the strategic structure of a company.

Session 15 Strategic structure – II

Each syndicate to tackle another syndicate's case study (which must, of course, contain enough data for a cruciform chart to be drawn up).

Session 16 Strategic structure – II

Syndicates report back to full session. Summary and conclusions as to strategic structures.

Session 17 Evaluation

Lectures on Sensitivity Testing, Risk Analysis and models.

Session 18 Models – I

Syndicates each build a model to demonstrate how a company's use of loan capital can be used to increase ROCE and ROSC and to show what happens to dividend cover when profits fluctuate.

Session 19   Models – II
Participants visit company or consultants where computer model is in full and effective use in corporate planning.

Session 20   Organization – I
Lecturer describes organization structure of a company having 1000 employees and no corporate planning.
Each syndicate is asked to list the advantages and disadvantages of various changes of organization – thus Syndicate A will consider the appointment of a corporate planner to this company, Syndicate B will consider the Overlord system, Syndicate C will look at a Matrix Organization for it, etc.

Session 21   Organization – II
Report back
Discussion.

Session 22   Forms and documents
Discussion on the design of forms and documents needed, if any.

Session 23   Lecturer to obtain agreement as to list of salient problems that participants will face on rejoining their companies. Suggested solutions.

Other Sessions   Visiting lecturers and private periods of study will no doubt be interlaced at convenient points in the course.

Session 30   Conclusions
Participants to state how far the purpose of the course has been achieved, i.e. to prepare them for a job of corporate planner with their company, in which they are to guide and advise very senior executives through the process of corporate planning.

Sources of information

While it may be legitimate for the tactical planner to rely mainly on information concerning his company, the strategic planner has to rely heavily on information concerning its environment. It is an essential part of the education and training of any person engaged in strategic planning that he should be aware of the sources of information outside his company. The most important of these may be Planning Societies (which should be able to advise him both on planning methodology and on specialist sources of information). But he may also wish to consult experts outside his company on target setting, on forecasting, on computer models, and so on. I give below a very brief, but I hope, useful list of sources of information on these topics.

Planning societies

Society for Long Range Planning,
132 Terminal Buildings,

Grosvenor Gardens,
London, S.W.1
(I think it is generally accepted that this is the premier planning society in the world. It has 1,000 members, issues a monthly news letter, organizes conferences, courses, etc. and issues the highly professional *Journal of Long Range Planning*).
Association Française pour la Planification d'Entreprise, Paris.
Associazione Italiana Pianificazione Aziendale, Milan.
Corporate Planners Association, San Francisco.
European Society of Corporate and Strategic Planners, Brussels.
Midwest Planning Association, Chicago.
North American Society for Corporate Planning, New York.
Southern California Corporate Planners Association, Los Angeles.
Vereeniging voor Strategische Beleidsvorming, The Hague.

Commentators on proposed targets

The decision as to which objectives shall be adopted together with the target level of achievement to be aimed at is usually taken by the company's senior managers. I believe this could be unhealthy unless they take pains to sound out the opinion of people outside the company. Among them may be these:

A merchant bank
A joint-stock bank
A major institutional shareholder
A shareholders' committee
A survey of shareholder opinion
A stockbroker
A reputable financial consultant
An inter-firm comparison study of such financial statistics as those published by Dun and Bradstreet or Moodies.

Long Range Forecasts

A quite incredible number of organizations whose sole or main activity is long term forecasting now exist. They cover the social, demographic, technological, marketing, political and economic fields.

According to a wide-ranging survey published in *L.R.P.* (Vol 5. No. 2 June 1972) there are 293 organizations engaged in forecasting in Europe alone. In this survey Nicolaus Sombart lists some of these under the various headings – sociology, education, politics, and so on – in the various nations of Europe. No list can be exhaustive and it remains valid only for a short time. Sombart does not mention the Battelle Institute for example, nor, under 'economic development' does he mention the UK's National Economic Development Office nor the National Institute for Economic and Social Research. Nor does he mention any of the large companies which regularly make studies of areas of interest to themselves and who occasionally publish their results – Unilever, for example, on the changing patterns of consumer spending and the Post Office on communications. Nor does he mention all the commercial organizations and universities who will, for a fee, undertake forecasting (and monitoring) assignments such as, in UK, The Economist Intelligence Unit nor the various specialist consulting firms throughout the world, who undertake market research and other forecasting.

Rather than attempt to list all these organizations, I would suggest the following rather crude rule of thumb for corporate planners; before commissioning a major forecasting study, spend some time finding out if it has already been done.

Ideas for New Products, Markets, Strategies

In addition to such internal sources of ideas as Employee Suggestions Schemes, Brainstorming Sessions and Delphis, there are a large number of outside sources of ideas to be tapped:

Patents Office
Departments of Trade and Commerce
Government Trade Journals
Think Tanks
Research Institutes
Trade Journals
Business opportunity advertisements in the press
Industrial Design Consultants
Merchant Banks
Professional Institutions and their Journals
Competitive Products
Suppliers and customers
Market Research Consultants
Foreign Trade Delegates
Product Development firms and Consultants.

Computer Models

The following well-known organizations offer computer models suitable for use in corporate planning:

Honeywell offer two models, Credit and Redcap specifically designed for capital investment appraisal and PA 300, an optimizing modelling system with which the user may build his own model using basic computer language.

International Computers Limited (ICL) offer several models of which Prosper is the best known. This is a modelling system with which the user builds his own model using a high-level computer language. It is not an optimizing model but sensitivity testing and risk analysis may be performed.

Metra Consulting Group offer a model called Capri specifically designed for the optimizing of investment plans. It has no risk-analysis or sensitivity testing facilities.

Rio Tinto Zinc Consultants, Ltd. offer several models, one of which, called FMP I briefly described on page 278. There is also the rather similar FPS and there are the Chemical Bank/RTZ financial models designed for financial evaluations but having somewhat limited facilities for risk analysis and sensitivity testing.

(An excellent survey of computer models and modelling systems appeared in the *Computer Bulletin* of September 1972 by J. C. Higgins and D. Whitaker.)

Exercises

I have included these exercises partly to help the student to test whether he has understood the fundamentals of corporate planning but chiefly to help those who teach the subject on courses, in schools and colleges. I find they are sometimes at a loss for suitable prototype questions in this subject area.

1.0   General

Q 1.1   List the reasons behind the recent rise in interest in corporate planning.

Q 1.2   List the alternatives to corporate planning. Why is the Overlord system inadequate.?

Q 1.3   Consider the present state of IBM. Does this company face a corporate planning problem or has it only got marketing problems or technological problems or finance problems?

Q 1.4   How does corporate planning differ from all other types of business planning?

2.0   Systems

Q 2.1   Why does W. W. Simmons say that the environment should be studied before objectives are set in his article in *L.R.P.* (Vol. 1, No. 3, December 1968)?

Q 2.2   Why does Argenti keep insisting on putting objectives first? Does it matter where they come in the system?

Q 2.3   Is the Systems Analysis approach to management really any different from the old budgetary control approach? What *is* the Systems Approach anyway and what is so wrong with cutting one's coat according to one's cloth?

Q 2.4   From time to time *L.R.P.* publish accounts of the methods of corporate planning used in various well known organizations (for example in Nestle's in Vol. 5 No. 2 June 1972 and the British Prison Department in Vol. 5 No. 3 September 1972). Examine not less than three of these systems and (a) note similarities if any and (b) suggest one good reason why these systems (not the procedures or the strategic contents of course) should be so different.

3.0 Objectives

Q 3.1 Study the article on planning for Britain's prisons by John Garrett and Norman Hare in *L.R.P.* Vol. 5 No. 3 September 1972. What is a prison for? How are the budgets drawn up? Would they be drawn up differently if we knew what objectives to set for a prison service? What do the authors say about objectives?

Q 3.2 What are the main social responsibilities of companies today in the Western Democracies? Are they any different in India, say, or Turkey? Why?

Q 3.3 Why does Argenti think there is a fundamental difference between corporate objectives and partial or departmental objectives? Even if he is right, does it matter?

Q 3.4 Is there any difference between a public company (i.e. one quoted on a stock exchange) and a nationalized company? How would an advocate of the Stakeholder Theory describe the difference?

4.0 Targets

Q 4.1 Company C's earnings per share has risen from £1·2 in 1962 to £1·6 in 1972. Determine a suitable long term financial target for this company which, incidentally, is in the shipbuilding industry in the UK.

Q 4.2 Would you feel more at ease having set a single point target for your company or having set a performance–risk curve even if only two or three parts of the curve are specified? Set a point target for your company. Set a performance–risk curve for your company.

Q 4.3 Which of the several possible indicators have your company used to express its financial aims? If it has only used one – ROCE or e.p.s. for example – why was that one chosen? If it has set two or more, can you prove (a) that the choice of the figures was not entirely arbitrary ('the numbers game') and (b) that they are mathematically compatible?

Q 4.4 Has your company determined a maximum threshold target level for complaints from its customers? Has it determined a similar level of complaints from employees? What indicators might it use to do this?

Q 4.5 Cuckoo Conglomerates Limited has a group growth target of 20% per annum for earnings per share. It has three subsidiaries of which A earns $100,000 on net assets of $1,000,000; B earns $200,000 on net assets of $500,000; C earns $400,000 on net assets of $2,000,000. (a) Assuming current performance is a good guide to the future select a target for each subsidiary. (b) Now devise a simple financial model to determine what results your chosen targets would have on group earnings in five years' time. Do you wish to change your answer in (a)?

5.0 Forecasts

Q 5.1 What does Ackoff mean by 'Wishful Projection'? Is what Ackoff calls a projection the same as a mere extrapolation or is it a forecast?

Q 5.2 Invite several colleagues to forecast when something definitive is going to happen each using a different method of forecasting. For example, when will fifty per cent of popular cars be powered by a Wankel engine using (a) trend analysis (b) life cycle analysis (c) Delphi? Compare and discuss.

Q 5.3 Taking the figures shown below for the past 5 years prepare a forecast of profits up to year 10

Year		1	2	3	4	5
Selling price per unit	$	31	31	31	32	32
Sales volume in units 000s		124	130	140	145	150
Cost of Material A per unit	$	11	11	11	10	10
Cost of Material B per unit	$	3	4	4	5	6
Cost of Fuel per unit	$	2	2	3	3	4
Cost of Labour per unit	$	8	9	8	8	7
Total cost per unit	$	24	26	26	26	27
Therefore Contribution p.u.	$	7	5	5	6	5
And Total Contribution $000		868	650	700	870	750
Overheads $000		310	322	340	350	370
Therefore Profit $000		558	328	360	520	380

Q 5.4 If you did not do so above, now prepare the same forecast but this time show the probable errors.

Q 5.5 Study the Annual Report of any company of your choice. From the first nine years of its ten-year financial record try to forecast the profits in the tenth (i.e. the latest) year. Notice the size of the error.
Invite a colleague to forecast the same year's profits but give him only the first five years' figures so he has to forecast five years ahead. Notice the size of the error.

Q 5.6 List five methods of reducing errors in a forecast. Which of these would be most useful in minimizing the errors in a social forecast?

Q 5.7 The most interesting and relevant case study is always your own company. Examine the past ten years' history of your company and make an F_0 forecast. Invite your colleagues to do the same, independently of course. Compare and discuss.

Q 5.8 Which methods of forecasting would you use to make a forecast of political changes in Africa during the Eighties? Which organizations do you think might already have made such a forecast?

6.0 Internal and External Appraisals

Q 6.1 From the description below list the strengths, weaknesses, threats and opportunities for Mortons Electric Motor Company Limited.
When John and Arthur Morton were demobilized in 1948 they set up in business together as manufacturers of electric motors – John was an electrical engineer and Arthur, although having no formal qualifica-

tions, was good at all things mechanical. The company grew rapidly, obtained a stock-exchange quotation in 1958 and for several years the dividends and share valuation increased by about 12% p.a. In the mid-Sixties pressure of competition began to be felt and profits have remained largely static for the past few years. As so often happens, competition is strong enough to preclude the raising of selling prices while inflation pushes costs up and Mortons' margins are being continually squeezed. Fortunately this is just about being balanced by rising sales (the market is growing by 6 or 7% p.a. although it is difficult to give an accurate figure because for some sections of the market and for some types of motor the figures are rather different).

Mortons buy in most of their components although they do cast their own casings and bedplates, and their motors range in size from $\frac{1}{2}$ hp up to over 200 hp. They are well built and reliable and their customers thoroughly appreciate their good delivery record and the sturdy if conventional character of the company and its products – nearly all their 26 customers have traded with them for many years. Sales have been rising at about 4% p.a. in recent years. Mortons do not export because of the wide variation in voltage requirements and climatic conditions throughout the world.

There are about 300 employees, mostly female assemblers and facilities are good. There have been two strikes in recent months. The senior staff are competent, the 58-year-old sales manager having been with Mortons for 15 years while the production manager and chief buyer were taken on about 18 months ago (to give the company some new blood) when John and Arthur realized that they were approaching 60. They are the only two active directors; John acts as Chief Executive and Arthur is Research Director. His main preoccupation in the past few years has been the development of an ingenious mobile diesel electric generator for use on outlying farms and other remote sites but the work has been held up by the difficulty of keeping the engine cool in hot climates.

Draw up a Cruciform Chart. Should the Mortons make any change to their strategic structure?

Q 6.2 List the strengths, weaknesses, threats and opportunities and draw up a Cruciform Chart for any well-known company (including your own). Invite several colleagues to do the same, then compare and discuss.

Q 6.3 Assume that the standard of living in your nation will rise at 5% per annum in real terms. This means that any of your employees now earning $2000 a year will be earning well over $3000 in 10 years' time and anyone earning $20,000 will be earning over $30,000.

(a) How will this affect your employees and the jobs they will be doing then?

(b) How will it affect your customers?

(c) What changes would you expect to see in the life styles of people now earning $2000 and $20,000?

(d) Classify the items in your answers above into threats, opportunities and either.

Q 6.4 List the trends and events that will lead to the decline and extinction of (a) mechanical engineering and (b) trawling and deep-sea fishing. When will these two activities start to go into a decline and when will they become virtually extinct as a means of livelihood? How and when will this affect your company?

Q 6.5 At what level will the Dow Jones Index stand in two years time? How will this affect your company?

Q 6.6 What evidence do you have that your company is any good at all at (a) R & D, (b) purchasing supplies and (c) financial control. Is there any evidence that IBM, Shell, Woolworths, ITT are any good at these either?

7.0 Strategic Structure

Q 7.1 Select a pair of very well-known companies (Shell and Exxon for example or Ford and General Motors) and carefully note the differences in their strategic structures. Is one of their structures more appropriate than the other for the 1970s and 1980s? Is there any evidence that either of these companies are making any effort to alter their structures? What changes are they making and why; or, if not, why not?

Q 7.2 You have just been appointed corporate planner of British Leyland Motors. Assuming BLMC have an earnings growth target of, say, 15% per annum, what changes in the strategic structure of the company would you make? How urgent are these changes?

Q 7.3 How would you describe the strategic structure of ICI? Over what time horizon would you recommend ICI to make forecasts and plans? What changes would you recommend in ICI's structure during that period?

Q 7.4 Go to your local tobacconist's shop. What is the strategic structure of this organization? In view of the threats and weaknesses do you think a change is necessary ? What does the proprietor think? If he disagrees what was the factor that you left out of account?

Q 7.5 Why does Argenti think that the concept of the strategic structure and the concept of performance–risk are so closely complementary? What is a portfolio of strategies?

Q 7.6 Marks & Spencers have outmanaged almost all their competitors for two decades. What is their strategic structure now? Can they continue to beat the competition without a major change to this structure? What change should they make?

Q 7.7 Study any medium-sized company of, say, 2000 employees. Why is it still independent? Ought it to invite a bid from a larger company? If so which company might make a suitable bidder? If not, what makes you think that the shareholders would agree with you?

Q 7.8 Study a well-known company whose share values are depressed on the stock market. For how far ahead does this low opinion remain valid

– i.e. is the company only in short term trouble or ought the management to be considering a structural change?

Q 7.9 Study a company whose shares are valued highly on the stock market. Should they begin to change their structure by adopting some low risk strategies?

8.0 Evaluation

Q 8.1 In what way do the criteria for evaluating Strategic Structures differ from those for individual strategies?

Q 8.2 Carefully study D. H. Allen's article in *L.R.P.* (Vol. 5 No. 2 June 1972). Would you recommend your Research Director to read this article? Would you, if you had the authority, insist that he at least tried to use Credibility rather than Probability in his next R & D proposals to you?

Q 8.3 What would you say to a senior colleague who refused to use d.c.f. on the grounds that he did not know the true cost of capital and did not think anyone else knew it either? Can you honestly claim to know what it is for your company at this point in time? If not, where does that leave d.c.f.?

Q 8.4 What are the advantages and disadvantages of using computerized optimizing models for strategic planning?

Q 8.5 Develop your own manual model to show how a company's stock turnover (i.e. the ratio of capital tied up in inventories to sales turnover) affects the ROCE.

Q 8.6 Get in touch with one of the well-known organizations listed on page 302 for permission to study their computer model. To whom would you recommend it and for what purpose?

9.0 Monitoring

Q 9.1 In 1965 a company adopted a strategic plan designed to raise the rate of growth in earnings per share to 15% per annum. No new equity has been issued over the ten year period and the annual earnings from 1960 to 1965 were $113,000; $108,000; $141,000; $136,000; $184,000. From 1965 the earnings were $209,000; $246,000; $228,000; $248,000; $355,000. Did they achieve their target? At what rate were earnings growing from 1960 to 1965? By what year could the company have been reasonably sure that its new strategy was having the desired effect?

Q 9.2 You have just been appointed corporate planner to Unilever (or Nestlé). You ask your staff to bring you the latest edition of the monitoring documents for the Group. Do you expect them to bring you a document of two pages or two hundred? How long ago would you expect it to have been prepared? Would it contain any technological forecasts? How many copies would have been issued and to whom?

10.0 Organizing

Q 10.1 Draw the organization chart of any company of your choice. What changes do you think it should show from (a) when there was no corporate planning to (b) when corporate planning was introduced to (c) ten years after.

10.2 Explain, as if facing them across your desk, how the work of the corporate planner differs from that of the Marketing Director.

10.3 Select an interesting and colourful company in your geographical area. As a student, request that you be allowed to study its strategic decision-making procedures. Write a report for the chief executive recommending three major improvements.

10.4 List the qualities that a corporate planner must display.

10.5 Can there ever be a justification for (a) a corporate planning department employing more than a dozen people? (b) a corporate planner answerable to anyone but the strategic planning committe or the chief executive (c) a corporate planner in a subsidiary but not in the group headquarters?

Bibliography

By far the most comprehensive bibliography on corporate planning and its related disciplines is to be found in Steiner's *Top Management Planning*; his list runs to hundreds of titles. The bibliography below contains only two dozen items which is approximately ten times as many titles as most students of this subject will have time to read. I have limited the list to the best of the established books on corporate planning plus a few of the most recent.

One obvious disadvantage of bibliographies is that they so quickly become out of date: the serious student may keep in touch through the *Journal of the Society for Long Range Planning*. In June 1972, for example, this Journal published its very comprehensive *European Bibliography of Corporate Planning* 1961-71.

Anderson, R.G.   *Management Strategies*
McGraw Hill, 1966

Ackoff, Russell L.   *A Concept of Corporate Planning*
Wiley Interscience, 1970

Ansoff, H. Igor   *Corporate Strategy*
McGraw Hill, 1965

Ansoff, H. Igor   *Business Strategy*
Penguin Books, 1969

Argenti, John   *Corporate Planning—A Practical Guide*
Allen & Unwin, 1968

Chamberlain, N.W.   *The Firm in Time and Place*
McGraw Hill, 1968

Cannon, J.T.   *Business Strategy and Policy*
Harcourt, Brace and World Inc, 1968

Denning, Basil W.   *Corporate Planning—Selected Concepts*
McGraw Hill, 1971

Ewing, D.W.   *The Practice of Planning*
Harper & Row, 1968

Ewing, D.W.   *The Human Side of Planning*
Macmillan, 1969

Henry, Harold W.   *Long Range Planning in 45 Companies*
Prentice-Hall, 1967

Halford, D.R.C.   *Business Planning*
Pan Books, 1968

Hussey, D.E.   *Introducing Corporate Planning*
Pergamon Press, 1971

Katz, R.L.   *Management of the Total Enterprise*
                                Prentice Hall, 1970
Miller, Ernest C.   *Advanced Techniques for Strategic Planning*
                                American Management Association, 1971
Novick, David   *Programme Budgeting—Program Analysis and the
                                    Federal Budget*
                                Harvard University Press, 1965
Perrin, Robert   *Focus the Future*
                                Management Publications, 1971
Payne, B.   *Planning for Company Growth*
                                McGraw Hill, 1963
Presanis, A.   *Corporate Planning in Industry*
                                Business Publications, 1968
Ringbakk, K.A.   *Organized Corporate Planning Systems*
                                Madison, Wisconsin, 1968
Steiner, G.A.   *Top Management Planning*
                                Macmillan, 1969
Scott, Brian W.   *Long Range Planning in American Industry*
                                American Management Association, 1965
Stemp, Isay   *Corporate Growth Strategies*
                                American Management Association, 1970
Walley, B.H.   *How to Apply Strategy in Profit Planning*
                                Business Books, 1971
Warren, E. Kirby   *Long Range Planning: The Executive Viewpoint*
                                Prentice Hall, 1966
Weinwurm, E.H. and G.F.   *Long Term Profit Planning*
                                American Management Association, 1971
Wolfe, H.D.   *Business Forecasting Methods*
                                Holt, Rinehart and Winston, 1966

Index

After graduating from Oxford University in 1949, John Argenti worked for a major British company for many years, latterly as Works Manager and finally as Head of Planning Services. He is now an independent consultant in corporate planning operating in the U.K. and Europe. He has written and lectured widely on this and other management subjects. He was a founder of the Society for Long Range Planning. In 1968 his first book *Corporate Planning—A Practical Guide* was published, followed in 1969 by *Management Techniques* and in 1972 by *A Management System for the Seventies*.